Animal Labor and Colonial Warfare

Animal Labor and Colonial Warfare

James L. Hevia

The University of Chicago Press CHICAGO & LONDON

The University of Chicago Press, Chicago 60637
The University of Chicago Press, Ltd., London

Published 2018
Printed in the United States of America

27 26 25 24 23 22 21 20 19 18   1 2 3 4 5

ISBN-13: 978-0-226-56214-8 (cloth)
ISBN-13: 978-0-226-56228-5 (paper)
ISBN-13: 978-0-226-56231-5 (e-book)
DOI: https://doi.org/10.7208/chicago/9780226562315.001.0001

Library of Congress Cataloging-in-Publication Data

Names: Hevia, James Louis, 1947– author.
Title: Animal labor and colonial warfare / James L. Hevia.
Description: Chicago ; London : The University of Chicago Press, 2018. | Includes bibliographical references and index.
Identifiers: LCCN 2017054498 | ISBN 9780226562148 (cloth : alk. paper) | ISBN 9780226562285 (pbk. : alk. paper) | ISBN 9780226562315 (e-book)
Subjects: LCSH: Pack animals (Transportation)—India—History—19th century. | Camels—India—History—19th century. | Donkeys—India—History—19th century. | Pack transportation—India—History—19th century. | India. Army—Transportation. | India. Army—Environmental aspects. | Transportation, Military—India—History—19th century. | India—Politics and government—1857–1919. | Afghan Wars—Environmental aspects—India.
Classification: LCC UC205.14 H38 2018 UC350 | DDC 355.4/24095409034—dc23
LC record available at https://lccn.loc.gov/2017054498

♾ This paper meets the requirements of ANSI/NISO Z39.48-1992 (Permanence of Paper).

CONTENTS

FIGURES AND MAPS

FIGURES

MAPS

PREFACE

On the eastern edge of Hyde Park in London stands the Animals in War Memorial.[1] As can be seen in figure 1, the monument itself is unusually multifaceted. On its long left-hand panel, as the visitor approaches it, is a bas-relief depiction of a host of animals credited with participating in wars—elephants, mules, donkeys, horses, dogs, carrier pigeons, and one-humped and two-humped camels. At the head of this procession, to the immediate right of the pigeons and elephants, is a gap between the panels, toward which two cast-bronze statues of heavily weighted ordnance mules seem to move, one taking labored steps and the other straining forward. As the visitor proceeds ahead of them through the gap and out to the other side, an alert dog and a formidable saddleless horse, reminiscent of Michael Morpurgo's *War Horse*, are seen.[2] They seem to be moving away from the monument, leading both the mules and the animals in the relief toward some distant point ahead (fig. 2).

1. The monument, officially dedicated in 2004, takes its name from Jill Cooper's book *Animals in War* (London: Heinemann, 1983). Cooper was very critical of the use of animals in wars. While writing her introduction, she reported, she had gazed at the dogs sleeping under her work table, the cat lying in her in-basket, and the cows, horses, and sheep grazing in the valley below her front window. She concluded, "This is how animals should live, not dragged, terrified and suffering, into our human conflicts" (11). Also see Hilda Kean, "Animals and War Memorials: Different Approaches to Commemorating the Human-Animal Relationship," in *Animals and War*, ed. Ryan Hediger (Leiden: Brill, 2013), 237–62.

2. Michael Morpurgo, *War Horse* (New York: Scholastic, 1982), which was repurposed as a "major motion picture" and a stage play at London's National Theater.

FIGURE 1. Bronze statues of ordnance mules at the Animals in War Memorial, London. Author's photograph.

This striking visual imagery of animals in war is complemented by text on the monument's right-hand panel that explains the installation's purpose. The monument is dedicated to "all animals that served and died alongside British and allied forces in wars and campaigns throughout time." Next to this dedication, the monument baldly asserts: THEY HAD NO CHOICE. As if these declarative statements are not enough to capture the attention of the casual observer, the reverse side of the panel contains even sterner rhetoric:

> MANY AND VARIOUS ANIMALS WERE EMPLOYED TO SUPPORT BRITISH AND ALLIED FORCES IN WARS AND CAMPAIGNS OVER THE CENTURIES AND AS A RESULT MILLIONS DIED. FROM THE PIGEON TO THE ELEPHANT THEY ALL PLAYED A VITAL ROLE IN EVERY REGION OF THE WORLD IN THE CAUSE OF HUMAN FREEDOM—THEIR CONTRIBUTIONS MUST NEVER BE FORGOTTEN.

And yet for some visitors, even this unusually long textual guide to the monument seems not to have been enough. When these pictures were taken

FIGURE 2. Bronze statues of a horse and dog at the Animals in War Memorial, London. Author's photograph.

in 2013, a group of wreaths made up of plastic poppies lay at the base of the monument (fig. 3). Each provided an addendum citing an animal that was absent from the bas-relief. For example, a plastic-covered card on one of the wreaths reads, "In Memory of Able Sea Cat 'Simon' RN, HMS Amethyst" and "Ordinary Sea Cat 'Togo' RN, HMS Irresistible." Photographs of the two cats accompanied the text.

The words on both the monument and the wreaths suggest an affinity between animals and humans, some kind of shared ontological status and common experience: companions in war, as it were, with animals now finally being remembered for their humanlike sacrifices. The monument corrects, therefore, an injustice, but this was a correction that itself required correcting, with the volunteered memorial wreaths. Yet the emphatic charge to viewers to remember the important sacrifices of animals obscures certain discriminations and contradictions embedded in the monument's representational organization. For example, the bronze figures of horse, dog, and mules make a very clear distinction between "beasts of burden" and the "companion animals"

FIGURE 3. Wreaths placed at the base of the Animals in War Memorial, London. Author's photograph.

that are somehow more free.[3] As they move vigorously beyond the monument toward some beyond of the animal world, the horse and the dog are not marked in any way by signs of military service. On the frieze, meanwhile, the various animals march along without distinction, all their services made to seem identical. Are we really to understand that there is no difference between the service of a carrier pigeon and that of the beasts of burden which make up the bulk of the other animals? If we reflect for a moment on some of these oddly flattened differences, we might be tempted to wonder what it is, exactly, that "must never be forgotten."

Moreover, for a monument with so much expressive language chiseled into it, it is curious that two important words regarding the presence of animals in

3. The distinction made between animals that have close emotional bonds with humans, namely pets, and those that work for humans has varied across time and space. Here I am following Donna Haraway's observation about the types of animals generally considered at present to be companions of humans; see *When Species Meet* (Minneapolis: University of Minnesota Press, 2008), 16.

war are missing. In 1914 in Great Britain, for example, horses were "requisitioned" for military service, and nearly half a million were sent to France and Belgium over the course of World War I. Throughout the nineteenth century in India, camels, mules, donkeys, ponies, bullocks, and elephants were "impressed" into service. Reference to either of these military practices would have helped clarify the claim that the animals had no choice.

Before the total wars of the twentieth century, when conscription for adult males became the norm for the first time, animals, unlike humans, had "no choice" because governments like those of Great Britain and British India reserved the right to force them to serve.[4] The hard fact is that until the invention and deployment of mechanical transport, such as trucks and trains, armies needed pack animals to transport their supplies. Animals were thus forced labor—labor that was repaid with very little beyond sometimes insufficient fodder. As elements of militarized animal populations who were often in the line of fire, mules, camels, bullocks, donkeys, and occasionally horses were made to carry the materiel of war and the supplies that allowed armies to move "on their bellies."

These contradictions and absences invite several questions. Does the idea of service obscure more than it reveals about human-animal relations? What could animal service possibly mean? How are we to understand the deaths of nonhumans "alongside" British and allied soldiers "throughout time," or interpret the assertion that animals played "a vital role" everywhere in the world "in the cause of human freedom"? Why must their "contribution," seemingly anthropomorphized by the rhetoric on the monument, "never be forgotten"? What are we to remember about the sorts of labor these animals performed, especially when we recall that animals such as camels, mules, and elephants were used in colonial wars of conquest, and campaigns of retribution, in Africa and Asia?

This book attempts to deal with questions like these. It is less concerned with the purported sacrifices animals made in the cause of human freedom than with the ignoble conditions under which animals by compulsion participated in human conflicts. Understanding those conditions may help to

4. Because of its all too human connotations, Jonathan Burt wonders if the word *choice* is "appropriate"; see his review of the memorial and the Animals in War Exhibition at the Imperial War Museum, London, in *History Today* 56, no. 10 (October 2006): 70–71. In harsher terms, George Monbiot charges that this and other war memorials recently unveiled in London have contributed to the "Disneyfication" of war, allowing viewers to ignore the "real savagery" of armed conflicts; see "The Disneyfication of War Allows Us to Ignore Its Real Savagery," *Guardian* (Manchester), October 23, 2006.

explain why and how millions died; where they actually marched; and why most of the animals that perished were transport animals. I hope it serves to provide a more detailed and historically nuanced correction to the monument in Hyde Park. I also hope that it serves to challenge any neat binary distinction between humans and animals.

ABBREVIATIONS

ARARD	Administrative Report, Army Remount Department
ARD	Army Remount Department
ARPCC	Annual Report, Punjab Canal Colonies
ARS&T	Administrative Report, Supply and Transport Department
CVD	Civil Veterinary Department
CTC	Camel Transport Corps
IJVSAH	*Indian Journal of Veterinary Science and Animal Husbandry*
IOR	India Office Records
JTVS	*Journal of Tropical Veterinary Science*
JUSSII	*Journal of the United Service Institution of India*
QJVSI	*Quarterly Journal of Veterinary Science in India and Army Animal Management*
USI	United Service Institution
VS	veterinary surgeon

Introduction

> The human-animal relationship is one of the most historically consequential of all past phenomena. Understanding that relationship and how it changed is crucial to the study of any place and any time.
>
> ALAN MIKHAIL[1]

This study had already been in the works long before I visited the Animals in War Memorial in 2013. It began while I was completing research on *The Imperial Security State*, when I learned to my surprise that in the first year of the Second Afghan War (1878–80), British losses of camel transport animals totaled around sixty thousand dead and missing. How was it possible, I wondered, for the British Indian Army to have lost so many camels in so short a time? As will be clear in chapter 1, one answer to this question is that the animals were badly treated in the mountain campaigns, either by British soldiers themselves or by animal handlers whose neglect of their charges the British ignored or tolerated. But there were other, less obvious reasons as well, and as I explored these, new questions about military and working animals emerged.

For those of us living in the global North, our world is one in which virtually all animal labor has been replaced by machine functions. In addition, most of us are protected from direct experience of armed conflict. How are we to recover an understanding of the historical uses of animals, particularly transport animals, in human warfare? When armies were still very much reliant on mules, camels, and even elephants to move supplies, how did humans relate to the animals used in this way? Did they imagine a difference between a horse pulling a farmer's wagon to a nearby market, or hitched to a coach traversing city streets, and hundreds of camels and mules weighed down by war materiel, following armies as they headed to a battlefield? Is there, in other words, some

1. Alan Mikhail, *The Animal in Ottoman Egypt* (Oxford: Oxford University Press, 2014), 1.

way of distinguishing forms of brute labor from one another, or is all transport work equivalent as abstractable animal labor?

At a more specific level, what did it mean in practice to rely on local animal populations when launching large-scale military operations such as an invasion of Afghanistan, or smaller-scale punitive expeditions like the ones that took place along the North-West Frontier of British India? How did rural life in northwestern India change under the pressure of pack animal impressment? Because all the animals used in the British invasion of Afghanistan in 1878, for example, were locally sourced we might wonder how agriculturalists and camel herders worked with their animals at the time. How did they cope with the forced labor and loss of the animals in military expeditions? Were laboring animals thought of in the same way in colonial India as they were in Great Britain?

In order to answer these questions, it has been necessary to move beyond the Second Afghan War and the camel casualties of 1878–80 and explore the continued use of animal labor in colonial warfare well into the twentieth century. In addition to many campaigns along the North-West Frontier of India between 1880 and 1939, Indian army transport units participated in a third war with Afghanistan in 1919; were active in nineteenth-century campaigns in Abyssinia, Egypt, and the Sudan; and were present in Persia, Mesopotamia, Gallipoli, and the Sinai and Palestine campaigns of World War I.[2] These conflicts generated a rich, and thus far almost untouched, archival record of the disposition of animal transport in warfare. The center of my concerns, however, lies not with the battles themselves or the strategies of commanding officers. Instead, I focus on the routinized role of pack animals in these

2. On the World War I campaigns, see chapter 9. Indian Army transport animals were shipped from India to Africa to participate in several campaigns, beginning with the one against the Abyssinian king Tewodros II in 1868. See Maj. Treven Holland and Capt. Henry Hozier, comps., *Record of the Expedition to Abyssinia* (London: Harrison and Sons, 1870), 2 vols. Figures given in volume 1 indicate that of the 5,735 camels disembarked at the port of Zula, only 40 were returned to India; the figure for mules and ponies was 17,675 disembarked, 4,126 returned (p. 234). During the effort to rescue Charles Gordon at Khartoum in 1884–85, Indian Army units and several thousand camels, mules, and bullocks were shipped from India to the Sudanese port of Suakin on the Red Sea. The units were disbanded soon after the rescue attempt failed. See the report of Gen. Gerald Graham in NA/WO 32/6129, especially pp. 2 and 20, where he discusses the composition of transport, which included over 7,000 camels (some locally sourced) and 1,700 mules. Few if any of the camels seem to have made it back to India (they were mostly shipped to Suez for sale), but several of the mules and bullocks did; see IOR/L/MIL/7/6942: Relief of Suakin garrison by other Indian regiments, 1885.

events, and the ramifications of their use in warfare across the reach of the British Empire.

After the carnage of 1878–80, for example, owners of camels in northwestern India attempted as best they could to hide their animals from the assessing eyes of British officials. Some even seem to have left India, with or without their own camels, to work as camel men in Australia.[3] In Britain at the same time, the deaths of vast numbers of animals in the Second Afghan War raised outcries and produced a scandal that, as I will show, contributed to the fall of Benjamin Disraeli's government. A similar outcry occurred in 1897, when thousands of camels, mules, donkeys, and ponies were impressed into service in order to support a series of campaigns to put down uprisings all along the North-West Frontier. There were good reasons for the clamor. Great Britain's powerful lobby advocating the rights of all animals to humane treatment was already in place by 1880. The Society for the Prevention of Cruelty to Animals had been founded in London in 1824. The first law protecting domestic and farm animals was passed in 1835, and was strengthened by new legislation in 1849 and 1876. In 1840, the society received Queen Victoria's patronage and hence was renamed the Royal Society, or RSPCA. By the end of the century, chapters of the organization had been founded in North America and in many of Britain's colonies.[4] This well-established British interest in animal welfare also spawned the antivivisectionist movement, which took as its target the use of live animals in scientific experiments. These nineteenth-century developments in Britain are echoed in the concerns expressed by the Animals in War Memorial. But the fact that the anticruelty and antivivisectionist movements had long been so vocal in England also makes the treatment of animals in the harsh conditions of colonial warfare seem even more peculiar. It was as if there were two standards—one for the civilian world, another for the military; one

3. See Christine Stevens, *Tin Mosques and Ghantowns: A History of Afghan Camel Drivers in Australia* (Melbourne: Oxford University Press, 1989). The feral camel population of Australia is made up of the descendants of camels shipped out of western India from the 1870s into the early twentieth century. See Tom McNight, *The Camel in Australia* (Melbourne: Melbourne University Press, 1969), 56–61.

4. On the early history of the RSPCA, see Edward Fairholme et al., *A Century of Work for Animals: The History of the R.S.P.C.A., 1824–1924* (London: John Murray, 1924). Also see Harriet Ritvo, *The Animal Estate: The English and Other Creatures in the Victorian Age* (Cambridge, MA: Harvard University Press, 1987), 125–66; and Chien-hua Li, "Mobilizing Christianity in the Antivivisection Movement in Victorian Britain," *Journal of Animal Ethics* 2, no. 2 (2012): 141–61.

for home, another for the colonies. If so, how did people live with these ugly contradictions?

Recent scholarship on human-animal relations begins to answer some of these questions. In work spanning the last two centuries of human-animal interactions in Great Britain, North America, and continental Europe, scholars like Harriet Ritvo, Margaret Derry, and Sarah Franklin have explored the variety of symbolic values attached to domestic animals in Euro-American culture, and examined the radical interventions humans have made in animal life to scientifically engineer their "improvement."[5] What these scholars observe about human-animal relations shows that the latter have been subordinated in a variety of ways to the former. Animals have tended to be the mute dependents of humans[6] even when they are the objects of human benevolent and sentimental paternalism—the language of both the RSPCA and the Animals in War Memorial reflect this. Alternatively, farm and domestic animals could simply be known as material property, to be used as owners see fit. A particular human-animal symbolic divide, these authors suggest, was less a product of nature than a potent cultural construction that took form in the long nineteenth century. Moreover, such constructions, as Alan Mikhail has suggested, have varied enormously over time and space. Ottoman officials, for example, made no distinctions in their records between the human and the animal forms of labor involved in state-funded projects. "Humans and nonhumans," he adds, "were thus abstracted by the Ottoman administration as possessions of the state to be enumerated, moved around, and configured as needed for Egypt's irrigation network."[7] This treatment of animal labor is far closer to that of the British military in India in the late nineteenth century than to the sentiments to be found on the Hyde Park monument.

The orientations that have emerged from studies of the history of human-animal relations not only open new areas of research but help strengthen a point made by cultural theorists and anthropologists working along similar lines. The commonsense notion that neatly divides humans from other living

5. Harriet Ritvo, *The Animal Estate: The English and Other Creatures in the Victorian Age* (Cambridge, MA: Harvard University Press, 1987) and *Noble Cows and Hybrid Zebras: Essays on Animals and History* (Charlottesville: University of Virginia Press, 2010); Margaret Derry, *Bred for Perfection* (Baltimore: Johns Hopkins University Press, 2003) and *Horses in Society: A Story of Animal Breeding and Marketing, 1800–1920* (Toronto: University of Toronto Press, 2006); and Sarah Franklin, *Dolly Mixtures: The Remaking of Genealogy* (Durham, NC: Duke University Press, 2007).

6. Lynn Hunt, *Writing History in the Global Era* (New York: W. W. Norton, 2014), 92.

7. Mikhail, *The Animal in Ottoman Egypt*, 31.

entities obscures the degree to which human lives are entangled with those of other species, and the ways in which human and animal relations in particular are frequently organized in relations of codependence or are products of coevolution.[8] This codependence operates from the microscopic level (microorganisms in the mammalian body)[9] to the macroscopic level (the irreducible shepherd-sheep-sheepdog unit).[10]

Such recognition encourages us to rethink a great deal of what we take for granted about the essentially human. In colonial India, the civil and military leaders of the colony tended to regard indigenous animals in mainly functional ways; that is, they asked what human uses these creatures were good for. Horses could be employed by civil officials to expedite their inspections and enumerations of the land and its people, while for the army, horses were essential in border security activities and internal policing schemes that called for nimble, mobile cavalry units. Both civil and military colonial officials thought in terms of the tasks to be performed, and they sought out certain kinds of horses bred with the desirable qualities to meet these criteria. Moreover, officials and soldiers often developed close bonds with their steeds. The ideal horses for civil and military operations, though different—one initiating the very process of colonial control, the other protecting the activities of the civil officials from external threats—were both important as they produced a codependent collaboration between man and beast. Only an official mounted on horseback could command the land and its people.[11] Only an army capable of moving quickly could protect the frontier from raids and other threats. When we think about colonial human-animal relations as complex forms of codependency, animal service needs to be moved to the center of the story. The examples invoked here also suggest a distinction, in both functional and affective terms, between the official or the cavalryman on their mounts and the "beasts of burden" they witnessed operating along the army supply lines.

Thinking in terms of human-animal codependencies also helps clarify the category of animal itself. Clearly, the relation of codependency need not be

8. Helen Leach, "Human Domestication Reconsidered," *Current Anthropology* 44, no. 3 (2003): 349–68; and Donna Haraway, *When Species Meet* (Minneapolis: University of Minnesota Press, 2008).

9. Haraway, *When Species Meet*, 31.

10. Donna Haraway, "Value-Added Dogs and Lively Capital," in *Lively Capital*, ed. Kaushik Sunder Rajan (Durham, NC: Duke University Press, 2012), 103 [95–120].

11. Here I am thinking of Captain Birch riding through the countryside in the Bengal region so that the people could see who their master was; see Gayatri Spivak, "The Rani of Sirmur: An Essay in Reading the Archives," *History and Theory* 24, no. 3 (1985): 253–54.

one of equality, yet the asymmetrical relations of power—the man rides the horse, after all—are not identical in every case. Humans view certain animals more favorably than others: the bronze dog and horse as well as the ships' cats in the volunteered tributes at the Animals in War Memorial suggest as much. In contrast, militarized pack animals occupy a lower position in human calculations, as we shall see; they tend to be reduced almost exclusively to their carrying capacity, and when involved in shooting wars they are reduced even further to examples of mere brute existence. And even though soldiers depended on pack animals for their lives, camels, ponies, and sometimes even mules and donkeys seem to have been treated mostly like "unloved others."[12] Whatever affective bonds existed between humans and pack animals during military campaigns seem to have been experienced mainly by the animal handlers, the indigenous "drivers" of the camels and mules.

The presence of this third party, the human who actually marched with and cared for the pack animals, further calls into question the representations on the monument in Hyde Park. Where are the "drivers," necessary to British Empire military activities? They seem much like the service-providing camp followers of colonial military campaigns, almost all of whom remained invisible in official accounts and in the subsequent histories of imperial campaigns. In the case of military operations in northwestern India and Afghanistan, the native camel handlers, or *sarwans*, were absolutely essential to any efforts to supply armies, and yet they seem to appear in writing only when being denigrated by British soldiers. From a historiographic point of view, we are left with the troublesome question, can the *sarwan* speak? One of my tasks, therefore, is to tease out of the historical record as much as is possible about this particular human-animal relation, that between camel handler and camel.

On the side of colonial rule, other troublesome issues arise. The day-to-day human management of transport animals presented many problems for civilian and military officials in India, especially when notions of rational efficiency, as opposed to the chaotic condition of arbitrary impressment and forced labor, became watchwords for a series of army reorganizations. Although the contrast between the cavalry horse and the "beasts of burden" such as camels and mules remained relatively stable after the Second Afghan War, by the beginning of the twentieth century a host of changes in the material and administrative conditions in colonial India reconfigured knowledge about pack animals and reorganized their disposition within the Indian Army.

12. I borrow the notion from Deborah Bird and Thom van Dooren, "Guest Editors' Introduction," *Australian Humanities Review* 50 (2011): 1–5.

From at least 1885 forward, many of Britain's colonies were transformed by a kind of "constructive colonialism," as Michael Worboys has termed it—a process of applying modern sciences there, with the aim of creating new resources for economic development.[13] Among the applied-science efforts were large-scale engineering projects, including road, bridge, and railroad construction, as well as hydraulic endeavors that refashioned whole river systems. They also included scientific agricultural schemes, and developments in human and animal medicine. Germ theory, for example, had arrived in India by the 1880s and led to the emergence of what physicians and veterinary surgeons referred to as "tropical science." Inevitably, these engineering and health-related projects had effects that transformed the ecologies of large areas, reconfiguring human relations to land and to other species, including insects and microbes,[14] as well as transforming the lives of domesticated animals. Given the scale of interventions in colonized territories and the multiple kinds of knowledge deployed—from trigonometric surveying, to animal breeding, to hydraulics for irrigation, to microbiological medicine—it becomes difficult to untangle or "partially detach" science from colonialism.[15] Such an endeavor would perhaps be undesirable—we are only now beginning to understand the complex nature of change that results when humans intervene in environments in order to reformat them.

One example may suffice to make this point. In *Rule of Experts*, Timothy Mitchell provides a case study of constructive colonialism: the British effort in the late nineteenth century to improve agricultural production in the Nile valley of Egypt by reengineering the river. In the process of remaking the river, a heterogeneous set of elements, such as hydraulic engineering, chemical fertilizers in the cotton and sugar industry, mosquitoes and parasites, and Anglo-Egyptian political relations, were linked; together they caused, among other things, a malaria epidemic in northern Egypt. This event took place during World War II in a region where the disease had not existed before. How did this come about? Mitchell argues that in order to understand the epidemic, we need to incorporate nonhuman actors into the analysis, and explore the relations between engineering, agricultural science, cotton and sugarcane plants,

13. The source is Worboys's dissertation and is cited by Mark Harrison in his "Science and the British Empire," *Isis* 96, no. 1 (2005): 57.

14. Good starting points for thinking about insects and microbes as agents are Hugh Raffles, *Insectopedia* (New York: Pantheon, 2010), and Heather Paxson and Stefan Helmreich, "The Perils and Promises of Microbial Abundance," *Social Studies of Science* 44, no. 2 (2014): 165–93.

15. William Beinart, Karen Brown, and Daniel Gilfoyle, "Experts and Expertise in Colonial Africa Reconsidered: Science and the Interpretation of Knowledge," *African Affairs* 108, no. 432 (2009): 418.

mosquitoes and microbiology, capitalism, and international relations, rather than treat each of these "factors" as discrete entities with separate historical trajectories.[16] In bringing these elements into the same analytic field, Mitchell is able to demonstrate how human interventions can have catastrophic ecological impacts that not only make malaria possible where it never was before, but also have consequences for human health and environmental quality that are felt right down to the present.

Mitchell's approach to colonial development projects is pertinent to the present study in several ways. First, an equally ambitious hydraulic engineering project was begun in the Indus River basin (map 1) in the 1880s.[17] The British administrators in India had a goal similar to that of their counterparts in Egypt: the improvement of agricultural output, particularly of commercial crops. Through modernization of a few existing irrigation canal systems, and the extension of new canals into arid "wasteland," the British sought to achieve this increase by opening vast new lands to production and moving the "surplus" population from nearby districts to work the irrigated land. As in Egypt, this meddling by engineers with an irrigation system that had long been adapted by humans to the regularities of the region's climate pattern had a number of negative consequences,[18] including the spread of malaria and flyborne animal diseases and the waterlogging and salinization of soil.

Unlike Egypt, however, the canal colonies created in the Indus River basin were administratively linked to the Indian Army's need for transport animals. Some plots of land were granted to those who agreed to raise camels and mules as part of their agricultural work. These camel and mule grantee plots were then connected to a new transport reserve scheme designed to eliminate the need for impressment of pack animals. Should mobilization of reserve units become necessary, the grantee animals would automatically enter service. This heterogeneous set of elements—ambitious public works projects, commercial agriculture development, animal breeding, and army transport needs—produced a complex recolonization of the Punjab and adjacent territories. It also created a newly hospitable environment for some nonhuman agents to flourish, while others, such as plants adapted to the arid zone, found their lives suddenly

16. Timothy Mitchell, *Rule of Experts* (Berkeley: University of California Press, 2002), 27.

17. David Gilmartin, *Blood and Water: The Indus River Basin in Modern History* (Oakland: University of California Press, 2015).

18. On Nile River irrigation before the arrival of the British, see Alan Mikhail, *Nature and Empire in Ottoman Egypt: An Environmental History* (New York: Cambridge University Press, 2011).

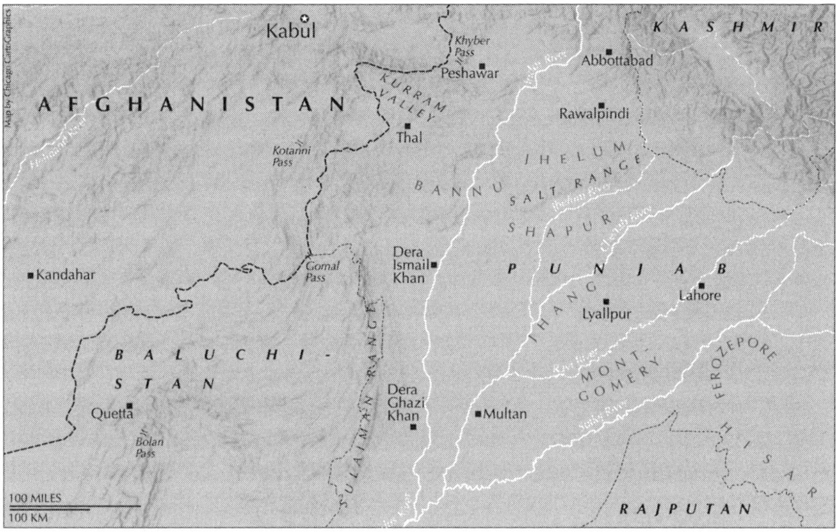

MAP 1. The Indus River basin and the North-West Frontier.

threatened. As in the Nile basin, some of the nonhuman agents that benefited from irrigation expansion in the Punjab were mosquitoes and the protozoan parasites that cause malaria in humans. But they also included various species of biting flies, which served as vectors of a protozoan blood parasite of the *Trypanosoma* genus. The latter insect-microbe partnership, important in its own right, took on added significance for administrators in the early twentieth century, because the disease caused by trypanosomes, known locally as *surra*, threatened the new military transport structure. Surra was capable of killing large numbers of camels, mules, ponies, and horses, the key animals in the Indian Army security scheme on the North-West Frontier. This disease threat mobilized another group of actors, veterinary surgeons, who quite literally went to war on flies and microbes. The challenge posed to army transport by groups of nonhuman agents reminds us that not all relations between humans and nonhumans are benign; some are agonistic, especially when the wholesale death of animal workers is a result. What, then, are we to do with "awkward creatures" like the biting flies and the protozoa they carried?[19] How do they figure into a history of animal labor, frontier warfare, and colonial improvement?

19. The issue of problematic entities like life-threatening microbes is taken up by Franklin Ginn, Uli Beisel, and Maan Barua, "Flourishing with Awkward Creatures: Togetherness, Vulnerability, and Killing," *Environmental Humanities* 4, no. 1 (2014): 113–23.

This plethora of agents, human and nonhuman, included colonial officials, soldiers, farmers, and pastoralists; transport animals such as camels, mules, donkeys, and ponies and their human handlers; the plants of the "wasteland" that nourished camels, but also sometimes killed them; standing and flowing water, biting flies, and pathogenic microbes; and professional animal managers and veterinary scientists. All are present in this study. The actions of this "multispecies/multiagent" complex, when considered as a distributed network, had distinct, massively important effects on the British colonial project.[20] Some of those effects worked in tandem with the goals of the colonial state, while others undermined "rational" planning and practices, causing what the British termed "frictions" or "turbulence" within the colonial order.

It is not unprecedented to make nonhuman agents visible in the historiography of colonial India. This book builds on recent work in South Asian studies concerning animals. Scholars such as Saurabh Mishra and Pratik Chakrabarti, for example, have explored not only human-animal relations in colonial India but veterinary medicine there as well.[21] And they have both been highly critical of the colonial state for its greater concern with military animals over domestic ones. I agree with them in general that the domestic scene and the animals of the Indian peasantry clearly took a backseat to the

20. A multiagent approach broadens the array of creative agents involved in any kind of interaction between living entities in a material environment, while deemphasizing human exceptionalism. Hence, it is more concerned with how entities with differential attributes and capacities interact in encounters to create "mutual ecologies" and coproductive environmental niches like the "wastelands" of the Punjab region. See Eduardo Kohn, "How Dogs Dream: Amazonian Natures and the Politics of Transspecies Engagement," *American Ethnologist* 34, no. 1 (2007): 3–24; and S. Eben Kirksey and Stefan Helmreich, "The Emergence of Multispecies Ethnography," *Cultural Anthropology* 25, no. 4 (2010): 545–76.

21. See, for example, Saurabh Mishra, "Beasts, Murrains, and the British *Raj*: Reassessing Colonial Medicine in India from the Veterinary Perspective, 1860–1900," *Bulletin of the History of Medicine* 85, no. 4 (2011): 587–619, and *Beastly Encounters of the Raj: Livelihoods, Livestock, and Veterinary Health in India, 1790–1920* (Manchester: Manchester University Press, 2015). Also see Pratik Chakrabarti, "Beasts of Burden: Animals and Laboratory Research in Colonial India," *History of Science* 48, no. 160 (2010): 125–51, and *Bacteriology in British India: Laboratory Medicine and the Tropics* (Rochester, NY: University of Rochester Press, 2012). In addition, for broader histories of animals in South Asian traditions, see Wendy Doniger, *On Hinduism* (New York: Oxford University Press, 2016), 409–508; Francis Zimmermann, *The Jungle and the Aroma of Meats: An Ecological Theme in Hindu Medicine* (reprint, Delhi: Motilal Banarsidass, 2011); and Fabrizio Ferrari and Thomas Dahnhardt, eds., *Charming Beauties and Frightful Beasts: Non-human Animals in South Asian Myth, Ritual and Folklore* (Sheffield: Equinox, 2013).

military priorities of the state. But this situation seems understandable to me as yet another example of the state's construction of a comprehensive security regime after 1880,[22] one that was deeply embedded in the North-West Frontier regions and had the effect of militarizing not just horses to be used as cavalry mounts but also vast numbers of pack animals. Hence, I focus on the military, and on working animals in particular.

And while this study shares certain archival sources with these other works, it also opens up a variety of other ones to be found in the military sections of the India Office Records in London. As I have argued in previous work, much more than military history can be produced with sources like Indian Army records. This is especially the case for approaching how professionalization in the military led to new organizational and planning structures (e.g. war games), and for discerning schemes for organizing statistical and topographical data (military intelligence). As will be clear in the latter part of the study, the process of professionalization was keenly felt in the units responsible for army logistics and in the veterinary corps, the two key sites in the army where military pack animals were of central importance and clearly legible. And knowledge production stimulated by animal transport problems led to the creation of new service manuals or handbooks for military transport and animal management, and for the identification and treatment of animal diseases.

This book is divided into two parts, moving from the chaos of colonial impressment (1878) to the institution of a rationalized transport and animal management regime (ca. 1902–3). Chapter 1 seeks explanations for the mass death or disappearance of thousands of camels during the Second Afghan War, and notes the various responses of the British to this catastrophe. Chapter 2 then reverses the gaze by exploring the dense "moral ecology" in which camels and other working animals were embedded in the Punjab and the Sind in the nineteenth century. This reconstruction of a more "natural" camel life will, I hope, highlight the often disastrous effects that impressment and colonial warfare later had on rural life in western India. One response of the Indian government to transport problems generated by large-scale military campaigns was to create a more formal army transport system in the early 1880s, designed to be more reliant on mule rather than camel labor. However, in order to make the relatively scarce mule the primary pack animal in army transport, mules had to be either bred in India or found outside the colony. Both approaches are discussed in chapter 3, along with the consequences of mule-breeding programs

22. James Hevia, *The Imperial Security State: British Colonial Knowledge and Empire-Building in Asia* (Cambridge: Cambridge University Press, 2012).

for the region's animal populations. The veterinary surgeons who took charge of mule breeding began to recognize that one reason so many camels died in 1878–79 was because veterinarians had no authority or resources to remove sick or exhausted pack animals from service. Chapter 4 discusses how some of these veterinarians lobbied for a more rational animal management regime while at the same time attempting, with minimal success, to change attitudes toward their profession by introducing the latest developments in microbiology from Europe. It also traces how, through more direct engagements with camels, veterinarians began to alter colonial views of the animal and its special attributes when it was properly cared for. Part 1 ends with an exploration of a repetition, with a difference. In 1897–98, rebellions against British rule broke out along the North-West Frontier, and thousands of animals were forced into service. Unlike in 1879, however, impressment of animals became a political issue in Britain, forcing the Government of India to consider basic reforms to army transport. Moreover, because of a substantial amount of documentary material produced during these operations, I am able, in chapter 5, to provide a clearer picture of what impressment was like on the ground.

Part 2 begins by exploring commissions of inquiry into army supply and transport using the results of their reports, all of which called for a thorough restructuring of army transport. Chapter 6 takes up a second effort at transport reform and covers the changes instituted by Lord George Curzon's government at the beginning of the twentieth century. The key elements created in the new order were permanent transport units and a robust reserve corps. The combination of a new law authorizing impressment and administrative restructuring, the integration of the army's demand for pack animals with the ambitious irrigation project in the Indus River basin, and the creation of an animal management regime that gave veterinarians unprecedented authority to determine animal fitness for service produced something that looked very much like a pack animal biopower regime.

From around 1905, the reformed transport corps was threatened by a new "enemy." This was not a human threat but a microbial one that killed a great many camels, horses, ponies, and mules. The veterinary corps was mobilized to address the threat of the disease that native *sarwans* (camel men) called *surra*. Chapter 7 discusses the war on surra and the emergence of tropical veterinary medicine in colonial India, a development that created a research network linking India with other parts of the British Empire in Asia as well as with French, German, and American colonies in Africa and Asia. As discussed in chapter 8, British veterinary surgeons in India found themselves as part of global colonial network to stamp out infectious diseases of animals. In addition to producing new knowledge about the surra parasite, those transcolonial linkages became important in several ways. For example, the one occasion on which the reformed transport system was made fully operational occurred not because of disturbances in India or along its frontiers, but as a result of the declaration of war in Europe in 1914. Indian Army transport units were dispatched to the fringes of the Ottoman Empire and operated along the thick network of relations connecting India to Singapore and beyond in the East, and to Egypt, Mesopotamia, and parts of Africa in the West. Chapter 9 discusses the war, and evaluates the extent to which the new transport system created under Lord Curzon might have corrected the mismanagement and inequities of previous wars.

The final chapter provides another kind of assessment. To what extent, it asks, are the forms produced under colonial governance in British India still evident in contemporary Pakistan? Exploring this question helps resituate the monument in Hyde Park. One of its major shortcomings, I suggest, is not the animals missing from the monument but the way in which this representation of animals in war ignores empire. This is especially the case when we consider the bronze mules. They are not a vague reference to war across all time. Most specifically, their very presence recalls colonial mountain warfare, like that fought across the North-West Frontier of British India.

* Prologue to Part One *

Warfare and Logistics in Saharasia

The variety of supply and transport issues the British Indian Army faced in the nineteenth century was neither unique nor unprecedented. Other powers that attempted to dominate the subcontinent had faced similar challenges. More important, with the possible exception of river steamers and an improved halter for draft animals, the technologies of transport, as well as the topography of India, had changed little from the time of Alexander's invasion of Afghanistan and the Indus River basin in the third century BCE.[1] The region

1. There were, of course, many invaders from the West. I mention Alexander here because some British officers were keenly aware that they were retracing the footsteps of the Macedonian warlord. For example, in his account of the First Afghan War, William Hough noted that outside Kabul were two inscribed pillars that had been put up by Alexander. He also made reference to the route in Afghanistan taken by Alexander's army; see *A Narrative of the March and Operations of the Army of the Indus in the Expedition into Afghanistan in the Years 1838–1839* (Calcutta: W. Thacker, 1840), 288, 94, 353. In his diary from the Second Afghan War, Col. Augustus Le Messurier explained that the Afghan city of Kandahar was founded by Alexander, and provided a Greek root word for the city's name; see *Kandahar in 1879: Being the Diary of Major Le Messurier, R.E.* (London: W. H. Allen, 1880), 246. Others, like Gen. Donald Stewart, the commander of the Kandahar column in the Second Afghan War, mentioned Alexander in letters home to loved ones. In Stewart's case, he told his wife that it was known from accounts of Alexander's campaign through Kandahar that there were no trees in a certain area near the city; see G. R. Elsmie, ed., *Field-Marshal Sir Donald Stewart, G.C.B, G.C.S.I., C.I.E.: An Account of His Life, Mainly in His Own Words* (London: John Murray, 1903), 277. Also see David Arnold, *The Tropics and the Traveling Gaze* (Delhi: Permanent Black, 2005), where several examples are given of nineteenth-century British travelers in India noting sites where Alexander's army had passed.

itself was part of an ecological continuum of arid tracts stretching across North Africa, through the Middle East, and well into India. Sometimes referred to as Saharasia, the region's low levels of rainfall have meant that large-scale human habitation has been sustainable only along river systems such as the Nile, the Tigris-Euphrates, and the Indus and its tributaries. Over hundreds of years, much of the rest of the land was thinly populated, if at all, by nomadic pastoralists and their animals.

Nevertheless, the riverine agrarian populations were not completely isolated from one another or from larger forces shaping the region, such as Islamic proselytizing, religious pilgrimage, and interactions with war bands of various stripes. In addition, substantial and sustained commercial intercourse fashioned links between the Levant and South Asia, as well as across North Africa from Cairo westward. Overland caravan trade also connected the Mediterranean with equatorial Africa, and with cities and towns across Anatolia and Central Asia. In the case of northwestern India, trade flowed through passes leading to northern and southern Afghanistan and on to Silk Road cities in Central Asia and the markets of eastern Persia. Much of this commerce was made possible through the exploitation of the labor power of an animal unique to the region: the dromedary or one-humped camel, whose many breeds had adapted to variations in plant life and topographies found in different parts of Saharasia. In a landscape where water and flora were scarce, the capacity of camels to live off the plants of arid regions was perhaps the critical element that made long-distance trade and communication possible. Where there was sufficient plant life for camels to graze on, the amount of grain, fodder, and water a caravan needed to carry in order to sustain its pack animals could be much reduced.[2] Caravan operators thus needed an intimate knowledge of routes and plants across the arid plains in order to make adequate plans for supply requirements. An understanding of desert vegetation and its impact on camel physiology was thus basic knowledge among pastoralists. According to one source, for example, Tuareg camel herders of the Sahara identify forty-

2. According to one of the few English-language sources to address the question of camel rations, if grazing is not available for them, they require a daily diet of 10 pounds of grain, preferably barley, and 25 pounds of chopped straw. Given the average carrying capacity of an adult camel (350–400 pounds), one camel would be required to carry the food for approximately ten other camels each day. See Maj. Arthur G. Leonard, *The Camel: Its Uses and Management* (London: Longmans, Green, 1894): 153. Regarding water rations, one authority estimates approximately eight gallons a day for both horses and camels; see Donald W. Engels, *Alexander the Great and the Logistics of the Macedonian Army* (Berkeley: University of California Press, 1978), 145.

seven species of herbs, shrubs, and trees that their camels eat, and they know the effect of these plants on the taste and quality of camel milk.[3]

If such logistical knowledge was unavailable, then travelers, be they merchants or armies, had to obtain it by seeking out local informants or by employing advance scouting parties. Large-scale operations, like those of Alexander the Great, whose cavalry and infantry forces have been estimated at over sixty thousand men, used such methods as they moved across Mesopotamia toward India. In his study of the logistics of Alexander's Macedonian army, Donald Engels has calculated that supplying this force each day required 1,492 camels (or the equivalent in horses and mules, each of which had about half the carrying capacity of a camel) to carry a little over half a million pounds of supplies comprising food and grain for humans and fodder for animals. If water was not readily available on the army's route of march, an additional 7,000 pack animals would have been needed. Alexander also supplemented supplies where possible by marching the army near the coastal ports and rivers to which grain and other foodstuffs could be moved by ship. In addition, he frequently launched the start of a campaign soon after grain crops had been harvested—this was the case for the passage of his forces in and through Afghanistan, for example.[4]

The sources used by Engels to reconstruct Alexander's logistics are limited in some respects. It is, for example, difficult to discern how the Macedonian army acquired its pack animals and supplies (did they commandeer them, hire animals, or purchase them?) as well as how supply and transport were organized. Far more source material is available for the study of more recent campaigns in Asia. For instance, the logistical operations of the Ottoman and Mughal Empires have been studied with particular attention to how armies were formed and maintained in the field. In both these cases, Ottoman and Mughal military leaders were often operating in territories about which they were much more knowledgeable, and where they enjoyed greater command of resources, than seems to have been the case for the Macedonian army. Nevertheless, Ottoman and Mughal armies were challenged by the same geographic,

3. See Ilse Köhler-Rollefson, Paul Mundy, and Evelyn Mathias, *A Field Manual of Camel Diseases* (London: ITDG, 2001), 5.

4. Engels, *Alexander the Great*, 145, 65–66, and 93. Engels also provides helpful calculations on overland supply and nutritional requirements of humans and pack animals; see pp. 16–22. He makes his estimates based on Leonard, *The Camel.* for camels, and Army Veterinary Department General Staff, War Office, Great Britain, *Animal Management* (London, 1908), two sources I use extensively below.

agricultural, and transport animal constraints faced by the ancient Greeks and their own Saharasian predecessors.

In the Ottoman case, supply and transport issues were extremely complex, given that the empire's armies fought on two fronts: one in Europe, the other in the East against the Safavids of Persia and others.[5] One solution Ottoman planners found was to take advantage of preexisting Roman and Saljukid road systems in the Balkans and Asia Minor respectively. Along these roads, the Ottoman commissariat placed grain storage depots. When, however, campaigns ventured farther from the road and depot system,[6] the army had to rely on extra animal power, primarily camels, to deliver food for soldiers and fodder for cavalry horses and other transport animals.[7] In such areas, the army also, like the Macedonians, relied on light cavalry units (in the Ottoman case, Tatars) to scout for water and fodder along the line of march (67).

As for the transport animals themselves, the Ottoman army faced the same conundrum that all premodern armies faced. To what extent should the state maintain its own transport corps, as opposed to hiring animals as needed? The former scheme, as Rhoades Murphey points out in his study of Ottoman warfare, left the care, feeding, and general upkeep of pack animals and their trained caretakers in the hands of the state. In such a system, while state actors were in a position to ensure the quality and health of the pack animal force at any given time, the structure was costly (74). Hiring transport was generally cheaper than year-round maintenance of a pack animal workforce, but prices could be unpredictable, and there was little or no control over either the quality of the animals and their handlers or the costs. The state could ameliorate the vicissitudes of the market in part by granting various kinds of tax relief to guarantee a certain amount of reserve transport for hire; or it could plan military action far in advance to ensure that campaigns were launched when

5. David Quataert observes that in general, horse transport dominated the European theater, camels the Asian theater. But he also notes that camel transport was used by the Ottoman army in the Danube basin; see *The Ottoman Empire, 1700–1922*, 2nd ed. (Cambridge: Cambridge University Press, 2005), 121–22.

6. The introduction of rail lines in Anatolia slightly altered this situation; Ottoman armies were still reliant on camel transport to move supplies from rail heads to forces in the field. See the discussion in Quataert, *The Ottoman Empire, 1700–1922*, 125.

7. Rhoads Murphey, *Ottoman Warfare, 1500–1700* (New Brunswick, NJ: Rutgers University Press, 1999), 70, 74. I make subsequent citations from this source in the text, placed within parentheses. Parenthetically, Murphey's estimates of camels' daily rations gleaned from Ottoman sources are virtually identical to those cited by Engels; see p. 71.

weather conditions were at their best, minimizing the need for additional transport.

But regardless of how well transport was organized, the scale of requirements was in all cases daunting. Murphey estimates that on average, 11,500 camels were required for the transport of the Ottoman sultan and his personal army, the Janissaries. This was only part of the force that took the field, however. There were also auxiliaries and allies, as well as irregular cavalry forces, termed Tamirot, who would muster when called on in exchange for tax relief (36). The addition of these forces to the sultan's army could raise the number of pack animals to fifty thousand or more, with a substantial number of them supported by camp followers made up of grain transporters, merchants, food suppliers, and sutlers (48). These vast numbers of followers, as Murphey and others point out, made the army in the field much like a mobile city, one that wherever it might come to rest provided a stimulus to local economies (82).

Mobility was a key feature of Mughal rulership as well. Whether it involved warfare, hunting, imperial tours, or the seasonal movement of the court from India to Kabul in Afghanistan, Mughal emperors spent about 40 percent or more of their time away from Delhi, often in shifting camps near the military campaigns or sieges under way.[8] Mughal mobility was completely dependent on animals, from their cavalry warhorses to their transport camels, mules, and bullocks. Various sources indicate that there were large numbers of animals involved in these activities, including over one hundred camels and elephants to carry the royal treasury and administrative records alone.[9] Like other groups who emerged from Central Asia and established empires and khanates in southern and western Asia, the Mughals were primarily a horse cavalry army. By the reign of Akbar (r. 1560–1605), the warhorses that made up the imperial Mughal cavalry, all of whom required special provision of fodder supplies when on the move, numbered some 12,000.[10] Maintaining the number of cavalry horses was, however, a challenge for the Mughal court. Because of the scarcity of grazing lands and the poor quality of many Indian grasses, few of the Mughal warhorses were bred in India, however. It was more common for members of the court to purchase Central Asian horses in

8. These are rough figures and vary by imperial reign. I take them from Jos Gommans, *Mughal Warfare* (London: Routledge, 2002), 101–3.

9. Ibid., 105, 109.

10. Henry Blochmann, the translator of Abu al-Fazl's *A'in-i Akbari* (1927; reprint, Lahore: Quasain, 1975), provided this estimate; see p. 256.

the markets of Kabul when they wintered there.[11] Others were bought at markets in, for example, Lahore and Peshawar from Afghan and Persian traders, who were given incentives by the Mughal court to bring their animals into India.[12] Most of the horses were Turkic breeds from Central Asia and Persian breeds, but there were also horses from Arabia who arrived by sea at Indian ports.[13] In addition to the court's cavalry, the *mansabdars* (feudal lords) were required to maintain a reserve force of some 26,000 horses, almost two-thirds of which had to be Persian and Turkic according to Mughal regulations.[14] Shireen Moosvi has estimated that in order to maintain the cavalry of the court and the mansabdars, around 22,000 horses from Persia and Central Asia were required.[15]

In addition to the horses of the imperial cavalry, a large and shifting number of horse soldiers with their own animals could be included in the war band of the Mughal court. These were auxiliaries who mustered when the overlord called on them to join in a campaign. The largest group of auxiliaries comprised warlords, hereditary rulers, and recruitment brokers who were collectively known under the aforementioned term *mansabdar*. The holders of mansabs pledged fealty to the Mughal emperor and were bestowed with a certain status, often in the form of a *khilat* (robe of honor) and/or emoluments.[16] Mansabdar ranks and statuses were based on the number of horsemen the

11. On horse breeding in India and the horse trade market in India and Afghanistan, see Jos Gommans, *The Rise of the Indo-Afghan Empire c. 1710–1780* (Leiden: E. J. Brill, 1995), 71–74, 79–89. The trade in Central Asian horses did not begin with the Mughal but was common among the Turkic dynasties referred to as the Delhi sultanate (1206–1526). On the sea and overland trade between India, Persia, and Central Asia during the sultanate, see Simon Digby, *War Horse and Elephant in the Delhi Sultanate* (Oxford: Orient Monographs, 1971), 29–36.

12. R. B. Azad Choudhary, "The Mughal and the Trading of Horses in India," *International Journal of History and Cultural Studies* 3, no. 1 (2017): 12–13.

13. Ibid., 7–11.

14. Arup Banerji, *Old Routes* (Gurgaon: Three Essays Collective, 2011), 96.

15. Shireen Moosvi, *The Economy of the Mughal Empire c. 1595* (Delhi: Oxford University Press, 1987), 376. For her discussion of how she arrived at these figures, as well as imperial and mansabdar expenditures on horses, see pp. 277–381.

16. On the *khilat*, see F. W. Buckler, "The Oriental Despot," *Anglican Historical Review* 10 (1927–28): 238–49; and Bernard Cohn, *Colonialism and Its Forms of Knowledge* (Princeton, NJ: Princeton University Press, 1996), 114–17. Cohn explains that the cloth used in items like this was graded hierarchically, which suggests that distinctions could be made between ranks of mansabdars based on the quality of the cloth.

recipient could put into the field when called on.[17] In turn, mansabdars could rely on a large pool of armed peasants and itinerant fighting men in the Indian countryside to fulfill their quotas.[18] In addition to filling their ranks with fighting men, the mansabdars were responsible for provisioning them and supplying the necessary pack animals—camels and mules—to carry supplies.[19] A second kind of auxiliary force was made up of part-time combatants termed Silladars. When called on, these men were expected to appear for service with their weapons and one or more horses.[20] The Mughal emperors could also count on a host of adventurers and mystical warriors, such as Turani, Afghan, and Persian freebooters attracted by the promise of plunder, as well as armed Sufi and Hindu ascetics in search of religious fulfillment; all of these came with their own animal transport.[21]

Whether it was the court displaying its wealth, splendor, and power during inspection tours or the emperor making pilgrimages to Sufi shrines[22] or joining his army on campaign, the number of animals required to carry the food, armaments, tents, and equipment of the Mughal emperor or court and its standing and auxiliary armies was formidable. For its part, the imperial household had several thousand elephants, some of whom were used in military engagements and others for transport. But the bulk of transport relied on camels, mules, and oxen, the last of which required reasonably decent roads on which to pull their carts. For imperial tours, the oxcarts functioned fairly well, but for military campaigns, camels had the great advantage of being able to not only traverse roadless tracks but keep up with the cavalry. They could

17. Gommans, *Mughal Warfare*, 42. Blochmann included a chart of the establishments and salaries of the mansabdars, which he took from the *Padishahnama* from the reign of Shahjahan; see Abu al-Fazl, *A'in-i Akbari*, Blochmann translation, 256–58.

18. See Dirk H. A. Kolff, *Nauker, Rajput and Sepoy* (Cambridge: Cambridge University Press, 1990). According to Abu al-Fazl, there was a pool of some 4.4 million men with military qualifications in Mughal India; see Gommans, *Mughal Warfare*, 74.

19. Gommans, *Mughal Warfare*, 116. In addition to the kinds and numbers of horses and elephants each rank was to provide, the mansabdar supplied a certain number of *qatars* (strings of camels and mules). Each *qatar* was made up of five animals. In the case of a commander of ten thousand men, 160 *qatars* of camels, 40 *qatars* of mules, and 320 carts were prescribed; see pp. 257–58.

20. See William Irvine, "The Mughal Army," *Journal of the Royal Asiatic Society* (January 1896): 549.

21. Gommans, *Mughal Warfare*, 42–51.

22. Akbar, for example, visited the Chisti shrines at Ajmer, Pakpattan, and Sikri. Ibid., 109.

in many terrains live off the land, reducing the amount of animal feed the army had to carry, while their dung could be used as fuel for cooking fires.[23]

Estimates are that Akbar's standing army maintained a transport force of six thousand to seven thousand camels.[24] According to Abu al-Fazl in the *A'in-i-Akbari*, the royal camel corps was divided into *qatars*, and each of these small groupings had a *sarban* (*sarwan* in later British sources), or camel driver, whose primary duty was to care for and properly load his camels. To ensure that this job was being done properly, imperial camels were periodically inspected by soldiers and court officials. They were also fed and supplied with equipment paid for by the imperial treasury, and medicated: they were given an annual injection of sesame oil, brimstone, and buttermilk via their nostrils.[25] This concoction may have been a preventive to deal with nasal bots, or botflies that commonly could block the nasal passages of many kinds of animals.[26]

For either imperial inspection tours or military campaigns, the numbers of camels available to the court would be supplemented from other sources. During Akbar's reign and perhaps earlier, the court formed relations with camel breeders among the Baluchi chieftains around Dera Ismail Khan and Dera Ghazi Khan in the Punjab, as well as with the Raibari camel breeders in the Indus valley. In discussing these sources of camels, Abu al-Fazl noted that to guarantee a supply, the court provided allowances to these herders for camel feed. He added that the Raibari bred multiple kinds of camels. One sort, probably bred to work in the mountains, was produced by crossing the two-humped Bactrian male camel with the single-humped lowlands female. Fifty of these lowland females, a Bactrian, and two one-humped male camels, called *loks*, comprised a breeding herd overseen by one of the Raibari herders. The *loks* were also of interest to the Mughal because the Raibari trained some of them to run; the Mughal used these swift animals to carry messengers.[27] As for the other key transport animal, the mule, Abu al-Fazl had little to say. But if the figures noted in the *A'in-i Akbari* for mansabdar transport are considered, they suggest that the ratio of camels to mules was approximately four to one.

23. Francis Bernier, *Travels in the Mogul Empire*, trans. Irving Brook (London: William Pickering, 1826), 2:104, 119.

24. Moosvi puts the number at 6,223 in Akbar's time; see *The Economy of the Mughal Empire c. 1595*, 238.

25. Abu al-Fazl, *A'in-i Akbari*, Blochmann translation, 152–55.

26. Köhler-Rollefson, Mundy, and Mathias, *A Field Manual of Camel Diseases*, 132–33.

27. Abu al-Fazl, *A'in-i Akbari*, 155–56.

Supply for both the court and the army was, however, not exclusively in the hands of the imperial household or the mansabdars. Camp followers, a population perhaps twice the size of the court and army together, made up a substantial element of the imperial entourage. Like the Ottoman camp followers, the Mughal assemblage was composed of grain transporters, merchants, and food suppliers, as well as grass cutters, who sold their gleanings to the cavalrymen.[28] Francis Bernier, a seventeenth-century French physician who participated in the emperor Aurangzeb's (r. 1658–1707) inspection tour to Kashmir, estimated that there were some 150,000 animals—warhorses and pack animals—50,000 of which were camels. His estimates included the animals of camp followers from the bazaars of Delhi.[29] In addition, the court might also be followed by a multitude of itinerant ox herders known as *banjara*, who regularly carried foodstuffs, salt, sugar, and textiles and other finished goods all over India. During his campaign to Kandahar, the Mughal emperor Jahanjir noted that upwards of one hundred thousand banjara oxen were following his army from Multan into Afghanistan.[30]

The scale of the Mughal court and war band assemblages speaks to the ability of a succession of rulers to attract followers to their imperial forays. To sustain regional domination at such a scale, the court relied on exploiting the agrarian revenue and agricultural resources of India while assembling an army drawn from the Indian armed peasantry, nomadic mercenaries and freebooters, and martial and spiritual glory hunters. With specific reference to the Mughal war band, Jos Gommans has argued that this diverse collection of soldiers was held together more by shared interests than by tribe, caste, or other binding social affiliations.[31] When such interests were no longer relevant, the band would dissolve, leaving a core made up of the court's own cavalry and

28. Bernier discusses the grass cutters as well as camels allowed to forage at the end of a day's march; see *Travels in the Mogul Empire*, 120.

29. Ibid., 118–20. Roughly a century after Bernier was in India, Richard Cambridge made similar observations about the scale and pomp of Indian armies in the field, in this case that of a lesser prince on campaign in the south. See his *An Account of the War in India* (London: T. Jefferys, 1761), iv–vii. Cambridge also noticed the grass cutters, but claimed that they were attendants attached to individual cavalrymen.

30. Jean Deloche, *Transport and Communication in India prior to Steam Locomotion*, trans. James Walker (Delhi: Oxford University Press, 1993), 1:247–52. Among other sources, Deloche notes that British generals recorded the presence of this form of transport in their campaign reports (249).

31. Gommans, *Mughal Warfare*, 39.

a coterie of soldiers (Ahadis) loyal to the emperor and sustained by imperial allowances.[32]

This rather loose structure, whose most formal elements involved either direct ties to the emperor or indirect ones through the mansabdar system, was generally interpreted by the British as a weakness, chiefly because there was no division of the army into regiments.[33] Early on, beginning with the East India Company, the British innovated by introducing not only the regimental form, including military ranks, but infantry drill and military discipline. At the same time, they set about systematically suppressing the peasant-based markets for military labor. In so doing they made the army a profession.[34] Yet even if they found the Mughal and, probably, other Saharasian political formations wanting, the British, as will be seenbelow, borrowed from Mughal military systems, often without admitting it.

For example, up until the end of the nineteenth century, when a formal supply and transport structure for the army was fully institutionalized, the Indian Army in the field was routinely accompanied by camp followers, a collection of service providers often numbering up to twice its size. The British Indian Army also continued to rely on camel transport, often obtaining animals through either impressment or hire from the same camel herders in the Punjab as those the Mughal court had patronized. And they appropriated Mughal terms while redefining them. For instance, the Indian Army used the term *Silladar* to designate the reserve camel transport corps that was maintained after 1900. On the other hand, the British had difficulty producing and sourcing horses and mules, and for whatever reason were never able to exploit the sizable Central Asian horse markets. While they eventually learned who the camel breeders of Rajasthan, the Indus basin, and Baluchistan were, they never established an allowance system like that of the Mughals, which might have ensured a supply of camels when needed. But perhaps most important, the British, while seldom acknowledging it, came to understand the limits and constraints placed on an army by its reliance on animal transport. Camels laden with hundreds of pounds of supplies had to be judiciously cared for or they would break down, imperiling the advance corps of armies and disrupting lines of communication. The Mughals had learned this through

32. Abu al-Fazl, *A'in-i Akbari*, Blochmann translation, 259–60.

33. See, for example, William Irvine, *The Army of the Indian Moghuls* (London: Luzac, 1903), 57.

34. Kolff, *Nauker, Rajput and Sepoy*, 178.

their campaigns into their ancestral Central Asian homeland, from which the Uzbeks had once driven them.[35]

The British eventually learned their lesson as well, in Afghanistan and in the campaigns along the North-West Frontier of India, but only after facing several disasters. The army began to learn about the logistical difficulties posed by the northwestern part of British India during the First Afghan War (1839–42). Its invasion of Afghanistan in 1839 brought into focus a number of transport problems that would trouble the Indian Army to the end of the century. To begin with, the British found it difficult to hire camel transport and so resorted to purchase, but found it a challenge to fulfill all their requirements in this manner. Exacerbating the shortage of camels was the fact that the army had more camp followers in its wake than soldiers, including the wives of sepoys and whole families of the indigenous support staff along with the large kits of supplies and equipment that officers insisted on carrying into the field.[36] Everyone needed animal transport. Further, pack camels were often stolen by mountain tribes along the route of march into Afghanistan.[37] And a third problem arose with the care and handling of pack animals. As Alexander Morrison has shown, the British were not only ignorant about the particulars of maintaining transport camels in good health—they also failed to hire competent camel men or sarwans for fear that these caretakers might prove disloyal in the field. Instead, the British preferred to hire natives, whether they knew anything about camels or not, from areas already subjugated to the British.[38] As a result of overloading and overwork, combined with a diet of unfamiliar plants and shortages of feed, camels died in droves. One observer estimated that between Quetta and Kandahar, a staggering twenty thousand transport camels, or two-thirds of the animals sent into the field, were lost.[39] The line of march was strewn with their decomposing carcasses, the stench from which

35. See Gommans, *Mughal Warfare*, 179–87.

36. Alexander Morrison, "Camels and Colonial Armies: The Logistics of Warfare in Central Asia in the Early 19th Century," *Journal of the Economic and Social History of the Orient* 57 (2014): 475. In this piece, Morrison compares the Russians' campaign to Khiva with that of the British in Afghanistan and concludes that they faced almost identical supply and transport difficulties.

37. James Atkinson, *Expedition into Afghanistan* (London: W. H. Allen, 1842), 155, 192; and Charles Rathbone Low, *The Afghan War, 1838–1942: From the Journal and Correspondence of Major-General Augustus Abbott* (London: Richard Bentley and Son, 1879), 90.

38. Morrison, "Camels and Colonial Armies," 468–69.

39. Low, *The Afghan War, 1838–1942*, 84.

was described as "pungent and fetid beyond description."[40] Four decades later, British participants in the Second Afghan War (1878–80), to which I now turn, would witness an almost identical scene of camel death and decomposition, but on a much greater scale. And like their predecessors, these witnesses too would note the suffering of creatures necessary and critical to the Indian Army's war-making capability.

40. Atkinson, *Expedition into Afghanistan*, 101.

CHAPTER 1

"Slayers of Camels": The Second Afghan War and Pack Animal "Wastage"

In November 1878, Lord Lytton, the viceroy of British India, decided that the amir of Afghanistan, Sher Ali Khan, was now siding with the Russians against the British in Asia; he ordered an invasion of his country. Almost immediately, the governors of Bombay and the Bengal region received orders from the Government of India to acquire some thirty thousand camels for immediate transport.[1] Civil administrators, sometimes in collaboration with members of the Indian Army Commissariat, sent out calls for camel owners to report with their animals to staging areas, where they would be "hired" for transport service. But since owners risked punishment if they refused to appear, the collection process amounted to military impressment. Compensation, should the animal die in service, was promised, although little actually materialized. This chapter explores the consequences for both animals and humans of this forced procurement or impressment of the camels, ponies, and mules of the Punjab and the Sind.

1. Robert Temple testified before a special parliamentary committee that as governor of Bombay, he was asked to supply twenty thousand camels in October 1878 and another twenty thousand in early 1879. See East India (Military Accounts): *Report of the Committee Appointed by the Secretary of State for India, by Minute Dated 2nd July 1880, to Enquire into the System of Military Account and Estimate in India* (London: House of Commons, 17 February 1881), 82. Cited hereafter as EIMA.

CAMEL CASUALTIES AND THE PROBLEM OF ACCOUNTING

It is evident from subsequent documentation that the process of collection and transfer of animals into the transport service was chaotic—so much so, in fact, that Commissariat personnel, according to Col. Thomas Sibley, a transport officer on the Kandahar-Quetta communication line, were never able to produce a fully accurate list of the number of animals impressed.[2] After two years of British Indian Army operations in Afghanistan, the best transport officers could do, according to the documentary collection termed the *Proceedings*, was to estimate that some eighty thousand camels had been either hired or purchased for service.[3] The main reason for the absence of precise numbers was that the commissary general of Bengal, one Col. J. L. Willes, the official responsible for keeping track of the animals, had no control over procurement and little if any control over the animals once they were put into service. Willes was, in other words, in the impossible position of being responsible for the animals in the Commissariat's care yet having in effect no authority to manage them. Why this was the case requires some explanation. What was the nature of the command and control problem, and why is it significant for an understanding of why so many pack animals died or went missing?

On the procurement side, the civilian officials who collected the animals were supposed to write a receipt containing the name of the owner and the particulars of the hire. But that procurement apparently occurred under such intense time pressure that these records were poorly kept. Afterward, Willes could only speculate that at some later point, when owners made claims for lost animals, for example, receipts might turn up.[4] But at no time, it would

2. Testifying before the same committee as Temple (31 July 1880), Sibley noted that after September 1879, purchases of camels were completely controlled by civil officials, and the numbers purchased or hired and the expenditures were not reported to the army Commissariat. EIMA, 49. Sibley's testimony runs from p. 45 to p. 51.

3. The full title of this twelve-volume collection in the India Office, British Library, is "Government of India Military Proceedings on the 'Kabul Expedition' (Second Afghan War), 1879–1880." It includes correspondence between forward and rear areas; battle accounts; records of troop movements, intelligence operations, transport, and supply; and reports on various aspects of the campaign. Each volume contains documents gathered over a three- or four-month period beginning in March–June 1879 and ending in October–December 1881. These are organized in categories, such as Commissariat and transport, and indexed by these categories at the end of each volume; see IOR/L/MIL/5/678–88.

4. See L/MIL/5/687, September 1881, p. 17.

seem, did he ever receive full and regular reports from civilian procurers. On the distribution side, there was a similar problem of reporting. Willes had enormous difficulty locating and collecting what were called "returns." These were periodic reports from transport officers in the field that should have recorded the numbers of active, disabled, dead, and replacement animals in their units.

But the problem of inaccurate enumeration emerged not only because of a lack of coordination between civilian and military officials, or bad record keeping under pressure of time. It also involved a muddled relationship between Commissariat officers and the regiments comprising the field force. The forces themselves were divided into three separately commanded groups—the Peshawar and Kurram columns advancing toward Kabul in the north, and the Kandahar Field Force advancing from Quetta toward the southern Afghan city. Hardly any of the transport of these columns was under the direct control of the Commissariat.

Furthermore, from the archival sources available in the India Office Records, it is very difficult to determine any clear chain of command in reporting on supply issues. There was certainly no one in the Commissariat who could make irrevocable decisions about how resources were to be managed on the lines of communication. As Sibley put it in his testimony before the Parliamentary Committee, "A great deal of confusion has arisen by there being several different authorities appointed to carry out the one duty of the transport, without any intercommunication or any special offices where such information would be collated."[5]

The "several different authorities" referred to by Sibley looked something like this: general officers commanding the three field forces or their designated subordinates often overrode decisions made by transport and veterinary officers on the communication lines. In addition, there were multiple officers filing reports that contained figures on pack animals, but no clear authority existed above the field commanders to make decisions on transport questions, including Commissary General Col. Willes. Even above Willes, authority was unclear. His main correspondence with a superior was with Col. H. K. Burne, who was the military secretary to the Government of India. Yet Burne's position was essentially advisory to the viceroy of India. He does not appear to have had much authority beyond demanding regular returns from Willes. In turn, Burne carried on a lively correspondence with Gen. Peter Lumsden, adjutant general of the Indian Army, who fed Burne information on conditions

5. See EIMA, 50.

along the lines of communication that Willes may or may not have seen, but which Burne doesn't seem to have shared with Willes. Burne also received reports from Lt. Col. William Lockhart, an assistant quartermaster general, who forwarded returns on the condition of transport with both the Peshawar and Kurram Field Forces.[6] There is no indication that Lockhart also communicated with Willes or that Burne passed reports from Lockhart to Willes. In Latourian terms, Indian Army transport lacked a "center of calculation," which meant that no one had an overview of what was happening on the ground.[7] Or, to use the parlance of the times, the "frictions" in the transport system made collation impossible.[8]

Perhaps nothing depicted the fragmented nature of the transport system more clearly than an incident in April 1879. Upon hearing that a column under command of Gen. Michael Biddulph was withdrawing from Afghanistan through Thal, Burne asked Willes to provide him with information on the strength of the transport Biddulph had with him. Two weeks later (5 May 1879), Willes responded that no one could give an account of Biddulph's numbers, because various units of his force had picked up carriage along the way and were now arriving back in India piecemeal. Meanwhile, other reports circulated that Biddulph was losing fifty camels a day, and that his column was being supplied with stores and pack animals not by the Commissariat but through the efforts of the political officer in Baluchistan, Robert Sandeman.[9] The transport disorderliness within the column Biddulph commanded apparently was repeated along all three lines of communication, indicating the extent to which transport and any hope of its orderly accounting were unlikely. But how had matters come to this—was it simply another case of the fog of war?[10]

6. See, for example, IOR/L/MIL/5/679, September 1879, pp. 60, 84.

7. Bruno Latour, *Science in Action: How to Follow Scientists and Engineers through Society* (Milton Keynes, Buckinghamshire: Open University Press, 1987), chap. 6, especially 232–37.

8. On friction and the second law of thermodynamics, see the prologue to part 2 below.

9. IOR/L/MIL/5/680, October 1879, pp. 112, 143, 148. In March, Willes had received a report from Sibley about Sandeman's initiatives; see p. 145.

10. There was at least one instance where a commander seems to have attempted to escape the "fog" by moving his regiment up a hill to breathe "pure mountain air." Unfortunately, the maneuver was so poorly executed that the pack animals bolted, with the loss of virtually the entire baggage train and the supplies they carried. See the court of inquiry for Gen. Frederick Appleyard; the court's decision was that Appleyard never again be placed in a position where he could assume command based on seniority; see IOR/L/MIL/5/680, November 1879, pp. 162–87.

As a way of addressing this question, let me begin by explaining how Commissariat personnel imagined the transport system would work once civil officials had placed the animals in their hands. Transport officers on the Kandahar and Kurram lines, and perhaps the Peshawar line as well, had attempted from the onset of the invasion of Afghanistan to establish an *etappen* (staged resupply) system. Camels would travel a certain distance to a point where their packs would be transferred to fresh camels, and then they would return to their original starting point, where they would rest and graze, if possible. The *etappen* system had been perfected by the Prussian army in the 1860s, and the British Commissariat officers were keen on testing it. It broke down almost immediately, however. Willes received a report on 2 January 1879 that although stages were established along the line from Jacobabad to Dadur, no British officers were present at these sites to supervise the process. As a consequence, desertion among the hired camels was rampant. In addition, no food or fodder was provided for the animals, no personnel were available to return them to their starting point, and perhaps worst of all, regiments who had lost their own pack animals for whatever reason simply commandeered the Commissariat transport. There was no authority to stop them from doing so, and, more important, no means for Commissariat officers to keep track of animals assigned to them any longer once reimpressment had occurred.[11]

The situation on the Kandahar line particularly highlights the difficulties transport officers faced. This was the communication line Col. Sibley was in charge of. When he became aware that animals were not being returned to their departure points, Sibley proceeded toward Kandahar to find out what had gone amiss. He apparently continued past Quetta and well into Afghanistan in seeking an answer, because on 24 January 1879, Willes received a dressing-down from Burne. Somehow, Burne had gotten word that Sibley had traveled all the way to Kandahar, where Gen. Donald Stewart and his division were now holed up for the winter. Why, he wanted to know, hadn't Sibley established a place where "he could superintend and control the whole of the supply operations on which the entire force was dependent"?[12] Willes was unable to reply until June, at which time he forwarded to Burne a detailed account he had received from Sibley.[13]

11. IOR/L/MIL/5/682, May 1880, pp. 449–51.

12. Ibid., pp. 455–57.

13. IOR/L/MIL/5/682, June 1880, p. 36. In his parliamentary testimony, Sibley mentioned how slow communication was between transport officers in the field and those they reported to. See EIMA, 48.

In his message to Willes, Sibley explained that while he had made certain estimates of the number of camels needed at the outset in November, it turned out that because soldiers had to carry a large stock of provisions themselves, extra transport had been assigned to the regiments, leaving initially only seven thousand camels for the transport corps. He still thought, however, that he would have had enough camels to move supplies up to Quetta had the animals continued to carry only stores, but "convoys, instead of being returned, were constantly being broken up and taken to complete the military equipment of regiments which had become inefficient owning to desertions and death."[14]

Sibley then referred to one of the Transport Rules of the Government of India (rule 4), which required officers to ensure the integrity of carriage. While he granted that it was impossible to control camel mortality in the winter in Afghanistan, "it was not expected that desertions would have been permitted to so large an extent." On 15 December 1878, Sibley explained, he had sent a message to Stewart to make him aware of the problem and of the paramount importance of maintaining the convoy capability for the security of his forces in Kandahar. He then proceeded toward Kandahar to inspect what was going on, as no camels were returning down the line. Most of the desertions, he said, were occurring in Dadur and in the passes leading into Afghanistan. As he approached Kandahar, he realized that all the reserves were being absorbed. Exacerbating matters was the quality of the roads: they were too rough for cart bullocks to proceed along the track to Kandahar, which meant that camels were being used to haul ammunition instead of just food supplies.[15]

But the disorganized nature of transport was not the only problem threatening the Commissariat's ability to supply Indian Army forces in Afghanistan. Far more disturbing was that camels impressed from the Punjab and the Sind were dying at an alarming rate. In corresponding with his wife, Gen. Stewart repeatedly returned to the extraordinary numbers of camels being lost. After noting the cold and "cutting" wind that appeared to have a profound effect on pack animals, he told his wife in a letter in early March 1879 that

> it is impossible to march, and the camels will suffer more than ever. Out of curiosity I asked Brigadier Hughes to count the skeletons of camels lying on the road from Kelat-i-Ghilzai to Candahar, and the list was 1924. This was what we lost out of a division transport of about 3,500. Many more disappeared, but there is no doubt about these, as the carcasses were counted by officers. If our

14. IOR/L/MIL/5/682, June 1880, pp. 37–38.
15. Ibid.

> Division lost this number, what will the losses of the army be? We have already got a mortality return of over 9000 camels, and this does not include the deaths in the train between Sukkur and Dadur. More than half of these deaths is due to starvation.[16]

By October, he was wondering if his name would go down in posterity as the "slayer of camels."[17]

If anything, Stewart underestimated the extent of the catastrophe. Along the Kandahar line, up to the beginning of July 1879, over 16,000 camels were reported to be dead,[18] out of a total of 36,688 that Willes estimated had been hired.[19] To use the terminology of the Commissariat, this was a "wastage" rate of 44 percent. But even this extraordinary number seems too low. In a report of 10 May 1879, Willes told Burne that in an initial count based on the returns he had in hand, 15,362 camels had been purchased since the beginning of the invasion and another 65,659 hired or impressed, for a total of 81,021 camels. From these same returns, Willes could account for only 15,311 camels still alive. Thus, by these figures, 65,710 camels had been lost—a wastage rate of 81 percent. While that number seems difficult to believe, it is supported by the only extant report on wastage I have been able to locate. The source is Maj. James A. S. Colquhoun, a transport officer, who provided a return on camel carriage employed by the Kurram Field Force in his published account of the war. According to Colquhoun, between October 1878 and May 1879, 10,861 camels were brought onto the rolls. At the end of May, only 2,033 remained. The other 8,828 camels had either died, deserted, been abandoned, strayed, or been carried off by bandits—a wastage rate of 81 percent.[20] How did this

16. G. R. Elsmie, ed., *Field-Marshal Sir Donald Stewart, G.C.B, G.C.S.I., C.I.E.: An Account of His Life, Mainly in His Own Words* (London: John Murray, 1903), 224, 237, 243, 245, 248, 250, 255, and 289. Also see Stewart's explanation of events in IOR/L/MIL/5/682, June 1880, 44–46.

17. Elsmie, *Field-Marshal Sir Donald Stewart, G.C.B, G.C.S.I., C.I.E.*, 289.

18. IOR/L/MIL/5/686, March 1881, Lockhart to Burne, 3 July 1879, pp. 322–23. The official history of the war gives a figure close to 12,000. Intelligence Department, Army Headquarters, *The Second Afghan War, 1878–1880*. Abridged Official Account (London: John Murray, 1908), 165. How this number was arrived at by Intelligence Department officers so long after the fact is impossible to ascertain.

19. IOR/L/MIL/5/686, March 1881, Willes to Burne, 10 May 1879, p. 293. None of the returns Willes alluded to are in the India Office Records of the campaign.

20. James Andrew Sutherland Colquhoun, *With the Kurram Field Force, 1878–79* (London: W. H. Allen, 1881), 400.

happen? How was it possible for such an extraordinary number of camels to have been lost in this relatively brief period of time?

The initial explanation, at least from some quarters, was that the number of deaths could be attributed to the camels themselves. One argument along these lines was environmental in nature. Willes, for example, noted as early as January 1879 that the plains camels impressed from the Punjab and the Sind were ill suited for use in the mountains during the winter. He also was one of the first to add a related cause: that the bulk of the plains camels impressed were of an inferior quality within the type.[21] Here Willes might have been pointing both to the physical characteristics of the plains camel and to the fact that many of those impressed were only two to three years old, an age considered inappropriate for hauling heavy loads.[22] The proper camels—the ones acclimatized to conditions in the mountains between Afghanistan and the Punjab—were ones referred to as Powindah camels. These were the animals used by traders who plied the routes into northwestern India. But the Powindah camels were not only difficult to hire.[23] As Willes reminded Burne, during the First Afghan War these camels and their owners had deserted in droves as the British army approached Kabul.

Yet if Willes's argument basically boiled down to the wrong camel for the job at hand, a few observers found additional reasons for the high death toll. Colquhoun's account of the campaign also contains a report by Maj. W. C. Anderson, the assistant adjutant general of the Kurram Field Force. In addition to pointing to the problem of using plains camels in the mountains, Anderson noted that grazing for the camels was scant and not what they were accustomed to.[24] This is probably a reference to mountain plants called

21. Col C. C. Johnson, quartermaster general, may have been the first to draw attention to the qualities of the plains camels; see his memo to Burne dated 4 January 1879 in IOR/L/MIL/5/678, May 1879, p. 103. Willes first mentioned this factor in a memo to Burne dated 23 January 1879; see IOR/L/MIL/5/678, May 1879, pp. 109–10. Also see the comments of Gen J. Watson in IOR/L/MIL/5/685, February 1881, p. 206.

22. On the age issue, see IOR/L/MIL/7/834: Report on the Veterinary Department Kurram Field Force, memo from Collins to under secretary of State, India Office, dated 12 September 1881.

23. Willes noted in a memo to Burne on 14 January 1879 that hired Powindah camel owners were refusing to go into Afghanistan or work beyond Peshawar or Jellalabad; see IOR/L/MIL/5/678, May 1879, p. 111. As he noted later, when pressed, these camel men simply deserted; see ibid., p. 112.

24. Colquhoun, *With the Kurram Field Force, 1878–79*, 393.

"bushwood" in several accounts.[25] Camels acclimatized to the mountains seemed to have no difficulty with these plants, but to the plains camels they were poisonous.

No doubt the arguments about environmental adaptations and the young age of the camels do account for some of the deaths. But these reasons shifted the cause of deaths to the animals themselves and obscured the chaos of impressment and the disorder on the supply lines. In contrast, Anderson laid a good portion of the blame on the humans responsible for the animals, and he provided examples of mistreatment. Many of the animals, he observed, had loads on their back upwards of twelve hours a day, when the norm seems to have been seven or eight, and they were often left standing fully loaded for hours. Moreover, when they arrived in camp at the end of the day, there was often nothing for them to eat.[26] Hence, many were progressively weakened.

A general ignorance about camels and how to manage them was noted in at least one other report. Gen. John Walker, commander of the Punjabi Chief's Contingent,[27] observed that little was understood about the "nature and constitution of the camel," with the result that no one knew what to do when the animal became ill.[28] Such ignorance was partly a function of inexperience, but it was also because those who did know something about the constitution of the camel, the veterinary surgeons, were very few in number and extremely overworked—there are at least two recorded cases of surgeons being invalided home in a state of exhaustion and frustration. Moreover, the veterinarians were seldom listened to by either the Commissariat personnel or the officers responsible for transport in regiments. What did the surgeons know that others didn't or chose to ignore?

At least two fragmentary reports by veterinarians are included in the *Proceedings* along with a large, comprehensive one by G. A. Oliphant, who was assigned to the Kurram line of communication from late 1879 to the beginning of October 1880. The reports of Oliphant and the other surgeons tell a

25. Joshua Duke, *Recollections of the Kabul Campaign, 1879 and 1880* (London: W. H. Allen, 1883), 78. Also see Henry Hanna, *The Second Afghan War, 1878–79–80: Its Causes, Its Conduct and Its Consequences* (Westminster: Archibald Constable, 1904), 2:130. In the Quetta area, Hanna noted that another plant he termed "southernwood" was also devastating to the camels from the lowlands; see 1:318.

26. Colquhoun, *With the Kurram Field Force, 1878–79*, 393.

27. These were native militia groups who were used to protect the lines of communication into the Kurram valley; see Colquhoun, *With the Kurram Field Force, 1878–79*, 388–93.

28. See IOR/L/MIL/5/685, February 1881, p. 206.

FIGURE 4. Camels left to die along the road to Kandahar. *Graphic* (London), March 27, 1880.

substantially different tale from what has been presented to this point. Consider first a series of memos written by Charles Steel, veterinary surgeon on the Kandahar line, in January and February 1879.[29] Observing that bodies of dead camels were strewn all along the line of advance (figs. 4 and 5), Steel noted that the largest numbers were collected at the top of an acclivity like the Bolan Pass, indicating that they had dropped while attempting to climb to higher elevations. The dead were mostly very young (two to three years of age, he estimated). All had come from the plains and had probably died of exposure and exhaustion.[30] After performing autopsies, Steel discovered additional causes of death. Many had died of congested and inflamed lungs. As he noted, "In every case I examined the lungs were the *viscera* affected, and it points out how especially intolerant is the camel of the plains of any violent change of climate."[31]

29. Steel's reports were forwarded by Adj. Gen. Lumsden in two batches to Burne in early May 1879; see IOR/L/MIL/5/680, December 1879, pp. 71–76.

30. Steel's observations were supported by others. In a report published four years after the war, another veterinary surgeon argued that the chief causes of the enormous mortality among the camels were that they were far too young, insufficiently clothed, and fed poorly or with indigestible grain; see *QJVSI* 2, no. 6 (1884): 211.

31. IOR/L/MIL/5/680, December 1879, p. 76.

FIGURE 5. A vultures' feast. *Graphic* (London), March 15, 1879.

In other cases, Steel observed a deficiency of bulk food or an excess of indigestible materials in the stomachs of the dead, either of which could result in starvation. Still other autopsies indicated that animals had choked on dry *bhoosa* (straw) and diffused it into their lungs, which caused congestion and inflammation. Hence, a substantial number of the deaths could be ascribed to the ignorance of those who were managing the animals. Steel was especially harsh on native attendants, or sarwans, on the campaign. As it turned out, most of these were not professional camel men. Later, after he had been invalided home, Steel wrote F. F. Collins, the principal veterinary surgeon of the Bengal Army, about a variety of contagious diseases in camels, including cases of mange so serious that he requested permission to put the animals down. He also noted rinderpest in army cattle and scab in sheep.[32] These animals were used to feed the army in the field.

The ignorance that Gen. Walker had observed regarding the constitution of camels became for Steel a kind of cruelty in which obviously unfit animals were forced to march on with loads that were seldom reasonably apportioned. When, at the beginning of the day, the animals were too exhausted to raise themselves after being loaded while in a kneeling position, they would be loaded while standing up. And if they failed to rise when ordered, the transport personnel considered them obstinate. Those so designated might have fresh slits for ropes cut into their nostrils, "to torture them into advancing a mile or two further eventually to fall down dead."[33] No one, Steel might have

32. The letter is part of Collins's memo of 12 September 1881; see IOR/L/MIL/7/834.

33. IOR/L/MIL/5/680, December 1879, p. 76.

added, intervened to prevent such mistreatment. On the other hand, the notion of the camel as an obstinate beast of burden gained currency.

Soon after he left the campaign, Steel was asked by the editors of the *Journal of the United Service Institution of India* to contribute an article about camels used during the Afghan campaign. The piece rehearsed much of what appeared in his official report, reiterating that a general ignorance of the camel and the refusal of senior officers to take the advice of veterinary surgeons were contributing factors in the number of deaths. He then concluded the piece with a series of questions that succinctly summarized the primary causes of camel death.

> How many were killed by want of provision for proper feeding, when arrangements might have been made, had *some one* remembered that the ruminating stomachs require special accommodation? How many succumbed to unnecessary over-driving? How many were willfully killed by negligent Surwans [sarwans]? How many water stores, as it has amused physiologists to call them, were allowed to run dry? I must repeat that Officers' camels enjoyed considerable immunity from all these evils, and leave readers to speculate, if it please them, as to the number that *might* have been saved.[34]

This last observation about camels that carried the officers' kit is telling. It suggested not only that officers closely supervised their camel handlers, but that the camels of the Sind, where Steel indicated that most on the Kandahar line had come from, were not of as delicate a constitution as some had claimed. Second, his reference to officer supervision of camel handlers pointed to a much larger problem that he identified—a complete lack of disciplined organization in transport, which included the absence of the most basic drugs for treating animals in the field.

Another veterinary surgeon who reported some of his observations was J. P. Adams. After also being invalided home like Steel, Adams wrote to Collins about what he had witnessed while with the Kurram Field Force. Adams had been assigned to an artillery unit and was unable to operate outside it. In his unit alone, 450 out of 1,200 camels died. By October 1879, he was in Kabul, where he set up a veterinary hospital that soon was inundated with over 10,000 sick animals. Adams found himself without medical supplies, the aid of other veterinarians, or cooperation from the army.[35]

34. Charles Steel, "Camels in Connection with the South Afghan Expedition 1878–1879," *JUSII* 8, no. 39 (1879): 455–62. The quotation is on p. 462.

35. The letter is part of Collins's memo of 12 September 1881; see IOR/L/MIL/7/834.

Steel also reported on the absence of cooperation from army officers. He claimed to have been told by a transport officer when attempting to inspect some animals along the Kabul line that he should go back where he came from. The primary reason for this attitude, as Steel seemed to have been aware, was the enormous pressure coming from superiors to keep the supplies moving regardless of the condition of pack animal transport. Some of this pressure came from Gen. Sir Michael Kennedy, who had been appointed on 20 September 1879 to a new position, controller-general of supply and transport, for the purpose of bringing order on the supply lines to Kabul. Kennedy complained about the number of animals being rejected by veterinarians for physical reasons. He argued that although many of the animals were not all that could be desired, the need for transport took precedence.[36] His evocation of necessity would seem to have placed matters precisely where they were at the beginning of the war—the need for military transport outweighed all other considerations.

For the veterinary surgeons, however, it was clear that if necessity was to be the criterion, the army would continue to have to deal with extraordinary levels of animal deaths—and not just among camels but mules, donkeys, bullocks, and horses as well. Even more disturbing from the veterinarians' point of view, the pressure of necessity obscured other major causes of death, the chief ones being communicable diseases such as mange, glanders (a contagious and often fatal respiratory disease caused by the bacterium *Burkholderia mallei*), anthrax, foot-and-mouth, and a debilitating disease known as surra to the camel men of the Punjab. About the last, virtually nothing was known.

In the longest extant report on conditions along the supply lines in 1879, First Class Veterinary Surgeon G. A. Oliphant reiterated the observations of Steel and Adams, and concluded that the fundamental problem was that there was no system in place and precious little knowledge or understanding of animal diseases to deal with transport problems. One example he gave was a case in which an animal with glanders was moved from the front to the rear of the line, spreading the disease all along the way. In another instance, he found animals with foot-and-mouth being sold off to villagers along the Kurram line. Government-owned animals were often starving, and Oliphant suspected that the army's animal feed was being sold to the owners of hired camels. By the time he was posted to the Kurram line, orders had been issued to create hos-

36. See IOR/L/MIL/7/834. Steel's comments are in Collins's memo of 12 September, while Kennedy's can be found in "Telegram from Sir Michael Kennedy, Controller-General of Supply and Transport to Principal Veterinary Surgeon, Jhelum, 27th January 1880."

pitals or depots to care for sick or injured animals. He spent time at three of these and provided statistics on admissions, discharges, and deaths. What his numbers showed was that with treatment, rest, and proper diet, the vast majority of animals, with the exception of camels, could be put back in service. At the Shalozan Hospital, the rate of deaths to admissions was as follows: 1.95 percent of the 3,485 mules and ponies, 2.24 percent of the 1,384 donkeys, 7.5 percent of the 2,764 bullocks, and 45 percent of the 4,054 camels.[37]

Oliphant sent his report to Collins, who combined it with those of Steel and Adams to provide evidential support for a recommendation he then made to the secretary of state for India in September 1881.[38] Collins asked that an administrative veterinary officer be assigned at the divisional level in the field, much as was common in European armies. His intent seems clear. If the veterinary service was to have any effect at all on the treatment of pack animals, if the "appalling" loss of transport animal life was to be avoided in the future, an officer of sufficient rank and authority was required: one who could oversee hospitals on lines of communication, be authorized to separate diseased from healthy animals, and presumably have a say in the selection of transport animals.

To bolster his recommendation, Collins included ample evidence that veterinary surgeons were not held in particularly high esteem by either physicians or the officers responsible for transport in the various regiments. At least one prominent doctor, J. M. Cuningham, the surgeon general of India, argued that the veterinarians were uniformly poorly trained and lacked the "necessary scientific qualifications,"[39] while transport officers did not like veterinarians present because they knew that they would try to pull sick or weary animals out of service. As one officer put it, presumably in an effort to dismiss the observations of veterinary surgeons, "there has been nothing in the casualties of the animals which in any way would have been prevented by professional opinions, as the causes are alone self-evident viz.; want of clothing, forage, supervision and establishment."[40]

37. See IOR/L/MIL/7/834, pp. 4–12 and 40–41. Oliphant's statement is dated 26 December 1880. This report was later published in the *QJVSI* 1, no. 2 (1882: 214–59, and 1, no. 3 (1883): 387–420.

38. See Collins to the secretary of state for India in IOR/L/MIL/7/834, with various enclosures.

39. See IOR/L/MIL/7/834: report of J. M. Cuningham, surgeon general of the Government of India, 20 April 1881.

40. IOR/L/MIL/7/834: Lt. Col. A. H. Murray, deputy adjutant general, to F. F. Collins, 14 February 1879.

Such attitudes probably only worsened when the veterinarians tried, as we have seen, to set up hospitals along the lines of communication.[41] Moreover, as was noted above, Commissary officers such as Willes did not want veterinarians involved in the initial selection process of transport animals—if they were, it would have been impossible to meet the high demand for these animals on short notice, because the veterinarians would oppose, among other things, the impressment of camels either too young or too old for effective service. Willes was no doubt right on this score. But as in the case of procurement and deployment of transport, the fundamental issue remained a lack of clear lines of communication and sufficient authority to make binding decisions in the field. The absence of veterinary authority in particular meant that there was no one who could override the indifferent, sometimes brutal treatment of transport animals and curtail practices that spread contagious diseases through their ranks.

The veterinarians' inability to have a more profound impact on the treatment of pack animals is quite evident in the records collected in the *Proceedings*. Beyond the observations of the veterinary officers, no explicit statements in these by army officers linked the ignorance of the constitution of the camel and the prevalence of communicable diseases to animal death and suffering. A similar absence is evident in the official history of the campaign compiled by Charles MacGregor, a history that, while published, was initially suppressed; it appeared in print, and then in a much-abridged form, only in 1908. Instead, MacGregor's history seems to have been primarily concerned with the problem the death of transport animals posed to the effective operations of the field forces.[42]

Something else also did not make it into the official history—the personal testimony of a number of participant-observers on the plight of the pack animals, much of which appeared in campaign memoirs. Published almost immediately after the end of the war, these accounts provide some sense of human reactions to the animals' suffering. In particular, memoirists noted the state of exhaustion of the animals and how many died of exposure to the harsh

41. See, for example, Steel's comments in the report of J. M. Cuningham, surgeon general of the Government of India, 20 April 1881; IOR/L/MIL/7/834.

42. Charles M. MacGregor, comp., *The Second Afghan War, 1878–80*, 6 vols. (Simla: Government Central Branch Press, 1885–86), a copy of which can be found in the India Office Records at the British Library. MacGregor's six volumes were later reduced to two; see Intelligence Department, Army Headquarters, India, *The Second Afghan War, 1878–80*, 2 vols. (Simla: Government Central Branch Press, 1908).

weather of the mountains. One, for example, observed that any number of camels were frozen to the ground overnight and were thus unable to rise in the morning.[43] This must have been an eerie scene for the sarwans and Commissariat personnel, because when the camels were bedded down at day's end, they knelt in a circle facing inward.[44] In other cases, camels unaccustomed to the rocky hill tracks might fall, break a leg, and need to be shot.[45] Or, if young and inexperienced, they might break down carrying unfamiliar loads.[46] Still others died in battle or in raids along the route of march. Supply columns were attacked by the mountain people—Afridis and Waziris in the north, Baluchis in the south. They struck in the passages of twisting *nullahs* (mountain canyons). If the animals could not be carried off, their bellies might be slit open by the attackers.[47]

Also found only in the memoirs were reports of elephants, virtually eliminated as transport animals at this time, being used to haul carcasses of dead camels off roads (fig. 6) and themselves dying from exhaustion in the process, or of camel handlers vocally lamenting the death of their animal on the roadside. In addition, all these accounts spoke of the pervasive stench of death all along the lines of communication, and evoked the sad sight of a camel finally released from its load thinking it was free, only to wander off to its death.[48] Also absent from the official record are references to the slow stages of the camel's death, which culminated in its refusal to rise again no matter how many times it was whipped and kicked. Missing too are the statements attributed to camel handlers that when a camel perishes, he turns his head toward Mecca.[49]

The unofficial works recording the conditions under which pack animals, especially camels, labored and died also testified to an affective response to their plight. Many officers took pity on them while also being angered by the

43. T. C. Hamilton, *Diary of the March of the 15th "the King's" Hussars to Kandahar: October 1878 to April 1879* (Meerut: "Charles & Co." Medical Hall Press, 1879), 35.

44. Charles G. Robertson, *Kurum, Kabul and Kandahar: Being a Brief Record of Impressions in Three Campaigns under General Roberts* (Edinburgh: David Douglas, 1881), 164.

45. Duke, *Recollections of the Kabul Campaign, 1879 and 1880*, 78–79.

46. Henry Francis Brooke, *Private Journal of Henry Francis Brooke: Late Brigadier-General Commanding 2nd Infantry Brigade Kandahar Field Force, Southern Afghanistan, from April 22nd to August 16th, 1880* (Dublin: William Curwen, 1880), 20.

47. Colquhoun, *With the Kurram Field Force, 1878–79*, 159.

48. Richard Gillham-Thomsett, *Kohat, Kuram, and Khost; or, Experiences and Adventures in the Late Afghan War* (London: Remington, 1884), 135, 141, 167, 238, 248.

49. Duke, *Recollections of the Kabul Campaign, 1879 and 1880*, 78.

FIGURE 6. Elephant removing a dead camel. *Graphic* (London), March 15, 1879.

great wrong that had been done them. Maj. Augustus Le Messurier, a royal engineer on the Kandahar line, summed up the sentiments of many when he exclaimed in his diary, "Poor beasts, what a tale they could tell of our want of care and forethought! And will the broad hint of their dead carcasses have any effect on our future campaigns?"[50]

But this was a sentiment generated from the vantage point of horseback, from the position of an educated officer, a participant having the foresight to keep a personal record of the campaign. The bulk of the army was made up of ordinary soldiers who entered Afghanistan on foot and left few if any records of what the war looked like at ground level. There is, however, a diary kept by a Pvt. William Atkinson of the South Hampshire regiment. With fresh units moving into Afghanistan in February 1879, Atkinson recorded seeing many camels drop from exhaustion and starvation all along the line of march, their carcasses ripped apart by "jackals and other wild beasts and large birds of prey," leaving their skeletons glaring in the broiling sun. Yet even amid this carnage, he also spoke admiringly of the qualities of the camels. "The camel," he tells us,

> is a very hard working animal and will go as long as the poor thing can get one leg before the other and fall down and die rather than shirk their work and so it was often remarked by my comrades as also by myself was as these the poor camels are just like the poor soldiers they will go on as far as they can until they

50. Col. Augustus Le Messurier, *Kandahar in 1879: Being the Diary of Major Le Messurier, R.E.* (London: W. H. Allen, 1880), 150.

> drop. And from that fact the soldiers during our trying marches compared ourselves with the poor camels.[51]

Not the grammar of an officer, to be sure, but perhaps as close as we will get to an affective response that seems like fellow feeling rather than mere superior pity.

But if the actual conditions faced by pack animals in the campaign of 1878–79 received scant attention in the official record, civil and military leaders did attempt to provide some semblance of order to the otherwise chaotic transport situation. Following the early September 1879 killing in Kabul of the British resident Pierre Cavagnari with his staff and guards, Lord Lytton ordered the army to reenter Afghanistan. At that time, Gen. Michael Kennedy had been named controller general of supply and transport. This action not only centralized decision making over transport on the Kabul lines of communication but placed an officer of the same rank as those who commanded field forces in charge of transport. In addition, Col. W. S. A. Lockhart was named road commandant of all traffic on the Khyber and Kurram roads leading to Kabul.[52] During this second phase of the war, some 76,500 animals were either purchased or hired. Apparently, after the experience of the previous year, few owners were willing to hire out their animals. Of the 59,503 camels, mules, and ponies procured, 54,305 had been purchased.[53]

While such accounting was a positive development for the transport system, no figures seem to have been kept on the number of animals lost in the second phase of the war. There was also a significant and relatively ignored problem arising from the earlier deaths. If the situation at Quetta is any indication, the carcasses of dead camels had created an alarming public health problem. The army was without the manpower to bury these, and so a pestilence set in that lasted into 1880.[54] About the only indications in the *Proceedings* of the extent of the environmental impact of animal deaths was a comment by Veterinary Surgeon Oliphant that some effort seemed to have been made in the Kurram valley to deal with the carcasses of the dead. Oliphant noted

51. IOR/MSS Eur D1093, 30.

52. IOR/L/MIL/5/681, March 1880, pp. 23, 26.

53. Figures are available for the animals purchased and hired between September 1879 and September 1880. The replacements included 24,740 purchased and 3,981 hired camels; 6,718 purchased and 719 hired mules; 22,847 purchased and 498 hired ponies; 9,000 hired and purchased bullocks; and over 8,000 donkeys. See IOR/L/MIL/5/688, October 1881, 253. The report is from Willes and is dated 12 September 1881.

54. Hanna, *The Second Afghan War, 1878–79–80*, 2:124.

that many had been buried. Unfortunately, he also observed that perhaps they had not been buried deeply enough, because organic matter appeared along the banks of streams that flowed into the Kurram River.[55] The only other indication of the environmental effects of mass death can be found in a request from an unnamed officer for permission to purchase three hundred maunds[56] of wood "for the purpose of burning the carcasses of camels lying about the neighborhood of Quetta."[57] Hence, just as it had neglected the suffering of the camels and other pack animals, the official record also ignored the problem of the sanitary disposal of the dead.

FINAL ACCOUNTING

The scale of camel deaths and the prosecution of the war did not go unnoticed in Great Britain. Newspaper coverage, including drawings in the *Graphic* of London of rotting camel carcasses, repeatedly returned to the high number of dead camels and the monetary cost of the war.[58] Parliament, however, seemed more concerned about the latter and especially the vast gap between the budget estimates of the Government of India and the actual expenditures. The discrepancy, as determined by the Parliamentary Committee cited at the opening of this chapter, was partly a function of the Government of India's accounting method. No actual disbursements were listed as expenditures until after an audit had been completed; hence, there would always be a delay in accounts and an underreporting of expenditures at any given time as well as inadequate data on which to make future budgetary estimates. Under normal circumstances, the committee concluded, this might not have been a problem;

55. See IOR/L/MIL/7/834, 1880, 8.

56. A maund is an Indian measure standardized by the British as the equivalent of 82.2857 pounds. See Henry Yule and A. C. Burnell, *Hobson-Jobson: A Glossary of Colloquial Anglo-Indian Words and Phrases, and of Kindred Terms, Etymological, Historical, Geographical and Discursive* (1903; reprint, New Delhi: Munshiram Manoharlal, 1994), 564.

57. See IOR/L/MIL/5/678, part B, p. 2. The request is dated 28 March 1879; Rs. 200 were authorized for the purchase.

58. See the comments on the camels' plight in the *Manchester Guardian*, 26 May 1879; *Pall Mall Gazette* (London), 17 July 1879; and *Blackwood's Magazine* (1880): 369–70. Other newspaper sources are the *Glasgow Herald*, 9 and 26 April 1880. Questions were soon raised about the Indian Government's budget and the losses of camels mentioned in criticisms of it; see the *Pall Mall Gazette* (London), "The Bogus Indian Budget," 7 May 1880, which then circulated in newspapers outside London (e.g., *Hampshire Telegraph and Sussex Chronicle*, 12 May 1880, and the *Lancaster Gazette*, 30 March 1881).

but in wartime, with monies hemorrhaging from treasuries, auditing in any timely manner became impossible. This meant, among other things, that the Government of India had no concrete knowledge of what had been spent on the war or what its future needs might be when it prepared its budget estimates for 1879–80.[59]

But the questionable nature of the Government of India's budget estimates was not the only concern circulating in Great Britain. Also at issue were the reasons why the war was proving so costly. Dead or missing pack animals comprised a major expenditure, of course, and this was probably fairly well known from newspaper coverage of the war. But it is also clear from various sources that a number of unanticipated costs emerged as the war continued and expanded. In his testimony before the Parliamentary Committee, Col. Sibley pointed out that because forage for the animals was virtually nonexistent in Afghanistan, it had to be packed and shipped from India at an extremely high cost.[60] In addition to the cost of fodder, the government had to replace the pack animals lost in the 1878–79 campaign. And since owners were refusing to hire out their animals for the second campaign, the government was forced to purchase large numbers of them at inflated prices. Then there was the cost of wages for indigenous labor, or camp followers, to support the army in the field. Because of a growing dread of service in Afghanistan, the cost of labor was also on the increase. Finally, a reserve of supplies had to be built up and stored on the frontier, should they be needed in Afghanistan.

Ticking off these added costs of war in a minute dated 1 May 1880, Gen. E. B. Johnson, a member of the viceroy's council, added that in a war like this one, expenditures proceeded at a "progressive ratio." By this he meant that once materials were exhausted in Afghanistan and on the frontier, they had to be brought at ever-greater distances from various parts of India, adding costly transport figures to expenditures.[61] Last but not least, the army had to deal with compensation for those lost camels whose ownership could be proved. The Military Department of the Government of India estimated that compensation would be in order for some 32,659 hired camels that had died

59. EIMA, vi. On the same page, the committee also lamented that no one in any part of the administrative apparatus had taken the initiative to inform the viceroy and his council of the scale of the expenditures from their particular unit.

60. Ibid., 46.

61. *Correspondence Relating to the Estimates for the War in Afghanistan: Presented to Both Houses of Parliament by Command of Her Majesty* (London: Eyre and Spottiswoode for Her Majesty's Stationery Office, 1880), 89.

between September 1878 and September 1879.[62] Another 5,357 government camels were reported as having died during the same period. This figure of some 38,000 dead camels is as close as the Government of India ever came to an official count. Later estimates were close to 60,000. In addition to compensation for the dead, the overall costs of animal transport had to be calculated. In a retrospective report from 1898, Gen. Edwin H. H. Collen, the military member of the viceroy's council, set the figure of purchased animals at 71,000 camels, mules, ponies, and pack bullocks and another 55,000 hired animals, at a total cost of £379,963 or some Rs. 30 million.[63]

How much of this detail about the real cost of Lord Lytton's Afghan adventure was known in Great Britain in early 1880 is difficult to ascertain. What is clear, however, is that as a result of several bad domestic harvests that caused economic instability in Britain and vocal criticism of his Afghan policy,[64] the Conservative prime minister Benjamin Disraeli dissolved Parliament and called for a general election in March. When the returns came in during the early weeks of April, the Conservatives were decisively defeated by the Liberals—they lost 111 seats, leaving the Liberals with a 352-to-237 majority. The role that dead camels played in the Liberal landslide is difficult to assess. But John Bright, a Liberal campaigning in Birmingham, perhaps set the tone when, after citing the stoical virtues of the camel, he argued that "the cruelties inflicted upon him will be found written upon imperishable tablets by the recording angel."[65]

Soon after the election, Lord Lytton resigned as viceroy of India and William Gladstone became the new prime minister. Gladstone appointed Spencer Cavendish, the Marquess of Hartington and 8th Duke of Devonshire, secretary of state for India and made George Robinson, First Marquess of Ripon, the new viceroy. It was Hartington who organized the Parliamentary Committee to investigate the military accounts of the British Indian Army. While the committee was meeting, Lord Ripon telegraphed to London a revised estimate for the Afghan War, which included the cost of one of Lytton's

62. See IOR/L/MIL/5/687, 12 November 1880.

63. IOR/L/MIL/7/6688: "Transport Service of the Indian Army, 27th August 1898," 4. However, it is not clear in Collen's report where these numbers come from.

64. See, for example, the many editions of Capt. William Joseph Eastwick, *Lord Lytton and the Afghan War* (London: R. J. Mitchell and Sons, 1879). Also see William Gladstone's widely circulated pamphlet, *The Approaching General Election: A Political Catechism containing an Indictment and a Programme* (London: H. J. Infield, 1879).

65. Quoted in the *Morning Post* (London), 29 March 1880, and the *Pall Mall Gazette* (London), 1 April 1880.

pet projects—the extension of rail lines to the North-West frontier. The figure Ripon sent exceeded £17 million, about twice as much as Lytton's highest estimates.[66] For the next several years, Parliament would subsidize the Government of India to the tune of £5 million.[67]

Matters, however, did not end here. In the wake of another transport debacle in the Egyptian campaign of 1882, Charles Cameron, Liberal MP from Glasgow, made a motion for the creation of a select committee to investigate the procedures and practices of the Army Commissariat. The committee met in 1883, and eventually expanded its investigation into the recent Afghan campaign. No report emerged by the end of the session of Parliament, so in 1884 Cameron made a motion for reinstating the committee so its work could be completed. With the secretary of state for war and the Conservatives opposed, the motion was soundly defeated. Cameron then went public with a pamphlet based on the committee's minutes. In it, he rehearsed the failures of the Indian Army transport system, drawing from Willes's reports and information that came to him from unnamed sources. After reviewing the available data, he estimated that the cost of lost animals alone was comparable to one of the £500,000 "grants in aid" to the Government of India. Cameron also quoted sources indicating that veterinary surgeons' recommendations had been ignored by Indian authorities, and he revisited the horrors of conditions faced by camels and other pack animals. Moreover, Cameron was skeptical about the recent reforms to transport in the Indian Army; he doubted that they would ensure that there would be "no danger of any similar breakdown in the future."[68]

The reform scheme that Cameron had doubts about requires some attention (see chapter 3), but before doing so, it might be helpful to consider more closely what life was like for camels in the Punjab region before their impressment into service. In the next chapter, it will be one of my arguments that an ongoing ignorance about camels and the prevailing camel-human-environment relations in the Punjab and the Sind produced the disasters for pack animals encountered during the Second Afghan War. Such ignorance

66. *Further Correspondence Relating to the Estimates for the War in Afghanistan* (London: Eyre and Spottiswoode for Her Majesty's Stationery Office, 1881), 6.

67. See House of Commons Papers, "Afghan War (Grants in Aid)," 1880–81 to 1885–86. Initially, the sum of £2 million was remitted to the Government of India; the remainder was paid out in six installments between fiscal years 1880–81 and 1885–86.

68. Charles Cameron, *A Romance of War; or, How the Cash Goes in Campaigning* (London: Baillière, Tindall and Cox, 1884); the quotation is on p. 40.

was shared by colonial officials, military leaders, and, of course, British parliamentarians, regardless of political party. Their inability to understand the complexities of life in the region meant that reform schemes, always structured as formulations more rational than what had existed in the past, left out a major part of the reality on the ground.

CHAPTER 2

The Browsing Camel and the Edible "Wasteland": The North-West Frontier of British India and the Punjab Environment

The excessive deaths of camels and other pack animals in the Second Afghan War were accounted for in a variety of ways. One of the key explanations for camel deaths favored by some British observers was that once removed from their familiar natural environment, they became extremely vulnerable. This chapter explores these environments and the local conditions of camel life in the northwestern parts of the British Indian Empire. I hope to show that camels in northwestern India were embedded in a dense network of human-environment-animal relations that are not easily reducible to the environmental determinism argument made by some British sources. And while environmental displacement was a factor in some camel deaths, it will be my argument that far more important was their removal from an Islamic-influenced popular moral ecology that situated animal-human-plant relations in a logic of co-dependency and human ethical responsibilities for other forms of life. I begin by providing an account of place—the arid stretches of the northwestern and western parts of the Indian subcontinent.

THE PUNJAB TERRAIN AND ITS ECOLOGY

As noted earlier, parts of India are situated within Saharasia, a broad band of arid land stretching across North Africa, the Middle East, and South Asia. The northwestern part of this region (present-day Pakistan and Rajasthan) is alluvial plain and desert bounded on the north and west by the high mountains of the Pamir, Hindu Kush, and Suleiman ranges. Five rivers flow out of the northeastern parts of these highlands.[1] The Jhelum, Chenab, and Ravi merge north of Multan, join the Sutlej, and flow into the Indus south of Dera Ismail Khan. The Indus then flows due south to the Arabian Sea. All the rivers at the time covered by this study had shallow, sandy beds, and the volume of their flow was extremely variable. Between the Indus and the Jhelum was a vast salt range, while between the other rivers lay arid alluvial tracts called the *doab* (uplands between rivers) by their inhabitants and the Bar by the British. Further south and west were sandy deserts. The Himalayan snowmelt brought spring floods along with fertile silt. But with the exception of the Indus, after the seasonal flood the rivers became meandering streams with unstable courses. In some areas they flowed between low bluffs several miles apart, shifting course between them as a result of the flood.[2] As one British settlement officer put it when commenting on the changeable nature of the Sutlej, "It is impossible to say where it may be any one year. Whole villages,—indeed clusters of villages—are one week on the right bank, the next on the left." He observed further that "this capriciousness is the cause of considerable expense in keeping open the heads of inundation canals, and sometimes leads to the failure of the water supply in them when most needed."[3] By the end of the nineteenth century, such observations would become justifications for radical engineering interventions to discipline the rivers of the Punjab (Land of Five Rivers) and command its land for agricultural purposes.[4]

In other areas of the river basins, there were either permanent riverbanks or raised levees, such that the rivers moved about the countryside in more stable channels. All along the rivers, and around the canals built off them, farmers intensively cultivated crops, usually planting in the spring and fall. The *khalif* (springtime) crops included wheat, barley, gram (chickpeas), lentils, turnips, rape, tobacco, opium poppies, cumin, and vegetables. In the autumn, farmers planted *rabi* crops, such as millet, cotton, hemp, peppers, sugarcane, melons,

1. For an overview of the climate and vegetation of the region, see Hugh Kennedy Trevaskis, *The Land of the Five Rivers: An Economic History of the Punjab from the Earliest Times to the Year of Grace 1890* (Oxford: Oxford University Press, 1928), 1–5.

2. Clive Dewey, *Steamboats on the Indus: The Limits of Western Technological Superiority in South Asia* (Oxford: Oxford University Press, 2014), 13–15.

3. C. A. Roe and W. E. Purser, *Report of the Revised Land Revenue Settlement of the Montgomery District, in the Mooltan Division of the Punjab* (Lahore: Central Jail Press, 1878), 3.

4. On the notion of the engineering of water to command it, see David Gilmartin, *Blood and Water: The Indus River Basin in Modern History* (Oakland: University of California Press, 2015), 150ff.

and beans.[5] Occasionally, however, farmers' lives could be completely disrupted by the rivers. When runoff from the mountains was significant, rivers burst their banks and spread across the dead-level portions of the plain, flooding out farmsteads and villages and destroying the inundation canals in their wake. In the Dera Ismail Khan District that occupied both sides of the lower Indus, villagers tried to protect themselves by clustering homes close together and building embankments around the villages. But the river deposited silt, gradually raising the level of the land and turning some of the villages into depressions in relation to the rest of the plain. Eventually, when the Indus rose high enough, these settlements would be wiped out.[6]

Snowmelt from the Himalayan massif in the spring and summer was, however, only one source of water. With their land dry most of the year, Punjabi agriculturalists and pastoralists also depended on wells with animal-driven Persian wheel pumps as well as on summer rain that came with the southwest monsoon, moisture-bearing winds that blow across the subcontinent from the Indian Ocean. In the case of the Punjab, the volume of the monsoon would determine agricultural output, particularly of wheat, for the year. The rains also recharged plant life in the doab after the spring season, normally extremely hot and dry. In the fall and winter, the wind patterns reversed, carrying only a severely limited amount of moisture into the Punjab region.[7] Yet this pattern could be disrupted by an oceanic phenomenon off the Peruvian coast known as El Niño. El Niño events are caused by a periodic warming or cooling of the waters of the western Pacific, whose effect on the subcontinent is to reduce or expand the volume of water in a monsoon cycle. During what is known as an El Niño-Southern Oscillation, drought and sometimes famine were common occurrences in much of India. A reversal of this pattern (La Niña) might bring excessive rain and disastrous flooding. In the latter part of the nineteenth century, two major El Niño–related drought cycles occurred in the Punjab: one between 1876 and 1878, the other between 1896 and 1902.[8] Normal aridity punctuated by periodic drought, with an occasional excess of water, highlighted the general pattern of life in the region.

Precarious water availability led to uneven agricultural production across

5. I take the list from the information supplied in the *Gazetteer of the Montgomery District, 1883–4* (Lahore: Arya Press, 1884), 103–4.

6. H. St George Tucker, *Report of the Land Revenue Settlement of the Kohat District in the Punjab* (Calcutta: Calcutta Central Press, 1884), 9.

7. Trevaskis, *The Land of the Five Rivers*, 2–3.

8. See Mike Davis, *Late Victorian Holocausts: El Niño Famines and the Making of the Third World* (London: Verso, 2001), 13–14, chap. 7, and the climatological sources cited therein.

the Punjab. In the central part of the region, where the rivers and manmade canals flowed, a surplus could be produced. In the foothills of the Suleiman range, and in other areas where the soil was poorer, farmers could manage only subsistence agriculture. According to accounts in British gazetteers from across the region, most farming families lived simple lives. Their dwellings, located close to their fields, were made of mud brick, with one large room and a flat roof. Depending partly on the nature of the land, houses might stand alone, be clustered with two or three others, or exist as part of larger settlements. Front yards, equipped with cattle troughs, were fenced by a low mud wall or bramble bushes. Here cattle were kept, and perhaps a bullock, camel, or mule, along with other domestic animals. Invariably, the rear walls faced toward the outside of the settlement, and entrances opened inward toward neighboring houses, supposedly making cattle rustling more difficult.[9] The houses of wealthier families might have carved woodwork around doors and whitewashed exterior walls. Inside, there was generally one large bed where the family slept; a spinning wheel for making cotton thread; earthenware plates and cups; a cooking pot or two; implements for making *chapattis* (wheat bread); and a storage bin for grain. The staple food was wheat—with maize, rice, and barley making an occasional change. *Chapattis* were eaten at the day's two main meals, along with salt, buttermilk, *ghee* (clarified butter), and, on occasion, some vegetables. Meat was rare and eaten only on special occasions. And like dwellings and diet, clothing was simple—cotton cloth cut in various ways over which cotton-padded jackets were worn in the winter.[10] Lifeways like this could be found around and between the rivers, up to the point where the ground became too dry and irrigation ended. That is where the "wastelands," as the British mistakenly called them, began.

The wastelands of the Punjab were the doab, the areas between the "ca-

9. Brian Caton has demonstrated the prevalence of cattle theft in the Punjab, a practice, he argues, was an accepted form of social mobility; see his "The Transition from Animal Capital to Land Capital in the Colonial Punjab, 1850–1900," *Capitalism Nature Socialism* 26, no. 3 (2015): 64–72.

10. My description of housing and diet comes from Punjab District gazetteers produced in the mid-1880s, under the direction of Denzil Ibbetson. They were organized in a uniform format that, from this point forward, was standard. Each of them contained a section titled "Social and Religious Life," in which housing, diet, and clothing were described, with varying degree of detail. See *Gazetteer of the Jhelum District (1883–4)* (Calcutta: Central Press, 1884), 54–56; *Gazetteer of the Dera Ismail Khan District, 1883–4* (Lahore: Arya Press, 1884), 51–55; *Gazetteer of the Montgomery District, 1883–4* (Lahore: Arya Press, 1884), 49–51, 54; and *Gazetteer of the Shapur District, 1883–4* (Calcutta: Central Press, 1884), 36–37.

pricious" rivers. They contained the same rich soils as the riverbanks, but scarce rainfall meant that these tracts were little cultivated. Instead, the doab was traversed by nomadic pastoralists, whose animals—mainly camels, goats, cattle, and sheep—lived off the uncultivated shrubs and grasses, as well as the leaves of the rare trees of the drylands. Unlike the nomadic herders from Afghanistan and Baluchistan, who moved between the plains in the wet winter season and the mountains in the dry season, those of the doab moved their animals from the drylands in the summer to the rivers in the winter, where they set up encampments.[11]

Nomadic pastoralists relied on agriculturalists and their nearby towns for finished goods and for markets to sell their camels and sheep, and goat and camel milk. But they also peddled a variety of services to the farmers. Some had sidelines as artisans, making pots and iron tools (plows, knives, etc.), providing carpentry, or serving as herbalists providing medical care for humans and animals. Others enhanced daily life by performing seasonal entertainments such as storytelling (legends, romances, poetry) and musical performances. The Qalandars (see below) entertained with trained monkeys, while other groups tumbled, juggled, and performed magic. A group known as the Sansi traveled from village to village as hereditary genealogists, keeping track of marriages and lines of descent from memory as well as telling fortunes. Some groups specialized in making and selling baskets made of grass and reeds, while others, such as the Bhubaliyas, peddled axes and spades, hoes, spoons, needles, plowshares, and iron fittings for carts. After establishing lasting relationships with particular farmers in villages, itinerant peddler-pastoralists were willing to perform services or sell on long-term credit. They timed sales and debt collections to the rhythms of the agricultural season, performing services, selling goods, and collecting on the previous year's financial commitments only after the harvests.[12]

As these multitasking pastoralists moved through the districts they frequented, farmers relied on some of them as a source of camels and bullocks to plow their fields and carry their goods to market. Merchants in towns were often dependent on the same source for camels to link them with interregional

11. For a description of the encampments, see the *Gazetteer of the Montgomery District*, 51–52.

12. Neeladri Bhattacharya, "Predicaments of Mobility: Peddlers and Itinerants in Nineteenth-Century Northwestern India," in *Society and Circulation: Mobile People and Itinerant Cultures in South Asia 1750–1950*, ed. Claude Markovits, Jacques Pouchepadass, and Sanjay Subrahmanyam (Delhi: Permanent Black, 2003), 166–72.

trade networks. In turn, the regional pastoralists, along with pilgrims and other nomadic peoples, participated to a greater or lesser degree in the ritual life of the towns, much of which was centered on a number of Sufi shrines (see below),[13] typically located where settlements and pastoralists' activities intersected as well as at nodes along trade routes.[14]

The seasonal movement of herders from Afghanistan and Baluchistan paralleled patterns of long-distance commerce into the region. The Punjab was connected to Persia and Central Asia and eastern India by a caravan trade with deep historical roots. Some of the trade was short-distance commerce between Afghan and Punjab towns carried out via the Khyber, Gomal, and Bolan passes of the Suleiman Mountains. Other trade involved long-distance caravan activity. As will be discussed shortly, much of this trade was in the hands of pastoralists who moved goods as well as their camel, goat, and sheep herds in and out of India seasonally. Other aspects of the trade were controlled by Indian merchants, some of whom traveled into Russia, Persia, and Central Asia and set up shop in towns like Samarkand and Bokhara.[15] After the Second Afghan War, both long-distance and local trade expanded, with more pastoral groups becoming involved, as a result of British development projects in the Punjab.[16]

Among the caravan businesses, perhaps the most intriguing in the eyes of the British was that of the Powindahs, a name given to groups of martial nomadic merchants and herders who migrated annually to India from Afghanistan.[17] Primarily Pathan tribesmen from eastern Afghanistan, the Powindahs moved goods from Bokhara in Central Asia through the eastern cities of Afghanistan and into the Indus River basin. In October, many of them would

13. Richard Eaton, "The Political and Religious Authority of the Shrine of Baba Farid," in *India's Islamic Traditions, 711–1750*, ed. Richard Eaton (Oxford: Oxford University Press, 2003), 269–70.

14. Gilmartin, *Blood and Water*, 22–23.

15. For a study of these pan-Asian commercial connections drawn primarily from indigenous sources, see Muzaffar Alam, "Trade, State Policy and Regional Change: Aspects of Mughal-Uzbek Commercial Relations c. 1550–1750," *Journal of the Economic and Social History of the Orient* 37, no. 3 (1994): 202–27. Also see Arup Banerji, *Old Routes* (Gurgaon: Three Essays Collective, 2011), and Claude Markovits, "Indian Merchants in Central Asia," in *India and Central Asia: Commerce and Culture, 1500–1800*, ed. Scott C. Levi (Oxford: Oxford University Press, 2007), 123–51.

16. Klaus Ferdinand, *Afghan Nomads: Caravans, Conflicts, and Trade in Afghanistan and British India, 1800–1980* (Copenhagen: Carlsburg Foundation, 2006), 253–70.

17. For a discussion of the tribal affiliations and lifeways of various groups designated as Powindahs, see J. A. Robinson, *Notes on Nomad Tribes of Eastern Afghanistan* (1934; reprint, Quetta: M/S Nisa Traders, 1978), 2–3.

leave highland pastures and congregate around Ghazni in Afghanistan, where other travelers, seeking the protection of a caravan, often joined them. These might include merchants; itinerant workers who found construction, canal dredging, and other kinds of physical labor jobs on the British side of the Suleiman Mountains; and religious pilgrims. Grazing in the lowlands during the winter, visiting family or medical specialists, or making pilgrimages to Sufi shrines were also part of the Powindah seasonal migration into India.[18]

Once a Powindah caravan had grown large enough, the group journeyed, with armed guards on their flanks and rear, through the Khyber, Kurram, Gomal, and Bolan passes into India,[19] sometimes skirmishing with hill tribes attempting to abscond with their goods and their camels. Once through the mountains, such caravans would camp for several months in large numbers. In the area around Dera Ismail Khan, for example, they numbered 50,000 or more, with some 70,000 camels and 100,000 sheep, in the 1880s.[20] Here and in settlements further east they sold silks, gold, and furs from Bokhara; pistachio nuts and fruits from Kabul; almonds, nuts, dried fruits, and wool from Kandahar; and wool, *ghee*, and tobacco from Ghazni as well as medicinal herbs, handicraft products, silks, Turkistani horses, dyes, saffron, goat and camel hair, and sheepskins. In Indian markets, they exchanged these things for English cotton goods, chintzes, Kashmir shawls, drugs, and spices.[21] Some were involved in the carrying trade in and around Dera Ismail Khan and Dera Ghazi Khan, hauling firewood, building materials, and local goods on their camels, while others ventured out of the Punjab and moved further east, trading on credit and lending money.[22] A few made annual treks to Bombay,

18. Daniel Balland, "Nomadism and Politics: The Case of Afghan Nomads in the Indian Subcontinent," *Studies in History* 7, no. 2 (1991): 209.

19. For an overview of the Powindah routes and camping areas in the Punjab, see Robinson, *Notes on Nomad Tribes of Eastern Afghanistan*, 4, 32–51.

20. I take the figures from Bhattacharya, "Predicaments of Mobility," 184. Citing census data for ten-year intervals beginning in 1881, Robinson provides a figure of around 200,000 total migrants initially, with a dropoff to around 110,000 by 1931; see *Notes on Nomad Tribes of Eastern Afghanistan*, 6.

21. H. St George Tucker, *Report of the Land Revenue Settlement of the Dera Ismail Khan District of the Punjab, 1872–79* (Lahore: W. Ball, 1879), 184–92; and the account of the Powindahs in Edward Emmerson Oliver, *Across the Border; or, Pathan and Biloch* (London: Chapman and Hall, 1890), 75–86. Also see Balland, "Nomadism and Politics," 219; and Bhattacharya, "Predicaments of Mobility," 185.

22. Balland, "Nomadism and Politics," 219. On the carrying trade, see Robinson, *Notes on Nomad Tribes of Eastern Afghanistan*, 25–26.

Calcutta, and Assam, collecting debts or trading in asafetida (an herbal preparation used as a digestive aid). As money lenders, Powindahs were noted in the Punjab for their use of the *danda* (a stick used as a weapon), while in the Bengal region, as one observer put it, novels and plays were incomplete without reference to the annual visit of the "Kabuli" with his heavy bamboo staff used to encourage debt payment.[23]

The British also knew of the Powindahs in another way. During the Second Afghan War, Powindah camels, like those of the Brahui, another transmountain trading and haulage group, were admired by army transport officers. Unlike the Brahui, however, the Powindahs were not inclined to hire themselves and their animals out for military transport service. When the Indian Army became desperate for camels in 1879, some of those belonging to the Powindahs were impressed into service. The Powindah reaction was to raid the area around Tank, a site on the supply lines into Afghanistan. Tank was burned, and the British found themselves struggling to maintain communications with their forces on the Kurram and Kabul lines.[24]

CAMELS AND THE PUNJAB ENVIRONMENT

Camels were distributed fairly well, though unevenly, across the Punjab. Census returns from the early 1890s put the population at around 213,000. About 45 percent of the total occupied the districts of Hissar, Multan, and Dera Ismail Khan. Jhang, Ferozepore, Montgomery, and Muzaffargarh all had populations between 11,000 and 13,000, while Rawalpindi, Bannu, and Jhelum had numbers ranging in the low eight thousands. The remaining nine districts of the province varied between Lahore's 3,400 and Hoshiarpur's 1,500. Although the overall census numbers seem low, and may be the result of either poor counting or the demographic effect on the camel population as a result of the casualties of the Second Afghan War, they do provide some sense of where in the Punjab camels constituted a significant part of domestic life.

23. On the *danda*, see Neeladri Bhattacharya, "Lenders and Debtors: Punjab Countryside, 1880–1940," *Studies in History* 1, no. 2 (1985): 306. On the "Kabuli" moneylender, see Robinson, *Notes on Nomad Tribes of Eastern Afghanistan*, 28.

24. See Henry Hanna, *The Second Afghan War 1878–79–80: Its Causes, Its Conduct and Its Consequences* (Westminster: Archibald Constable, 1904), 2:164. The official account of the incident made no mention of the seizure of Powindah camels; instead, the Powindah motive for attacking Tank was that they "could not resist the temptation to plunder"; see William Henry Paget and A. H. Mason, *A Record of the Expeditions against the North-West Frontier Tribes since the Annexation of the Punjab* (London: Whiting, 1884), 593.

In most districts, Baluchis were the primary camel herders, but they were by no means the only ones. In Dera Ghazi Khan, for instance, large herds were kept by chieftains and merchants, while the dominant sarwan group was the Muslim Jats. In the district of Hissar, which had the largest population in the Punjab, camels were almost exclusively owned by Raibaris, while Multan, with the second-largest population, numbered owners among the Langrials, Gabhesars, Dhuddis, and Dhas people as well as Baluchis and Brahuis. In some cases, camels were used only for local work within a district; in others they moved across the region in short- and long-distance hauling, or, in some instances, pulled the plows of their agricultural owners.[25] Some of these groups, as was noted earlier, had close ties with the Mughal court.

Yet wherever they were located or regardless of in whose care they resided, most of the Punjab's camels browsed the plants of the wastelands (chewing off bits and meandering on) for a good portion if not all of their diet. The monsoon rains usually regenerated the vegetation of the doab, thus providing a sufficient supply of the plants on which camels and other animals could feed at various times of the year. "Leaves of all thorny trees and shrubs, saline and prickly grasses" as well as camel thorn, tamarisk bushes, and mimosas were all eaten by camels, one source tells us.[26] Others indicate that a favorite was the leaves of the *shisham*, or Indian rosewood, which grew all around the plain.[27] Perhaps the richest source on local flora and fauna related to camel browsing is the gazetteer of Multan (a district lying between the Chenab and Sutlej Rivers). According to it, camels fed on the foliage of the four principal trees of the district: the *farásh*, *karril*, *van* (an evergreen which yielded a widely eaten fruit), and *jan*. These trees could withstand long seasons of drought and also kept the local markets supplied with fuel. Camels were also fond of *lani* (*Suaeda rudiflora*), a salt-tolerant shrub that when burned yielded a type of barilla, or soda ash, used in the manufacture of soap and glass. And along with goats, camels ate two varieties of the *lai* plant, *Tamarix gallica* and *Tamarix dioica*. The former, known as the *kokan*, was found in saline soils, whereas the latter was encountered in the alluvial deposits of the Punjab plain. *Bhakra* (*Tribulus terrestris*, sometimes called devil's weed) too was found throughout the Multan District. Camels, goats, and sheep all fed on it, and its powdered

25. The source of this paragraph is IOR/L/MIL/7/6687: *Report of the Transport Committee, 1897* (Simla: Government Central Printing Office, 1897), 1:345–49.

26. Maj. Arthur G. Leonard, *The Camel: Its Uses and Management* (London: Longmans, Green, 1894), 159.

27. *Jhelum District Gazetteer, 1904* (Lahore: Civil and Military Gazette Press, 1907), 17.

BOX 2.1: The Camel's Stomach and Digestion

Camels are ruminants, a division of hoofed mammals that also includes sheep, oxen, giraffes, antelopes, deer, and goats. These kinds of animals have either three or four stomach compartments, the first of which processes unchewed herbaceous matter that is then regurgitated in masses and masticated while the animal is at rest. It is then reswallowed and passed through the first stomach to the other two or three for further breakdown by gastric juices. While animal physiologists usually use the same terminology for the separate chambers in camels' stomachs as those applied to other large ruminants (rumen, reticulum, omasum, and abomasum), the third and fourth of these are hardly distinguishable. More important, the camel stomach contains structures not found in other ruminants. Its rumen, for example, consists of a number of small chambers separated by mucosae, which themselves are covered by millions of tubular glands. Similar structures are found in the other parts of the stomach system. It is thought that the glands act as absorption and fermentation areas, as well as areas where digestive enzymes are secreted.

See R. T. Wilson, "Nutritional Requirements of the Camel" (1989).

fruit was used as a medicine to counter human urinary and kidney disorders. Camels and goats even fed on "weeds" such as *bokhat* (*Asphodelus fistulosus)*, a "troublesome" wanderer that encroached on productive fields and was found throughout the district. It grew in sandy soil, and flourished with great stubbornness during the monsoon season.[28]

Lists of Punjab flora with commentary, like those to be found in the Multan gazetteer, began to be assembled in the 1850s by British officials undertaking land settlement surveys. With their *munshis* (secretaries and translators), they queried the inhabitants of villages, gathering bits and pieces of local life that went well beyond matters of land use and ownership. Such data were then compiled into the Punjab gazetteers from the mid-1800s forward, providing a view of plant and animal life in the region. Taken together, these sources sug-

28. *Multan District Gazetteer, 1901–2* (Lahore: Civil and Military Gazette Press, 1902), 15–20.

gest three important things about the region's ecology. First, despite aridity, a thriving and diverse "wild" plant life was to be found outside and adjacent to cultivated areas, plant resources that were shared, in some cases, by animals and humans—camels ate *buin*, while villagers used it to treat boils![29] Second, from a dietary perspective, camels found a rich smorgasbord of plant species to browse and ruminate, providing themselves with a much more varied and nutritious diet than could be found for them in the grains humans cultivated. And third, goats seemed to have agreed with camels that there was much to be savored by an ecumenical ruminant in the wastelands and at the edges of cultivated fields along the rivers.

Yet as rich an image as the British colonial gazetteers provide of the abundance of plant life in the Punjab, belying their own characterization of the region as a wasteland, they do not tell us much about how herders and their camels interacted with this environment. Three decades after the gazetteer format was routinized by Denzil Ibbetson in the 1880s, Arnold Leese, a veterinary surgeon who had taken up the position of camel specialist assigned to the Civil Veterinary Department in 1907, began to catalog facts on camels, many gleaned from his close work with native camel experts. In a book on camels published in 1927, Leese devoted an entire chapter to the grazing and feeding patterns of these animals. He prefaced his comments with an injunction about how important such knowledge was for a veterinary surgeon or transport officer. "I strongly advise," he began, that

> anyone who finds himself with a responsible interest in the camel to become acquainted . . . with the principal camel-grazing plants of his particular locality, and to get to know their best seasons and how they fit available fodder-crops, and what *seasonal movements the camelmen make*, so as to take advantage of the best grazing within reach.[30]

Why would Leese emphasize a need to know the plants ideal for a camel's diet and the seasons in which certain fodder crops were available? Having observed the behavior of camel men from intimate on-the-ground study of camels in good and bad health, it became clear to Leese that the animal could not remain healthy and fit for work if it was not allowed to browse wild plants.

29. *Gazetteer of the Montgomery District, 1883–4* (Lahore: Arya Press, 1884), 20.

30. Arnold Leese, *A Treatise on the One-Humped Camel in Health and in Disease* (Stamford, Lincolnshire: Haynes and Son, 1927), 62; emphasis added. I make subsequent citations from this source parenthetically in the text.

Dried fodder, as Charles Steel's autopsies during the Afghan campaign had demonstrated, played havoc with a camel's respiratory and digestive systems. Fresh, green leafy plants that flourished at various times of the year across the Punjab were much more appropriate. Leese said they were slightly laxative and had a "cooling" effect (61), both of which kept the camel's complex digestive tract (see box 2.1), made up of four stomachs, in good order.

As important as knowing the qualities of the plants themselves was understanding the patterns of their consumption. Leese explained that camel men organized their movements based on the annual cycles of plants, matching different qualities of green fodder with work and rest periods for their camels. He summarized this human-camel-plant ecology in a succinct rule of thumb learned from the camel men: in crossing barren country, lengthen marches so as to lessen the period of scarcity; in traveling though good country, shorten marches so that the camels shall have plenty of grazing time (61). Such a rule was recommended regardless of the kind of work the camel was asked to do.

Green plants should make up only one part of the camel's diet, however, the other being various kinds of saltwort. These salty plants, according to Leese, comprised about a third of the camel's diet, particularly if the main green fodder plants were the most common ones of the plains, such as *kareel* (*Capparis aphylla)* and *jal* (*Salvadora oleoides*). After allowing their camels to enjoy a green diet for a few days, camel men would move their animals into saltwort beds two or three times a week to keep their constitution balanced (64). In areas where water might be more abundant, camels grazed on tamarisk, gum, jujube, and mulberry trees, and even grasses like *Tribulus* that appeared after rains (65–66). Further to the west of the Indus, in the valleys of the Suleiman Mountains and northwestern regions, camels grazed on other kinds of shrubs and trees, as well as thistle (66–67). But regardless of the place, the keys to fitness remained the same basic rules of a diet rich in green fodder with mild laxative qualities supplemented with salt plants, coupled with sufficient browsing and rest time for the camel to chew its cud. Ignoring these rules, Leese concluded, was what led to the "terrible suffering and mortality" of the Afghan campaign (61).

Leese's description and analysis help explain the seasonal patterns of life of Punjab pastoralists and others who bred and raised camels throughout the plains. Life was somewhat different, however, for those living on the western edge of the province, where a variation on the agriculturalist-nomad relation existed. Baluchi pastoralists, known on the plains as camel herders, exploited the runoff of mountain streams to combine herding with small-scale agriculture. According to David Gilmartin, Baluchi farming allowed for the creation of fixed tribal settlements, around which pastoralists circulated and where Hindu merchants traded.[31] Population pressure as well as conflict with other groups pushed some of these farmer-nomads out onto the plains, where they seem to have become strictly pastoralists in the doab region. At the same time, they were known as local experts on camels.

But because most of the British administrators considered doab areas to be a wasteland, they missed the delicate ecological relations between farmers and pastoralists, plants and animals, cultivated and uncultivated land, as well as between mixed-livelihood groups like the Suleiman Baluchi and those of the doab. And although the British Indian Army exploited camels for purposes of warfare, they knew precious little about them as a species. As I have argued above and as Leese emphasized, this ignorance cost many camel lives in military campaigns. On the other hand, there was at least one thing the British managed to figure out. Indian camels were dromedaries, or one-humped camels, as opposed to the two-humped Bactrians found through much of Central Asia and China. Beyond this simple classification, and with the exception of a few observant veterinarians, the constitution and nature of the camel remained a closed book into the 1880s.

CAMELS AND THE RHYTHM OF LIFE IN WESTERN AND SOUTH ASIA

Across North Africa, the Middle East, and the deserts and drylands of Mesopotamia and Persia, dromedary camels provided, for over two millennia, a very economical form of transport for long-distance travel and commerce. The commercial part of camel-human relations, as discussed above regarding groups collectively known to the British as Powindahs, was organized in the form of caravans, a collectivity permitting a degree of protection from bandit groups for both humans and animals. Towns and caravansaries (inns along trade routes) often took their location and form as determined by the rhythms and pace of the camel in motion as much as by the presence of water. Richard Bulliet, in his extensive study of camels, argues that the economic efficiency of this animal-human collaboration among the peoples of these regions produced a bias for the camel over wheeled vehicles.[32] This may explain why improved roads were rare outside main population areas.

31. Gilmartin, *Blood and Water*, 32–34.

32. Richard W. Bulliet, *The Camel and the Wheel* (Cambridge, MA: Harvard University Press, 1975).

Yet the economic import of camels was only one dimension of their overall relationship to pastoralists, desert inhabitants, and commercial traders. Within Egypt and Arabia, for example, they were arguably the most important animal with which humans had a relationship.[33] Camels provided food, transport, shelter, and hair and hides for clothing. Desert nomads like the Bedouins believed that the animal's appearance in dreams was an auspicious sign. After the arrival of Islam, camels took on additional meanings. They were among a special set of blessed creatures that included horses and bees. The Prophet Muhammad was said to have conversed with them, and pointed out on more than one occasion their importance in God's creation. Sarra Tlili, in a study of commentaries on the Qur'an, has even suggested that the camel is the exemplary animal in the Islamic tradition. Despite their great strength—they are loaded while they are on their knees and then rise up—camels are willing to serve those weaker than themselves, that is, humans. This apparent paradox is the sort of sign in which Islamic exegetes find the power and the richness of God's creation. Camels were seen as prime examples of such complexity. They provided milk as abundant and nutritious as that of cows, and meat for human sustenance as good as that of sheep. Moreover, unlike other animals, the camel could live off the meanest of fodder, like that to be found in the arid plains of the Punjab, and still be capable of traversing distances greater than any other animal.[34]

Such attributes of the camel's constitution found rich metaphorical purchase in ruminations on specially endowed humans, in particular Sufi saints. In addition to being recognizable to the camel's senses with greater facility than other humans, saints possessed the same sort of patience, pious obedience, and reproductive virility as the camel. Like a camel, a saint such as Sayyid al-Badawi (1200–1276) could support vast loads and endure great hardship.[35] Given the traffic in imagery between camel and human to be found in saintly hagiographies, it should not be a surprise that camels appear in other literature, such as Arabic and Persian poetry and stories, as well as in the poetry

33. Michel Tuchsherer, "Some Reflections on the Place of the Camel in Ottoman Egypt," 172–75, in *Animals and People in Ottoman Egypt*, ed. Suraiya Faroqhi (Istanbul: Eren, 2010), 171–85; and Alan Mikhail, *The Animal in Ottoman Egypt* (Oxford: Oxford University Press, 2014), 28.

34. Sarra Tlili, *Animals in the Qur'an* (New York: Cambridge University Press, 2012), 156–58.

35. Catherine Mayuer-Jaouen, "Badawi and His Camel: An Animal as the Attribute of a Muslim Saint of Mamluk and Ottoman Egypt," in Faroqhi, *Animals and People in Ottoman Egypt*, 113–28.

and folklore of other Muslim groups, such as those in the Punjab.[36] Richard Foltz has argued that certain poetic meters reflect the camel's gait.[37] Others have added that camels are ubiquitous in Arabic proverbs and poems, where they might be compared to the most beautiful of women, precious jewels, and fine weapons. The softness of the camel's cheek, the slenderness of its neck, its ears like those of a falcon, and its eyes as clear as mirrors provide imagery that suffuses the poetry of the region.[38] The camel's gait probably also provided rhythms for the songs and chants of caravan drivers or camel handlers, among them the sarwans of the Punjab.

It was as a result of the rise of Muslim dynasties in western Asia that the dromedary camel spread across Persia and, through Baluchistan, into the Indus River valley of India, being established there by the beginning of the second millennium CE. By the time the British moved into western and northwestern India in the mid-nineteenth century, important parts of local economies, both moral and material, were organized around seasonal regularities of the caravan trade between Persia, Afghanistan, and India, while Indus valley agriculture was reliant on symbiotic and material relation between farmers and nomadic herders of camels, sheep, goats, and, to a degree, cattle.

The camels that were part of this ecology did not simply survive on the wild brush and trees of the doab. They thrived on them. Before the Indian Army developed such a need for pack animals, an ideal camel life seems to have been free-ranging with other camels on the arid plains; browsing on prickly bushes,

36. The panegyrical ode, or *qasida*, was one poetic form in which camels appeared prominently. The poet frequently invoked, both literally and metaphorically, a long, grueling journey by camel across arid land. The *qasida* form began among nomad pastoralists and eventually became court poetry during the Umayyad and Abbsid dynasties; see Renate Jacobi, "The Camel-Section of the Panegyrical Ode," *Journal of Arabic Literature* 13 (1982): 1–22; and Julie S. Meisami, *Medieval Persian Court Poetry* (Princeton, NJ: Princeton University Press, 1987), 49–50. On animal nomenclature in general in Arabic poetry, see Jaroslav Stetkevych, "Name and Epithet: The Philology and Semiotics of Animal Nomenclature in Early Arabic Poetry," *Journal of Near East Studies* 45, no. 2 (1986): 89–124. Also see Michael Sells, "Mu'akkaqa of Tarafa," *Journal of Arabic Literature* 17 (1986): 21–33, for a poem rich in camel imagery. I am grateful to Elizabeth Sartell for making me aware of this scholarship. Early British studies undertaken in northwestern India commented on the presence of camels in Punjabi folklore and literature; see Thomas H. Thornton, "The Vernacular Literature and Folklore of the Panjab," *Journal of the Royal Asiatic Society of Great Britain and Ireland*, n.s., 17, no. 3 (1885): 373–414.

37. Richard Foltz, *Animals in the Islamic Tradition and Muslim Cultures* (Oxford: Oneworld, 2006), 11, 22–23, 66–70.

38. Hilde Gauthier-Pilters and Anne Innis Dagg, *The Camel: Its Evolution, Ecology, Behavior, and Relationship to Man* (Chicago: University of Chicago Press, 1981), 135.

such as camel thorn, as well as the many other bushes and trees they enjoyed nibbling on; and now and then rubbing up against another camel, a rock, or the occasional tree.[39] This kind of life kept domestic camels in good condition for either pack or farm labor; and camel owners in northwestern India mixed short periods of heavy work for their camels with extended periods of browsing and grooming. Grooming was especially important, because camels were susceptible to dry skin and mange, an ailment of the epidermis caused by the parasitic mite *Sarcoptes cameli* and transmissible under certain conditions to humans.[40] Brushing camels and treating their skin with conditioners helped keep them fit and free of mites. Such practices also indicate a tactile intimacy between sarwans and camels, one that was not unlike that between grooms and horses in Europe, though it seems to have been rare between the British and camels.

Camel owners also kept their animals fit in other ways. They might, for example, feed them revivifying preparations as a supplement to regular feeding. According to Arthur Leonard, a British army transport officer in India and Africa for sixteen years beginning with the Second Afghan War, the inhabitants of the Punjab mixed barley flour with

> the melted fat of Doomba[41] sheep, in proportions of three parts of flour to one of fat; also coarse wheat flour mixed with ghee (clarified butter), or with goor (coarse brown sugar) and ghee (in the same proportion), and made into balls, but given to the animal in emergent cases [of illness] only. The natives

39. This seems to have been a regular pattern of camel life regardless of their location. In the late 1850s, the US Army imported some camels from North Africa and field-tested them in the Southwest in anticipation of using them in campaigns against Native American tribes. While in San Antonio, the camels were herded onto hillsides covered with grass for grazing. They refused to eat the grass, preferring instead to browse on a "variety of bushes, hackberry, daisies, wild grapevines, thistles," and many other plants that Lt. Hartz, who observed their behavior, could not identify. See Forrest Bryant Johnson, *The Last Camel Charge: The Untold Story of America's Desert Military Experiment* (New York: Berkley Publishing Group, 2012), 284. In Australia, camel browsing habits could also lead to controversies between the overwhelmingly white population and the Punjabi camel handlers; see Tom McKnight, *The Camel in Australia* (Melbourne: Melbourne University Press, 1969), 91.

40. D. Richard, "Camel Mange," *Revue Scientifique et Technique* 6, no. 2 (1987): 475–77.

41. The Anglo-Indian lexicon *Hobson-Jobson* has it as the Doombur sheep, from the Persian *dunba*; it is a fat-tailed sheep found in west Asia and Africa. See Henry Yule and A. C. Burnell, *Hobson-Jobson: A Glossary of Colloquial Anglo-Indian Words and Phrases, and of Kindred Terms, Etymological, Historical, Geographical and Discursive* (1903; reprint, Delhi: Munshiram Manoharlal, 1994), 324.

> consider all three kinds very nourishing and more than equal to double the quantity of grain.[42]

There were probably seasonal concoctions as well, some of which were perhaps the special provenance or secret formulas of a camel specialist family.

When well cared for by their sarwans and treated decently, camels could be, Leonard noted, "a gregarious animal." They should be "ridden or driven" in pairs, he continued, because the animal showed

> a decided disinclination to part company from other camels, and at times will absolutely refuse to do so; and if beaten or bullied will throw himself on his knees and display great determination. If you happen to leave a convoy to go into the bush, as long as the convoy remains in sight he will try to get back to it, for he hates isolation—a strange fact given his coldness of character.[43]

Some time later, T. E. Lawrence also wrote about these seemingly affectionate relations between camels. In one memorable passage, Lawrence explained how he set off into the desert on his she-camel to find a lost member of his party. The camel's response to leaving her companions was a deep grumbling, a vocalization that Lawrence referred to as "a constant resource of ill-treated camels." He went on to explain that camels

> have been accustomed from calf-hood to go about in droves, and some got so conventional that they would not march alone; while even the best of them would not leave [without] their habitual loud grief or unwillingness, as mine was showing. She kept on turning her head back on her long neck and lowing to the rest, and walked very slow and bouncingly, needing careful guidance to keep her on the road, and a tap of my stick at every pace to keep her moving.[44]

This forced separation of his camel from her affinity circle meant that Lawrence had to find ways to keep her focused on the task at hand, and that required, as he put it, "careful guidance."[45]

42. Leonard, *The Camel*, 157.

43. Ibid., 50, 161.

44. Thomas E. Lawrence, *Seven Pillars of Wisdom: The Complete 1922 "Oxford" Text*. (Fordingbridge, Hampshire: J. and N. Wilson, 2004), 271.

45. The sociality of camels is mentioned in other sources. See, for example, Mohammad-Nasar Golamreza'i, "Camel," *Encyclopaedia Iranica* (London: Routledge and Kegan Paul, 1983), 4:374. Also see Maj. G. E. M. Hogg, "Camel Breeding," in *The Camel and Its Diseases:*

Few other British accounts mention these rather appealing attributes of the camel. Instead, as will be discussed in the next chapter, there was substantial bias against the animal. Even fewer accounts go into the kind of depth about the lives of camels that Arthur Leonard did, but even he missed a good deal. On the other hand, Leonard seemed well aware that part of a camel's gregariousness was probably based on the treatment received from its handler. Like some of the veterinarians and other transport officers, Leonard knew bad sarwans when he saw them. These were men who had no particular experience, but like the camels had been either impressed into service separately from the animals or hired as casual laborers from the bazaars. Leonard referred to them as "lazy, ignorant, scoundrels who have only been attracted by the high rate of pay."[46] There were others, though, who like the Raibari and Brahui lived in intimate contact with their camels. These camel men watched over them as they browsed the doab, bred them and raised the young, treated their afflictions, and loaded them judiciously for the hauling trade across the Punjab. It is to these aspects of camel life in the Punjab that I now turn.

INDIGENOUS VETERINARY MEDICINE, CAMEL AFFLICTIONS, AND SARWAN CARE

While postindependence research in rural Punjab by sociologists and ethnobotanists has demonstrated a broad understanding of the medicinal qualities of regional plants and herbs, including those used for treating the afflictions of domestic animals, there is little in this scholarship that addresses precolonial healing practices and theories.[47] Moreover, the emphasis in much of this work in the twentieth and twenty-first centuries has been to identify the active chemical agents in plants so that they might be used as a lower-cost alternative to products created by the transnational pharmaceutical industry. In most cases, "traditional" medicine is treated as a reclamation project, one designed to exploit indigenous knowledge for the purported benefit of the rural poor on the part of a benign and modernizing development state. Nevertheless, from such sources it is possible to discern the vast repertoire of local plants

Being Notes of Veterinary Surgeons and Commandants of Camel Corps, by Henry Eustace Cross (London: Baillière, Tindall and Cox, 1917), 29–44.

46. Leonard, *The Camel*, 48.

47. See, for example, S. S. Katewa, P. K. Galav, and Anita Jain, *Traditional Folk Veterinary Medicines* (Jodhpur: Scientific Publishers [India], 2010). This particular work attempts to be comprehensive and includes references to studies in Africa, Latin America, and rural European countries, but the authors' own research was done in India.

animal healers have used not only in the Punjab but in the camel country of East Africa as well.[48] Indigenous veterinary medicine is also present in the colonial archive, however, but in quite a different guise. In the writings of administrators and veterinary surgeons, it appears, like Ayurvedic medicine and Yunani tibb for humans, as a defective but seemingly omnipresent form of "folk" treatment that should now be superseded by European medical science. Yet in telling us what is wrong with folk practices and beliefs, colonial observers provide material with which to work in inferring characteristics of nineteenth- and twentieth-century indigenous knowledge.

So, for example, army transport and veterinary sources record indigenous formulary and preparation instructions, the uses of individual herbal preparations for certain afflictions, nonherbal treatments such as cauterization and bleeding, and information about all-purpose elixirs like the one Leonard recorded. Much of the information about native healing practices is presented as oral lore, or in some cases as unquestioned tradition or commonplace superstition. There is no suggestion that any sophisticated schema or body of literate knowledge might support the practices recorded. Nor is there any sense that there might have been multiple and overlapping forms of treatment, or that treatments differed in various parts of the country, where they might be variations of older formulas adapted to local conditions and available plant life, such as Leese had observed.

Still, the colonial sources provide enough suggestive material to make some inferences regarding the nature of animal medicine in the Punjab. Here, for example, is Veterinary Surgeon G. J. R. Rayment writing in 1886 on sarwan treatments of camels:

> *A theory, which should be exploded as soon as possible, is that natives understand the treatment of these animals in sickness.* To mention some of their curative measures, let us take Dementia:—They tie the patient down, cover him up

48. For some geographically diverse studies of indigenous veterinary medicine in contemporary Pakistan, see Altaf Hussain et al., "An Account of the Botanical Anthelmintics Used in Traditional Veterinary Practices in Sahiwal District of Punjab, Pakistan," *Journal of Ethnopharmacology* 119 (2008): 185–90; G. M Shah et al., "Ethno-phyto-veterinary Medicines in Northern Pakistan," *Journal of Animal and Plant Sciences* 22, no. 3 (2012): 791–97; Muhammad Asif Raza et al., "Ethno-botanical Remedies Used by Pastoralists for the Treatment of Livestock Diseases in Cholistan Desert, Pakistan," *Journal of Ethnopharmacology* 151 (2014): 333–42; and Khalid Ahmad et al., "Ethnoveterinary Medicinal Plant Knowledge and Practice among the Tribal Communities of Thakt-e-Sulaiman Hills, West Pakistan," *Journal of Ethnopharmacology* 170 (2015): 275–83.

> with blankets, light two fires before and behind him, if there is in addition a hot sun all the better! Again cow's urine is a favorite draft, indigo is rubbed in wounds, sinuses are filled with common salt, a slit is made in the ear for colic, &c., &c.[49]

To Rayment's dismissive observation about native "understanding" could be added John Henry Steel's characterization of indigenous drug formulary. Steel began his critique by acknowledging that sometime in the unspecified past, the British too were rather benighted. Current "scientific Therapeutics" has demonstrated, however, that substances like orpiment (an orange-yellow arsenic-sulfide mineral compound)[50] and realgar (ruby sulfur crystal), while having "striking physical characteristics," have proved to be "devoid of useful therapeutical properties." The natives of India, he continued,

> like our Barber Surgeons, and Farriers *et hoc genus omne* [all of this kind], have long formulae, some comprising even a quarter of a hundred different ingredients, probably on the "hit or miss principle," but in blissful ignorance of chemical incompatibility. These ingredients were mixed and compounded with the greatest care and exactness as to amount, odor, method of admixture, and preparation, the solemn mystery of the "remedy" being extended even to the method of administration. Incantations were often essential to the due concoction of the potion, and the phases of the moon required careful attention from the native pharmacist.

The effectiveness of local drugs, he concluded, depended on superstitions shared by both doctors and patients, as did the belief in the effectiveness of "Cowrie shells," frog entrails, and "powdered bone." Whatever slight therapeutic value these substances may have, they would not be "perceptible" to "crude and pre-convinced" observers like the native animal handlers.[51]

49. V.S. [Veterinary Surgeon] Rayment, "With the Indian Contingent at Suakin," *QJVSI* 4, no. 15 (April 1886): 284–85; emphasis in the original.

50. On the uses of orpiment in Indian medicine, see George Playfair, trans., *Taleef Sereef; or, The Indian Materia Medica* (Calcutta: Baptist Mission Press, 1833), 173–75. This is but one of many examples of British interest in Indian drugs (see below). A few decades after Steel dismissed the medicinal usefulness of orpiment, physicians were treating sleeping sickness victims in French Equatorial Africa with it; see Deborah Neill, *Networks in Tropical Medicine* (Stanford, CA: Stanford University Press, 2012), 143, 172–73.

51. John Henry Steel, "Materia Medica Veterinaria Indica," *QJVSI* 1, no. 1 (October 1882): 102–3.

The impression given in these examples, both of which were written at a time in the 1880s when veterinary surgeons continued to have little authority within the army's transport system, is that local veterinary medicine was essentially quackery because it lacked a scientific method, was laced with superstition and magical beliefs, and was reproduced by the unquestioned authority of the "doctor" sarwans and the ignorance of other animal handlers. Moreover, Steel sought to make clear that the Indian practitioners were no better at their work than English barbers and farriers, practitioners of equally dubious "medicine." These folk practitioners had been displaced in Great Britain by modern physicians and veterinary surgeons trained in specialized colleges. Both Rayment and Steel were products of this new order there, in which legal codes prevented the open practice of medicine without a medical degree. Indeed, the very term they used for themselves, *veterinary surgeon*, indicated the boundary the men presumed existed between themselves and Indian sarwans.

Nevertheless, in their dismissal of sarwan practices, the two veterinarians provide some inkling of popular medicine and healing practices. In the Punjab, compilers of British district gazetteers also took note of some treatments and native drug formulas, in most cases those of hakims, Yunani medical practitioners.[52] Moreover, colonial interest in hakim practices extended beyond simply recording local data compiled into gazetteers. During the 1860s and 1870s, the government of the Punjab had looked to hakims as a means of moving medical care into rural areas. Officials hoped to graft a modicum of allopathic medicine onto their existing training and then set them up in rural health stations. Over time, officials were convinced, the hakims, with close supervision by district officers, would recognize the superiority of Western medicine over Yunani. Enlightened hakims would then attract the rural population to the new medicine and thereby provide better care while breaking down the superstitions of those living in farming communities.[53]

Yet, we might ask, what was it that officials of the colonial state were seeing when they looked at the hakims or the animal handlers and their practices?

52. See *Gazetteer of the Attock District, 1907* (Lahore: Civil and Military Gazette Press, 1909), 264–66. This unusually long entry gives several examples of treatment. Also see *Baluchistan District Gazetteer Series, Bolan and Chagai* (Karachi: "Mercantile" Steam Press, ca. 1868), 4:108–9.

53. John C. Hume Jr., "Rival Traditions: Western Medicine and Yūnān-i Tibb in the Punjab, 1849–1889," *Bulletin of the History of Medicine* 51, no. 2 (1977): 217–19.

Was there, in other words, something clearly identifiable as Yunani medicine that could be placed against Western medicine and other forms in India, such as Ayurveda? In looking at the medical traditions of South Asia, David Arnold argues that thinking in terms of medical systems obscures the plurality of forms of healing present on the ground in precolonial and colonial India. He adds that it is difficult to extract South Asian medicine from the "poetical and saintly idioms" in which they have been embedded. Nineteenth-century Yunani medicine, for example, ranged across Greek "humoralism, poetic aphorisms, astrology, aphrodisiacs, elixirs, dietary prescriptions, talismanic devices and exorcism."[54] Guy Attewell notes that in the markets of Hyderabad, one could find multiple forms of practice, overlaps between Yunani and Ayurvedic, and educated hakims who might call on a *jarrah* (barber surgeon, bonesetter) to cauterize, lance boils, and perform bloodletting on one of their own patients.[55] Some scholars, such as David Hardiman and Projit Mukharji, have gone further. Drawing from the notion of a "nomad science" proposed by Gilles Deleuze and Felix Guattari,[56] they argue for a subaltern science of "diverse and heterogeneous . . . therapies and practitioners" that use and misuse, borrow from and discard technologies, practices, and ideas forming highly eclectic assemblages.[57] Such a mixture, I would suggest, was the case with animal healing in the Punjab, where the sarwan's skills were more akin to those of the *jarrah*, but not devoid of some theory of how animal bodies functioned and how to treat their ills.

Much medical knowledge, including the use of herbs, for instance, was passed on through oral traditions or embodied in the idiosyncratic practices of individual healers. The procedures that resulted could be quite local, in part because environment was understood to have a strong influence on the

54. The quotation is taken from an unpublished paper entitled "Plurality and Transition," cited in Projit Mukharji, "Symptoms of Dis-ease: New Trends in the Histories of 'Indigenous' South Asian Medicines," *History Compass* 9, no. 12 (2011): 890.

55. Guy N. A. Attewell, *Refiguring Unani Tibb: Plural Healing in Late Colonial India* (Hyderabad: Orient Longman, 2007), 16–18, 102. Also see Helen Lambert, "Plural Traditions? Folk Therapeutics and English Medicine in Rajasthan," in *Western Medicine as Contested Knowledge*, ed. Andrew Cunningham and Bridie Andrews (Manchester: Manchester University Press, 1997), 191–211.

56. Gilles Deleuze and Felix Guattari, *A Thousand Plateaus* (Minneapolis: University of Minnesota Press, 1987), 362.

57. See their introduction in David Hardiman and Projit Mukharji, eds., *Medical Marginality in South Asia* (London: Routledge, 2012), 18–26.

constitution of all life.[58] But there were also well-established textual sources in Persian and Arabic that were used to train some hakims, if not animal healers, which dated to the beginnings of Islam's eastward expansion. Some of these same sources had also been translated into Latin and European vernaculars so that the Greek or Galenic tradition was simultaneously a resource in early modern Britain, parts of continental Europe, North Africa, the Middle East, and South Asia. In Britain, the transmission was from Latin translations of Arabic texts into vernacular sources such as Nicholas Culpeper's *Galens Art of Physick* (London, 1657) or almanacs.[59]

These were the bodies of knowledge and practice that British barbers and farriers partook of, and which was being displaced in the nineteenth century by medical science. Indeed, as Deepak Kumar has pointed out, when European physicians in the seventeenth and eighteenth centuries engaged their counterparts in places like Goa, they shared a humoral heritage and together could acknowledge that diseases were environmentally determined. Where they differed were in areas of practice. As Kumar argues, while the Europeans might prefer bloodletting, the Indian practitioner relied on "urine analysis and urine therapy." At the same time, they exchanged information about illnesses as well as drugs and plants themselves.[60] Well into the twentieth century, British veterinarians would remain dependent on local medicines as well as on drugs produced from plants imported from Europe that had been assimilated into local practices.

Indian practitioners and medical texts moved west, while Arabic and Persian texts and practices were disseminated by Islamic Sufi physicians in India, where Yunani tibb took root.[61] Why this was the case can be accounted for,

58. See, for example, Francis Zimmerman, *The Jungle and the Aroma of Meats* (Delhi: Motilal Banarsidass, 1988).

59. See Louise Hill Curth, *The Care of Brute Beasts: A Social and Cultural Study of Veterinary Medicine in Early Modern England* (Leiden: Brill, 2010), 34–40; on almanacs, see Curth's *English Almanacs, Astrology, and Popular Medicine: 1550–1700* (Manchester: Manchester University Press, 2007).

60. Deepak Kumar, "Adoption and Adaptation: A Study of Medical Ideas and Techniques in Colonial India," in *Science between Europe and Asia*, ed. Feza Günergun and Dhruv Raina (Dordrecht: Springer, 2011), 236–37.

61. In his study of Galenic medicine in India, Fabrizio Speziale argues that the path of the transmission of Greek or Yunani medicine into India was via Central Asian urban centers like Bukhara and Shiraz. The Mongol invasions of the thirteenth and fourteenth centuries seem to have triggered the moves of a number of Sufi adepts and their families into northern India. See Speziale's "The Relation between Galenic Medicine and Sufism in India during the Delhi and

not only because of humoral medicine's emphasis on local environments as the causes of afflictions, but because of the patronage Yunani tibb enjoyed from Muslim rulers, including the Mughal. It may also be accounted for because of Arabic medicine's strong moral code, linked directly to the Qur'an and the consequent injunction that humans care for animals.[62]

There are, however, no clear connections in scholarly studies of South Asian medicine linking Yunani tibb and veterinary medicine. Indeed, one of the few available studies of veterinary medicine influenced by the humoral tradition is geographically and temporally removed from the place and period of this study. Nevertheless, in his work on veterinary medicine under the Mamluk sultanate in Cairo (1250–1517), Housni Shehada provides an overview of Galenic or humoral medicine and its application to animal care, one that resonates with some of what we know about animal medicine in the Punjab.[63]

Galenic medicine regarded illness as an imbalance in the body's humors and treated this imbalance through a set of practices, techniques, and substances that could restore humors to their natural state. Rebalancing the system could be achieved by a variety of means involving both the purging of humoral excess through bloodletting or encouraging their flow out of the body's orifices, hence restoring the quality and proper quantity of the humor that had become excessive or deficient. So, for example, an excess of black humoral bile could affect the brain, causing unusual behavior. The application of heat could move the excess black bile out of the body. Hence, Rayment's description of the treatment for dementia, securing the camel and heating its body, appears to have been one consistent with humoral theory. Other practitioners might treat the same ailment with cauterization, on the theory that intense heat on a specific location would draw out the black bile.

According to Shehada, in treating afflictions of animals, Mamluk physicians began by clarifying the difference between the temperaments of humans and those of animals, which led to the development of a theory of treatment. Humans were to be treated with complex medicines that had gentler qualities,

---

Deccan Sultanates," *East and West* 53 (December 2003): 149–50. On Sufi migration into north India as a result of Mongol expansion, also see Muzaffar Alam and Sanjay Subrahmanyam, *Indo-Persian Travels in the Age of Discoveries, 1400–1800* (Cambridge: Cambridge University Press, 2007), 48–51. Also see Kumar, "Adoption and Adaptation," 236.

62. Housni Shehada, "Arabic Veterinary Medicine and the 'Golden Rules' for Veterinarians," in Faroqhi, *Animals and People in Ottoman Egypt*, 318, 323–28.

63. Housni Shehada provides an excellent overview of the key principles of Galenic medicine in *Mamluks and Animals: Veterinary Medicine in Medieval Islam* (Leiden: E. J. Brill, 2013), 226–31.

while large animals, because of their stronger temperaments, could be treated with simpler, more powerful drugs or combinations of drugs. Bloodletting to eliminate excess quantities of humors was commonly used in both humans and animals. Moreover, because bloodletting was a broadly accepted form of treatment, it was important to know the circulatory system of humans and animals in order to gauge the proper insertion of needles into the body.[64]

Mamluk physicians also understood the importance of maintaining health and preventing illness. Hence, a general tonic, a variation of which Leonard described, made up of camphor, musk, roses, and saffron was given to some animals in springtime. In addition to drug formulas and bloodletting, magical signs and numerology might be brought to bear to deal with particularly difficult cases. In other instances, whispering or chanting verses from the Qur'an might be used when evil forces, such as genies or *jinn*, were suspected. Lastly, cauterization, sometimes involving many burns organized into geometric patterns, was used to deal with humoral excesses or to dry a body thought to be too moist or flaccid.[65]

Elements of the Mamluk veterinary canon are suggested in Steel's and Rayment's observations about sarwan practices. But they were not the first to draw attention to such practices with respect to camel care. Other British sources recorded native veterinary practices and found some of them useful. For example, one of the earliest published treatises on the diseases of the camel was by William Gilchrist, a surgeon in India in the 1840s. Like Steel and Rayment, Gilchrist often commented negatively on some of the native treatments he witnessed, such as blowing smoke into camels' nostrils to increase the flow of mucus, because he deemed them "inert"; that is, they had no discernible power to address the animal's actual affliction. Quite often, he corrected native treatment by providing one of his own. On the other hand, like native healers he freely used bleeding and purgatives, that is, individual drugs or formulary that humoral medicine would have understood as removing excesses of humors from the body.[66] In other cases, Gilchrist prescribed alternatives to

64. Ibid., 233–45.

65. See ibid., 288, 396–402, 412–13.

66. Gilchrist's use of bloodletting might not be too surprising, however. In Great Britain, humoral veterinary medicine had been common in the past, while bloodletting and the use of leeches on human subjects continued to be practiced in Europe and the United States well into the nineteenth century. On early modern veterinary medicine in Great Britain, see Curth, *The Care of Brute Beasts*—chapter 2 deals with humoral medicine in England.

indigenous treatments,[67] but he also provided native drug formulas to treat afflictions for which he could offer no alternative. These include treatments for a form of madness, rheumatism, paralysis, colds, and itch (mange?).

For such native recipes, Gilchrist's formulary included quantities of drugs, transliterated names of Indian drugs, and the drug in local script. So, for example, in treating a "dropsical affliction" (inflammation or swelling of the body) termed *Zaarbadh*, he provided three different formulas, number three of which contained fifteen items. Several of the ingredients were to be powdered and then the whole made into balls or "mussals" and administered over several days.[68] For "itch" (*kaareesh*), the sarwans mixed six ingredients to make an ointment. The first four were to be powdered; the fifth, a nut, was to be boiled in the sixth ingredient, an oil. Then they were all to be mixed together and rubbed over the animal's body. Gilchrist's formula section is twenty-four pages, the largest section of his treatise.[69] With such a book in hand, a surgeon could purchase the ingredients in a bazaar, prepare them as Gilchrist instructed, and treat camels with or without the aid of sarwans. But the key point to be made is that until the 1880s, it would seem that many of the indigenous treatments were being drawn from by British veterinary surgeons.

Punjabi sarwans as well as camel men in North Africa continued to rely on such preparations and local herbs, many of which came from the wastelands. A half a century after Gilchrist published his treatise, Arthur Leonard, in his book *The Camel*, provided many examples of Indian and African treatments for conditions ranging from injuries caused by improperly loading camels (saddle galls) to itch, mange, and internal afflictions such as colic and catarrh. Like Gilchrist, Leonard learned details about camel illnesses and the various drugs used to deal with them from native sarwans. But in contrast to Gilchrist, or Rayment and Steel for that matter, he expressed his debt to native camel men and acknowledged that they knew far more about treating camels than he did.[70] And although he didn't understand its purpose or effect, Leonard reported that sarwans treated a disease called *Taplarja*, something they at-

67. William Gilchrist, *A Practical Memoir on the History and Treatment of the Diseases of the Camel, with Instructions for Preserving Its Efficiency as an Animal of Transport and a General Outline of Its Anatomy, Also, an Account of the Medicines Used in the Cure of Its Diseases* (Calcutta: G. H. Huttmann, Bengal Military Orphan Press, 1843). The alternatives he provided include calomel and tartar emetic, the former of which he preferred to aloes; pp. 25 and 27.

68. Ibid.; on *Zaarbadh*, see pp. 13, 37–38.

69. Ibid., 51, for the itch ointment recipe; the formula section runs from p. 28 to p. 52.

70. Leonard, *The Camel*, 212–40.

tributed to wind, by cauterizing the head and flanks of the afflicted camel. Itch was treated with mustard oil, iris root, and brimstone.[71] Leonard felt that the efficacy of these treatments partly lay in the camel men's faith in them and the fact that they drew from the plants and materials that were at hand. Sometime later, Arnold Leese averred that the indigenous treatment for mange was "difficult to improve upon." And while he leveled the same sorts of objections to cauterization as his predecessors, he also argued that camel men ought to be carefully listened to; it was up to the listener to sort the wheat from the chaff of their explanations. Moreover, Leese recognized that many drugs and herbal preparations used by sarwans were highly effective for some common ailments found among camels.[72]

The contrasting reactions to sarwan knowledge may be no more than the difference between a transport officer who was willing to admit his own ignorance and veterinary surgeons who had elite training in allopathic medicine. But was this simply a matter of differences of professional expertise? Leonard spent sixteen years in army transport, all of it around camels. In that time, he had come to depend on and respect the native handlers while expressing no doubt about his authority over the natives. Veterinary surgeons, on the other hand, were uncomfortable with their dependence on native knowledge of camels, frequently denying that any such knowledge existed while also dealing with the fact that they had limited authority within the army transport scheme. Perhaps more to the point, as Leonard's account made clear and as the Afghan campaign certainly demonstrated, army transport was highly dependent on competent sarwans. In their absence, the scale of animal deaths and the cost to the Indian government rose astronomically. At the same time, however, to grant experienced sarwans a modicum of authority would, at least by the time Steel was writing in the 1880s, have been like giving stable farriers a status similar to that of trained veterinary surgeons. This was a dilemma that both the veterinarians and those in charge of army transport faced. Still, there was no getting around the fact that as long as there were to be camels in army transport, the British were reliant on the camel men of the Punjab, be they Brahuis, Baluchis, or Raibaris.

When in the late 1890s the British Indian Army was compelled to consider the creation of a permanent transport system in the Punjab, the sarwan issue came into the foreground. If there was to be a regular army camel transport corps, wouldn't native handlers be needed to ensure that government camels

71. Ibid., 226–27.

72. Leese, *A Treatise on the One-Humped Camel in Health and in Disease*, 142, 155.

were kept in proper condition? If sarwans were to be part of the new scheme, where would they come from? How was the army to identify or create competent sarwans? At that time, one of the investigative subcommittees involved with exploring the matter asked a number of local notables in the Punjab if they thought it might be possible to train a cadre of camel men for military service. The question put to them attempted to circumscribe camel handlers' duties as knowledge of how to water, feed, saddle, and load camels. All the respondents agreed that these were basic skills, but they differed in the length of time—from a month to a year—it would take to train someone to undertake these tasks competently. Those questioned then added that there was more to a sarwan's duties than this short list of tasks. Camel doctoring, for example, was "a practice which every practically-experienced *sarwan* understands." Acquiring skills associated with camel care on this order, they thought, would take a year or two of training.[73]

The actual training, however, required the government to gain the cooperation of the families who taught sarwans. Ali Baksh, a revenue collector from Rawalpindi, suggested the following method:

> There is no difficulty in training an ordinary Punjabi to look after a camel, but it would be necessary for such a man to learn his trade from living with *sarwans* for a year. From eight to ten families of the witness clan [?], which were formerly *zamindari* (government recognized land-owners), have gone in for keeping camels (20 in all). They learnt from a relative who had long been a camel-owner and who remained with them while they learnt. Such learners must be young men.[74]

Here perhaps is one of the few indications in colonial sources of how "young men" became sarwans. They underwent a period of apprenticeship under an older, experienced camel man, either a relative or a member of the same extended clan. The training took upwards of a year and required the apprentice to live with the master. Given what is known of the training of hakims, what was imparted to the apprentice was special and perhaps even secret knowledge about camels, their habits, and the remedies for keeping them healthy.

Once trained, the young man might remain with the family as one of the attendants to their camels. Or he might be hired by a landowner who could afford such expertise, or by commercial pack animal firms. Any such arrange-

73. IOR/L/MIL/7/6687: *Report of the Transport Committee, 1897*, appendix D, 228.
74. Ibid.

ments were probably also tied to connections through extended networks of family and clan relations. For the poor small holder, on the other hand, camel knowledge probably came from experience handed down from father to son or from itinerant herbalists or bonesetters who circulated through rural villages. In any case, as Ali Baksh's testimony suggested, well-trained camel experts would bring a broad range of knowledge to bear, and would be the ones that the British transport and veterinary officers could rely on for an understanding of the animals brought into government service.

Although the subcommittee didn't pursue the matter further at the time, it no doubt would also have been clear to the local notables queried that trained sarwans would probably also know the best ways for managing camels on the march. Unlike the untrained hired men who used brute force to move impressed camels, experienced handlers certainly used a variety of techniques to maintain orderly pack trains and keep them moving at a regular rate. In his memoir, Leonard was one of the few to observe how well managed caravans were when in the hands of competent natives.[75] One of the techniques sarwans used to keep camels moving and content was to make use of their positive response to music, especially singing or musical chanting. According to one source, camels preferred singing to shouting and moved more "cheerfully" to rhythmic sounds. Caravan managers might hire singers if there were no adequate ones among the camel handlers.[76] Although army transport and veterinary sources make no mention of such matters, sarwans also seemed to have known how to keep camels content during the monotonous and arduous labor involved in caravan commerce.

75. Leonard, *The Camel*, 132, 198. Also see Ahmed Hassanien, *The Lost Oases* (New York: Century, 1925), 101, who also commented on the strong bond between camel driver and camel (139–40).

76. George P. Marsh, *The Camel: His Organization, Habits and Uses* (Boston: Gould and Lincoln, 1856). Marsh cited Joseph von Hammer-Purgstall, whose essay "Das Camel" appeared in *Denkshriften der Kaiserlichen Akademie der Wissenshaftern*, vol. 70. According to Marsh, Hammer-Purgstall drew from some sixteen Arabic works on the camel, cited many Persian and "Oriental" works of prose and poetry that deal with camels, and concluded with references to the Qur'an and the Bible; see pp. 28–29. In his recent study of the camel, Robert Irwin, citing other materials, makes a similar observation about the camel's love of music; see his *Camel* (London: Reaktion Books, 2010), 31–32. Much earlier, Ibn Khaldun, the fourteenth-century historian, noted instructors in Egypt that specialized in teaching camel chants. See *The Muqaddimah: An Introduction to History*, trans. Franz Rosenthal (New York: Pantheon Books, 1958), 2:348. Among other examples, Ibn Kaldun presented the teaching of camel chants as a sign of a "perfected and refined" civilization. Also see Hassanien, *The Lost Oases*, for some examples of songs sung to camels (126–27).

Given the examples presented above concerning indigenous camel care, intraspecies affinities, and the central role of sarwans to camel life in the Punjab, we might better understand the toll that impressment and forced labor exacted on animal-human relations in the region. From the extant reports of the Afghan campaign over the winter of 1878–79, it seems fairly clear that once camels began assembling at collection centers, the animals, most of whom were either far too young and ill prepared for pack work or clearly beyond their prime, found themselves in what charitably can be described as a thoroughly disorienting situation—their world had literally been turned upside down. They had been force marched from rural grazing lands to the noise, bustle, and chaos of collection centers, many of which seem to have been located near city bazaars. For most of the animals, therefore, the sense of traumatic separation may have been quite pronounced. And such feelings of longing and disorientation might have been exacerbated when, for instance, they were placed in the hands of strange camel handlers who knew little about them—how to load and unload them, how to respond to their ailments and discomforts, especially on the grueling march into Afghanistan, and how to ensure that they got proper food, rest, and protection from the elements. At least one British officer was bothered enough by the carnage to ask his personal attendant, Biloch by name, what could be done to alleviate the situation for the living animals. Biloch responded that the poor treatment the camels had received since the beginning of the campaign had broken their hearts; nothing the British could do now would change matters.[77]

Biloch's response speaks to the plight of camels forced into service, animals that in most cases were permanently lost to their owners. Precisely what impact this had on those who raised or kept camels is difficult to gauge, but one land settlement report written in the mid-1880s indicated that impressment and loss changed local practices. Deputy Commissioner H. St. G. Tucker, the settlement officer, wrote that the Kohat District had been picked clean of camels during the war. By 1884, however, the camel population appeared to be recovering, but Tucker could provide no precise numbers because a census was impossible. "Since the late war," he explained, "it has been a common practice for camel-owners in the district to try to pass off their camels as the property of some Afridi or other trans-border man in order to avoid impressment for military or other service, the rule being that camels belonging to trans-border

77. Col. Augustus Le Messurier, *Kandahar in 1879; Being the Diary of Major Le Messurier, R.E.* (London: W. H. Allen, 1880), 104. Le Messurier thought that Biloch knew a good deal about camels.

men are only to be impressed in the cases of extreme emergency." Exacerbating matters, according to Tucker, were Afridi salt merchants who grazed their camels with those of local sarwans, making it impossible to distinguish one from the other![78]

The people Tucker referred to in frustration here may well have been Powindah traders, some of whom entered India through passes further north and grazed their camels in areas around Peshawar, Kohat, and Bannu rather than Dera Ismail Khan.[79] And, as Tucker made clear, they mixed their camels in with those of the local sarwans, hiring the latter to watch over their caravan herds as they themselves moved eastward to engage in trade and money lending. What these camel encounters were like we can only guess. But recall Leonard's observation about the gregariousness of camels. We can imagine these Powindah camels rubbing up against the camels of the plains, perhaps even interbreeding with them. Or we can imagine them encountering these others as the Powindahs rode them to visit *ziarats*, the holy shrines that dotted the region,[80] or while engaged in local carrying trade during their winter stay. And perhaps a sarwan or a local storyteller, seeing the camels mixing as they browsed, crafted a song or poem based on the differences between hill camels and plains camels. But whether this was the case or not, the many kinds of camels that populated the hills and lowlands of the Punjab were very much part of a rich cultural scene that only partially had to do with their being beasts of burden or, as one recent scholar put it, animal capital.[81] Like sheep, goats, and cattle, camels were active participants in the human-constructed cultural-symbolic universe, along the edges of which they also browsed.

SUFI SAINTS AND POPULAR BELIEFS

Music-loving camels browsing the Punjab and meeting others of their kind down from the high country might be an appropriate place to end this chapter. But before moving on to a discussion of the colonial transformations of the region and their impacts on human-animal-plant ecological relations, there is one other important element of life in the region to consider. Camels as well as other domestic animals were enmeshed in a rich symbolic world of popular

78. Tucker, *Report of the Land Revenue Settlement of the Kohat District in the Punjab*, 125.

79. Robinson, *Notes on Nomad Tribes of Eastern Afghanistan*, 32–36.

80. Robinson mentions these visits as well as particular Sufi brotherhoods (see next section) to whom they made offerings. See ibid., 9–10.

81. Caton, "The Transition from Animal Capital to Land Capital," 65.

beliefs that, like medicine, were a mixture of Islamic and Hindu beliefs and practices, folk cults, and the culture of shrines. Probably the most prominent of these were the cults of Sufi saints that centered on the aforementioned *ziarats*, burial sites of holy men who were believed to have special powers for interceding with God on behalf of their worshippers. Pilgrims, including Mughal emperors,[82] came from across the region to these shrines, where they sought solutions to family and clan problems, the poor health of humans and animals, fertility issues, and possession by the many kinds of spirits and demons that caused chaos in human lives.

The idea of a holy person with a special relationship with God dates to the beginning of Islam, but the particular forms these relationships took changed over time. Persons recognized as saints had achieved this position through rigorously following a mystical path of study with spiritual superiors, fasting and meditating in ways that eventually led them to a union with God.[83] Much like Buddhist bodhisattvas, the saint's special powers remained potent on earth as an aid to others less fortunate or disciplined than they. Sufism remapped the Punjab as a sacred geography, fixing the transcendence and permanence of saintly power over that of earthly lords such as sultans, khans, or rajas.

The charismatic power centered at the tomb complex, or *dargah*, was understood to be potent enough to emanate outward for some distance, attracting supplicants. From the shrine, poems about the saint and simple tales from the Qur'an circulated into everyday practice, often taking the form of songs sung by village women carrying out household tasks.[84] In this way, the powers of the saint were literally in the air and spread by word of mouth. Pilgrims came to the shrine seeking the aid and blessings of the current *pir* (head of the shrine), who was usually a descendant of the saint and perhaps of the Prophet as well.

In addition to addressing individual problems, such as illness and bar-

82. The Mughal emperors Akbar and Jahanjir worshipped at the shrine of Khwaja Mu'inuddin Chishti and bestowed donations and special privileges on the shrine. See S. A. I. Tirmizi, "Mughal Documents Relating to the Dargah of Khwaja Mu'inuddin Chishti," in *Muslim Shrines in India: Their Character, History, and Significance*, ed. Christian W. Troll (New Delhi: Oxford University Press, 1989), 48–59; and Nile Green, "Stories of Saints and Sultans: Re-membering History at the Sufi Shrines of Aurangabad," *Modern Asian Studies* 38, no. 2 (2004): 419–46.

83. Nile Green, *Making Space: Sufis and Settlers in Early Modern India* (Oxford: Oxford University Press, 2012), 5–17.

84. See Richard Eaton, "Sufi Folk Literature and the Expansion of Indian Islam," *History of Religions* 14, no. 2 (1974): 119.

renness, the *pir* or his followers handed out *amaliyat* (amulets) containing prayers or passages from the Qur'an. The amulets retained saintly power and continued to address the supplicants' needs after they left the shrine. They might also be placed on other humans or animals, such as camels, to protect them from disease or misfortune or to heal them. Such activity was heightened on the anniversary of the saint's death. On that occasion, the *'urs* (literally, "wedded to God") ceremony was understood to be the most propitious time for visiting the saint.[85] The *'urs* celebrations might draw thousands of pilgrims, and were accompanied by market days, feasts, and entertainments.[86] Vendors sold objects said to have been blessed by the saint through the keepers of the tomb. According to one account, the ill were fed from copper pots and plates rather than the earthenware plates and cups used in their homes, and sick children were placed in cradles bought at the shrines.[87] The *'urs* also drew non-Muslims to the tomb. Sikhs, for example, venerated Shaikh Baba Farid, and marginal groups and "criminal" castes patronized many of the shrines.[88] Such festive gatherings may also have been occasions on which wealthier pilgrims adorned their camels, and perhaps other transport animals as well, in rich garments, jewelry, and protective amulets.[89] In some cases, certain tombs became known for specialties, such as the curing of insanity, the exorcism of demons, or the healing of burns and snakebites.[90] When requests

85. For a translation of a guide to the *'urs* ceremony at a saint's tomb, see Carl Ernst, "An Indo-Persian Guide to Sufi Shrine Pilgrimage," in *Manifestations of Sainthood in Islam*, ed. Grace Smith and Carl Ernst (Istanbul: Isis Press, 1993), 43–67.

86. Green, *Making Space*, 35.

87. Iqtidar Husain Siddiqui, "The Early Chishti Dargahs," in Troll, *Muslim Shrines in India*, 22.

88. Anna Suvorova, *Muslim Saints of South Asia: The Eleventh to the Fifteenth Centuries* (London: RoutledgeCurzon, 1999), 2. Having established, in their own minds at least, strict divisions between castes, ethnic groups, tribes, and religions, the British were continually surprised by Hindus joining "Musalmen" to pay homage at the shrines of Muslim saints; see, for example, Maj. Cecil Henry Buck, *Faiths, Fairs, and Festivals of India* (Calcutta: Thacker, Spink, 1917), 214.

89. In his book on camels, Leonard noted that "Orientals invariably decorate their camels thus, also with cowries (shells) and silver neck and head ornaments." See *The Camel*, 54.

90. While treating all such beliefs as superstition, Oliver recorded several examples of the powers of shrines to be found on the Afghan-India border; see *Across the Border*, 134–36. Carl Ernst provides some examples of contemporary guides to specialties of certain shrines; see *Sufism: An Introduction to the Mystical Tradition of Islam* (Boston: Shambhala, 2011), 75.

were granted, worshippers gave thanks, often in the form of alms, and spread the word of the efficacy of the saint, thus attracting others.[91]

By the time the British moved into the Punjab in the mid-nineteenth century, Sufi healing and teaching shrines were well established. As British administrators carried out land settlements in the northwest, they began to discover the vast number of shrines that existed at every administrative level. Rather than alter the preexisting relations between shrines and the state, colonial authorities tended to follow the lead of their predecessors, in part because the saintly families that controlled the shrines were often large landholders in their districts, with many peasant tenants who maintained allegiance to them. By allowing the *pirs* to retain their hereditary holdings, the British first gained their allegiance and then were able to coopt them into the colonial regime.[92]

Not all shrines were of such an august stature as those of Sufi saints. The land settlement officials found all sorts of worship sites in and between villages, and right up into the mountains and highlands to the west and north.[93] Settlement officers kept careful track of many of them, and their findings eventually found their way into district gazetteers, where they were later compiled into works such as *A Glossary of the Tribes and Castes of the Punjab and North-West Frontier Province* (1911). It is clear from this compilation that what was identified as a shrine often included a great variety of sites. Villages had ancestral shrines to specific lineages and shrines to village founders. But there were also the graves of dead Brahmins, holy men of various stripes, warriors, and the malevolent dead, all of whom required propitiation. Other sites harbored dangerous spirits who might cause smallpox or plague among humans or harm cattle, sheep, goats, and camels if not properly cared for. Sometimes a new shrine had to be built because of recurring calamities; other times spir-

91. See Desiderio Pinto, SJ, "The Mystery of the Nizamuddin Dargah: The Accounts of Pilgrims," in Troll, *Muslim Shrines in India*, 112–24.

92. Some of the heads of shrines took up positions on provincial councils, while their sons were admitted to colonial colleges and law schools. Later, many joined the Unionist Party that supported the British establishment in the Punjab; see Green, *Making Space*, 195. Gilmartin dates the greater involvement of the British colonial government with shrines to the period after 1857, at which time many saw the advantage of both participating in the religious life of the shrines and taking advantage of the authority shrine leaders had with the rural population; see *Empire and Islam* (Berkeley: University of California Press, 1988), 46–52, 68–71.

93. See Lal Shah, "Notes on Some Frontier Shrines," *Indian Antiquary* 35 (1906): 119–25; and Aubrey O'Brien, "The Mohammedan Saints of the Western Punjab," *Journal of the Royal Anthropological Institute of Great Britain and Ireland* 41 (1911): 509–20.

FIGURE 7. Camels passing under the Qur'an. *Graphic* (London), February 22, 1879.

its were content to remain in trees or in jungle areas, provided they received regular offerings.[94] Spirit propitiation, be it at established shrines, at a pile of rocks near a sacred stream, or at the base of a tree inhabited by *jinn*, was complemented by a rich folklore on witchcraft, the evil eye, omens, taboos, and the meaning of dreams. Popular beliefs like these incorporated many kinds of invisible entities into a sacred geography of the Punjab that linked land, environment, animals, and plants, each of which required human care and respect.

British officials tended to see these popular beliefs as the superstitions common to benighted "Orientals." And while it seemed unlikely to "enlightened" British settlement officers and district administrators that such notions could easily be eradicated among "ignorant" peasants, they could not help but record these beliefs and, when the opportunity arose, challenge claims that went with amulets, magical objects, and the shrines themselves. Now and then, perhaps because they seemed to embody the "strange" beliefs of the local people, images of indigenous practices would make their way out of India and into the popular media in Britain. During the Second Afghan War,

94. See H. A. Rose, comp., *A Glossary of the Tribes and Castes of the Punjab and North-West Frontier Province* (Lahore: Civil and Military Gazette Press, 1911), 1:203–58; and the examples given in Buck, *Faiths, Fairs, and Festivals of India*, 210–18.

for example, the *Graphic*, a London illustrated newspaper, published a picture of camels being led under a Qur'an that had been wrapped in cloth and suspended between two poles (fig. 7). Two decades later, during campaigns along the North-West Frontier, an almost identical picture was published; this one was titled "A Strange Cure for Sick Camels" (4 December 1897).

*

This chapter has attempted to provide an overview of the complex human-animal-plant ecology that gave the Punjab its unique character. Camel life was thoroughly enmeshed in these relations, and the camel was privileged in many cases because of the special place the animal held not only in Islam but also in the moral economy of the pastoralists and farmers. In this sense, it should be clear that the impressment and forced labor undertaken by the British Indian Army were far more complicated than simply a military-economic relationship. Suffering and dead camels evoked, for the natives of the Punjab, an excess on the part of humans that was difficult to reconcile with their own moral and ethical universe. British attitudes toward camels and their modes of life did eventually change, but not their acceptance of Punjabi beliefs. As we will see in the next two chapters, change had more to do with the necessities of the army transport system and new knowledge about camels produced by veterinary surgeons than it did with any appreciation of native "superstition" or the "disorderly" life of pastoralists and nomads.

CHAPTER 3

Jackasses for India: Transport Reform and the Global Traffic in Mules

Gen. Michael Kennedy's appointment as controller general of supply and transport during the latter phase of the Second Afghan War did not solve the problems in the existing transport system in the British Indian Army. The central issue, brought glaringly into focus by thousands of dead camels, mules, and bullocks, was the virtual absence of an organization capable of mobilizing transport in a manner that did not result in logistical disasters. This chapter explores the army's initial responses to conundrums of institutionalizing transport logistics, including its efforts at reform. One outcome of such efforts was a preference for the mule over the camel as the ideal pack animal for transport.

TRANSPORT REFORM: FIRST ITERATION

For most observers, the heart of the Indian Army transport problem lay in the absence of trained transport officers, competent and abundant animal handlers, and a peacetime organization capable of rapidly and efficiently mobilizing for war. Observers concluded that a more formal organization was required. From this perspective, animal labor should no longer be governed by an ad hoc arrangement made up of mass impressment, an unclear chain of command, and murky relations between civil and military officials. The

I take the title of this chapter from a file in the IOR; see the correspondence of September 1904 in IOR/L/MIL/7/1056: Arrangement for Purchase of Donkey Stallions in the United States, 1902–1906.

nature of the desired organization became a subject of debate almost immediately upon the cessation of hostilities. The site through which the debate proceeded was not a parliamentary committee or an internal investigative body but a publication of the Indian Army, the *Journal of the United Service Institution of India*.[1]

One of the journal's preferred formats for stimulating discussion was the essay contest. Sometime in 1880, the editorial staff put out a call for essays addressing "A Transport Service for Asiatic Warfare." The top three entries were published in a special issue, along with extracts from several others (156 pages in all).[2] All the essayists were in agreement that something on the order of a permanent establishment was required, one that would be directed by specialists trained in supply and transport. Most also agreed that depots should be created in order to facilitate the expansion of transport during wars. Overwhelmingly, the authors favored the mule over other transport animals, although they could imagine camels working efficiently behind the lines in a staged system of transport. As one of the essayists put it, the mule was "best suited for military transport work, being docile, hardy, surefooted and enduring; is little subject to epidemic diseases and thrives on all kinds of food."[3] In light of this widely shared perception of the mule, the authors almost unanimously recommended the creation of a mule-breeding program in India, and the importation of donkey sires to improve the Indian stock. All of them also imagined that individual regiments would remain the primary units of organization for transport, and that these regiments would mainly be those on or near the North-West Frontier.

In addition to the recommendations to be found in the winning essays, several officers sent proposals directly to army headquarters in Simla. For example, Charles MacGregor, head of the Intelligence Branch in the Quarter-

1. The institution had begun publication of the journal in 1871 and used it for informing Indian Army officers about matters specific to Indian conditions, the state of armies in European and Asian countries, recent military campaigns within and outside India, and the latest military technologies. Through its regular meetings and the production of its journal, the United Service Institution of India functioned as a place where ideas could be exchanged over issues of importance to the army. It was in the pages of the journal, for example, that articles appeared advocating the creation of an intelligence branch for the Indian Army. See James Hevia, *The Imperial Security State: British Colonial Knowledge and Empire-Building in Asia* (Cambridge: Cambridge University Press, 2012), 66–69.

2. *JUSII*, special number (1880).

3. Col. H. Moore, "A Transport Service for Asiatic Warfare," *JUSII*, special number (1880): 148. Also see pp. 125, 132, 136, and 156, where the virtues of the mule are extolled.

master General's Department, proposed a scheme calling for an active-duty transport establishment in regiments one-fourth the size for wartime. Active-duty units would involve one attendant for every three transport animals of a particular kind, with a reserve pool of transport animals of 10 percent.[4] Meanwhile, Gen. Kennedy devised a scheme of his own that differed in a number of important ways from those circulated in the essays. It called for the creation of a commissariat and transport department for all of India, removing the responsibility for transport from the regimental level, except for units located on the Indian frontiers. Instead, several transport depots were to be established at fifteen strategic sites. At each of these sites, five hundred mules would be kept, with that number to be doubled in time of need. The depots would also contain a permanent establishment of officers charged with maintaining a thorough knowledge of animals in their district; familiarizing themselves with animal fairs and local pack animal contractors; maintaining rolls of influential Indians who would aid in procuring pack animals; drawing maps with statistics on animals available for hire in each village; providing inspectors to register animals and ensure that returns from districts were accurate; and maintaining lists of natives willing, if needed, to enter service as animal handlers. Kennedy felt that this scheme—parts of which resemble that of the Mughal Empire in the Punjab—also would make it possible to eliminate the most onerous elements of impressment. Instead, a rational quota system could be set up so that procurement would not be oppressive for any one group or village.[5]

Kennedy's scheme and those to be found in the essays and other proposals highlighted a fundamental tension in these discussions: would transport remain at the regimental level under the authority of the regiment's commanding officer, or would it be centralized in a single transport department? According to a later report, the matter was placed in the hands of Col. R. C. Low and a small committee to reconcile differences of opinion and come up with a workable structure. The upshot of these deliberations was a recommendation for a mixed system. First, certain units, such as the Punjab Frontier Force, would maintain animal populations at half the amount meeting regimental needs, which could then be quickly mobilized and rapidly deployed. Second,

4. IOR/L/MIL/7/6668: Col. R. C. Low, "Scheme for the Transport Service in India," 28 July 1882. MacGregor's scheme is dated 27 December 1881.

5. See Lt. Gen. M. Kennedy, *Memorandum Proposing a Permanent and Organized Transport Service in India* (Simla: Government Central Branch Press, 1880), 17, 21, 33, and 37, in IOR/L/MIL/7/6666.

depots would be established where skeleton crews would be maintained. Supplied with animals procured by civil authorities in the districts, the cadres in depots could expand on mobilization. Civil administrators were also given the responsibility to keep track of potential animal recruits in their district by familiarizing themselves with breeders and local transport contractors. Upon any mobilization, these civilian animals would be either purchased or hired.

Low also recommended that a formal pack animal registration system be introduced in the Punjab, but the idea was opposed by British officials there who thought it was too cumbersome and expensive.[6] As a result, it was decided that rather than introduce a costly new system, "it would be better to trust to the ordinary action of demand and supply."[7] In the end, much emphasis was placed on cooperation between military and civilian officials, but without creating any clear lines of authority. In other words, the problems associated with enlisting additional animals and keeping track of them as they entered the transport service were, as in the past, left to civilian procurement officials.

Beyond rethinking the problem of transport as one that involved a disciplined ordering of relations between army and civilian authorities and some sort of mechanisms for locating animals for procurement, little if any consideration was given to the animals themselves. Conspicuously absent in all the proposals was a meaningful role for veterinary personnel in decision making about transport animals, and no attention was paid to the question of how to develop an understanding of the nature and needs of the camel. Instead, camels remained in the position of having dubious value as a transport animal. Col. H. Moore seemed to sum up the general view when in his transport reform essay he wondered "whether their habits and structure suit them to the necessities of modern warfare."[8] And that view held into the twentieth century.[9]

The new transport scheme, with its emphasis on the mule over other trans-

6. IOR/L/MIL/7/6668: Low, "Scheme for the Transport Service in India."

7. The quotation is from an 1898 report of Gen. Edwin Collen on the history of army transport. See IOR/L/MIL/7/6688: "Transport Service of the Indian Army," 27th August 1898, 6–8, 19.

8. Moore, "A Transport Service for Asiatic Warfare," 147.

9. As the first army animal management manual explained, the mule "is capable of great endurance, tolerates thirst well, can put up with changes of climate and food, and is not fastidious regarding the latter." In addition, with attendants who understand them, they "are by no means troublesome." See Army Veterinary Department, General Staff, War Office, *Animal Management* (London: His Majesty's Stationery Office, 1908), 270.

port animals, was not universally praised, however. Almost immediately upon its announcement, a critique appeared in the pages of the United Service Institution's journal. The critic was Lt. Edmund George Barrow, an Afghan war veteran and the author of the journal's Gold Medal essay on transport in 1880. Barrow's basic argument was that while creating a transport corps and depot system was a positive step, the structure that had been authorized by the government was insufficient for a wartime mobilization on the order of the recently completed Afghan campaign. As Barrow put it, "the chief . . . most striking blemish in the scheme" was the failure to recognize that what was needed in peacetime was trained men, not trained animals. Only by building a well-trained cadre of officers and animal handlers would the transport corps be able to expand rapidly in time of war. Even the depots were suspect, he thought, because instead of serving as a reserve force, their resources would be absorbed quickly to meet the immediate needs of deployment. Furthermore, he implied that the failure to establish a training regime meant that after a brief respite, frantic impressment of both animals and untrained handlers would ensue, and the disasters of 1878–79 would repeat themselves.[10] For the time being, however, Barrow's concerns were ignored, and the new scheme was put in place. In it, mules were given a prominent position, and camels were relegated to one of lesser importance overall in logistical planning.

ENTER THE MULE

As Low's depot and reserve scheme indicated, the animal around which the new transport system would be built was the mule, or, more precisely, two kinds of mules—a transport mule to pull carts or haul loads on its back much like a camel, and an ordnance mule (like those depicted in the Hyde Park monument) to carry field guns and ammunition on steep mountain paths. Much of this interest in the mule may have emerged as a result of Gen. Frederick Roberts's iconic forced march from Kabul to Kandahar with a pack train

10. Lt. E. G. Barrow, "The Government's Transport Scheme," *JUSII* 12, no. 55 (1883): 109–10. When he wrote his prizewinning essay, Barrow was attached to the Quartermaster General's Department, Rawalpindi division. Later, he became a member of the Intelligence Branch of the Indian Army, where he authored pieces concerning frontier defense and mountain warfare logistics. On his later publications, see, for example, *The Military Geography of Afghanistan* (Simla: Government Printing Office, 1893). For his prizewinning essay, see "A Transport Service for Asiatic Warfare," *JUSII*, special number (1880): 1–30.

primarily composed of mules.[11] It may also have come from offhand comments like that of the veterinary surgeon Charles Steel, who had noted that in one pack train made up of 800 camels and 80 mules, 150 of the former and 76 of the latter made it to their destination in Afghanistan.[12] But it was probably based as well on the fact that the mule, being a hybrid kind of horse, was a known and understandable quantity to British observers, unlike the camel.

The mule's positive characteristics were presented in a variety of other sources in the 1880s and 1890s, harkening back to the transport reform essays of 1880.[13] One of those authors, a Maj. G. A. Furse, had previously published a piece in which he emphasized that mules were capable of carrying heavy burdens equal to those by a horse (the standard carrying capacity was generally understood to be around half that of a camel, or 160 pounds) and of "enduring long-continued fatigue"; later, he added that mule transport had proved to be most efficient in the Abyssinia campaign and the China campaign of 1860.[14] But perhaps most important, certain kinds of mules seemed especially adapted for the mountainous terrain on India's northern borders and in Burma. Those with thick shanks below the knee and ample chests and girth (circumference of the body behind the front legs) were seen as the ideal animal for hauling ordnance and supplies along difficult mountain paths. The sure-footedness and endurance of particular mules, combined with the fact that large mules could perform well on more level ground, made them the most desirable for Indian Army transport. There was, however, one fundamental problem—neither ordnance mules nor transport-quality mules were particularly plentiful in India, and the ones that did exist were deemed only marginally adequate. The initial solution to this dilemma was to find ways of breeding better mules in India.

11. The march and the battle that followed near Kandahar effectively ended the Second Afghan War. On the march, see E. F. Chapman, "The March from Kabule to Kandahar in August and the Battle of the 1st September, 1880," *JUSII* 25 (1881): 282–315, especially 289–90.

12. Charles Steel, "Camels in Connection with the South Afghan Expedition 1878–1879," *JUSII* 8, no. 39 (1879): 462.

13. See, for example, Maj. Arthur G. Leonard, *The Camel: Its Uses and Management* (London: Longmans, Green, 1894), 286–88; W. B. Tegetmeier and Charles Lindsay Sutherland, *Horses, Asses, Zebras, Mules, and Mule Breeding* (London: Horace Cox, 1895), 71–78; and John Lockwood Kipling, *Beast and Man in India: A Popular Sketch of Indian Animals in Their Relations with the People* (London: Macmillan, 1904), 202–6.

14. The quote is from Maj. G. A. Furse, "Various Descriptions of Transport," *JUSII* 7, no. 34 (1878): 464; and "A Transport Service for Asiatic Warfare," *JUSII*, special number (1880): 125.

HORSE AND MULE BREEDING IN INDIA

Military mule breeding in India was intimately connected with the breeding of horses for the army. This was in part because in order to produce mules, a donkey sire and either a horse or a pony mare were required. Hence in theory, with the addition of a few male donkeys, mule production could be appended to whatever facilities were being used to produce horses and ponies. Since at least the beginning of the nineteenth century, and especially because of the cost of shipping horses by sea from other parts of the world, the British army in India had sought ways of supplying itself with locally bred horses. In 1818, the first stud depot was established at Hapur, followed by two more: one in Saharunpur (1843) and the other at Kurnal (1862). From its outset, the organization of the horse-breeding system was a joint government and private enterprise; it is worth reviewing because of certain parallels with mule breeding.

At the depots, the government owned both the breeding stallion and the horse mares, and their progeny were raised on-site until, at the age of five years, they could be distributed to regiments. A second scheme involved government-owned animals, but the mares were farmed out and their colts raised by local contractors. A third system, the zemindary, involved the government's offering free stud services to mare owners. By 1869, however, the British were experiencing the same problems as the Mughals had before them.[15] As J. H. B. Hallen, general superintendent of horse-breeding operations in India, explained in an 1887 address before the United Service Institution on the history of British breeding efforts: after some initial positive signs, the quality of the remounts, as the replacement horses were called, gradually declined and the numbers fit for service were drastically reduced.[16]

Hallen went on to explain that in 1872, the viceroy of India, Lord Northbrook, charged a special committee to investigate the horse and mule supply chain. The committee reported that the remounts produced in the current scheme cost almost three times more than horses imported from Persia and Australia, with the latter country being the primary overseas source of horses

15. In addition to Jos Gommans, *The Rise of the Indo-Afghan Empire c. 1710–1780* (Leiden: E. J. Brill, 1995), 68–73, see R. B. Azad Choudhary, "The Mughal and the Trading of Horses in India," *International Journal of History and Cultural Studies* 3, no. 1 (2017): 2, on environmental constraints to horse breeding in India.

16. J. H. B. Hallen's address can be found in *JUSII* 15, no. 76 (1887): 177–97; his reference to the deterioration of the breeding establishment is on p. 179.

for the army, exporting approximately 2,500 annually in the 1890s.[17] The reason for the high cost of domestically bred as opposed to imported horses, the committee argued, was government interference in horse breeding, which had "paralyzed private enterprise."[18] A second committee was tasked with setting up a new system. On its recommendation, two new departments were established: the Department of Army Remount Operations, which was responsible for procuring horses as needed by the army, and the Horse-Breeding Department, which was in charge of a new procurement format built around privatization and imperial patronage.[19]

The idea behind this new scheme was to reduce the size of the army stud establishment and instead provide European-bred stallions to local breeders free of charge. In order to ensure that the best Indian mares participated in the scheme, they would be inspected and branded for future identification by veterinary surgeons like Hallen.[20] The government would then encourage breeders to enter the progeny produced by the European stallions in annual fairs, where the best would be given prizes and where the army could purchase remounts.[21] Along the way, the planners expected that horses in India would gradually be improved, with more and better remounts becoming available to the army. Indian farmers would, of course, have to be persuaded to participate. But the expectations of the new scheme's designers were that prizes and the profits to be made from raising horses would quickly educate Indians on

17. The Persia trade seems to have been the only instance in which the British tapped the earlier scheme of the Mughals. On the formidable Australian horse trade with India, see Alexander Yarwood, *Walers: Australian Horses Abroad* (Carlton, VIC: Melbourne University Press, 1989). Yarwood indicates that a total of 50,174 were imported in the 1890s. Although he doesn't provide figures for the army in subsequent years, the total number of horses imported for the thirty-year period from 1901 to 1930 was 229,000; see pp. 90–93, 198, and 200.

18. Hallen, "Address," 179.

19. See IOR/L/MIL/7/9627 and 9628 for the committee report and the documents related to the abolition of the Stud Department and creation of the Remount and Horse-Breeding Departments. The privatization element sounds much like conclusions drawn by several Parliamentary Commissions in Great Britain. Regardless of army needs, a succession of commissions concluded that horse breeding in England should be left to the free market. See the discussion in Margaret Derry, *Horses in Society: A Story of Animal Breeding and Marketing, 1800–1920* (Toronto: University of Toronto Press, 2006), especially 103ff.

20. See "Extracts from Resumé of Horse and Mule Breeding Operations in India, 1880," *JUSII* 11, no. 51 (1882): 139–40. This report indicates that by 1880, there were 9,275 branded mares on the rolls (142).

21. Hallen, "Address," *JUSII* 15, no. 76 (1887): 181.

the advantages of breeding, and end the paralysis introduced by government interference in the market.

A few years later, this approach to equine breeding would repeat itself when donkey sires from southern Europe were introduced to encourage the expansion of mule breeding in India. By that time, the Horse-Breeding Department had begun to generate annual reports on the impact of the new breeding regime. In his address, Hallen summarized the progress to date. The numbers of horses born over the first decades of Northbrook's reform program, he began, was cause for optimism about India's capacity to eventually achieve self-sufficiency in horse breeding. Yet this prediction of a bright future was tempered by the fact that the British Indian Army continued to rely on remounts imported from Persia and Australia.[22]

Why was India still dependent on external sources for its remounts? Hallen pointed to three kinds of problems as the reason. The first involved the long-standing historical problem of a shortage of pasturage, which meant that colts had limited areas to graze and mature physically through field exercise. The second issue had to do with Indian farmers' continued use of oxen for agricultural work. Hallen argued that it had been shown that mares were just as proficient as oxen on the farm and had enormous value added—they could also be used to breed horses or mules. Yet according to him, the government had done very little to encourage Indian farmers to shift from ox to mare labor.

Lastly, Hallen pointed to a contradiction in policy. The key idea of the new horse- and mule-breeding system had been to encourage private enterprise while limiting government expenditures on military animal replacements. Unfortunately, the government, because of the latter concern, undermined incentives by setting a ceiling on how much it would pay for a horse or mule. As a result, it seemed that some farmers did not pursue breeding these animals, even when the government offered free stud services, because of the inelasticity of the market.[23] This meant, according to one observer, that the priorities of the Remount Department—acquiring horses for immediate use—took precedence over the breeding program.[24] Such countervailing tendencies, with

22. And the trend of foreign imports continued. Between 1891 and 1905, the state of New South Wales alone shipped almost eighteen thousand horses to India, or roughly a little over a thousand a year in a fifteen-year period. See *Official Yearbook of New South Wales* (Sydney: Government of New South Wales, 1907), 391.

23. Hallen, "Address," 187–91.

24. Walter Gilbey, *Horse-Breeding in England and India and Army Horses Abroad* (London: Vinton, 1906), 59. Gilbey also cited here a critique of the breeding program by Gen. John Watson, who found the system of diffusing breeding stallions around India to be the program's

one policy vitiating another, often in the form of different parts of the colonial administration finding themselves at odds with each other, would continue to plague the breeding program. Well into the twentieth century, conflicting policy agendas would continue to have profound effects on economic development programs that relied on civil and military cooperation.

There was one other problem with the new system, one that Hallen did not address in his speech: the limited number of veterinary personnel participating. In addition to Hallen, only three other veterinary surgeons were to cover all the northwest, Rajputana (present-day Rajasthan), and the Bombay Presidency, a geographic area comprising approximately half the British Indian Empire. As will be seen shortly, this made it difficult for Hallen to produce an accurate assessment of the mule-breeding program's performance in India. He did not have the personnel to keep track of what was happening on the ground.

FOREIGN DONKEY STUDS AND MULE BREEDING

Problems not unlike those related to horse breeding also developed in the army's mule-breeding program. As with efforts to improve Indian horse stock by importing European stallions, the Government of India had decided by 1880 to purchase what were understood to be superior donkey studs from southern Europe and the Mediterranean. The first efforts at government-sponsored mule breeding were, however, less than successful. A pilot program was begun at six sites in the Madras Presidency in 1879. The rules laid down by the Government of India for breeding were that the stud services would be provided to mare-owning farmers free of charge; in return, the government would have first choice of the progeny produced, to be purchased at fair market prices. There were to be no monetary or other kinds of incentives to encourage participation beyond these market features.

Fourteen donkey studs were procured, four identified as European and the other ten as Orientals, or "Bokhara" and "Arab" donkey sires. However, it was soon clear in some of the districts where the studs were located that owners had little interest in participating in the breeding program. One local official reported that in his district, people knew nothing about mules and found the crossing of ponies with donkeys "objectionable." In another area,

main problem. Also see IOR/L/MIL/17/TN 544: *Report of the Horse and Mule Breeding Commission, 1900–1901*, which concluded that "supervision and method" were wanting, and that India was a country in which breeding was not maintained "for the love of the thing" (61).

the program was more successful because local officials were paying owners to breed mules with their ponies—in direct violation of the Government of India's rules for breeding. Perhaps more disturbing were the statistics on the number of pony mares "covered" by each donkey stallion, and the number of foals "dropped."[25] Between 1879 and 1883, the 14 donkey sires covered a total of 533 mares. This disappointing annual average, from the point of view of the British administrators, of only 10 coverings per donkey per year produced even more dismal results—a grand total of 15 mules, all of whom were deemed unfit for army work! Soon afterward, the program was abandoned,[26] and all mule-breeding operations, and much of the horse breeding as well, shifted to northwestern India. In the Punjab and areas of Rajputana, it was believed that local ponies were of a better stock and owners more willing to participate in breeding programs. Moreover, in many of the major cities of the region, annual fairs where horses and camels were sold were commonplace.

*

As should be clear by now, to make mules, one needed donkey sires, or jacks, as they were called (hence the term *jackass*). Before 1880, the mule breeding that existed in India used "Arab" and "Bokhara" donkey sires.[27] In 1880, the Madras experiment had introduced the first "European" donkey sires into India. The India Office in London hired Charles Leslie Sutherland to procure these animals.[28] Over the next two decades, Sutherland bought donkey sires in Spain, Italy, France, and eventually Cyprus, and shipped them to India. A renowned breeder of donkeys and mules, first in Surrey and later in Kent, Sutherland had worked in the War Office from 1858 to 1860, and apparently competed in animal fairs from the 1860s onward. One of his jackasses placed first in the Royal Agricultural Society's annual show of 1874, and his mules finished first, second, and fourth in that show.[29] In 1876, he was one of the

25. These are standard euphemisms for *copulated* and *birthed*.

26. *Résumé of Pony and Mule Breeding Operations in the Madras Presidency* (Madras: Superintendent, Government Press, 1888), 8–14. The statistics for each site are on p. 13.

27. See "Extracts from Resumé of Horse and Mule Breeding Operations in India, 1880," 147.

28. Sutherland first appears in the Military Department Records of the India Office in correspondence that began in 1874; see IOR/L/MIL/7/1001: Employment of R. Sutherland, 1874–1879.

29. *Journal of the Royal Agricultural Society* 10, 2nd ser. (1874): lix. A list of Sutherland's prizewinning animals is provided in Tegetmeier and Sutherland, *Horses, Asses, Zebras, Mules, and Mule Breeding*, following p. 158.

British commissioners to the Philadelphia Centennial Exhibition, and was a juror of breeding competitions at the Paris World's Fair of 1878.

Equally significant, Sutherland was a major promoter of the use of mules as laboring animals. In Britain, as a review of the 1874 Royal Agricultural Society show observed, there was an apparent prejudice against breeding asses and mules,[30] an attitude that Sutherland was making it his life's work to change. Part of his enthusiasm for mules seems to have come from his travels through continental Europe, where he encountered them being used for both haulage and field work; but he was also well aware that a large mule population in the United States was being used for draft and pack work in mining, transport, and railway construction, as well as for basic agricultural work such as plowing and hauling.

In 1881, Sutherland made his first major purchase of donkey jacks in Italy, sending 20 to India that November and following up with another 10 from Cyprus the same year. Through 1888, he purchased and shipped from Italy, France, Spain, and Cyprus on average 30 donkey studs annually, paying around £65 for them on the Continent and £14 on Cyprus.[31] The animals were transported in British naval ships when possible (otherwise by commercial steamer), and once in India they were put under the supervision of the Horse-Breeding Department, which then dispersed them initially to Madras and later to districts in the northwest.

In 1888, Supt. Hallen was asked by the government's military secretary to report on the number of mules taken into mountain artillery and transport units as a result of the mule-breeding program. While he could not give exact numbers because of a shortage of personnel to brand and register mules, he did know that the army was seeing visible results, and estimated that about five-sixths of its 14,493 mules were the progeny of imported donkey studs. Hallen attributed the program's success to two factors within India. The first was that over time, it was discovered that ordinary-quality mares when crossed with superior donkey studs could produce quality mules. The second factor was that "moral objections" on the part of Indian breeders to crossing their mares with imported donkeys had diminished. Apparently far more rational actors than Sutherland's compatriots in Britain, Indians curtailed their

30. Tegetmeier and Sutherland, *Horses, Asses, Zebras, Mules, and Mule Breeding*, 162.

31. IOR/L/MIL/7/1018: Mr. Sutherland's Purchase of Four Italian Donkey Stallions, 1890–91; and L/MIL/7/1016: Reports on the Results of Mule-Breeding, 1886–89. The total cost for donkey studs in the 1880s was £15,027, according to a Military Department minute of 18 November 1896 in this file.

objections once it was demonstrated that the progeny of these "objectionable" matings drew good prices at the Rawalpindi fair. Thus, by 1888, as a result of a fortuitous discovery and the natural operation of market rationality, the program to import donkey studs for mule breeding appeared to be a success.

As for the donkeys themselves, Hallen thought that the Catalan and Italian versions produced the best ordnance mules, while the French donkey, "being too coarse and heavy of class," proved ill suited to the Indian climate. In addition to these assessments, Hallen was able to provide figures on the geographic distribution of the donkey studs: about two-thirds of the 334 he could account for were in the Punjab, another third on the North-West Frontier, and the remainder scattered throughout Bombay and Rajputana.[32]

Some of Hallen's optimism might also be ascribed to the limited bits of data he did have. Veterinary Surgeon G. J. R. Rayment, assistant superintendent of the Horse-Breeding Department for the Northwest Provinces and Rajputana, provided Hallen with statistics from his region (table 3.1). These results indicated a much higher percentage of successful pregnancies than had been the case in Madras for the same period, and the success rate had recently improved. More important, perhaps, Rayment's numbers suggested that mule breeding was indeed spreading in the areas under his supervision; moreover, since there was no hint to the contrary, presumably this growth was occurring under Government of India provisions for breeding. Not all the 5,542 foals produced in Rayment's districts were bought by the army at annual fairs, of course; but given Hallen's estimate of around 12,000 locally produced mules in army service, it seems reasonable to conclude that a good number came from the northwest and Rajputana.[33]

At the same time, however, the picture as reported by his two other subordinates looked somewhat different in their regions of responsibility. For example, J. C. Dawyer, assistant superintendent of the Horse-Breeding Department in the Punjab, argued that the far cheaper Arab and Persian donkey studs were second only to Sutherland's Italian jacks. In other words, the Spanish and Cypriot donkey sires, from Dawyer's perspective, were not as good as the more locally bred ones. Another of Hallen's subordinates, J. K. Gardener, Superintendent of the Horse-Breeding Department in the Bombay Presidency, took issue with his superior's assertion that Indians' prejudices toward the program had disappeared. He reported that in his area, "higher caste men

32. IOR/L/MIL/7/1016: Reports on the Results of Mule-Breeding, 1886–89. Hallen's memo is dated 15 May 1889.

33. Ibid., 4.

TABLE 3.1 Mule production, 1881–88

Year	Donkey stallions	Pony mares covered	Foals	Percentage foals to coverings
1881–82	30	1,110	244	22
1882–83	35	1,886	403	21
1883–84	65	2,754	546	20
1884–85	70	3,343	796	24
1885–86	82	4,249	908	21
1886–87	79	3,834	1,343	35
1887–88	84	3,678	1,302	35

Source: IOR/L/MIL/1016, *Report on Mule Breeding 1896*; enclosure in Hallen memo dated 15 May 1889, 4.

have religious objections to crossing species with a view to the production of Hybrids."[34] Gardener's point is supported by other sources at the time.[35]

From these reports, it is impossible to determine whether Hallen or Gardener was right about Indian beliefs, or whether refusals to participate in the government-sponsored donkey import projects involved some other factors. It is equally difficult to determine if the program itself was producing an indigenous supply of mules sufficient for both the ordnance and the transport needs of the army. However, two kinds of evidence suggest that there were problems with the program other than "caste" prejudices. One such sign was that after its creation in 1892, the Civil Veterinary Department took over responsibility for mule breeding in India, while the horse- and mule-breeding establishment was placed under the control of civilian administrators in the Punjab Agriculture and Revenue Department. A second sign of difficulties was that by the 1890s, the army had narrowed its focus to the importation of almost exclusively Italian donkeys,[36] having found others less useful for pro-

34. See ibid., 3, 5–6.

35. See, for example, Kipling, *Beast and Man in India*. Kipling observed that Hindus thought mule breeding "unnatural and improper" (203). Also see "Extracts from Resumé on Horse and Mule Breeding Operations in India, 1880," 151.

36. Figures on imported donkey stallions are in IOR/L/MIL/7/1024: Italian and Cyprus Donkey Stallions, 1895–1898. They show that from 1880 to 1886, donkey stallions were imported from Spain, France, Italy, and Cyprus. Between 1885 and 1888, they were imported only from Italy and Cyprus. About 30 to 34 were brought in each year, followed by a two-year hiatus between 1888 and 1890, when Sutherland was ill. When imports resumed, the donkey

ducing adequate animals, especially for ordnance. Yet by the mid-1890s, even the Italian imports had become a perceived problem.

In an 1896 report to the secretary of the Military Department of the Government of India, Veterinary Surgeon Col. Alfred E. Queripel, inspector general of the Civil Veterinary Department, observed that although the height of mules remained roughly the same, the newest population showed a decline in girth and shank thickness (the bone below the knee—a thick shank bone being essential for mules operating in mountainous terrain). A subordinate in the Northwest Provinces, he added, had noted that "the old Italians in the district show much more bone and substance than the new ones," a reference to leg circumference and other qualities of donkey bodies. Similar reports had come from the Punjab, which led Queripel to argue that the current purchasing system was not producing animals adequate for ordnance. He suggested that new fields for purchase be found.[37] Two years later, the mule-breeding system became even more strained. During several military expeditions along the North-West Frontier in 1897–98, Queripel reported that he feared a large reduction in foals in the coming year, because some 3,599 pony mares from the Punjab and another 1,016 from the Northwest Provinces hade been removed for transport duty.[38] That same year, the Punjab Civil Veterinary Department's report argued that perhaps mule breeding should be suspended for "some years to come," and expressed doubt that influential agriculturalists would embrace breeding even if studs were provided to them. The report added that equine breeding was a decidedly secondary concern for most farmers, their primary one being cures for or prevention of cattle diseases.[39]

In addition to identifying key problems with breeding transport and ordnance mules in India, these reports provided something more. In Queripel's case, for instance, his evaluation of mules used words like *girth* and *shank*, *bone* and *substance*, technical terminology not simply employed for organizing mule attributes of significance for pack and ordnance work but also applied to the larger arena of animal breeding in both colonial India and Great Britain. Not surprisingly, perhaps, it was terminology associated with the horse. That

stallions, with the exception of 4 from Spain, were imported exclusively from Italy. Moreover, the numbers were erratic—4 one year, 12 another, and 47 in 1894–95.

37. IOR/L/MIL/7/1025, file labeled "Italy and Cyprus, 1896"; Queripel's report is dated 4 August 1896.

38. IOR/V/4378: *Annual Administrative Report of the Civil Veterinary Department of India for the Official Year 1897–1898*, 22.

39. *Provincial Report of the Civil Veterinary Department, Punjab, 1897–98* (Lahore: Civil and Military Gazette Press, 1898), 5.

is, measurements and physical characteristics, or what were called "points" of an animal, were easily transferable from horse to mule, with proper adjustment for desirable functional characteristics. For example, horses were measured in "hands," roughly the four-inch distance across the palm of the hand with fingers and thumb closed, with the height from hoof to top of shoulder or base of neck being the primary measurement. Such tactile standards of measurement and points of the animal, easily applied by any transport officer, set a common language for organizing and classifying mules, for sorting the appropriate ordnance mules from the inappropriate ones. But it also suggested a kind of intimacy with mules in which one felt for muscle and bone, and didn't simply apply a measuring device, be it hand or measuring tape.

Hence, features or points of a mule could be correlated with the kinds of labor to which the animal would be subjected. As noted above, mules in India were used for pulling carriages, carrying packs on more or less level ground, or carrying field guns, ammunition, and other supplies on mountain paths. The last of these tasks, and perhaps the most important to the army, required a mule of around twelve to thirteen hands, broad chested and well girthed with a thick, solid shank. Given that so many army mules had to be custom produced by then, it would have been logically and perhaps even linguistically impossible under such circumstances to conclude that the problems Queripel and his subordinates identified lay in the mules themselves—they lay, rather, in the quality of the donkey studs and the horse or pony mares. To put this another way, veterinary surgeons and Army Remount Department officers had a general set of comparative categories for organizing mule knowledge and for critiquing the quality of animals produced in the "jackasses for India" initiative.

When veterinary surgeons applied these evaluative categories, it became disturbingly evident that the quality of the mules being produced in India had declined by the 1890s. The cause of this decline did not lie wholly within India, however. It could be attributed to a shortage of superior donkey studs coming from southern Europe. The reason for this shortage, as Sutherland made clear in 1899, was that the best Italian donkey studs were being siphoned off by American buyers, who were able to outbid the British.[40] Moreover, the mule-breeding operations in the United States were producing over 150,000

40. IOR/L/MIL/7/1035: Improvement in Breed of Stock, Cyprus 1898–1904. Sutherland to the Secretary of State for India, 29 April 1899. Sutherland had been having difficulties acquiring Italian jacks since 1891, when he shipped only four; see the figures in IOR/L/MIL/7/1024: Italian and Cyprus Donkey Stallions.

animals per year nationwide, roughly 150 times more than were being produced in India.[41]

Thus, when it became clear in the 1890s that importing donkey sires could meet only a part of the army's need for transport animals, the Army Remount Department sought other sources of mules. In July 1895, Col. Deane, department director, wrote the military secretary for the Government of India, requesting that British consular officers around the world report on the availability of mules, especially ones fit for ordnance work, in their respective countries.[42] The request was forwarded to the India Office in London for distribution through the Foreign Office, and by the end of the year Deane had his answers.

The communication from London indicated that mules were available in parts of the United States, Mexico, Central America, and South America. There were also figures for Spain, Italy, and Greece, although the quantities were much smaller than in the Americas. Reports also came in from Persia, where the army had purchased some mule transport in 1891, and from Mesopotamia.[43] In addition to these consular reports, the Remount Department was privy to a detailed report by Lt. F. A. Thatcher, the assistant commandant of a military police detachment at Moguang, Burma, on mules from Yunnan Province in China.[44] A few years later, Maj. M. E. Willoughby augmented Thatcher's report with more details on the Yunnan mules. Although the Chinese animals were relatively small in stature (11.2 to 12.2 hands), he noted that some forty thousand were involved in a vast highland commercial network. The mules carried up to two hundred pounds each over rough mountain terrain, swam rivers, jumped in and out of ferryboats, and did not need to be led because they followed the sound of gongs. He emphasized their "endurance,

41. J. L. Jones, a renowned American mule breeder, indicated the numbers of mules foaled in 1889 to be 157,000 in twenty-one different states. See Tegetmeier and Sutherland, *Horses, Asses, Zebras, Mules, and Mule Breeding*, 117.

42. IOR/L/MIL/7/1026: Purchase of Mules in Foreign Countries, 1891–93.

43. IOR/L/MIL/7/1028: Purchase of Mules in Italy, 1897–1898. The latter gave figures for mules that could be purchased in Baghdad, and suggested that they could be shipped by mail steamer from the port of Basra.

44. For the results of the consular reports and a report on mule purchases in Persia, see IOR/L/MIL/7/1026: Purchase of Mules in Foreign Countries. On China, see IOR/L/MIL/7/1023: Mule Breeding across the Chinese Frontier. On the Burma-Yunnan highland trading networks, see C. Patterson Giersch, "Across Zomia with Merchants, Monks, and Musk: Process Geographies, Trade Networks, and the Inner-East-Southeast Asian Borderlands," *Journal of Global History* 5, no. 2 (2010): 215–39.

surefootedness, docility and intelligence," and thought that approximately one thousand such mules could be obtained annually, particularly if a Chinese partner at Kohn and Company, based in Bhamo, Burma, was employed.[45]

With this collection of reports in hand, the Remount Department began an ambitious mule procurement project that, when combined with the pre-existing horse import schemes (stallions from Europe, cavalry mounts from Australia), literally spanned the globe. Some of these purchases were from old sources—250 ordnance mules were purchased in Italy, for example.[46] But others came from the opposite side of the world. In March 1902, Maj. Gough of the Bengal Cavalry, accompanied by four native soldiers from the Remount Department and seventeen men from a mountain battery, arrived in Kansas City, Missouri, with the objective of purchasing 500 mules for India. By November, Gough was able to deliver this quantity to India as well as a dozen donkey studs, followed by 21 more studs the next year. He made at least one other trip to the United States in 1907, when he purchased 1,500 mules and 47 donkey sires.[47] In between his US visits, in 1904 Gough journeyed to Argentina, where he bought some 1,000 mules through Thomas Bracht and Company, and ordered another 5,500. Records, though scant, also indicate that Gough developed a relation with Bracht's competitor Tetley, Howard and Sons, and that up until the start of World War I, this company shipped at least 2,000 mules to India, but perhaps many more.[48]

While Gough worked the rich mule markets of the Americas, others procured mules in northern and southern China, Persia, and the Transvaal. In the case of Persia, the quantities varied from the low sixties to over eight hundred in 1908. In China between 1911 and 1913, some three thousand were imported, mostly, it would seem, from the northern region. Some of the mules went to the Supply and Transport Department, while others were sent to mountain

45. IOR/L/MIL/7/1061: Maj. M. E. Willoughby, *Report on the Mules and Ponies of the Province of Yunnan (West China)* (Calcutta: Office of the Superintendent of Government Printing, India, 1905), 1, 2, 9.

46. IOR/L/MIL/7/9665: Army Remount Department, *Annual Administrative Report of the Bengal, Punjab, Madras, and Bombay Commands* (Simla: Government Central Printing Office, 1898), 10. Hereafter, the reports will be cited as ARARD, followed by the date.

47. See IOR/L/MIL/7/1051: Deputation of Maj. Gough to USA to Buy Ordnance Mules, 1902; and 1068: Report on Mule Purchasing in North America, 1907. On the additional donkey studs, see IOR/L/MIL/7/9665: ARARD (1904), 20.

48. IOR/L/MIL/7/1060: Purchase through Bracht & Co. of Mules from Argentina, 1904–1906; and 1070: Purchase of 1,000 Transport Mules in Addition to Ordinary Requirements, 1910.

batteries stationed along the Afghan-Indian frontier.[49] The network remained viable through World War I and provided thousands of horses and mules to British forces in France and India, as well as units campaigning in western Asia (see chapter 9).[50]

There is little question that the British Indian Army required these additional mule resources. One of the driving forces behind this demand was the extension of the frontier security scheme into the Suleiman Mountains and deep into Baluchistan, calling for the expansion of mountain warfare units, including mountain artillery and demolition units (Sappers and Miners). The latter, in particular, were of importance because of the way in which the British punished "unruly" mountain tribes. The normal course was to destroy their fields and orchards, and blow up their sturdy stone houses and lookout towers. These kinds of "punitive" measures required mobile cavalry units and ordnance- and pack-mule trains that could move swiftly into the valleys on the North-West Frontier occupied by Pathan clans.[51]

It is also clear that despite a regular investment in donkey studs from Europe and North America, mule production in India could not keep pace with the expanding security regime. By 1911, the Remount Department was estimating that it required around 2,600 additional mules a year, and could purchase only 20 to 30 percent of them in India.[52] Although it is unclear what "normal" pregnancies entailed in other parts of the world where mules were bred, in India the annual percentage of births to number of mares "covered" seldom exceeded 30 percent. In addition to low birthrates, two other kinds of problems plagued the mule production program. Over the first decade of the twentieth century, the Indian Army underwent major structural change (see below), including the creation of a permanent transport corps with a robust number of active and reserve pack-mule units.

Yet for much of the first decade of the new century, the Army Remount Department relied exclusively on temporary-duty officers to buy mules at the

49. See the following files for imports from China and the other countries mentioned here: IOR/L/MIL/7/9691: ARARD (1908), 3; IOR/L/MIL/7/9696: ARARD (1909), 3; ARARD (1912), 9; IOR/L/MIL/7/9700: ARARD (1913a), 4; and ARARD (1913b), 4–5.

50. See IOR/L/MIL/7/1079: Supply of Ordnance and Transport Mules from Argentina, in which memos for 1917 indicate thousands of animals being imported from Australia, China, Argentina and the United States.

51. See Army Headquarters, India, *Manual of Operations on the North-West Frontier of India* (Calcutta: Government of India Central Publication Branch, 1925), and *Frontier Warfare—India* (Delhi: Government of India Press, 1939).

52. IOR/L/MIL/7/9700: ARARD (1913a), 4.

many annual horse fairs in the Punjab. The result was a lack of continuity from year to year in the procurement program, and certainly inconsistent standards of judgment regarding mule attributes among the temporary procurement officers. A second problem was related to the fact that purchasing officers could offer only those sums fixed by the Remount Department, so they regularly found themselves outbid for the best mules by brokers and Swati dealers. This situation was exacerbated by a global rise in the prices of mules over the same period.[53]

The problems related to mule production in India found their solution in the communication and transportation links that gave the Army Remount Department a unique global reach. The Royal Navy and British merchant marine were a presence in the Mediterranean and the western Atlantic worlds as well as on the China coast, regions the Indian Army could exploit for fresh donkey and mule bodies. And where Britain's commercial and naval presence did not reach, such as Kansas City, the army could tap other resources by hiring local transport firms to move mules to embarkation points. Moreover, unlike horse procurement, which seems to have been limited to Persia and Australia, mule purchases spanned the world.

Thus, by the beginning of the twentieth century, the Indian Army Remount Department had established a global network for mule trafficking. This network included diplomatic and consular staffs, foreign purchasing agents, the Indian Army Intelligence Branch in Burma and north China, international financial institutions for transferring money, land and water shipping companies, and regional insurance brokers.[54] Through the network, mule breeders in Persia, north and southwest China, the American Midwest, Argentina, southern Europe, and the Transvaal were linked into a military transport system centering on northwestern British India. Put simply, whatever mule-breeding constraints the army faced in India could be addressed by integrating Indian Army mule requirements into the transnational connections fashioned by imperial Britain's global military and economic power. Mules who would have found their labor used in commerce or farming were now not only far removed from familiar territory but mobilized into a structure where their sole duty was to support the military adventures of the British Indian Army in Asia and Africa.

53. IOR/L/MIL/7/9697: ARARD (1910), 5.

54. The India Office clerks placed all the documents—bills of sale, wire transfers, insurance agreements, shipping documents, and so forth—in a single file for each purchasing mission. See, for example, IOR/L/MIL/7/1051 on Gough's mission to the United States.

CHAPTER 4

Veterinary Science and the Partial Rehabilitation of the Camel

In the last two decades of the nineteenth century, veterinary medicine in India was transformed. A key benchmark was the creation of the Civil Veterinary Department in 1892. The fact that the unit was given responsibility for government-sponsored horse- and mule-breeding operations in India signaled a change in status for veterinary surgeons. Contributing to this change were the activities of a small group of veterinarians determined to alter perceptions of veterinary medicine and demonstrate the professional skills of its practitioners.[1] In 1883, three of these men launched the *Quarterly Journal of Veterinary Science in India and Army Animal Management* with the goal of establishing the legitimacy of their vocation in India. In addition to providing a platform for the work of British veterinary surgeons in that country, they sought to encourage scientific research on animal diseases and to introduce the latest developments in veterinary medicine in Europe and North America. This chapter explores this undertaking and the impact it had, not only on

1. On the low esteem in which veterinarians were held in the nineteenth century, see Ann M. Greene, "The Now-Opprobrious Title of 'Horse Doctor': Veterinarians and Professional Identity in Late Nineteenth-Century America," in *Healing the Herds*, ed. Karen Brown and Daniel Gilfoyle (Athens: Ohio University Press, 2010), 42–58. Also see Douglas M. Haynes, "Social Status and Imperial Service: Tropical Medicine and the British Medical Profession in the Nineteenth Century," in *Warm Climes and Western Medicine*, ed. David Arnold (Amsterdam: Rodopi, 1996), 208–26, who argues that medical men in general, most of whom came from the British lower classes, were extremely class conscious and sought social recognition from "genteel society."

the development of veterinary science in India but on British knowledge and understanding of the camel.

PROFESSIONALIZING VETERINARY MEDICINE IN INDIA

The journal's editors had all been trained in London veterinary colleges. The eldest, Charles Steel, was a Fellow of the Royal Veterinary College and superintendent of the Army Veterinary School at Puna. Recall that he was also the veterinarian on the Kandahar line during the Second Afghan War, and thus was well aware of the limited influence veterinarians had on the army's transport system. The other two editors were his son, John Henry Steel of the First Madras Light Cavalry, and John's classmate at the London Veterinary College in the 1870s, Frederick Smith of the Twelfth Royal Lancers. The three appear to have shared both a commitment to the professionalization of veterinary medicine in India and a desire to link India-based veterinary science with laboratories and journals in Europe and North America.[2] The two younger men in particular were keenly aware of scientific changes occurring in continental Europe as a result of the work of Louis Pasteur in France and Robert Koch in Germany. Given these interests, it should come as no surprise that they not only were advocates of germ theory but also introduced terms such as *bacteriology*, *parasitology*, and *microbiology* in India, and published abstracts of studies conducted under these rubrics outside India.

Moreover, the three men's insistence on foregrounding research as much as was practicable in the journal may not only have been a consideration when they included the words *veterinary science* rather than *veterinary medicine* in its title—their effort might also be seen as distinct from the prevailing attitude toward research among veterinarians in Britain. According to Michael Worboys, at virtually the same time that the Steels and Smith were breaking new ground for the field of European veterinary science in India, veterinarians in Britain tended to emphasize "stamping out" animal diseases through quarantine, culling, and the tight control of the movement of animals into the British Isles. And while they generally accepted germ theory, they regarded experi-

2. All three editors published a number of pieces based on their own research, but Smith was the most prolific. In addition to books on veterinary medicine and his many research articles, he was a historian of the profession. See Frederick Smith and Fred Bullock, *The Early History of Veterinary Literature and Its British Development*, 4 vols. (London: Baillière, Tindall and Cox, 1919–33). I am indebted to Clare Boulton, head librarian, RCVS Knowledge, for sharing information on these three veterinarians.

mental research as incorporating challenges to "firm policing measures."[3] It is worth bearing this contrast in mind, because it suggests that developments in the colonies did not mesh neatly with those in the imperial center.

The journal was published without government support, relying instead on advertising and private subscriptions for financial resources. During its short life (it was published only between 1883 and 1890), the editors used it as a platform to promote a wide array of causes designed to improve the status of veterinary medicine in India and of veterinarians in the army. Their primary aims included the expansion of the army veterinary service and an increase in the veterinarians' authority; the formation of a civil veterinary department to tend to the domestic animals of Indian farmers; the creation of public schools to train Indians in veterinary medicine; and the development of veterinary knowledge concerning India's flora and fauna, particularly the camel. In each of these cases, they made practical and pragmatic arguments about the many advantages that would accrue to the colonial state if it instituted their suggestions.

Yet unlike many of the scientific journals outside India, the Steels and Smith did not view their quarterly as a purely scientific enterprise. Harkening back to the elder Steel's experience in Afghanistan, the second half of the journal's title acknowledged concern for creating a rational structure that would organize animal labor within army transport. Because of their two priorities—animal science and animal management—the editors often found themselves at odds with the policies of both the Government of India and the British Indian Army. They used the journal's lead editorials to criticize what they felt to be official indifference or ignorance, obstacles to creating a more professional and organized army transport system. They also used editorials to better educate their readers about the work of army veterinarians and the particulars of the profession. So, for example, in the journal's second year, the editors published two important pieces, one comparing and contrasting the work of veterinarians in India and Great Britain, the other comparing human and veterinary medicine.

In the latter piece, the Steels and Smith showed how animal medicine was built on the study of human anatomy and pathology. They noted the similar anatomy of "higher" and "lower" mammals, and how all mammals are affected positively and negatively by bacteria and other microbes. Hence, through the study of diseases in animals, where researchers could "experiment more

3. Michael Worboys, "Germ Theories of Disease and British Veterinary Medicine 1860–1900," *Medical History* 25 (1991): 323, 326.

boldly with [their] patients than human practitioners" could, it was possible to find cures or treatments for diseases that also affect humans. In addition to describing the similarities between animal and human physiology, the editors mentioned that many prominent veterinarians began their education in medical schools, shifting to animal studies later in life. Given the "community of interests" existing between veterinary and human medicine, they predicted that the "study of diseases of animals in relation to the health of mankind" promised to bring the two biological domains even closer, particularly through ongoing research into diseases of the blood, where the study of parasites offered a promising field for comparative pathology.[4]

These ruminations seem to indicate an early form of human-centered animal experimentation—one could use animals both to better understand the physiological effects of certain pathogens that cross the human-animal divide and, as Pasteurian methods promised, to develop vaccines or serums to treat diseases in humans. By taking this position, the editors also signaled their commitment to germ theory at a time when the value of this approach to disease was still subjected to much debate.

In their explication of veterinarians' duties in Great Britain and in India, the Steels and Smith produced a list of army veterinary surgeons' responsibilities that contrasted sharply with those of their counterparts in Great Britain. In addition to treating sick animals, veterinarians in India were called on to advise the government and Indian agriculturalists on animal breeding; help establish training schools for teaching veterinary medicine to Indians; make decisions about casting government-owned animals from service; and participate in military campaigns. And they did all this with extremely limited resources, low pay, and limited recognition from the government. These veterinarians also exposed themselves to the rigors of life in India, which included, as the editors noted, exposure to many diseases not common in Europe. As a result, they periodically found themselves invalided home. From this profile of veterinary life in colonial service, no reader could have missed the point that these men not only served the greater needs of the British enterprise in Asia but made significant personal sacrifices to do so.[5]

Along with its advocacy for the veterinary profession and for a more rationally organized army transport system in India, the journal, from its inception

4. "Editorial: On the Inter-relations of Human and Veterinary Medicine," *QJVSI* 2, no. 7 (April 1884): 308–21.

5. "Editorial: On the Specialties and Scope of Veterinary Science in India," *QJVSI* 2, no. 6 (January 1884): 169–82.

in 1883, performed two other significant functions. It collected, edited, and circulated a mass of material produced inside and outside India on animal diseases and veterinary medicine, and it presented veterinary medicine as equal to human-based biomedicine in legitimacy and professionalism. In the latter instance, the editors grounded the viability of their "science" in contradistinction to indigenous practices in India as well as to popular animal treatments to be found in Great Britain, where physicians and veterinarians condemned folk practices as quackery.

Recall John Henry Steel's comparison between English barbers and farriers and Indian practitioners (chapter 2). Any astute reader of that passage would have understood the contrast between an unscientific and unregulated set of practices, built on inherited folk traditions, faulty reasoning, and exaggerated claims, and the knowledge and practices of contemporary medicine. The latter was firmly situated in state-regulated licensing, a body of legal codes, and the sound scientific practices of physicians and diploma-bearing veterinary surgeons.[6]

As they made their case for veterinary science, the editors of the *Quarterly Journal*, clearly sensitive to what Charles Steel once described as a rude rebuff by a general officer while he was merely doing his duty,[7] became vocal advocates, like their counterparts in Great Britain, for the professional authority and legitimacy of the veterinary surgeon.[8] In the journal's premier issue, Charles Steel, Frederick Smith, and John Henry Steel criticized Government of India plans to reduce the size of the army veterinary corps, and observed that veterinarians frequently found their functions usurped and their advice ignored.[9] Moreover, during the first few years of the journal's run, the editors made a point of printing from the Parliamentary Papers the questions and comments of Dr. Charles Cameron, MP from Glasgow and a major critic of army transport in India.

The journal carried parliamentary notices of the select committee Cam-

6. In the case of veterinary medicine, a series of parliamentary acts separated farriers from college-trained veterinarians. The most recent of these, passed in 1881, forbade anyone without a degree from a legally recognized veterinary school from using the initials *V.S.* after their name, under penalty of fine. For the laws and charters related to the veterinary profession, see http://knowledge.rcvs.org.uk; accessed 1 October 2017.

7. Charles Steel, "Camels in Connection with the South Afghan Expedition 1878–1879," *JUSII* 8, no. 39 (1879): 461.

8. Worboys, "Germ Theories of Disease and British Veterinary Medicine 1860–1900," 327.

9. *QJVSI* 1, no. 1 (October 1882): 1–4.

eron had requested to "inquire into the workings of the Transport and Commissariat Services of the British and Indian Armies in the recent Egyptian and Afghan Campaigns."[10] Its editors subsequently reproduced a number of Cameron's observations concerning army veterinarians. For example, Cameron claimed that "Veterinary Science in the Afghan, as in the Egyptian Campaign, was utterly ignored by the Indian authorities. There was no veterinary organization—nothing but the grossest mismanagement as far as animals were concerned."[11] A year later, when the British government was preparing to send a military expedition to the Sudan, Cameron asked, with respect to the Indian contingent, if any arrangements had been made to "prevent the disregard of veterinary superintendence characteristic of Indian Army administration."[12]

In presenting Cameron's comments and publications, the journal's editors reprinted his views without comment. But then, they had already pointed out in the very first issue that the bleached bones of immature camels in Afghanistan, witnessed personally by Charles Steel, testified to the dire consequences of official disregard for veterinarians' informed views.[13] When, seven years later, the journal presented the contents of Cameron's pamphlet, *The Romance of War*, little if anything had changed. Each time British government ministers and army officials were asked to address the question of transport problems and veterinary authority, they responded with the same trite formulas. The secretary of state for India and his subordinates claimed either that earlier problems had been corrected in India, or that the exigencies of war prevented more efficient management of supply and transport. Officials also complained that veterinary surgeons' standards as to the capacity of pack animals to serve were much too high.[14]

Such dismissals of veterinary expertise seem to have only energized the Steels and Smith to expand their journal's thematic scope. They included news items concerning the profession in and outside India; carried descriptions of surgeries performed by veterinarians in India; abstracted scientific advances culled from professional journals in Europe and North America; and carried on correspondence concerning veterinary research and medicine in Europe and North America. They also published reports by veterinary sur-

10. *QJVSI* 2, no. 8 (July 1884): 545.
11. *QJVSI* 7, no. 28 (October 1889): 367.
12. *QJVSI* 3, no. 12 (July 1885): 545.
13. *QJVSI* 1, no. 1 (October 1882): 4.
14. *QJVSI* 7, no. 28 (October 1889): 367, 369.

geons who participated in Indian Army military operations; printed statistics on the supply of animals available to the army for the cavalry and transport service, and data on the prevalence of animal diseases in India; published research on Indian grasses useful as animal fodder, and on plants as medicines; culled army news and the postings of veterinary surgeons in India from various sources; and printed letters and queries from readers.

Clearly, this eclectic mix of news, advocacy, scientific developments, and reporting on the activities of veterinarians in the Indian Army was assembled to keep informed a readership dispersed across India and Burma. And there was certainly a need for such a journal. The primary army publication at the time was the *Journal of the United Service Institution of India*, but it seldom if ever contained anything related to medicine, and addressed transport issues only when a major crisis was perceived, such as the Afghan campaigns of 1878–80 and the Chitral campaign in 1895 (see chapter 5). But the *Quarterly Journal* did more than fill an information gap; it also was meant to elicit an audience, and to help individual veterinarians think of themselves as part of a community and a much larger endeavor. It is not difficult to understand why its editors might have felt their publication was necessary. Only about sixty veterinary surgeons were in India at the time the journal was launched, and they were scattered through the three presidencies of Bengal, Madras, and Bombay, as well as in the Punjab and Burma. Moreover, veterinarians were not attached to a veterinary department, because none existed. Instead, they were assigned to army units, where they answered to the commanders of infantry, artillery, and cavalry regiments. As such, individual veterinarians could be quite isolated from one another, and ignorant of the kinds of developments occurring in their field.

But it wasn't simply the lack of professional authority or respect that agitated the editors; they also felt that veterinary surgeons in India were beleaguered on a number of other fronts. British veterinarians in India frequently complained about overwork, unrealistic expectations on the part of government, shortages of veterinary surgeons on the ground, limited resources for training local students, and a general lack of appreciation for their accomplishments. In the area of education, they lobbied for resources that would allow veterinarians to familiarize army officers with common animal diseases. They also advocated vastly expanding the number of schools for training an indigenous cadre of veterinarians who, like "native" missionaries, could spread the word about the benefits of veterinary science throughout India, function as trusted go-betweens with farmers and stock raisers, and eventually supplant native healers and their dubious methods.[15] The veterinarians were, in other words, in line with other "modernizing" British officials in India who saw rational management and scientific development as keys to Indian progress. And like their critical counterparts in other units of the colonial administration, they bridled at what they saw as official indifference on the one hand and native obstruction and superstition on the other.

Superstition could be dealt with by demonstrating to Indians the practical benefits of scientifically managing their domestic animals. Combating official indifference was more difficult and required rhetorical strategies to nudge superiors toward reform. In this regard, the journal's editors were not without resources. They could point to the costly Afghan Wars and argue that wiser animal management might have saved the imperial state money. Or they could point to the rapid progress being made in veterinary science in Europe. The new field that sprang out of germ theory and microbiology and its subfields of bacteriology and parasitology promised to produce novel ways for addressing common diseases that plagued domestic animals in India as well as the army's cavalry horses and transport animals. Here too was another argument for how government investment in veterinary science would pay dividends in the long run.

Charles Steel, Frederick Smith, and John Henry Steel kept their readers abreast of developments in microbiology and, more important, provided examples of its application by the younger veterinarians now in India. One of their most prominent examples involved John Steel's confirmation of the pathogen discovered by Veterinary Surgeon Griffith Evans as the cause of equine relapsing fever, or surra (see chapter 8). Steel had found the microbe in the blood of sick British army pack mules in Burma.[16] Since the disease also affected camels and horses, it became a primary target of research by military veterinary surgeons in India. But the key point for both Evans and Steel

15. On the theme of veterinary medicine as a kind of civilizing mission in India, see John Henry Steel, "Materia Medica Veterinaria Indica," *QJVSI* 1, no. 1 (October 1882): 101.

16. The journal carried a notice of Steel's confirmation of Evans's discovery in April 1885; see *QJVSI* 3, no. 11 (April 1885): 401. The report that Steel wrote on his findings in Burma as well as Evans's own report on surra can be found in IOR/V/27/541/15. A summary of Steel's findings also appeared in the *Veterinary Journal and Annals of Comparative Pathology*; see John Steel, "On Relapsing Fever of Equines," 22 (1886): 166–74, 248–57. It is also available online under the title *Report of Veterinary Surgeon J. H. Steel, A.V.D., on His Investigation into an Obscure and Fatal Disease among Transport Mules in British Burma*, at http://www.biodiversitylibrary.org, accessed 8 October 2017.

was that they had identified the cause of relapsing fever with the use of a microscope and Pasteurian methods.[17] At the same time, however, neither man could account for how the pathogen moved from animal to animal, with the result that older notions of transmission continued to circulate in their own work. In his research on anthrax, for instance, Evans was fully aware that the disease was caused by a bacillus. Yet when trying to explain its transmission, he repeated a much earlier argument about how diseases spread. Anthrax, he argued, was probably moved in windblown emanations from swampy ground—an interpretation associated with miasma theory.[18] The tension between older views of how diseases spread and new ideas emerging from bacteriology and parasitology would run into the twentieth century.

Nevertheless, it is perhaps worth emphasizing that Evans and Steel's identification of a pathogen that would prove deadly not only to camels and mules but to all equines marked, in a sense, the advent of animal microbiology in India—or, as the title of the journal indicated, the arrival in India of new scientific theories and methodologies. So, for example, stimulated by nutritional science, veterinarians in India sought to better understand how diet helped maintain animals' condition and support their capacity for sustained and healthy labor. Hence, they needed to know more about the kinds and qualities of edible plants found in India, and which were best for browsing animals such as camels.

In the first year of the journal's publication, 1882, Veterinary Surgeon Thomas Symonds began a series of pieces about the grasses of the Madras Presidency. Symonds located each species he identified within a global taxonomy, providing Latin names and notices by other authors of their presence in different parts of the world; thick descriptions of their characteristics; and drawings of each grass.[19] And although he did not dwell on the nutritional value of the grasses, his entries appeared under the rubric "dietetics," a new food science that divided digestible matter into three primary categories: carbohydrates (fuel), albuminoids (body heat), and fats-salts (tissue builders).[20]

17. Griffith Evans, "Autobiographical Memoir," *Annals of Tropical Medicine and Parasitology* 12, no. 1 (1918): 5.

18. *QJVSI* 1, no. 1 (October 1882): 49.

19. *QJVSI* 1, no. 1 (October 1882): 105–11; 2, no. 5 (October 1883): 120–27; 2, no. 6 (January 1884): 251–57; 2, no. 7 (April 1884): 378–84; 2, no. 8 (July 1884): 509–14; 3, no. 9 (October 1884): 75–79; and 3, no. 10 (January 1885): 236–38.

20. See, for example, J. Milner Fothergill, *A Manual of Dietetics* (New York: William Wood, 1886). Fothergill was a physician at the London Hospital for Diseases of the Chest and held honorary degrees and fellowships at teaching colleges in Chicago and Philadelphia.

In other words, Symonds situated his research in relation to scientific developments outside India while incorporating the specificities of India into a universal classification.

That even straightforward reporting like Symonds's grasses of Madras was informed by developments within an international scientific community was perhaps made most clear in its juxtaposition to an article by Frederick Smith entitled "Veterinary Hygiene."[21] Subtitled "Food," it comprised elements that later became a much expanded chapter in Smith's book on veterinary hygiene published in 1887.[22] In this work, Smith added sugars, starches, and cellulose to the categories of the chemistry of food. He then evaluated the nutritive value of food in a discussion of the "co-efficient of digestibility" of grasses, hays, straws, grains, and legumes, the basic kinds of animal feed in Europe and, to a degree, India. He concluded his essay with a discussion of "green herbage," enfolding Indian grains and grasses into a larger body of source material drawn from European publications and from the "Agriculture" entry in the eighth edition of the *Encyclopaedia Britannica*. Thus, in the case of both Symonds and Smith, their objective seemed to have been to add local Indian plants to an expanding imperial global "database" on nature. This pattern was repeated by other contributors to the *Quarterly Journal*, writing on other subjects.

At roughly the same time that he was publishing on nutrition, Smith turned his attention to army animal management. Over the course of the first four years of the journal's existence, he produced a series of articles about saddles meant to address the medical issue of sore backs and galls, that is, sores created by riding or pack saddles.[23] Eventually, he published his findings and recommendations in *A Manual of Saddles and Sore Backs* (1891). Two other publications, each of which went through multiple editions, were the result of work that first appeared in the pages of the journal—*A Manual of Veterinary*

21. *QJVSI* 3, no. 10 (January 1885): 206–36; 3, no. 11 (April 1885): 336–60; and 3, no. 12 (July 1885): 496–524.

22. *QJVSI* 3, no. 12 (July 1885). The book in question is *A Manual of Veterinary Hygiene* (London: Baillière, Tindall and Cox, 1887). The food chapter is 127 pages long. Smith dedicated the work to George Fleming, then principal veterinary surgeon of the army, editor of the *Veterinary Journal and Annals of Comparative Pathology*, and vice president of the Royal College of Veterinary Surgeons. This is the same Fleming who visited Manchuria in the early 1860s and commented on Chinese veterinary medicine (see below); he would later contribute an entry on the mule to the tenth edition of the *Encyclopaedia Britannica*.

23. *QJVSI* 1, no. 1 (October 1882): 111–18; 1, no. 2 (January 1883): 263–73; 1, no. 3 (April 1883): 445–53; 1, no. 4 (July 1883) 566–76; and 2, no. 6 (January 1884): 217–29.

Hygiene (1887; 5th ed., 1911) and *A Manual of Veterinary Physiology* (1892; 5th ed., 1920).[24] Thus, Symonds and Smith, along with Steel, demonstrated a textual strategy similar to that of their journal—the alignment of new knowledge being produced in India with knowledge generated outside India and, in Frederick Smith's case, the publication and revision of authoritative veterinary resources and training materials. In this formulation, the three men seemed to be arguing not only for the relevance of veterinary science but for the intrinsic value of research being done in India. These themes and textual strategies set a standard for India-based veterinary publications from the 1880s forward.

In the production of new knowledge, one advantage veterinary surgeons in India had over their counterparts in Great Britain was that they saw animals in many different conditions of distress, particularly during military campaigns. During the journal's existence, the British and Indian Armies were involved in several campaigns on the North-West Frontier of India and in expeditions to Egypt and the Sudan. The journal printed the field reports of the veterinary surgeons who accompanied these operations. These reports from the 1880s indicated that despite the restructuring of army transport, little had changed concerning veterinarians' lowly status in the army or their limited authority in the field. Moreover, transport operations in each of the expeditions were only marginally less chaotic than those during the Afghan War, and the army continued to lose many camels in each campaign.[25] On the other hand, some veterinary surgeons began to change their views on camels, arguing that the main problem these animals presented was not so much their natural recalcitrance or environmental sensitivity as it was British ignorance of their constitution and needs.[26]

The notion that there were things to be learned about indigenous animals in India had a corollary in attitudes toward indigenous knowledge of various other kinds. While John Steel in particular was dismissive of Indian animal

24. For an overview of Smith's contributions to veterinary medicine and a partial bibliography of his publications, see John Hickman, "Sir Frederick Smith—his Life and Work," *Equine Veterinary Journal* 16, no. 5 (1984): 403–10.

25. See, for example, Veterinary Surgeon Rayment, "With the Indian Contingent at Suakin," *QJVSI* 4, no. 15 (April 1886): 284–85; "Editorial," *QJVSI* 4, no. 13 (October 1885): 4; V.S. Alfred Queripel, "Nile Expedition," *QJVSI* 5, no. 17 (October 1886): 44–58; "Nile Expedition (continued)," *QJVSI* 5, no. 19 (April 1887): 213–34; and V.S. Fenton, "Veterinary Report on the Suakin Field Force, 1886," *QJVSI* 7, no. 26 (April 1889): 127–36.

26. See V.S. Robert Pringle, "Report on the Working of the Veterinary Department of the Zhob Valley Field Force," *QJVSI* 4, no. 13 (October 1885): 82–84.

doctors and treatments prescribed by camel handlers,[27] he was also aware of certain British dependencies concerning knowledge about medicinal plants. Indeed, as noted earlier concerning the publications of William Gilchrist in the 1840s, Indian plants and medical formulas were, with the help of Indian interlocutors, being appropriated and redeployed in English-language veterinary materia medica. There was, of course, nothing particularly new about such appropriations. As Mark Harrison has shown, early British Orientalists took a keen interest in Indian medicine and its formulary, in part because in the late seventeenth century, European medicine had much in common with Ayurvedic and Yunani tibb, including their shared emphasis on climate as a major cause of illness and the use of local drugs as the proper treatment for such illnesses.[28]

Moreover, the Indian practice of using local medicines to treat disease continued well into the nineteenth century, as Gilchrist's publications indicated. Before Steel began a journal column about Indian medicinal plants in the 1880s, Dr. Edward J. Waring had led a committee that produced the *Pharmacopeia of India*, which appeared in London in 1868.[29] The following year, Moodeen Sheriff, with Waring's blessing, published the *Supplement to the Pharmacopeia of India*, which provided transliterations and native script in fourteen Indian languages for several hundred common plants to be found in Waring's text.[30] It was this combination of transliteration and native script that seems to have attracted Steel. By using Sheriff's formulations as they now appeared in the Materia Medica section of the journal, Steel argued, any veterinary surgeon could obtain the drugs he might need from Indian bazaars.

In many ways, this was a practical admission on Steel's part that British veterinarians could not do without either Indian plants or knowledge about their properties. As he put it, "We must not prove exclusive in our selection of remedies." And he admitted that his efforts in the journal were a modest start-

27. Steel referred to them as "ignorant and superstitious." See "Notes on the Camel as an Animal of Transport," *QJVSI* 4, no. 14 (January 1886): 161–62.

28. Michael Harrison, "Tropical Medicine in Nineteenth-Century India," *British Journal of the History of Science* 25 (1992): 301–2.

29. Edward J. Waring, *Pharmacopeia of India* (London: Allen and Sons, 1868).

30. Sheriff, a graduate of the Madras Medical College, had noticed errors in the vernacular synonyms found in a number of English-language works on Indian medicines and botany. In his supplement, Sheriff used the system of Sir William Jones to transliterate native plant names. See Moodeen Sheriff, *Supplement to the Pharmacopeia of India* (Madras: Government Gazette Press, 1869).

ing point that acknowledged a degree of reliance on local resources. Yet this dependency seems to have stopped with the kind of local knowledge Sheriff had produced—that is, knowledge that would allow a veterinary surgeon to enter a bazaar in much of India and find desirable plants for specific afflictions.[31] This instrumental approach to native knowing, and its confinement to indigenous plants, was an imposed limit demanded, it would seem, by the endeavor to make veterinary medicine into veterinary science. It was difficult, in other words, for Steel to accept local knowledge about disease and its causes because, as he insisted, the knowledge and practices of the *salootries* (horse attendants), sarwans (camel men), *mahouts* (elephant handlers), and hakims (Yunani tibb doctors) were colored by "alchemical tendencies, witchcraft, 'hit and miss' practice, and a complete absence of accurate and exact information."[32]

As a result, Indian knowledge of herbal treatments had to be carefully cleansed of these polluting influences, isolated and cordoned off from indigenous practices that would occlude the actual agency at work in veterinary practice—the rational investigation into the active, healing component of any plant. The problem scientifically oriented British veterinary medicine faced was thus twofold. On the one hand, as Charles Steel, Frederick Smith, and John Henry Steel repeatedly reminded their readers, more resources were required, ones that in this case would allow research to produce scientific understanding of the active ingredients in Indian plants. On the other hand, this had to be done in such a way as to avoid local informants muddling the discovery process. And the latter sorts could not be easily excluded from the veterinary system without vigilant supervision of Indian subordinates by British officers and the training of Indians in proper veterinary schools. Sheriff's pharmacopeia supplement was a step in that direction, but much more work and conversion needed to be done.

During the *Quarterly Journal*'s second year of publication, certain signs began to appear that matters were moving in a more desirable direction. Rahim Khan, professor of materia medica at the Lahore veterinary school, was

31. Shopping for medicinal plants in Indian bazaars was not a new idea. Moreover, some Indian plants had entered British materia medica at least a century earlier. On eighteenth-century Indian bazaars, see Pratik Chakrabarti, "Medical Marketplaces beyond the West: Bazaar Medicine, Trade and the English Establishment in Eighteenth-Century India," in *Medicine and the Market in England and Its Colonies, c. 1450–c. 1850*, ed. M. Jenner and P. Wallis (New York: Palgrave Macmillan, 2007), 196–215.

32. Steel, "Materia Medica Veterinaria Indica," 104.

reported to have published a work in Urdu on veterinary medicine. The journal noted its publication and saw it as a "hopeful sign." As the editors put it, the book "will be found of great value to the increasing number of Hindustani reading and speaking Veterinary Students and Practitioners in this country, and, from the examination which we have made of it, we believe that the matter has been carefully and judiciously selected and arranged."[33] Khan's work was, in other words, devoid of the errors that, as Steel put it earlier, had previously marked Indian vernacular-language publications on medicine.[34]

This kind of "progress" ran parallel to the overall objective of focusing on materia medica publications. The journal's editors sought to redirect the meaning and understanding of medicinal plants in India and scientifically characterize how they operated to alter pathogenic patterns in organic life. The target was the complex drug formulas common in Yunani humoral medicine, Ayurvedic medicine, and other Indian healing traditions. Recall that British veterinarians like John Steel tended to see Indian formulary as a corollary to the concoctions of seventeenth- and eighteenth-century rural British farriers. Steel and others thought they observed the same misguided notions of cause and effect in the sarwans of the contemporary Indian present. In either case, because neither farrier nor sarwan could explain in chemical terms the elements that interacted to effect a change in a body—an alleged failure of reason that opened the door to supernatural agents—the only explanation for established effectiveness in local medicaments was "hit or miss."

If we look at a contribution by Steel to the Materia Medica Veterinaria Indica section of the journal, we can see how general processes of exclusion, appropriation, and reduction were worked out textually. Steel's prose sought to capture the object in minutely descriptive terms and then reduce its medicinal meaning to its "most active constituent." His first entry, on "bhelamay," the marking nut, also known as the malacca bean or marsh nut, is illustrative of what might be called an imperial editing practice.

> They are dark brown or black bean-like bodies, frequently somewhat shriveled over the surface, having the remnant stalk well marked at one end, and rounded or roughly pointed at the other. They are plano—or concavo-convex, with thick rounded margins; each consists of an outer fleshy part and an inner thin

33. *QJVSI* 2, no. 7 (April 1884): 327.

34. Steel found an "amateur stamp" and "quack medicines" in much of what was published on medicine by Indians; see "Materia Medica Veterinaria Indica," 105.

> stony coat; from the former and from between the two oozes a blackish viscid fluid; the cavity is occupied by the large solitary seed.[35]

When the juice or the seeds are boiled, we are told, their "active constituents" work as a "stimulant or excitant" for elephants and camels that show debilitation—the scourge, as Steel had noted earlier, of all animals subjected to India's climate. Gilchrist is cited as an authority on this drug. In fact, all authorities referenced in subsequent entries are British ones, while dosage is given in *tolas*, a variable Indian measure standardized by the British in 1843 as a base unit of mass fixed at three-eighths of a troy ounce. Subsequent entries follow this pattern, with the "local" enfolded into a universal taxonomy, measured in a redefined terminology, and carefully separated out from the "adulterations" of Indian formulas. There was, in other words, no thought given to the possibility of drug interactions in formulas or to the consideration that the animal body on which the sarwan worked might be conceptualized differently from the body of anatomical medicine.[36]

Steel's mode of appropriation through translation proved difficult for him to sustain in the journal over time, however. After the second year of publication, he turned over the Materia Medica section to Thomas Symonds. Initially, Symonds's entries retained native names in multiple languages and included the thick description of plant, seed, and fruit. He added a new touch—color illustrations showing phases of a plant's life cycle, a throwback to eighteenth-century botanical representation.[37] But this visual enhancement was offset by little if any information about the active agents in a plant, the uses of the drug, or the dosage. Instead, a host of new authorities appear, almost all of

35. *QJVSI* 1, no. 2 (January 1883): 522–23.

36. This was clearly the case with medical practices influenced by humoral theories (see chapter 2 above), but it was also the case in other medical traditions. See, for example, Judith Farquhar, *Knowing Practice* (Boulder, CO: Westview Press, 1996) on Chinese medicine and Francis Zimmermann, *The Jungle and the Aroma of Meats: An Ecological Theme in Hindu Medicine* (Delhi: Motilal Banarsidass, 2011) on Indian medicine.

37. For some examples of visual representations of plants in the eighteenth century much like those later produced by Symonds, see "The Botany of Empire in the Long Eighteenth Century," http://www.doaks.org/library-archives/library/library-exhibitions/botany-of-empire; accessed 2 October 2017. Steel and Symonds were, of course, hardly pioneers in their appropriations and redeployments of indigenous knowledge and the natural world of Asia, Africa, and the Pacific. See, for example, the essays in David Miller and Peter Reill, eds., *Visions of Empire: Voyages, Botany, and Representations of Nature* (Cambridge: Cambridge University Press, 1996).

whom are British materia medica and botanical works. The only "Indian" source Symonds cited was the government-produced *Pharmacopeia of India*, for which Moodeen Sheriff had compiled his supplement. The *Pharmacopeia* was, however, concerned only with drugs used to treat human illnesses, and its dosages were given exclusively in British measures.

More to the point, the *Pharmacopeia* incorporated India into an imperial project the scale of which, as envisioned by the editors of the journal, was yet to be achieved. As Edward J. Waring had noted in 1868, the work was based on the British pharmacopeia, which, "while affording all the information contained in [the latter] of practical use in India, would embody and combine with it such supplementary matter of special value in that country as should adapt it to meet the requirements of the Indian Medical Department."[38] In other words, knowledge of Indian plants, much like Moodeen Sheriff's tables of indigenous names in fourteen languages, was positioned as a supplement to the universal and stood in a part-whole relationship to a much larger and more rationally organized world, that of Linnaean Latin-language taxonomy. As Waring suggested, this was an imperial knowledge project that would define what was "of special value in that country." It was also an authority that veterinary medicine at the time could only aspire to. Severely short of resources, Charles Steel, Frederick Smith, and John Henry Steel abandoned the pretense of producing equivalencies with the *Pharmacopeia*. The Materia Medica sections in the *Quarterly Journal* became shorter in 1888 and 1889, and disappeared completely in the final year of the journal's publication.

We might take this dropoff in the study of local flora as indicative of a general loss of energy in the journal project. In 1885, Charles Steel retired and returned to England. The following year, Frederick Smith took up a professorship at the Army Veterinary School, Aldershot; and although he remained as an editor of the journal, the bulk of the work seems to have been taken up by John Henry Steel. In 1888, however, Steel was invalided home with a liver abscess and did not return to India until 1889. The journal continued to publish, but without the strong editorial voice of previous years. There was, however, one exception.

An editorial on microbiology appeared in the April 1889 edition. The piece showed all the forceful, on-the-ground practicality that had marked the journal's editorial stance from its inception, and it made several key points.[39] First, the editor argued that microbiology was an all-encompassing concept for the

38. Waring, *Pharmacopoeia of India*, vi.

39. *QJVSI* 7, no. 26 (April 1889): 198–208.

study of microscopic life, including bacteria, bacilli, fungi, and parasites. Use of terms such as *bacteriology* or *parasitology*, he asserted, not only confused matters but signaled an unnecessary commitment of resources to overspecialized fields. Microbes were microbes, from the journal's point of view, and their lives ought to be studied to determine whether or not they were pathogenic. Such study could be done at very low cost; all that was needed was a small, sanitary setting, adequate microscopes, a gas supply and burners, an incubator (made locally under close supervision), glass tubing and pipettes, and a few chemicals. Such facilities would allow veterinary surgeons to do what they did best—combine laboratory study with the regular, systematic contact in the field with domestic animal populations for the purpose of reducing the impact of contagious diseases. From the identification of pathogens, new discoveries and treatments would result. But more practically, by identifying the agent of disease, veterinarians could move expeditiously to separate diseased animals from healthy ones. In an environment of limited resources where contagion was understood to be closely tied to unavoidably unsanitary conditions, it is not difficult to see why a priority on preserving lives through preventive measures, as opposed to seeking the final cures for diseases caused by microbes, made more sense than a heavy investment in research. And such an approach fit well with the journal's earlier commitments to the education of Indian veterinarians.

It is difficult to gauge the impact of the *Quarterly Journal of Veterinary Science in India and Army Animal Management*. One suspects it had a greater effect on veterinarians in India than on the army hierarchy. Yet beyond the involvement of veterinary surgeons in the Remount Department's horse- and mule-breeding operations, there seems to have been little other palpable effect on the army's thinking about its transport system. Nonetheless, despite its short life, the journal did set a tone and establish a set of principles to guide future veterinary medicine in India, ones that would carry well into the twentieth century. These principles were, first, that veterinary medicine should be scientific, with one foot in the laboratory and the other in the field in close proximity to military animals. Second, veterinary surgeons ought to set the standards for the proper management of military animals. Third, veterinary surgeons should be the final arbiters on whether an animal was fit for military service. Frederick Smith in particular exemplified these principles through his scientific publications, scholarship on the profession, and service in the Boer War and World War I. And although the journal ceased publication in 1889 with the death of John Henry Steel, the surviving editors could take a measure of credit with him for the Government of India's decision to create the Civil Veterinary Department in 1892.

Yet if the journal appears to have had little influence on animal management, it did make one significant contribution to pack animal life—in its pages, the ignorance that had surrounded British interactions with the camel began to be rectified. The camel, if not completely rehabilitated, at least came to be known in ways it had not been previously.

RETHINKING THE CAMEL

In the 1880s, the reevaluation of camels as transport animals involved a deeper exploration of camel life by transport officers and veterinary surgeons. Transport officers approached pack animals in terms of their efficiency in moving supplies, arguing that when they occupied an appropriate place in a multianimal transport scheme, camels, if properly managed, would prove their worth. Veterinary surgeons, in contrast, approached camels as puzzles to be solved through a better understanding of their physiology, anatomy, and dietary habits, as well as the diseases that affected them. Both parties assumed that the general problem the British faced was one of ignorance about the animal, and so they premised their reconsideration of the camel on the production of new knowledge. Such knowledge for transport officers involved, on the one hand, situating camel power within the mathematical equations that predicted investments in military supply logistics,[40] and on the other, learning from native camel handlers the techniques of camel care when on the march, as Maj. Arthur G. Leonard had demonstrated. Knowledge acquisition for veterinary surgeons involved scientific study of the animal under laboratory-style conditions that allowed autopsies, experimental treatments, identification of disease-causing microbes, and the appropriation of native knowledge purged of superstition, magic, and faulty notions of cause and effect.

Ironically, this process of learning about camels began virtually at the same time that the animals were being dismissed by many as unfit for serious trans-

40. See, for example, IOR/L/MIL/17/5/752: *Field Service Manual for Commissariat and Transport Officers of the Indian Army* (Simla: Commissary-General-in-Chief, 1887), 55–59. These pages deal with the appropriate size of loads for mules and camels; equations to calculate how many animals could travel daily in a staged transport system; and equations for determining the number of animals required to deliver a certain amount of supplies over given distances and times.

port service—that is, in the Afghan campaign itself. Recall the earlier discussion of veterinary reports on the causes of camel deaths. These included poisoning, improper feeding, overwork and insufficient rest, and exposure to the elements. One conclusion, drawn by First Class Veterinary Surgeon G. A. Oliphant, was that the camel, unlike the mule, had too delicate a constitution to survive the rigors of mountain warfare. Others concluded—and Oliphant certainly concurred—that camels raised on the plains of the Punjab and Baluchistan, especially young ones, were ill suited for higher-elevation and cold-weather service unless they had proper rest, warm blankets, and adequate food. Yet all agreed that a major factor in accounting for the scale of death was the brutal treatment of camels by government-hired drivers.

There was at least one exception to this pattern of assessment. It came from Lt. Samuel Spence Parkyn, whose *Transport in Southern Afghanistan* provides one of the most concise on-the-ground descriptions and evaluations of the shortcomings of army transport during the Second Afghan War. In one suggestive passage, Parkyn explained that he took great pains to discover why camel mortality among the hired camels of the Brahui was so much lower than in his own pack trains.[41] Recall that the Brahui were nomadic camel herders, much like the Powindah, and moved seasonally between southeastern Afghanistan and western Baluchistan (roughly from Quetta eastward).[42] During the war, they had been enrolled into transport duty by Sir Robert Sandeman, the British political agent in Baluchistan. Parkyn indicated that he had managed to converse with the Brahui about their care of camels, learning that they would work their animals hard for some two hundred miles, and then give them plenty of rest and "good feeding" before working them again. Instead of feeding them raw grain, the Brahui prepared food for them, although Parkyn offered no details. He added that these herders provided *jhools* (warm blankets) to all their animals that went into the hills. Then Parkyn contrasted these observations about the Brahui with how the British had handled camel transport. In addition to hiring drivers who had scant knowledge of the animals and then severely overworking and underfeeding them, the main cause

41. Lt. Samuel Spence Parkyn, *Transport in Southern Afghanistan, between Sukkur and Quetta, 1878–1880*, 2nd ed. (London: Harrison and Sons, 1882): 29.

42. The Brahui seem to be one of many indistinct nomadic groups on the frontier. According to a number of sources, they were of Dravidian origin, having migrated into Baluchistan sometime after the eleventh century. See the entry in *Encycopaedia Iranica*, http://www.iranicaonline.org/articles/brahui; accessed 2 October 2017.

of camel breakdown was sore backs, he noted; this he attributed to improper loading, a situation remedied by improving the pack saddle and making certain that the load on each camel was properly adjusted.[43] Presumably, Parkyn had learned these points from observing the Brahui.[44]

It is impossible to gauge the impact of Parkyn's small book. There may have been none. All we know is that it was printed by Harrison and Sons, the publisher for House of Commons committee reports in London. On the other hand, it may well have been the sort of publication that attracted the attention of Sir Charles Cameron, that staunch critic of Indian Army transport. Perhaps Parkyn's observations helped reinforce what was in Britain already a substantial consternation over the death of so many camels in service. Whether it shifted opinion about the animal's value is, however, another question. The dominant position—or at least the one frequently repeated in a variety of sources about camels—was that of William Palgrave, who seems to have become an authority solely by virtue of his published reminiscences about travel in Central Asia and Arabia in the 1860s.

"If 'docile' means stupid," Palgrave began a frequently cited passage, then "the camel is the very model of docility." He then proceeded to argue that

> if the epithet is intended to designate an animal that takes an interest in its rider so far as a beast can, that in some way understands his intentions, or shares them in a subordinate fashion, that obeys from a sort of submissive or half-fellow-feeling his master, like the horse or elephant, then I say that the camel is by no means docile; he pays no attention to his rider, whether he be on his back or not, walks straight on once he is set going, merely because he is too stupid to turn aside. . . . In a word he is an undomesticated and savage animal, rendered serviceable by stupidity alone. . . . One passion alone he possesses, namely revenge, of which he furnishes many a hideous example.[45]

43. Parkyn, *Transport in Southern Afghanistan*, 30.

44. Parkyn was not alone among veterinary surgeons in observing the care with which native drivers treated their animals. During the Nile River campaign of 1885, Alfred Queripel observed that "Arabs will not on any consideration work a fatigued or galled animal, they always halt during the heat of the day, and will not work in June or July. They march their camels in herds which tires considerably less than marching in file." See *QJVSI* 5, no. 19 (April 1887): "Nile Expedition, (continued)," 217–18.

45. William G. Palgrave, *Personal Narrative of a Year's Journey through Central Asia and Eastern Arabia (1862–63)* (London: Macmillan, 1869), 25–26. The original edition seems to have appeared in 1865 and was reprinted by Macmillan into the 1880s.

FIGURE 8. A "Bobbery" camel. *Graphic* (London), April 22, 1893.

Clearly, Palgrave was annoyed that camels paid so little attention to him. But more important than his bruised ego was his establishment of a set of negative camel characteristics that stuck. These features—stupidity, indifference to humans, savagery, and vengefulness—were repeated in reviews of Palgrave's book and continued to be cited in the camel entry of the *Encyclopaedia Britannica* into the twentieth century (11th ed., 1910, vol. 5).[46] And although other observers took issue with Palgrave's characterization, the allegations of indifference to humans, especially in comparison to the behavior of dogs and horses, did—as we will see shortly—prove bothersome. Other stereotypes also stuck, such as the camel's being difficult to manage while in the field (fig. 8). Far more common, however, was a general recognition paralleling that of Pvt. William Atkinson. Recall that during the Second Afghan War, he argued that camels would rather die than "shirk their work" (see chapter 1).

Arthur Leonard, the army transport officer and author of *The Camel*, was well aware of Palgrave's characterization of the animal, and appears to have wanted to set the record straight in his own book. From his "practical observation" of the animal in Afghanistan, Egypt, and the Sudan, he had developed

46. Early reviews include *Eclectic Review* 9 (1865): 141; and the *Quarterly Journal of Prophecy* 19 (1867): 335, both of which repeat the passage cited here.

a great deal of respect for the camel as a pack animal. He devoted lengthy passages in the early part of the book to disabusing his readers of negative camel attributes to be found in sources like Palgrave. The temperament of the camels Leonard had known was "decidedly passive," never the viciousness or vengefulness attributed to them by Palgrave.[47] Indeed, he wondered how an animal as stupid as Palgrave claimed it to be could also have the intelligence to avenge a slight. Obstinacy was another purported camel attribute he addressed head on. Leonard insisted, "It is only when he falls into the hands of men who do not know how to manage him and who vent ill-humour on him that he develops this characteristic, and once he does, his extremely passive dullness assists materially to intensify it." Here and in other passages, Leonard attributed the camel's supposedly negative characteristics to ill treatment by humans. And while the camel wasn't playful or sportive like some other animals, preferring instead to remain completely absorbed in his tasks, he was gregarious with other camels (46–48), as we saw earlier.

We have also seen that the kind of sociality Leonard discussed was also noticed by T. E. Lawrence and others. But Leonard added that this conviviality did not extend to humans, and he seems almost hurt by that fact. The camel, he explained, declined humans' advances, refused their offer of friendship, and would not identify with rider or driver in any way. "His eye never lights up with love or even interest at the approach or approval of his master—in fact, it never lights up at all with any feeling inspired by affection . . . [you] cannot appeal to him through his stomach . . . in fact, you cannot appeal to him at all, for he has no feeling to appeal to" (57). In other words, the camel was decidedly neither a horse nor a dog, and yet Leonard also recognized that the animal clearly did have some sort of feelings, if only for other camels.

The camel's greatest virtue, however, was his willingness to work for humans. Sometimes Leonard attributed this feature to the "brute's tenacity" and "pluck"; other times he saw it as an acceptance of "life and its conditions as inevitable with long-suffering passivity truly phenomenal." In other words, the camel displayed a kind of fatalism commonly attributed to Asian peoples. But if Leonard anthropomorphized the camel on some occasions, on other matters, much like Parkyn, he was utterly practical. He summed up his experience by providing a list of twenty-eight rules of the road for proper camel management, including feeding, knowledge of camel grazing habits, and proper loading techniques. At the same time, he could wax poetic and, like

47. Maj. Arthur G. Leonard, *The Camel: Its Uses and Management* (London: Longmans, Green, 1894), 44. I make subsequent citations from this source parenthetically in the text.

Atkinson, demonstrate a real empathy for the animal (53, 77, 267–69). One of the advantages of grazing, he explained, was the camels' freedom from "constraint and control,"

> when . . . out of the reach of brutality and cruelty, they can wander at will more or less, pick and choose where and when they like, stand here or kneel down there and ruminate; lie down, rest and chew the cud, maybe of morbid fancies, but more probably of some choice pickings that they have stumbled across; stretch themselves, and enjoy a good roll in some soft sandy spot; rub up against a rough prickly tree, a hard rugged boulder, or against another, indulging in the luxury of a mutual friendly scratch. Do just what they like, in fact, and feel in their own dense way that even their life is not altogether made up of hard knocks and blows and brutal drivers. (161–62)

But perhaps more extraordinary than this passage was Leonard's acknowledgment that his knowledge of camels came primarily from the camel men of Asia and northeastern Africa. They had taught him not only the habits of camels in different environments but the diseases and afflictions the animals were susceptible to. He devoted twenty-eight pages to discussing common ailments, and he was one of the few observers who accepted the validity of the native treatment of each of them (v, 212–40).

Leonard's crediting sarwans with a certain set of skills and acknowledging the value of their treatments set him apart from many others who wrote about camels. As we have seen, veterinary surgeons could be dismissive of and hostile toward indigenous animal handlers. They could also question native practices and ideas, while incorporating native plants into their treatments. One reason veterinary surgeons rejected local knowledge probably involved their contact with hired camel drivers during campaigns, as Charles Steel made quite clear. Leonard too found these handlers unredeemable.

But if veterinarians felt there was nothing to learn about camels from native animal handlers, much of what they did know came more or less the same way Leonard's had—in the field during military campaigns. Recall, for example, Charles Steel's reports on the causes of camel deaths during the Afghan campaign (chapter 1). In addition to his general observations concerning the ill treatment of the animals by both natives and British soldiers, he provided ample information about a number of afflictions while beginning to explore camel physiology. Steel was not alone in using military campaigns as a learning experience. For instance, in an article published in the *Quarterly Journal of Veterinary Science in India and Army Animal Management* concerning the

Zhob valley campaign of 1884, Veterinary Surgeon Robert Pringle extolled the virtues of properly managed camels. During the portion of the Afghan campaign in which he participated, however, he acknowledged that the camel was a "perfectly sealed book . . . none of us knew anything about him, neither how to feed him, work him, nor treat him in any way."[48] Service in Waziristan and now in the Zhob valley seemed to have opened Pringle's eyes. The mystery, he asserted, had ended; and with this demystification, the sort of lore that claimed the animal was capable of dying out of spite also went by the boards. Instead, Pringle found a hardworking creature that if well treated and cared for performed as well as any other pack animal. He then laid down some basic camelology.

While he doubted that Punjabi and Hindustani camels could handle high-elevation work, Pringle found Brahui and Pathan camels perfectly serviceable.[49] From contact with these sorts of camels, and presumably their expert sarwans, he concluded that it was essential to rest camels and allow them to graze freely for a day or two each week. In between, the animal should be given small amounts of grain and *bhusa* (straw). Without rest and grazing, he explained, camels quickly lost condition; they could not be expected to remain fit with rations of grain and *bhusa* alone. He also thought that if transport officers were properly trained in managing camels, there should be little difficulty with their use as transport animals. Yet Pringle noted that had he expressed these views during the Afghan campaign, he would have been laughed at.[50]

Even though his praise was limited to what were generally referred to as hill camels, Pringle's reassessment of the animals' value for army transport pointed to how camels could be reconsidered through working closely with them and learning from the techniques of experienced sarwans. The change in attitude that Pringle recorded echoed Charles Steel's earlier observation that few casualties occurred during the Second Afghan War among the officers' baggage camels—superior care and supervision mattered. Direct participation in military campaigns was thus one way that opinions changed. A second was to reduce British ignorance of the camel's constitution through published commentaries.

Charles Steel himself began this process in his reports during the Afghan

48. Pringle, "Report on the Working of the Veterinary Department of the Zhob Valley Field Force," 82–83.

49. Pringle provided the astonishingly low figure of 67 casualties out of 1,628 Brahui camels employed in the campaign; see ibid., 84.

50. Ibid., 83.

campaign and with the article he wrote for the United Service Institution journal. The new knowledge he presented in these writings came from direct observation as well as from autopsies he had performed in the field. It also came from listening to the views of his own sarwan, an older man who had been around camels all his life. In his journal article, Steel not only mentioned this source but went beyond his official reports to review the general characteristics of camels, including their complex digestive system of multiple stomachs. He also described their skeletal frame and general anatomy, including the fact that their skin had perspiratory follicles and ducts. In addition, he identified the different breeds to be found in India, and recapitulated the many causes of camel deaths along the route to Kandahar. It is perhaps worth reiterating that these causes included age—far too many were only about two years old—and the breakdown of camels' respiratory and digestive systems under conditions of overwork and exposure to the elements without proper rest and rations. At the time, Steel's article provided more information about the constitution of the camel and ill handling, as well as proper management of the animal, than was then available in a publicly accessible form.[51]

The production of new knowledge about camels was furthered by Steel's son, John Henry Steel, in the pages of the *Quarterly Journal*. Already by 1883, the younger Steel had dispelled some of the mystery surrounding elephants by providing a manual detailing their anatomy and diseases.[52] In 1886, he sought to do the same for the camel. In his first journal article on the topic, following a review of the kinds of camels to be found in India and their uses in military campaigns by other powers, he addressed the delicate subject of his fellow veterinarians' views about the care of the camel. Put simply, he abhorred the commonplace attitude among veterinary surgeons that sick camels should be left to the natives for treatment. We have seen what Steel thought of sarwans and native camel doctors. Here he reiterated those views, and charged veterinary surgeons with not knowing their proper business. "It is not fair to urge that the camel be unfit in Army transport on active service," he remonstrated,

> because he has succumbed to bad management in countries unsuited by geography and climate for him; nor [is it true] that we are unacquainted with his management although we have much information accessible; nor that we dislike and despise him. These arguments are more than counterbalanced by the

51. Steel, "Camels in Connection with the South Afghan Expedition 1878–1879," 448–55.

52. John Henry Steel, *A Manual of the Diseases of the Elephant and His Uses* (Madras: W. H. Moore, 1885). He also wrote similarly titled books about sheep, dogs, and oxen.

> facts that in some countries the camel is, under intelligent and sympathizing appreciative management, the most reliable animal for Transport in War and Trade.[53]

Having presumably gotten his reader's attention, Steel then ticked off the camel's virtues. The animal was enduring, patient, tolerant of water shortages and sun exposure, capable of carrying heavy and awkward loads, and, in the right environment, could forage for itself when on a military campaign. He was docile when well managed and developed close ties with his handlers. But he could also be "intractable and obstinate when handled unskillfully" or overloaded. And although a slow and deliberate worker, the camel could cover substantial ground daily and keep up with armies. These many positive attributes were tempered by environmental constraints, meaning that the army could not rely solely on camel transport. Nevertheless, for Steel, the camel's virtues outweighed this single limitation. It was simply a matter of using the animal in the right circumstances, combining him intelligently with other transport animals, and learning more about him.[54]

Over the next three years, Steel set about closing the camel-knowledge gap. Under the rubric "camel pathology," he published pieces in the journal about camel diseases in general, along with the camel's blood and its diseases, digestive system, various organs and circulatory system, surgery, and wound treatment.[55] He then combined the articles into a single volume, which was printed in India in 1890 as *A Manual of the Diseases of the Camel and of His Management and Uses*. The title mimicked that of the journal, with its dual emphasis on scientific inquiry and animal management. Like his work on the elephant, Steel thought of the camel book as only a beginning—there was much still to learn about camel diseases in India, as well as from researchers in Russian Central Asia and French Algeria, and from camel specialists in the Arab world.[56] Presumably, this knowledge could be obtained in the same way India's materia medica had been approached—by separating out the fantastical lore produced by superstitious natives and stabilizing sound empirical knowledge based on field and laboratory research.

53. John Henry Steel, "Notes on the Camel as an Animal of Transport," *QJVSI* 4, no. 16 (July 1886), 162.

54. Ibid., 162–71.

55. Articles about cameline pathology are in *QJVSI* 4, no. 16; 5, no. 17; 5, no. 18; 6, no. 23; 7, no. 25; and 7, no. 27, published between 1886 and 1889.

56. John Henry Steel, *A Manual of the Diseases of the Camel and of His Management and Uses* (Madras: Lawrence Asylum Press, 1890); see the preface.

Unfortunately, other demands, illness, and an early death ended Steel's efforts to make the camel more legible to army transport officers. And with the demise of the journal he helped found, a key venue for circulating practical knowledge obtained from military campaigns and from veterinary research on camels as well as other army animals also disappeared. When Leonard published his study of the camel in 1894, it stood with Steel's manual of camel diseases as the only works about the animal produced by soldiers or veterinarians stationed in India since William Gilchrist's work in the 1840s. On the other hand, through its varied publications, from veterinary reports on military campaigns to animal physiology, diseases, and proper management, the journal created by the Steels and Frederick Smith set new professional standards for Indian Army veterinarians. Their efforts made a strong argument for establishing the authority of veterinarians in the army, an authority based on knowledge of transport animals in health and disease and of their proper management.

*

Seventeen years would pass before anything like the journal edited by Charles Steel, Frederick Smith, and John Henry Steel appeared again in India. But when the *Journal of Tropical Veterinary Science* began publication in 1906, its very title signified a conceptual shift. No longer encumbered by the need to justify the importance of veterinary medicine as a handmaiden to imperial control in India or the task of arguing for rational animal management, its editors presented veterinary surgeons' work as an aggressive assault on the pathogenic microbes specific to the "tropical" areas of the world. As such, they saw themselves as part of a network of investigators operating across sub-Saharan Africa, India, Southeast Asia, and the Indonesian and Philippine archipelagos.

At roughly the same time that veterinary surgeons were beginning to constitute a new authority for their specialty, the army transport system again found itself in a state of crisis. The dire predictions made by Lt. Edmund George Barrow concerning the inadequacies of the new transport scheme became obvious in the mid-1890s. As a result of a succession of frontier campaigns, beginning with the Chitral expedition of 1895 and extending through open rebellions on the North-West Frontier in 1897–98, the standing and depot reserves were used up, and the British Indian Army was once again forced to impress camels and mules into service. As in the past, many camels died, and once again the transport system was in crisis. Also as in the past, there were calls for reform.

CHAPTER 5

Frontier Warfare and the Persistence of Impressment

On 2 August 1898, Thomas Baring, the Earl of Northbrook, rose in the House of Lords to call attention to a statement by the financial commissioner of the Punjab, Septimus Thornburn. The latter had been quoted in the *Civil and Military Gazette* in India to the effect that one hundred thousand animals and twenty-five thousand owners of these animals had been impressed into the frontier operations during 1897 and 1898. The earl called for the correspondence between the secretary of state for India and the Government of India on this matter. Two days later, in the House of Commons, Mr. Edward Pickersgill asked Lord George Hamilton, secretary of state for India, whether it was not the case that the impressment was done without "discrimination, system or organization"; he also asked who had authorized such a practice. Hamilton replied that he was in communication with the viceroy on the subject. When Pickersgill pressed him again a few days later to name the legal code that sanctioned impressment, Hamilton replied that the practice was "based on immemorial custom and usage." He added that he thought the numbers being bandied about were exaggerations, but provided no basis for that belief.[1] Few were satisfied with Lord Hamilton's response.

What is perhaps most intriguing about this exchange was how it differed from the situation during the Second Afghan War. Then, it will be recalled, the concern and critique emerging in Britain were about the sheer numbers of camels that had perished during the first year of the war. The questions posed

1. IOR/L/MIL/7/6683: Commissariat and Transport Department: Impressment of Men and Animals in India, Questions in Parliament, 1898.

by Northbrook and Pickersgill focused attention instead on how the Army of India was acquiring camels and other pack animals. Was there, in other words, a legal basis for impressment? And why was the requisitioning so chaotic? It is not clear if either Northbrook or Pickersgill ever got clear answers to these questions. On the other hand, investigations in India stimulated by these parliamentary queries produced a substantial amount of testimony about how impressment was working in the rural areas and villages of the Punjab.

This chapter uses the testimony of district officials, army transport officers, and native responders to impressment to provide an overview of the animal collection process and its impact on the animals and people of the province. The next chapter explores the deliberations and recommendations made by two committees for restructuring army transport, and concludes with an overview of the new system put in place in 1900–1901. I hope to show that there was nothing particularly new about arguments made for necessary changes—many of them had already been laid out by Lt. Edmund Barrow and Col. R. C. Low some twenty years before, and were repeated in a second essay contest run by the *Journal of the United Service Institution of India* in 1896.[2] What had changed was the introduction into the army of notions of professionalization and a newly urgent sense that Britain had fallen behind Germany, France, and other European countries in restructuring its military to meet the demands of modern warfare.[3] What had also changed was the appointment of Lord George Curzon, a firm believer in administrative efficiency and rational management, as viceroy of India. Curzon arrived in India in January 1899, when various transport committee reports and recommendations were just wrapping up.

INITIAL ASSESSMENT OF ARMY TRANSPORT

One of those reports contained a history of army transport problems dating back to the First Afghan War. It was assembled by Maj. Gen. Edwin H. H. Collen, the military member of the viceroy's council. Collen had arrived in India in 1873 with an education that included the University College School, London; the Royal Military Academy, Woolwich; and the Staff College at

2. The prizewinning essay was written by Capt. A. H. Bingley, an intelligence officer. See "The Improvement of the Present Transport Organization in India," *JUSII*, suppl. (July 1896): 1–32.

3. See my discussion in *The Imperial Security State: British Colonial Knowledge and Empire-Building in Asia* (Cambridge: Cambridge University Press, 2012), 34–52.

Camberley as well as service in the Abyssinian Expedition (1867–68). He was, in other words, one of the new breed of professional officers, and one of the first such experts to be posted to India. Once there, he helped organize the Intelligence Branch in the Quartermaster General's Department and served in supply and transport during the Second Afghan War. After the war, he took up a number of administrative appointments.

In his report, Collen provided a definitive explanation of the problem of transport for any campaign requiring the collection of a sizable number of additional pack animals. He began with the simple fact that the existing system, put in place after 1881, distributed transport in regiments stationed all over India. Hence, when a sudden flare-up occurred and the need for transport was greatest, it was impossible quickly and expeditiously to move the active units from one place to another. Using the Chitral mobilization of 1895 as his prime example, Collen explained that

> there were no cadres that could be expanded and still *remain organized units*; and some 20,000 pack animals had to be got together somehow, by hire or by purchase in as short a time as possible. It took about two months to hire and purchase 9,000 camels, although the work was carried on in sixteen districts. . . . The experience gained in accomplishing this task showed that we were no nearer any systematic plan, whereby large numbers of efficient transport could be rapidly collected to meet a sudden emergency, *than we had been before.*[4]

Collen's observations made two key points. First, there was no governmental mechanism in place to expand transport in an orderly fashion; hence, a chaotic situation was to be expected in rural areas when transport was required in an emergency. Second, the market mechanism that supposedly guaranteed a sufficient supply of pack animals beyond the existing transport corps did not work. Owners, perhaps because they recalled earlier instances when camels were lost and compensation was spotty, refused to voluntarily place themselves or their animals in service. This meant that force (i.e., impressment) had to be used to procure animals, with the consequent disruption of the rural order and the generation of ill feelings toward the government among animal owners.

4. IOR/L/MIL/7/6688: *Report of the Transport Committee, 1898* (Simla: Government Central Printing Office, 1899); Maj. Gen. E. H. H. Collen, "Transport Service of the Indian Army," 27th August 1898, 1:14–15; emphasis added.

Collen's comments were damning enough regarding the reformed transport system, but his observations about the civilian side of matters were equally unfavorable. Recall that under Low's scheme, civilian officials were to collect animals, with the army selecting from these the ones most appropriate for its needs. According to Collen, however, the information civil officials had about animals in their districts was "found to be unreliable," and the scheme of identifying such animals through district censuses "useless" even in the case of camels.[5] Collen's assessment of the situation identified two themes that would run through all subsequent deliberations on transport: (1) the present mechanism for expanding transport into organized units was inadequate, and (2) when the army had to turn to impressment, it could not rely on district officials, who apparently had other priorities, for aiding in the process.

When the frontier uprisings began in 1897, the only apparent difference from the Chitral mobilization was that civil officials responded more vigorously to the task of collection. W. M. Hailey, junior secretary to Septimus Thornburn, the head of the Punjab Financial Department, was the official responsible for writing the department's assessment of mobilization and impressment for the government of the Punjab. Hailey indicated that 31,889 transport animals were volunteered, of which 19,054 were either purchased or hired. Another 103,597 were impressed, 35,207 of whom were found fit for service.[6] Given the experience of 1895, these numbers seem staggering. How were they possible? As Hailey explained, the "sudden and peremptory" initial call for transport animals fell on deaf ears, which led to an order for owners to produce immediately all available pack animals at collection centers in the districts. That is, animal owners were compelled to deliver their animals, and possibly even themselves, or defy the colonial state. What then transpired, Hailey continued, was a predictable muddle.

> When demand followed demand in the Kohat District, and every transport animal and owner that could be discovered in the district or enticed over the border into British territory had been impressed, several thousand agricultural bullocks were taken for temporary employment, and of these no record has

5. Ibid., 15.

6. IOR/L/MIL/7/6687: *Report of the Transport Committee, 1897* (Simla: Government Central Printing Office, 1897); *W. M. Hailey to the Officiating Chief Secretary to Government, Punjab, 18th August 1898*, 2. This report, like a number of others, was made available to the Rawalpindi committee and became part of its supporting evidence. In what follows, I cite the page numbers of Hailey's report parenthetically in the text unless otherwise indicated.

> been kept. In many cases the district returns of "collected" are entirely wanting. The records for the Delhi District are only for animals actually taken by the Transport Department, not the actual collections, and the same is the case for Hoshiarpur and for Ferozepore [in other cases, there were no figures at all] . . . there is [also] doubt as to the figures which distinguish "voluntary" and "impressed" collections. There are no laws, rules or regulations dealing with impressment; there is no authoritative decision as to the *amount of compulsion that must be exercised before service ceases to be voluntary*. (2; emphasis added)

In other words, the situation was a repeat of 1878; and once more, impressed animals were the primary victims of human ineptitude.

IMPRESSMENT: REPORTS FROM THE GROUND

The nineteen thousand "volunteers" taken into service seem to have been primarily from Rawalpindi, Shapur, and the Jhelum District of the Rawalpindi division. Otherwise, volunteers were scarce. When the collection order was issued, the initial thought was to focus on animals held by professional carriers, but the effort proved fruitless, and soon every sort of animal was swept up (1–2). Or, as a Military Department report put it, the "halt, the maimed, and the blind" were collected, with many "undersized, half-starved and galled" animals indiscriminately included with healthy ones.[7] How this sweeping-up was accomplished, how it played out from village to village, is made clearer in Hailey's report. The intent was to have local officials carry out the collections, but in almost every case they delegated responsibility to *chaprasis* (menials), who according to Hailey were the most "rapacious harpies" employed in the districts.[8] "There are no regulations to bind their choice of animals," he continued, "and there is necessarily little supervision to restrict their exactions from owners. In the midst of law and order is introduced a Saturnalia in which the . . . chaprasis is lord of the situation." These menials used this unusual occasion of authority to collect old debts and squeeze money from any owners who tried to protect at least some of their animals. In other instances, the "passive resistance" of local officials and village heads stymied efficient collection. Some of them might claim to know little about the animals in their unit, while colluding with wealthy farmers and army pensioners to ensure that the

7. IOR/L/MIL/7/6688: *Report of the Transport Committee, 1898*; Letter from Military Department, India, to Secretary of State for India, 26th January 1899, 1:6.

8. IOR/L/MIL/7/6687: *Report of the Transport Committee, 1897*, 5.

animals of these local big men remained invisible to the colonial state.[9] The upshot was that the animals of the "poorest and most defenceless" were the first to be taken regardless of the animals' condition.[10] Almost all the district reports Hailey cited included similar tales of oppression and intimidation. Through these means, 103,597 camels, mules, donkeys, ponies, and bullocks were collected from the pack animal breeders and farmers of the Punjab (2).

Other difficulties resulted from the rules to be found in field service manuals. These stipulated that there be one driver for three mules; but what of the carrying trade owner with five or more? Did he accompany his three and turn over the rest to someone else for safekeeping? Did he give up an animal to strangers with the certainty that if he ever saw it again, it would not be in fit condition? Did he hire an additional driver, an extra cost to himself, to accompany three of his mules? Or did he simply bribe the collectors to avoid these dilemmas? Indeed, Hailey noted that among the few types of owners willing to offer their mules for hire were the hashish dealers who conducted long-distance commerce with Leh in the far north (4). In other words, those who were long-distance traders were more likely to sign up than animal owners who were farmers or breeders in the districts.

Once the animals were collected, they had to be taken to a "passing station," where the responsibilities of the civil authorities ended and those of army transport officers began. Their job was to determine if the animals were fit for hire and to dismiss those who weren't. First, however, owners or their sarwans had to get the animal to the station, and for many this was easier said than done. Some of the stations were great distances from where the animals had been found, and the caretaker had to provide for himself and his camels or mules along the way. When owner or caretaker and animals arrived at the assigned site, the process of selection for hire might be delayed, because the inspector was not always present. Again, expenses were incurred with little chance of compensation. In some cases, the owner or sarwan was forced to borrow money at high interest. Facing mounting costs, owners sometimes simply abandoned their animals, which would then be seized as government property. In other instances, when animals had been placed in the hands of a stranger because the owner was unable to accompany them, this person was entered on the rolls as the animal's owner (6–7), erasing the actual owner from colonial record keeping. The deputy commissioner of Umballa summarized the plight of many.

9. IOR/L/MIL/7/6688: *Report of the Transport Committee, 1898*, 2:145.
10. IOR/L/MIL/7/6687: *Report of the Transport Committee, 1897*, 5.

> Jat Singh's cart and bullocks are seized just as he is reaping the kharif and sowing the rabi [spring and fall crops]. He and his sons cannot spare time to go to Umballa. A *pali* [hired man?] is sent with the cart, and the cart is entered in the *pali*'s name. The *pali*, finding Khushalgarh cold and tiresome, deserts. The cart is sent on by some driver unknown. Jat Singh is still wondering whether he will ever hear of his cart again, and is whistling for hire while the Commissariat Officers are getting their affairs straight. (7)

With many situations like this, it became impossible to determine how many owners of animals chose to accompany them to the front. The little that was known indicated that all the camel volunteers hired in Shahpur were accompanied by owners or their relatives. But Shahpur seems to be an exception—of the several thousand mules, ponies, and donkeys, all of whom were impressed, few owners accompanied their animals. In other cases, very few camel owners were induced to go; and in still others, owners had to be coerced into accompanying their animals.

After registration, a month's advance payment was given to the animal's keeper, but this was soon spent on pack gear for the animal and the "cost of detention" while both were awaiting inspection. The result was that many owners found themselves paying the government for the "privilege" of having their animals "seized" (7). In other instances, where the animal and sarwan were enlisted for service, the month of advance pay was left behind with the sarwan's family, on the promise that rations would be plentiful along the line to the front. This was no small matter, because the Punjab and contiguous territory had at the time undergone two years of drought and famine. For some, therefore, the offer of food while in service was an unexpected boon for hard-pressed rural families. When, however, it turned out that no provision had been made down the line to feed men and animals, both would desert rather than starve.[11]

Further costs might accrue to the driver because the transport officers wouldn't send the animals forward until they had amassed a certain number. As if this were not hard enough for both animal and man to bear, the most egregious effects of registering attendants as owners became clear only later. As per regulations, the person responsible for the animal in the field received payment for his services. The owner, meanwhile, probably never saw any of this money or, in many cases, the animal itself again.[12] It is worth quoting in

11. IOR/L/MIL/7/6688: *Report of the Transport Committee, 1898*, 2:1n42.

12. IOR/L/MIL/7/6687: *Report of the Transport Committee, 1897*, 8.

some detail a report of the deputy commissioner in Hissar as to the fate of 148 camels "hired" from his district. "Since December [1897]," he began, "I have received constant petitions for payment of hire, for compensation for animals that have died, or for the return of camels taken." He continued:

> In most of these petitions neither I nor the Superintendent of the [Hissar] Cattle Farm, nor the Commissariat authorities at the front can give any answer owing to the impossibility of saying what had happened to each man's camel. Towards the end of January [1898] I was informed that out of the camels received from Hissar, which the Base Commissariat described as 66 in number, 16 had died, 10 had been lost, and 49 were being returned under the charge of a Sergeant and a Transport Agent. After the lapse of six weeks it appeared that they had been marched by road all the way from Peshawar. On or about 2nd March Sergeant Harris arrived in Hissar with 15 miserable skeletons in the shape of camels. Of the remainder, 34 had died or been shot on the march down. Two of the fifteen died a few days afterwards. The Superintendent of the Cattle Farm kept the remaining 13 . . . for a month till the news got abroad that some camels had returned from the front. We had no means of knowing to whom the animals belonged, but eventually the owners of the 13 survivors appeared and claimed them. Thus out of the 148 camels sent off from Hissar 13 have returned alive to their owner, 2 died in Hissar since return, 34 died in the course of a return journey from Peshawar to Hissar, 3 died in Rawalpindi, while 96 are either dead or unaccounted for. *In no single case has a penny of compensation been paid.* (8; emphasis added)

In army transport parlance, the Hissar camels suffered a wastage rate of 91 percent! As if this were not appalling enough, it is clear from Hailey's report that this was not an isolated case. In other instances, where animals survived and owners could not be identified, the animals were simply sold. Probably most worrisome is that the returns of transport officers show little indication of losses or disappearances on this scale. Perhaps this was because, as in the past, the men in the field could barely keep track of the animals in their charge, and they may well have had little idea of their fate when they returned to the bases at either Peshawar or Nowshera. Nor do we have a clear picture of the reactions—with only a few exceptions—of the many people affected by impressment. One of those exceptions involved what Hailey described as an "agitator" in Jagadhri. This owner had filed suit against the secretary of state for damages, and was urging others to do the same (8). In other instances, however, many seem to have thought that it was too time consuming and costly to pursue redress. Or, as T. H. Hoam, a civil official at Dera Ismail Khan, put it, "The reason why complaints are rare is due to the fact that the loss to individual owners is trifling compared with the trouble entailed in making complaints."[13]

The most disturbing element in Hailey's summaries of comments by district officials was, however, the utter failure of the rationale that had underpinned emergent animal acquisition. It had been assumed since the reforms of the early 1880s that when the government offered generous monetary terms for hire or purchase, herders and farmers would seize the opportunity to demonstrate their loyalty to the colonial state while also benefiting financially. By the time Hailey assembled his report, it was clear in almost all cases that owners had lost any commitment they may have had to the law of supply and demand. Most officials reported that no amount of money for an animal would persuade owners to hire them out to the state. Only the threat of impressment could persuade them otherwise.[14] Abuses of the poor and weak followed naturally upon this.

In the final sections of his report, Hailey summarized the problems and abuses of the current system as it related to the civilian collectors and the agents of the Transport Department (8–9). He then made a number of suggestions for reform and improvement, not the least of which involved a fairer distribution of animals hired based on something like per capita quotas. In this way, smaller and less wealthy villages would not carry the full brunt of impressment (10). He also recommended a standing reserve scheme that could be mobilized as needed, thus obviating the need for impressment (12).

The report, according to Hailey, was shown to Finance Commissioner Septimus Thornburn, who took issue with some of it. Most specifically, Thornburn concluded that owners who placed their animals into the hands of strangers in order to avoid service had no one to blame but themselves for losses. And he added that there was no other choice in the field than to treat the attendant as the owner (11). This rather callous conclusion completely ignored the sheer scale of the disorder introduced into the lives of animals and rural households affected by the "sudden and peremptory" actions of the Punjab government (1). It also suggests that Thornburn cared little about how the animals were procured, only that he had done his duty to supply transport animals as ordered by his superiors.

Hailey's report was only one among several on impressment that was seen

13. See IOR/L/MIL/7/6687: *Report of the Transport Committee, 1897*, 190.

14. Ibid., 9.

by the Rawalpindi Transport Committee. His sources were primarily civilian district officers, most of whom seemed to have known little about the animals themselves, relying instead on Indian functionaries located at the *tahsils*, administrative subdivisions of the district. But one of these other reports stands out, because it came from an army officer appointed to select animals for service. Capt. Brooke-Murray,[15] who had been assigned to the Rawalpindi division, provocatively concluded that the tahsil officers had, in fact, "completely hoodwinked" the civil officials on the Rawalpindi Transport Committee concerning "[the] class of animals, the time to collect them, and the existence of the required numbers in their tahsils." As a result, collection fell unevenly across the territory, with all the animals swept up on one farmstead and few or none on the one adjacent to it. Moreover, the tahsil functionaries took any quality of animal they could get their hands on simply to meet expectations that sufficient animals were available to be brought in (147). One response on the part of some owners, as Brooke-Murray indicated, was to blame the unfamiliar British official who had been deputed to the district (i.e., the army transport officer) for this "illegal oppression" and flee the scene, taking their animals into the jungles and *nullahs* (ravines) until the crisis passed (136–37). These observations not only support Hailey and his sources but go a long way in explaining why, as we shall see presently, rejection rates by "passing" officers were so high—the best animals were in hiding.

The problem of collection, Brooke-Murray thought, might have been mitigated were it not for the fact that the government had done so little to prepare anyone for the process. Like many other officers, Brooke-Murray had little experience with hiring or purchasing pack animals. Yet only two years before in the very area where he had been assigned, others had procured a good number of animals for the Chitral campaign. None of the information about this experience had been passed on to him, however. Moreover, the government made no effort to brief local leaders, such as landlords or tahsil officials, on the class of animal needed, probable quantities, or anticipated number of animals by class so that the collection would be evenly distributed. Nor was any effort made by the district officers to introduce the transport officer to local notables (136). This meant that as an outsider, the transport officer must have appeared not only as the coercive arm of the colonial state, but as the one official who would most surely disappear once the emergency had passed. The

15. Brooke-Murray's report is included in Hailey's at IOR/L/MIL/7/6687. I make subsequent citations from Brooke-Murray's report parenthetically in the text unless otherwise indicated.

implication was that the transport officer was pitted against the rural populace as an adversary. Putting this another way, the expected cooperation imagined as necessary between civil and military officials during emergencies was perfunctory at best.

But even in the hands of apparently responsible transport officers like Brooke-Murray, it did not necessarily follow that the animals and sarwans he handled were better off. In order to get animals from the passing stations to the base at Nowshera, most transport officers tried to move as many as possible by rail. Here too cooperation and coordination were lacking or completely absent. To begin with, there was no military authority over the rail lines, which meant that scheduling and decisions about the makeup of trains were completely in the hands of rail officials. This situation would have unforeseen consequences for many pack animals. For example, when his efforts to delay loading a group of fifty mules into metal boxcars until departure time were overruled by the station master at Jhelum, Brooke-Murray recalled how the animals were crowded in without food or water for thirty-two hours until their cars could be attached to a passing train (138).

But railroad officiousness was not the only obstacle transport officers faced. Within the British Indian Army itself, few protocols existed for asserting military priorities on the rail lines or addressing the mundane needs of men and animals. And the regulations in place were often inadequate. For example, buckets of water were required to be placed on trains for the animals. When the boxcars arrived in the Nowshera depot, the animals and the buckets were detrained. But since there was no regulation directing that the buckets be returned to their starting points, all available buckets eventually were at Nowshera, while the cars carrying mules and camels were without water receptacles (138). While the animals suffered in this way from official neglect or bureaucratic incompetence, their sarwans, having been forced to pay extortionate prices for bad food along the rail lines, arrived at their destinations with themselves and their animals requiring rest and rehabilitation before they could be sent into the field (143).

Compounding these problems was how various parts of the transport service appeared to be working at cross purposes with one another. After a bit of inquiry, Brooke-Murray had sorted out a means of attracting competent sarwans and their animals into service. The key was to obtain men from the same village or family, and promise to keep the group and their animals together during their service time. This worked well as a recruiting tactic, but ran into two major problems. One involved billets in the field. The British tents were extremely capacious, and many drivers were housed together. Unfortunately, no one gave much thought to the problem of billeting Muslims, Sikhs, and others in the same tent. Men discontented with these arrangements simply deserted. The other issue had to do with Brooke-Murray's promise to keep friends and family together. Once his recruits were out of sight, he had no control over their distribution in the field. Affinity groups were often broken up, and animals separated from owners. This was one sort of "breach of faith." Another was promising men that rations would be plentiful when they arrived at their destination; the Commissariat, it turned out, had no power to deliver on such a promise. By the "arbitrary rules" of the Military Accounts Department, the Commissariat could provide food or other supplies to the drivers of animals only through a petition for "special sanction," a process that took days and weeks to complete (142). When it was clear that they had been misled, again men and animals deserted.

Unlike Thornburn, Brooke-Murray concluded that the confusion and hardship caused by impressment had an extremely serious effect on British prestige at the local level. Not only did it lead to a "strong feeling of unrest and uneasiness" among the population, but it opened the door to litigation. He argued that in towns, there were more than enough "oily tongued gentlemen" who advertised themselves as "Failed B.A." These sorts exploited discontent and encouraged the spread of unfounded rumors. One of his solutions, as we saw, was to recruit affinity groups whenever possible and send them collectively into the field with their animals. The other was to call together local officers and village headmen to explain the selection process and dispel rumors that men would be impressed along with their animals (136–37).

The details to be found in Brooke-Murray's account of "hire and purchase" were substantiated by the reports of other transport officers. Many noted that initially, the quality of animals brought in was extremely poor; many were rejected. In fact, if we step back a bit from the ground-level view of Rawalpindi, the numbers are staggering. As noted earlier, during the voluntary phase of collection about 32,000 animals of all types were presented at "passing stations." Of these, 2,370 were purchased and 16,684 hired, or around 60 percent "passed." Parenthetically, all those who were not accepted, no matter the distances they had traveled or time they had spent away from their home areas, received no compensation whatsoever for "volunteering." During the second phase, which began near the end of 1897, when impressment was the rule, Hailey reported that over 100,000 were collected and 35,000 actually taken, more often than not without owners or familiar animal handlers.

But perhaps the more important point is that it is unclear by any measure or source how many among the 54,000 pack animals impressed died or dis-

FIGURE 9. Camel baggage convoy. From Maj. E. A. P. Hobday, *Sketches on Service during the Indian Frontier Campaigns of 1897* (London: J. Bowden, 1898).

appeared during service, and how many actually made it back home. In part, this was because record keeping of losses in the field was not much improved over the Second Afghan War. Part of the reason for this continued uncertainty concerning numbers has to do with the fact that there were six separate mobilizations in 1897–98—the Peshawar Valley, Kurrum-Kohat, Mohmand, Malakand, Tochi, and Tirah Valley Field Forces, all involving fighting in rugged mountain terrain (figs. 9 and 10). The deployments of these forces happened one after another over an eighteen-month period, and occasionally pack animals were demobilized from one of them and immediately mobilized into another. In addition to the confusion this must have caused for both sarwans and animals, the reports from supply and transport officers from each of the forces vary in format. All of these record animals procured and some provide wastage figures, but there is no comprehensive accounting that enumerates the total number of animals involved in the campaigns and the overall casualties. Moreover, while the limited figures that do exist paint a somewhat better picture than the first phase of the Afghan War, wastage rates were still high. The Tochi Field Force accounts indicate that 4,199 camels were bought or hired. Of these, 12.83 percent died and 1,338 were discharged as unfit. When

FIGURE 10. Ordnance mules with troops destroying refractory villages. From Maj. E. A. P. Hobday, *Sketches on Service during the Indian Frontier Campaigns of 1897* (London: J. Bowden, 1898).

other categories of losses are figured in, the wastage rate was 51.3 percent.[16] In a separate report, Gen. Edwin Collen gave the following figures for the Tirah Valley Field Force: 22,953 hired or impressed and 7,258 casualties, a wastage rate of 32 percent.[17]

These figures do not include other kinds of losses, however. Overall, it seems reasonable to conclude that wastage rates ran between 40 and 50 percent and perhaps even higher, because little account was taken of impressed ponies, for example. Then too, we also have the appalling case of the Hissar camels, among whom nine out of ten died or simply disappeared from official records. On the other hand, camel losses, as one report pointed out, could be as low as 13 percent among hired camels accompanied by owners or professional sarwans.[18] As we will see shortly, the fact that hired camels in the care of

16. IOR/L/MIL/17/5/1855: *Report of the Commissariat-Transport Arrangements of the Tochi Field Force, 1897–98* (Calcutta: Government of India, 1899), 127.

17. IOR/L/MIL/7/6688: *Report of the Transport Committee, 1898*, 1:270.

18. IOR/L/MIL/17/5/1855: *Report of the Commissariat-Transport Arrangements of the Tochi Field Force, 1897–98*, 70.

experienced handlers fared better than others would influence the subsequent organization of army transport.

But if it remains difficult to determine in any clear fashion the scale of pack animal losses during the fin-de-siècle North-West Frontier campaigns, coercion of one sort or another was clearly essential for making a system without order function at all. Also of significance, on this occasion impressment emerged as a political issue, one that created the conditions of possibility for an entirely new approach to army transport in India. It was equally clear that faith in a market mechanism that could obviate the need for impressment was wholly misplaced. As W. M. Hailey argued in his report, the Government of India had received a "decided and emphatic answer" from the districts where pack animals were abundant. "Our rates of hire," he explained, "had no effect whatsoever in inducing a free supply of carriage." And he concluded that "there is so far a unanimous belief that the most liberal terms could never do away with the necessity of impressment."[19] Not even the magic of the liberal free market, it would seem, stood a chance against the immemorial customs of empire.

Although the chaos of impressment may well have made older Punjabis recall the catastrophe of the Second Afghan War if not the more recent Chitral adventure, more than a few civil and military officials felt that as difficult and, perhaps, unfair as the process of collection was, the government had every right to make such demands. Some, like Thornburn, thought that impressment implied the compulsory "hiring" of man and beast. Hence, if an owner refused to accompany his animal into the field, it was his own fault if the animal were lost.[20]

This attitude and its accompanying draconian procedures, reminiscent as they seem to be of a feudal order, only appear questionable and odd because it was, after all, the end of the nineteenth century. A half century or more of Royal and Parliamentary Commissions had established institutions and procedures in Great Britain to make governance rational and more logically organized, with legible lines of authority and inspection mechanisms that made it possible to identify institutional defects and responsible parties.[21] Impressment as a practice did not seem to fit this new form of governance. Nor was it

19. IOR/L/MIL/7/6687: *Report of the Transport Committee, 1897*, 1, 9.

20. Ibid., 11.

21. See, for example, the discussion by Philip Corrigan and Derek Sayers concerning the role of official Commissions and inspection that altered British governance practices: *The Great Arch* (Oxford: Basil Blackwell, 1985).

consistent, as we will soon see, with notions of colonial improvement—hence the parliamentary questions of the Earl of Northbrook and Mr. Pickersgill concerning the basis of authority for impressment.

It would also seem that along the North-West Frontier—this flashpoint of indigenous resistance to British expansion—the improvement ethic of a new generation of colonial administrators came face to face with the fundamental contradictions of colonial rule. Impressment may not have been modern, but its rationale was not necessarily atavistic. Rather, it embodied an imperial state of exception that took precedence over law and rational governance, producing for animals and their caretakers a lawless, unregulated sphere in which they were left with a simple choice—serve or desert and, either way, suffer the consequences.[22] Moreover, no amount of rhetoric in colonial courts by a "Failed B.A." was going to alter this fact. The state of emergency trumped law and order.

What is perhaps most surprising and disturbing about this situation is that forced animal laborers, themselves often reduced to a condition of "bare life," whether locked in boxcars or starved along the line of communication, drew very little sympathy from the perpetrators of an impressment regime. Instead, more often than not, animal suffering and ill treatment was blamed on "untrained coolies"[23]—or, as a later report put it, the "riff raff" of bazaars, "a motley assemblage of cooks, sweepers, gardeners, bhistis [water carriers], etc.,"[24] whose only qualification was availability. But it was difficult, either in 1878 or 1897, to lay blame on coolies or lower-level Indian officials for impressment itself, or for the gross inefficiencies, waste, and suffering that came with it. The transport system, despite reforms, remained encumbered by a host of frictions, resistances that repeatedly created obstacles to any sort of order thoughtful transport officers might attempt to introduce. The question that the Government of India and its military now confronted was rather straightforward: what was to be done in order to avoid another transport debacle in the future? At the very least, the arbitrary practices of impressment and the faith of colonial authorities in rationalities of "supply and demand" required careful reassessment.

22. On state of exception and bare life, see Giorgio Agamben, *Homo Sacer: Sovereign Power and Bare Life* (Stanford, CA: Stanford University Press, 1998).

23. IOR/L/MIL/7/6687: *Report of the Transport Committee, 1897*; "Précis of the Portion of the Report of the Transport Committee, Rawal Pindi, 1897, Relating to Impressment of Transport," 29th July 1897, 4.

24. IOR/L/MIL/7/6694: From the Commissary-General-in-Chief to the Secretary to the Government of India, Military Department (Simla, 25th April 1899), 1.

* Prologue to Part Two *

Colonial Transformations

After the suppression of the Sepoy Rebellion of 1857, the 1850s penetration of the Punjab by the British colonial state accelerated. From that point forward, colonial officials inaugurated a succession of changes that fundamentally altered the political economy and ecology of the region. Driving these changes were widely shared notions of how colonies should be improved and economically developed. Joseph Chamberlain, secretary of state for the colonies between 1893 and 1903, is usually credited with having developed the policy of what some have called "constructive imperialism." Chamberlain's position was that economic development ought not to be left to the vicissitudes of the market. Instead, the state should use revenues and loans to invest in infrastructure—irrigation, sanitation, and railway and harbor construction—thereby generating new wealth and revenues in the colonies. E. H. H. Green argues that Chamberlain's initiative was the culmination of an argument that the imperial state ought to take on a greater role in the economic management and development of Britain's colonial possessions, particularly in areas that were—to use a more recent parlance—undeveloped. Green adds that the Conservative government's effort to promote state intervention in colonial economies was part of a broader attempt to break the fiscal constraints of the "Gladstonian minimal state."[1]

1. See E. H. H. Green, "The Political Economy of Empire, 1880–1914," in *Oxford History of the British Empire: The Nineteenth Century*, ed. Andrew Porter (Oxford: Oxford University Press, 1999), 3:352–53. Also see Robert V. Kubicek, *The Administration of Imperialism: Joseph Chamberlain at the Colonial Office* (Durham, NC: Duke University Press, 1969).

In the case of India, an improved Punjab and its bordering areas would be brought into the modern world through massive investment in canal irrigation, bridge and road building, rail line expansion, and the careful enumeration and management of a diverse population. With these state-directed undertakings, that region would become the testing grounds for and a stellar example of a new form of colonial rule—rational British colonial management by trained administrative managers and technocratic elites, including agronomists; entomologists; medical and veterinary scientists; road, rail, and bridge builders; and hydraulic engineers.

The administrative and development side of colonial rule in the Punjab was complemented by a military side that, during the last decade of the nineteenth century and the first decade of the twentieth, transformed the Punjab into a garrison state and produced a militarized pack animal–human polity. And while the rationale for this militarization could be found in persistent conflicts with peoples along the Indo-Afghan frontier, it also had been stimulated by developments outside the region. In global terms, it involved the emergence of new interregional powers—Germany, Japan, the United States, and Russia—and the decline of older empires such as Qing China and the Ottoman sultanate. The "decline" of these Asian empires, often referred to in Britain as the Eastern Question, or a succession of Eastern Questions, implicated British colonies in Asia in broad discussions of geostrategic shifts across the continent. In the case of South Asia, Russian expansion into and conquest of what had been Muslim khanates along the old Silk Road triggered anxieties and concerns about how to defend India. Critical to this discussion was fear that Russia was capable of employing historical invasion routes out of Central Asia, all of which traversed the Punjab. The militarization of the Punjab and its western frontier for the "defense of India" became, as a result, the keystone in what was imagined as the strategic defense of India.[2] The invasion of Afghanistan in 1878, as we have seen, was justified on the ground that Russian influence there threatened the security of all India. We have also seen that such fears were directly tied to concerns about British Indian Army dependency on Punjabi sarwans and camel transport, the result of which was the ambitious mule-breeding program discussed earlier.

The large-scale processes that would alter human and animal life in the

2. On the discourse of the Eastern Question and the defense of India, see James Hevia, *The Imperial Security State: British Colonial Knowledge and Empire-Building in Asia* (Cambridge: Cambridge University Press, 2012), 13–14.

Punjab began with land settlement surveys in which British statistics gatherers and surveyors sought to establish landownership for taxation purposes. The settlement was buttressed by the passage of the Punjab Tenancy Act in 1868 and the first Land-Revenue Act in 1871.[3] These land surveys also sought to establish the social and cultural makeup of the province. Tribes, castes, language and religious groups, human and domestic animal populations of towns and rural areas, landlords and tenants, and agricultural output were all enumerated. In some cases, as was noted earlier, descriptions of domestic dwellings, diets, eating utensils, and clothing were included in the enumerator's reports, as was physical geography, flora and fauna, and rivers and roads. Trigonometric survey mapping accompanied enumerations and empirical description. Surveys of the land served to fix exact boundaries of plots and establish locations for boundary pillars.[4] The settlement procedure functioned, in other words, to produce land and population in a systematic and consistent way on paper in the form of empirical narratives, statistical charts, drawings and diagrams, and precision maps. It also served to incorporate the Punjab, as well as Baluchistan and the Sind, into the universal grid of longitude and latitude, thus firmly situating the region in relation to other parts of the British Empire.

The effect of this process of enumeration and mapping was profound—it refigured the Punjab, to use James Scott's notion, as "legible" colonial territory.[5] Once established, such legibility was to be maintained through a regular process of inspection by officers responsible for revenue assessment, and by the daily keeping of village logbooks in both vernacular languages and English.[6] And because the same categories were used in each district to organize data about the human and physical terrain, all administrative units of the Punjab and the frontier territories were made into similar entities for the administrative eye.[7] In other words, on paper they achieved optical consistency,

3. On the revisions of the Land-Revenue Act, see James M. Douie, *Punjab Settlement Manual* (1899; reprint, New Delhi: Daya 1985), under Acts in the index.

4. On surveying methods, see ibid., 109–17.

5. James Scott, *Seeing Like a State* (New Haven, CT: Yale University Press, 1998).

6. Douie, *Punjab Settlement Manual*, 185–88.

7. These are, of course, processes made familiar in the work of Michel Foucault and James Scott. I have rehearsed their arguments in Hevia, *The Imperial Security State*, 4–8. The particular administrative genre generated through the settlement report, the district gazetteer, was the civilian counterpart to the military report discussed in my study of military intelligence; see chapter 6.

allowing their features to be compared or contrasted with each other.[8] Difference between one district or another was more a matter of degree (e.g., more Muslims here, fewer Sikhs there, superior and inferior soils) than of kind, making administrative rule—be it of human subjects, animals, or the land itself—a management problem to be solved by ever-more efficient administrative methods. The environment, meanwhile, as Septimus Thornburn quaintly put it with respect to water, was to be "trained" and "broken to harness."[9]

A second effect of the new land revenue system was to constitute agriculturalists as living in settled communities and reform them into ideal colonial subjects. Whether proprietor, tenant, or lessee, in the eyes of British administrators those who worked the land were seen as industrious and productive, in contrast with "lazy" pastoralists, who were described as perfectly content to wander barren wilderness or wasteland habitually, like vagrants or vagabonds. Disturbingly for administrators, in the nomadic state of nature, pastoralists could remain virtually free of their enumerating functions of rule. Wandering the wastelands, the nomad flouted the regulatory mechanism of census and revenue collection, premised, as it was coming to be, on land tenure.[10] These "disorderly" internal others were soon grouped with the long-distance nomad-traders, such as the Powindahs, and became known as "primitive" populations suspected of theft, spying, and various other nefarious activities,[11] all of which justified strict policing or ultimately elimination. Ideally, with the proper incentives and legal restrictions, the pastoralists could be refashioned into property owners and productive farmers. One strategy developed to achieve this end was to make it illegal for pastoralists to graze their herds on village lands. In the case of the Powindahs, efforts were made to limit

8. See Bruno Latour, "Drawing Things Together," in *Representation in Scientific Practice*, ed. M. Lynch and S. Woolgar (Cambridge, MA: MIT Press, 1990), 19–68.

9. S. S. Thornburn, *The Punjab in Peace and War* (Edinburgh: William Blackwell and Sons, 1904), 265.

10. See the discussion of British notions of property and deviant behavior in Neeladri Bhattacharya, "Pastoralists in a Colonial World," in *Nature, Culture, Imperialism*, ed. David Arnold and Ramachandra Guha (Oxford: Oxford University Press, 1995), 67–77.

11. Neeladri Bhattacharya, "Predicaments of Mobility: Peddlers and Itinerants in Nineteenth-Century Northwestern India," in *Society and Circulation: Mobile People and Itinerant Cultures in South Asia 1750–1950*, ed. Claude Markovits, Jacques Pouchepadass, and Sanjay Subrahmanyam (Delhi: Permanent Black, 2003), 198; Denis Judd, ed., *A British Tale of Indian and Foreign Service* (London: Radcliffe Press, ca. 1999), 117–18; and Daniel Balland, "Nomadism and Politics: The Case of Afghan Nomads in the Indian Subcontinent," *Studies in History* 7, no. 2 (1991): 217–21.

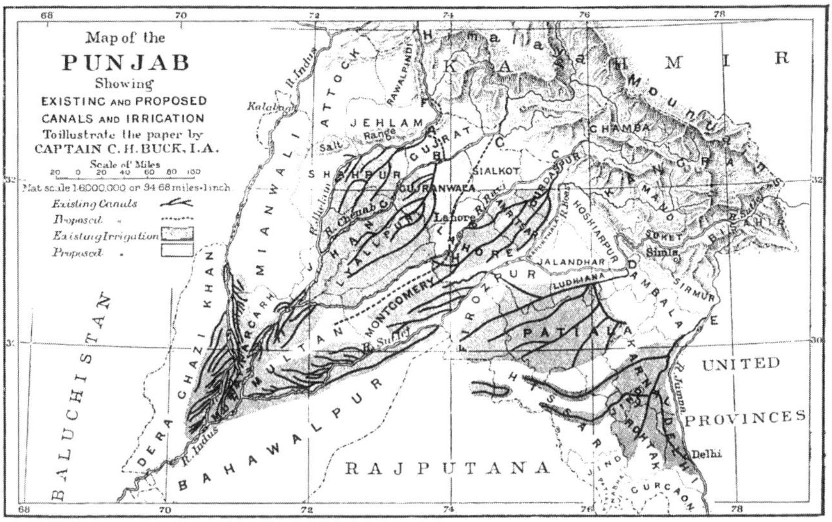

MAP 2. Punjab canals, existing and proposed (1906). From C. H. Buck, "Canal Irrigation in the Punjab," *Geographical Journal* 27, no. 1 (1906): 61.

their movement, tax their use of pasturage in India, and, through legal statutes, constrain their ability to lend money. If necessary, the Criminal Tribes Act of 1871 could always be invoked against Powindahs and other itinerants, since it made "habitual wandering" illegal.[12]

The other way of dealing with nomads and pastoralists involved the improvement and expansion of canals branching off the Punjab's major rivers (map 2). The river management and canal extension projects were part of a number of programs, like horse and mule breeding, launched by British administrators under the sign of improvement. While schemes for the material improvement of land and population had a long history in the United Kingdom,[13] by the 1890s improvement as an administrative concept was situated within a new notion of nature-human relations. Under the influence of the second law of thermodynamics, which posits that all natural systems, because of friction, tend toward disorder or entropy, a new breed of colonial administrators argued that

12. Bhattacharya, "Pastoralists in a Colonial World," 83.

13. Projects in Ireland and Scotland, for example, provided prototypes that were carried into the colonial world; see Patrick Carroll, *Science, Culture, and Modern State Formation* (Berkeley: University of California Press, 2006), and Paul Slack, *The Invention of Improvement: Information and Material Progress in Seventeenth-Century England* (Oxford: Oxford University Press, 2015).

technical interventions and expert management could work to maintain order, reduce friction, and limit the loss of energy resulting from entropy. This proposition provided the ideological foundation on which large-scale improvement projects—the expansion of irrigation, the organization of military transport, and so on—could be justified and initiated in the form of disciplined, regulated systems. In British India, the idea that nature could be technologically managed or "trained" informed action across many fields, including colonial administration, military intelligence, and land and revenue management, inaugurating, as Timothy Mitchell has put it, the "rule of experts."

The irrigation canal projects involving the rivers of the Punjab are a case in point. These were ambitious undertakings designed to extend "perennial" irrigation into the wastelands between the five rivers and thereby open vast new tracts of land to agricultural production. Canal irrigation had long existed along the Punjab's rivers; it had been supported and encouraged by the Mughal government. Modest in scope, these inundation canals served to spread the spring flood, with its restorative silt, some distance from the main flow of the rivers.[14] The British ambitions for irrigation to provide water year round were at a different magnitude of imperial ambition. From the perspective of the engineers who designed the new irrigation works, the rivers and their canals were understood as more than simply about delivering water to drylands—the project was conceptualized as one integrated system of efficient water regulation, one vast machine, each part of which was coordinated with the others, regardless of any local requirements or topographical differences.[15] This mechanization of nature, as we will see in later chapters, had enormous consequences for the ecologies of all life in the region. And it was also part and parcel of other grandiose projects that sought to discipline the space of Asia,[16] to make places like the Punjab not simply legible to the eye of the colonial administration but fully reordered into formats of measurable quantities, be

14. Indu Agnihotri, "Ecology, Land Use and Colonization: Canal Colonies in the Punjab," *Indian Economic and Social History Review* 33, no. 1 (1996): 40–42.

15. On the conceptualization of the Punjab's irrigation scheme as an integrated system, see David Gilmartin, *Blood and Water: The Indus River Basin in Modern History* (Oakland: University of California Press, 2015), 148–56.

16. I have used this term to describe the trigonometric mapping operations and reconnaissance surveys undertaken by army engineers and military intelligence officers in India, China, and western and Southeast Asia from 1880 forward; see Hevia, *The Imperial Security State*, 73–106. On another colonial project, this one in French Indochina, with equally grandiose ambitions, see David Biggs, *Quagmire: Nation-Building and Nature in the Mekong Delta* (Seattle: University of Washington Press, 2010).

they human, animal, or plant. Outputs (e.g., number of mules foaled, number of acres irrigated) became raw data for formulas that evaluated efficiencies and hence progress.

The reengineering of the Punjab's rivers as an integrated irrigation system was complemented by other large-scale projects, all of which were designed to create efficiencies by reducing entropic friction and thereby manage waste.[17] In India, the logic of reducing frictions led to road improvements and the extension and construction of railroad lines.[18] The main roads were paralleled by rail lines that by the beginning of the twentieth century ran as far as the passes on the invasion routes into Afghanistan, and linked the Punjab with Bombay and the port of Karachi in the Sind. The Grand Trunk Road, which linked Peshawar with Delhi, was upgraded all along its length, and large sections were "metalled" (i.e., stone beds were covered by a gravel and tar mixture). Where the Grand Trunk and other roads crossed rivers, new bridges were built with state-of-the-art materials. Where road and rail went, telegraph lines, postal services, and print technologies followed, connecting the Punjab to a communications network that joined the far-flung territories of the global British Empire.[19]

Transport and communication improvements had major military-strategic benefits as well. Improved roads and rail and telegraph lines linked many forts and military cantonments or bases that the British erected at key strategic points throughout the province and along the North-West Frontier. As a result, it was now possible for the British Indian Army to organize coordinated and comprehensive plans for the defense of the frontier and the management of populations moving into and out of the Punjab. It also became possible for the military strategists to rethink the kinds of animal transport appropriate for

17. Wise and Smith have demonstrated that there was a fundamental shift in thinking around the mid-nineteenth century away from a balanced notion of energy use to one that separated matter into work and waste, the latter being unavoidable entropic loss caused by friction or the inefficiencies within a system. The notion had wide application beyond mechanics and physics, informing most pronouncedly political economy and social engineering projects in the second half of the century. See M. Norton Wise and Crosbie Smith, "Work and Waste: Political Economy and Natural Philosophy in Nineteenth Century Britain," *History of Science* 27, no. 77 (1989): 263–301; 27, no. 78 (1989): 391–449; and 28, no. 81 (1990): 221–61.

18. On the expansion of the railroads in India after the rebellion of 1857, see Ian J. Kerr, *Building the Railroads of the Raj, 1850–1900* (Oxford: Oxford University Press, 1995).

19. Rajit K. Mazumder provides a detailed overview of the development of transport and communication in the Punjab; see *The Indian Army and the Making of the Punjab* (Delhi: Permanent Black, 2003), 50–64.

enhancing the mobility of the army. For example, better roads extending into mountainous areas might allow for a revision of attitudes toward camel and mule transport.

As colonial administrators were refashioning the relations between farmers, pastoralists, and animal populations of the Punjab, the new land for cultivation created by the canal projects reorganized the region's agriculture. Wheat production nearly doubled between 1871 and 1936, while other grains, with the exception of gram, either remained unchanged in output or declined. Barley, which had been a staple animal feed, showed a marked drop-off. Changes in grain diversity and yield can be accounted for not only by the expansion of wheat acreage but also by the planting of cash crops such as cotton and sugarcane. Into the post–World War I period, the Punjab increasingly functioned as an exporter of wheat, cotton, and sugar to Great Britain and the empire in general.[20] And while this may have seemed to be a boon from an economic development point of view, the commercialization of Punjab agriculture had more harmful long-term ecological consequences; these will be addressed in more detail below.

This combination of improvement projects also clarified for officials the continued "inefficiencies" within the colonial polity—the human-made frictions, as it were, of "customs" and "superstitions." Among the negative qualities noted were aspects of native character, such as the supposedly muddled thinking of native religion and medicine discussed earlier, which worked against the rationalizing practices of the colonial regime. Many peasants were in chronic debt, largely caused, from the British perspective, by their "improvidence" and extravagant spending on weddings and funerals,[21] or by their patronage of Sufi shrines, folk healers, and other forms of quackery. An additional problem was the continued presence of itinerant wanderers—"mad mullahs" or Muslim contraries, such as Qalandars, who were thought to stir up trouble among benighted peasants and encourage "fanatical outrages" against British officials.[22] Pastoralists, like the Powindahs, still migrated in

20. Mazumder provides gross statistics on agricultural output in the Punjab between 1871 and 1936; see ibid., 72–81.

21. The definitive study of the rural debt issue by a colonial official is Malcolm Darling, *The Punjab Peasant in Prosperity and Debt*, 4th ed. (Oxford: Oxford University Press, 1947). The work was updated in three subsequent editions. See especially his discussion of "unproductive" debt (19–20), and improvidence and extravagance (60–67).

22. For a catalogue of incidents in which British officials were attacked, usually by a lone assassin, see IOR/L/P&S/20/203: "Statement of Fanatical Outrages in the North-west Frontier Province and Baluchistan, 1905," Simla, 1 December 1905.

and out of the region, while camels, for those colonial officials still thinking about them, remained stubbornly unimproved. With shrinkage of wasteland brought about by canal expansion, some officials even wondered if camels might be in decline as a species (see below).

The efforts to wean the Indian Army transport of its dependence on camel power may be understood as one kind of improvement project undertaken by the colonial state. Mule breeding and the importation of mules from various parts of the world involved multiple kinds of expertise, rational calculation, and the exploitation of the new transport and communications technologies that connected the Punjab with networks of empire. Moreover, the reforms in the early 1880s appeared to have dealt adequately with frontier warfare. In a succession of campaigns between 1891 and 1895 (eight in all), the army was able to purchase or hire enough additional animals when needed with the help of civil officials. But the numbers of animals involved were small compared with earlier campaigns, reaching a high of 7,340 for the Waziristan Field Force (1894–95) and averaging around 3,000 in seven others.[23]

Hence, few changes were deemed necessary to improve the transport system itself, the primary one being the amalgamation of the supply and transport branches of the Bengal, Bombay, and Madras units into the Commissariat Department. Yet despite this centralization, regimental transport for some units remained autonomous.[24] Moreover, as in the past, few officers were actually trained in the rigors of transport management, and in times of need the number of experts available with any experience in the field was extremely limited. And, as we have seen in chapter 5, the active transport corps continued to be incapable of expansion in an emergency, except through impressment. This seems odd, given that at the same time, in both India and Britain, concern remained over a possible Russian invasion of India.

Indeed, the "defense of India" question spawned substantial speculation about the Russian threat and the status of the British Indian Army's ability to meet it. In a confidential study leaked to the press in Great Britain in 1884, Gen. Charles MacGregor, veteran of the Afghan War and director of the Intelligence Branch of the Indian Army, insisted that the Russians were planning

23. IOR/L/MIL/7/6687: *Report of the Transport Committee, 1897* (Simla: Government Central Printing Office, 1897), 6.

24. IOR/L/MIL/7/6688: *Report of the Transport Committee, 1898* (Simla: Government Central Printing Office, 1899); Gen. Edwin Collen, "Transport Service of the Indian Army," 27th August 1898, 1:8–9. Collen said that the Commissariat had authority over regimental transport, but mentioned only the right to inspect regimental transport units.

such an invasion, and that India was ill prepared to defend itself. The heated debate over Russian intentions and capabilities was stoked the following year when a Russian army defeated an Afghan force at Panjdeh, a small town north of Herat, which the amir of Afghanistan had claimed belonged to him.[25] The incident led to a panic in Great Britain and a mobilization order in India. After the crisis had cooled down, the War Office in London asked the Indian Army to clarify its mobilization plans for India's defense. A committee was duly set up, and it decided that the places to meet the Russians were north of the Hindu Kush and at Herat in northwestern Afghanistan. The entire exchange that ensued between the War Office and the Indian Army concerning this response need not detain us here.[26] For present purposes, the key point is that the military planners in India seemed to have a rather tenuous grasp on the logistical problems facing either Russian or British forces aiming to move across Afghanistan. And at the center of those problems was what ought to have been an obvious question: did the Indian Army have on hand pack animal transport capable of supporting a large field army hundreds of miles from their bases in India?

But army leaders continued to only partially grasp the intrinsic problems of pack animal transport and build them into their war plans. In his study, MacGregor almost completely ignored transport issues, and later assessments continued to avoid confronting the challenges large-scale frontier warfare posed to pack animal transport.[27] Nothing makes this clearer than what happened when in 1895 a British garrison in Chitral was besieged and another major mobilization of pack animals became necessary. The active transport units in the Punjab were soon exhausted, and impressment of large numbers of pack animals followed. Recall Gen. Collen's assessment of the ensuing chaos—the army, as he put it, was no nearer solving its transport issues than in the past. Hence, in the wake of the campaign, a transport committee was convened at Rawalpindi to make recommendations on how to deal with crisis situations.

25. On the incident, see J. M. Brereton, "The Panjdeh Crisis, 1885," *History Today* 29, no. 1 (1979): 46–52.

26. See my discussion of the exchange between London and the Indian Army in Hevia, *The Imperial Security State*, 155–64 and the sources that are cited therein.

27. As late as 1912, a strategic assessment of Russo-British conflict in Afghanistan noted in its summary that "a factor that was not taken into consideration is the difficulty of organization and control of efficient lines of supply based on animal transport." See IOR/L/MIL/17/13/7: General Staff Branch, Army Headquarters, India, *A Study of the Existing Strategical Conditions on the North-West Frontier of India* (1909; Simla: Government Monotype Press, revised to 1912), pt. 2, p. 56.

Amid the committee's deliberations, the North-West Frontier, as noted above, exploded in the largest concerted resistance to British rule since the 1857 rebellion. The disastrous mass impressment that then commenced sealed the fate of the Low and Kennedy transport system. In the chapters that follow, I explore the government's deliberations over transport reform, the inauguration of a wholly new transport scheme, and the subsequent transformation of animal life in the Punjab into something that looks, in hindsight, very much like a transport animal biopower regime.

CHAPTER 6

Indian Army Reform and the Creation of a Permanent Transport Establishment

Inquiries in Parliament and the turbulence caused on the ground by impressment forced the Government of India to deliberate further on remedying the disarray of transport in the British Indian Army. A new transport committee, chaired by Gen. G. E. L. S. Sanford, was appointed in 1898. In August of that year, Maj. Gen. P. J. Maitland, military secretary to the Government of India, communicated to Sanford the issues that required the committee's attention. Maitland explained that its purpose was to draw up a transport plan that would be economical and practical, and would thereby obviate the need for impressment of animals and their handlers. To help it proceed on this charge, Maitland indicated that the committee would have on hand the data, interviews, and initial recommendations of the Rawalpindi Transport Committee of the previous year, a history of Indian Army transport prepared by Gen. Edwin H. H. Collen, and all documents concerning transport available in the Military Department. He pointed out that certain aims had already been decided on, namely creation of both a peacetime establishment and a reserve system, but he added that questions about the legalization of impressment were outside the committee's purview.[1]

Apparently, the Sanford Transport Committee was told that impressment was not to be its concern because, as Collen's report had made clear, there were differing opinions among officials concerning the legality of impressment.

1. IOR/L/MIL/7/6688: *Report of the Transport Committee, 1898* (Simla: Government Central Press, 1899), 1:i–ii. As an officer in the India Army's Intelligence Branch, Maitland had led the intelligence unit that was part of the Afghan Boundary Commission of 1885.

Rather than embroil the reconstituted transport committee in such matters, then, Maitland wanted attention focused on what a peacetime establishment and a reserve system ought to look like, including estimates of what it would cost the colonial state. Moreover, he pointed out that because a more robust transport corps would undoubtedly demand additional financial resources, whatever the committee recommended would require approval in London.

Let me begin with the materials that the Sanford committee had in hand. A review of the evidence collected by the Rawalpindi committee will help clarify its successor's final recommendations for addressing the key issues noted by Maitland, and how it envisioned creating an economical and practical transport system. These developments are discussed in the second half of the chapter.

RAWALPINDI TRANSPORT COMMITTEE, 1896–97

Presided over by Septimus Thornburn, the Rawalpindi Transport Committee was constituted on 28 October 1896 and completed part of its report the following April. The materials it gathered, later placed at the disposal of the Sanford committee, were substantial. In addition to records presented in chapter 2 concerning sarwans and chapter 5 involving animal collection and impressment, they included a number of memoranda and communications between different parts of the army and the colonial civil establishment, as well as printed minutes, dispatches, and appendices totaling over four hundred pages. A précis preceded the report proper that framed the materials for readers. The authors of this summary, which included Maitland, made two key points at the outset. First, the Punjab had sufficient transport animals to meet a war on "a considerable scale." Second, the fundamental problem was not a want of animals but rather a complete "absence of organization" to deal with large-scale mobilizations of animals and men.[2] In the committee's report, these two points were supported by testimony, charts showing numbers of available animals in each district, and interviews with Indian officials in district and tahsil administrations about popular responses to various schemes the government might propose for a peacetime and a reserve system. In particular, the British were keen to find out what sorts of incentives would coax

2. IOR/L/MIL/7/6687: *Report of the Transport Committee, 1897* (Simla: Government Central Press, 1897); "Précis on Report of the Transport Committee, Rawal Pindi, 1897, Relating to Impressment of Transport," 29th July 1897, 6. The précis was written by F. G. Cardew, E. deBarth, and Maitland.

animal owners into a trained reserve corps. In what follows, I will address the main conclusions drawn by the 1897 committee and then take up native officials' assessments of some of the proposals that were put before them.

Summary Conclusions

Given the central importance of impressment for the existing transport scheme, the Rawalpindi committee prefaced its findings by noting that in all provinces of British India other than the Punjab, codes were in place that made impressment legal.[3] A similar code, designed to deal with the special conditions of the Punjab, was thus recommended (70). In conjunction with the code, the committee added, a transport animal registration scheme was also needed, one that should then be extended throughout India. Registered animals fit for service could be branded, making them easily identifiable if calling them up were to become necessary. Branding itself might be encouraged by compensation of Rs. 6 a year to the owners, plus exemption from *begár* (unpaid labor; 71–72).

Administratively, registration should be organized within at least four circles, one each around Delhi, Lahore, Rawalpindi, and Derajat, with Inspecting Transport Officers (ITOs) in charge of each area, aided by one or two assistants. In addition to registering and branding pack animals, the ITOs could set allotment figures for each district, ones that would be fairly distributed among households based on size and number of animals, thus ensuring that the poorest households were not overly exploited. The committee also envisioned that under certain circumstances, mainly those of large-scale mobilization, collection and passing stations might still be necessary (74–75). But with proper planning, and organization wholly in the hands of the army, members suggested that collection could be done in a less disruptive way than in the past. In other words, there would still be a role for civilian district and tahsil officials, but essentially only during emergencies.

The précis then turned its attention to a reserve system. Such a scheme, if of sufficient size, might obviate the need for impressment except under the most unusual conditions. The key to an effective reserve, the committee thought, was to guarantee the involvement of trained sarwans. It suggested that inexperienced young men from the "jungles" be recruited and trained at a new school to be established at Multan. Once trained, the sarwans would be

3. IOR/L/MIL/7/6687: *Report of the Transport Committee, 1897*. Hereafter, I cite the page numbers of the summary in the text.

registered and paid an annual fee of Rs. 18, with each sarwan and his family also exempted from *begár*. The committee cautioned, however, that

> regular reserves from men on the Government establishment cannot be formed until the present status and conditions of service of Government transport attendants are improved, and until they are subjected to military discipline and recruited from better classes. (79)

Improvement of conditions meant several things for the committee. First, it involved abolishing the use of transport agents and their minions (W. M. Hailey had referred to these agents as "harpies"), thus eliminating what was recognized as one of the more pronounced evils of the existing system. These private contractors had tended to gather up any and all animals and people, regardless of their qualifications for transport service. The second concern was the means of attracting experienced sarwans into service. The committee thought that candidates should be offered pensions and gratuities, on identical pay scales as applied to the regular army when called up for service, as well as furloughs on the same terms as native troops, without needing to provide substitutes. Discipline could be enforced by covering sarwans under the Indian Army Articles of War and by enlisting them from the same classes of people from which the Indian Army recruited. Lastly, sarwans and their animals should all be organized into troops of the same size and structure. Presumably, this last would involve a separate ranked military hierarchy, with commanding officers and noncommissioned officers serving above and supervising each of the reserve units (79).

These recommendations were in keeping with views that had been circulating since at least the early 1880s, many of which, as noted earlier, had been repeated in a group of essays that appeared in the *Journal of the United Service Institution of India* in 1896. But why did the committee and the essayists think that such a system might work? Change on this order would, after all, depend on the cooperation of landowners and herders, who had not fared well during the Indian Army's adventures on the North-West Frontier and in Afghanistan. For an answer to that question, we need to explore the native officials' responses to the government's desire to create a transport reserve.

Native Testimony on a Proposed Reserve Scheme

The people questioned by the Rawalpindi Transport Committee were from all the key districts in the Punjab. Almost everyone was either a military or a civil official. In the latter case, the largest group was Tahsildars (revenue collectors in tahsils), while a few others had experience at the district level. At least two were landowners who raised camels.[4] The officials were asked three basic questions: (1) how would camel owners respond to a registration scheme and the branding of their animals; (2) would owners be willing to enter service with their animals: and (3) what incentives might help induce them to do so? These questions were, from virtually any perspective, the key issues if the government was ever going to eliminate impressment.

In general, most responded that they thought owners would comply with government orders. But there were a few caveats. Some thought, for example, that Baluchi herders, the primary camel breeders of the region, would be uninterested in any scheme that committed themselves and their animals to a permanent system. In other cases, they pointed out, owners might be reluctant to register their animals for fear they would be unable to sell them afterward. Since all agreed that the central issue for owners was the possibility that they might be forced to accompany their animals into the field, traveling perhaps a great distance from their homes, respondents thought that owners might interpret registration of the animal as registration of themselves (216). Similar reservations were raised concerning the branding of animals (217).

On the other hand, several, such as Mirza Sultan Ahmed, a Tahsildar in Multan with prior service in Jhang and Lahore, suggested that although there might be resistance to registration and branding, the colonial state could do certain things to persuade owners to participate. For one, the state could enroll the aid of local luminaries to encourage people to come forward. Such appeals could be enhanced with positive rewards, such as exemption from *begár*, monthly stipends, and free grazing on government *rahks* (government-controlled forest reserves). Grazing issues, in fact, were mentioned by a number of the other respondents, and regarded as a critical incentive for some owners because of the recent reduction of grazing land due to the expansion of the Chenab canal colony (218–19, 223–24). Others, such as Yar Mahommed of Musaffargarh, thought that no incentive would work. He recalled that the people of his district had refused the good rates of hire offered during the Chitral campaign, so it was likely that few would be enticed now. He added that most had a greater fear of death in the military transport service and the consequent breakup of their homes and families than they had of government

4. IOR/L/MIL/7/6687: *Report of the Transport Committee, 1897*, appendix D (211–28); page references are cited in the text. In chapter 2, I used the testimony of these men to provide a sense of camel ownership across the Punjab and for observations about the means of training sarwans.

sanctions (220). This view was supported by others, who added that people would rather sell their animals than serve with them, especially small holders who had only one or two animals (221–22).

These negative to lukewarm assessments of the government's solutions for transport problems probably came as something of a shock to colonial officials, especially those who had deluded themselves into thinking that the Chitral rates of hire had generally been accepted by Punjabis. On the other hand, officials like Thornburn simply may have been unconcerned about what the colonial subjects thought. In his estimation, "reasons of state" were objective facts requiring no justification or explanation. But for someone like Mirza Sultan Ahmed, who seemed to see that impressment was experienced as despotic power, the issue was much more about how the government could persuade large- and small-scale owners of animals to willingly participate in a new scheme. Although there is little known about this elder official beyond what appears in the colonial records, he seems to have been one of the few who felt compelled to follow up on his testimony before the Rawalpindi Transport Committee. On 11 March 1897—that is, before the outbreaks on the frontier and another round of impressment—he submitted a letter to the committee in which he outlined his understanding of the central problems the government faced.

For Ahmed, the active and passive resistance of animal owners could be attributed to the coercion of impressment, especially its arbitrary exploitation of the weak and the poor. Hence, it was no surprise that the less powerful would run off with their animals and hide in the jungles; or that those wealthy enough would make payoffs to corrupt animal collectors to avoid impressment of their own animals. Ahmed's proposed solution to the trauma of impressment was gradual incremental change designed to build trust and to win over the population, and he advocated procedures that followed the rule of simple justice. To begin, the government needed to eliminate middlemen (agents, contractors, and procurers)—who were the source of so many abuses—and go directly to *zamindars* (large landowners and landlords) and camel owners to seek their assistance. In this way, small holders would be "saved" from molestation, and those who had abandoned raising animals would return to it. Such an approach, he argued, would not only enhance trust in government but also increase the number of pack animals in the province. Once such trust had been established, the government could then implement a registration scheme that people would support, one that would bring sarwans and their animals into a reserve system voluntarily. Over time, their participation could be ensured by exemption from unpaid labor and the granting of stipends. Meanwhile, through registration, the state would have an unambiguous accounting of the animals and men available for mobilization at any one time (231–32).

But perhaps the most important advice from Ahmed involved his conviction that in order for any new program to succeed, it must be built on the indigenous power structures from the village level up. This meant patronage in one form or another of village headmen and *maliks* (hereditary leaders) as well as the strengthening of the Tahsildars' authority. It also meant investing resources in getting the state's message to the rural people. As he put it, "The intentions of Government should be clearly made known to the public, and the concessions agreed upon should be printed in Urdu and Hindi and distributed . . . , after which a European military officer should commence the work in each district" (232). In sum, Mirza Sultan Ahmed asserted that the essential question was one of trust: the government needed to build confidence before it could proceed. Once trust was established, a well-defined system with clear lines of authority could be put in place and assured by assigning military officers to local points of contact with area leaders and animal owners.

To Ahmed's seemingly sound assessment of the problems and possible solutions a more permanent transport system faced can be added the additional testimony of other respondents. One of these, Chaudri Aurangzeb Khan, the assistant colonization officer in the Chenab canal colony, brought up the question of pack animal breeding. As was discussed in chapter 3, problems with mule breeding in the Punjab had become evident to the Civil Veterinary Department by the time the transport committee met in 1897–98. Khan thought he had a solution to address shortages in horse and pack animal breeding: he suggested using land grants in the new canal colonies as incentives for breeding or keeping such animals. Plots could be offered, on the condition that the colonists raised camels or kept a mare for horse or mule breeding. And he was particularly keen on directing grants to the nomadic Balochis. He imagined that sedentary Balochi villages would emerge over time, and they would become centers of camel breeding as well as of sarwan recruitment. In addition, he suggested that *takavi* or government loans be offered as incentives for those without the resources to buy a camel. Part of the monetary support for such a program could come from taxing owners who were not part of the reserve scheme. Additional camels might be bred, Khan thought, by maintaining a breeding stock of females at Tahsildar headquarters and allowing them to graze in nearby government *rakhs* (233–34).

It should be clear from this review that the solicitation of native opinion provided key elements that were incorporated in the recommendations of the Rawalpindi committee. Indian officials from the Punjab offered substantial advice on how to win native support, and they outlined the incentives that might be required to induce animal owners' participation in the transport program. Khan had even suggested a scheme that would join regional improvement projects to the needs of the army. Land grants keyed to maintaining cavalry horses and pack animals seemed to him to offer a way to channel a regular stream of animal and human recruits into a reserve transport service while also addressing the troubling problem of the nomad amid colonial modernity. The Balochis would be transformed into farmers and accessible experts in animal husbandry, whereas the sons of the land grantees would find a place and a certain status within an overlapping military structure. In this way, the commercialization of the Punjab economy and the militarization of its agrarian population would proceed in tandem. It is no small irony that the conceptual framework for such a "modernizing" transformation came from an indigenous Muslim official. But perhaps this was because Khan's recommendations were a variation on a Mughal theme, one that had worked well for Britain's imperial predecessors. When something like this structure was finally implemented, the British would even adopt the Mughal term *Silladar* to refer to its reserve cavalry and camel corps units.

SANFORD TRANSPORT COMMITTEE, 1898–99

Partly as a result of the military outbreaks of 1897–98 and perhaps also because of the insensitive comments of Septimus Thornburn at the same time regarding impressment, the questions confronting army reformers subtly changed. The new Sanford Transport Committee agreed with its predecessor that army transport must be placed on a "military basis, with properly trained and disciplined establishments," and that a registration scheme making animals visible and open to inspection by transport officers was desirable.[5] But the committee also had to deal with the fact that multiple outbreaks like those that had just occurred would pose strategic and tactical challenges for the British Indian Army that required careful consideration.

The army officers who made up the committee looked back over the last quarter century of Indian Army campaigns and concluded that any new transport organization had to have the capacity to deal with three situations simultaneously. It had to be capable of supporting a field force the size of the Chitral expedition while also enabling movable columns both to function along the North-West Frontier and to safeguard lines of communication

5. IOR/L/MIL/7/6688: *Report of the Transport Committee, 1898*, 1:68.

into Afghanistan. Presumably working with equations to be found in the field service regulations for supply and transport,[6] the committee estimated that 17,484 mules and 21,541 camels would be needed to fulfill these requirements.[7] The numbers were based on standard carrying weights, in place by 1887, of 2 maunds[8] for mules and ponies, 5 maunds for camels, and 10 to 12 maunds for bullock carts. Should a campaign in Afghanistan extend from two to three months, an additional 115,000 five-maund animals (camels) would be required; and 230,000 if the campaign extended for longer. Recognizing that these were rather staggering numbers, the committee noted that if the government was unwilling to take the necessary steps to finance such a military transport organization, the Indian Army ought to be reduced in size and its mission modified.[9]

If, however, the government remained committed to the size and mission of the Indian Army, which included the capacity to deploy forces outside South Asia, then a few basic things needed to be done. First and foremost, the committee argued, an infrastructure to facilitate rapid mobilization must be built. Supply depots linked by rail at key points like Peshawar, Rawalpindi, Jhelum,

6. These equations calculated the number of animals required to carry *x* amount of supplies over given distances. The calculations were based on the employment of stages on a line of communication. Convoys of animals would carry their loads a certain distance, at which point supplies should be transferred to fresh animals. See IOR/L/MIL/17/5/752: *Field Service Manual for Commissariat and Transport Officers of the Indian Army* (Simla: Commissary-General-in-Chief, 1887), 55–59, for the various mathematical equations used by transport officers.

7. IOR/L/MIL/7/6688: *Report of the Transport Committee, 1898*, 1:68.

8. On animal carrying weights, see *Field Service Manual for Commissariat and Transport Officers of the Indian Army*, 55. *Field Service Regulations, India (Provisional Edition)* (Calcutta: Superintendent of Government Printing, India, 1906) adds material about the marching pace of different transport animals and the space taken up on a road by a standard single-file column of transport animals (11).

9. The fact that these figures are so precise indicates that there were officers within the Quartermaster General's Department who were perfectly aware of the enormous number of transport animals required to sustain an Afghan invasion. This ought to have influenced thinking about the possibility of a Russian invasion of India, which would have required a far greater number of animals to combat the tsar's army. But this did not seem to be a consideration between the 1880s and 1914. On the controversy surrounding war planning and strategic thinking in India, see John Gooch, *The Plans of War: The General Staff and British Military Strategy, c. 1900–1916* (London: Routledge and Kegan Paul, 1974), 219–23; and James Hevia, *The Imperial Security State: British Colonial Knowledge and Empire-Building in Asia* (Cambridge: Cambridge University Press, 2012), 164–72.

and Shapur[10] were essential, as was pushing light rail lines further west toward the passes leading into Afghanistan. Second, the government would have to commit resources to the creation of a permanent active-duty transport corps backed up by a substantial reserve. Ideally, the latter would be composed of reserve cadres made up of trained sarwans enlisted in the army, along with pack animals organized through a mandatory registration system managed and inspected by trained transport officers.[11]

With respect to camel transport, the committee recommended the formation of reserve or Silladar units, each composed of 356 sarwans and 1,068 camels. In order for these units to change rapidly from peacetime to wartime service, sarwans and their camels would be required to train annually and occasionally participate in large-scale maneuvers. To accomplish this goal, the committee suggested a rotational system in which one-third of the sarwans and animals were on active service for part of the year while the others remained in their districts. It envisioned eighteen such units, or a total of 19,224 camels, upon mobilization. On the mule side of the transport establishment, it recommended that 19,512 mules be formed into an active-service corps for immediate use, and that a reserve of 2,244 be established.[12] The proposed structure thus reflected the Indian Army's greater faith in the mule. But it also indicated that few could contemplate a scheme that did not include a substantial number of camels, at least when full mobilization was required.

But how should the army get camel owners to buy into this scheme, especially given the doubts of native officers that had appeared in the Rawalpindi report? The Sanford committee decided that firm guarantees of compensation for deceased or disabled animals should be a basic starting point. But it also recognized that more incentive was needed. In addressing this issue, the committee adopted Chaudri Aurangzeb Khan's proposal to link a pack animal reserve with the canal colonies. "Whenever Government wastelands are brought under cultivation by the opening of new canals," it argued, "a condition should be attached to every grant of land to the effect that the grantee must keep up a specified number of camels or mules fit for transport."[13]

10. In addition to having some of the transport units based at the four corps centers, the committee recommended that subestablishments be created at Ferozepore, Jhang, Montgomery, Multan, Muzaffargarh, Dera Ismail Khan, Dera Ghazi Khan, and Hissar and in the Sind at Karachi and Hyderabad (IOR/L/MIL/7/6688: *Report of the Transport Committee, 1898*, 1:72).

11. Ibid., 74–76.

12. Ibid., 71.

13. Ibid., 76. For additional discussion of these grants, see Imran Ali, *The Punjab under Imperialism, 1885–1947* (Princeton, NJ: Princeton University Press, 1988), 123–51. Ali is perhaps

What the committee was calling for, in effect, was the expansion of an existing program (one that mirrored earlier Mughal patronage of mansabdars) that gave preferential land grants in areas where canals were built to the "martial races" within the Indian Army.[14] These populations were not only seen as desirable for army recruitment, but now also as made up of the kind of men who would provide reliable camel and mule drivers. Moreover, from the army's perspective, making the ownership of future land grants conditional upon ownership of pack animals not only expanded the military's role in what was understood to be a commercial land development project, but further entrenched the processes through which the North-West Frontier was becoming a militarized bastion protecting India's western flank. Like the German frontier of the Roman Empire, the Punjab was being transformed into an area experiencing military colonization in depth.[15]

Having laid out a rationale for a substantially larger transport corps, the committee then turned its attention to the question of animal registration. It thought that registration should be mandatory, but that owners ought to be told that their animals would primarily be used on lines of communication. The registration staff would periodically inspect registered animals, note changes in ownership, seek new sources of transport, and familiarize themselves with animals used on trade routes. Registration officers might share their records with civil officials, but they were clearly to be in charge of registration down to the lowest levels of the districts. They would also make themselves known to recruiting officers and use the existing system to enlist sarwans.[16]

To facilitate the effective movement of the reserve animals to the depots and forward areas, the committee suggested the formation of a rail corps, which, as in the German army, could take command and control of traffic on rail lines when mobilization had been ordered.[17] Military command of rail lines in time of war would not only expedite troop and supply deployment but obviate the kind of mistreatment of animals that had been reported by Capt. Brooke-Murray. Lastly, the committee stated the obvious—for the new estab-

---

the first scholar to explore the relation between expansion of the Indian Army transport corps, land grants, and the militarization of the Punjab.

14. Rajit K. Mazumder, *The Indian Army and the Making of the Punjab* (Delhi: Permanent Black, 2003), 67–68, 130–38. Also see Ali on "soldier settlement" in *The Punjab under Imperialism*, 110–23.

15. See Edward N. Luttwak, *The Grand Strategy of the Roman Empire: From the First Century A.D. to the Third* (Baltimore: Johns Hopkins University Press, 1976), 130–45.

16. IOR/L/MIL/7/6688: *Report of the Transport Committee, 1898*, 1:74–76.

17. Ibid., 78–79.

lishment to function effectively, it required trained personnel, from transport and registration officers through noncommissioned officers, administrative staff, and camel sarwans, mule drivers, and pony and bullock attendants. And with such changes, the committee concluded, a new name for the unit ought to be found—perhaps the Military Service Corps or Supply and Transport Corps.[18]

The Sanford Report, far more forcefully than that of the Rawalpindi committee, made clear that the watchword was *military*; any new transport system must be organized on *military* lines, which meant professionalizing each of its components, creating a uniform command structure, and introducing British military discipline to animals and their handlers who enlisted in the transport reserve. The implication of this professional militarization of pack animal life was that the entire transport system, including the means and methods of acquiring transport animals, would be in the hands of the army.

THE HORSE AND MULE BREEDING COMMISSION

The assertion by the transport committees that there were more than enough transport animals in the Punjab and the Sind was somewhat disingenuous. Recall that the Civil Veterinary Department, in charge of horse and mule breeding for the cavalry and transport respectively, had long been unable to supply enough cavalry horses and transport mules to the army. With respect to mule breeding, it would seem that there were two difficulties that the colonial state faced. One involved the problems attendant upon relying on an outsourcing system, which supposedly involved the free service of government studs and the purchase, at periodic fairs throughout the Punjab, of the mules so produced. The number of mules available in these markets proved, however, to be either insufficient in number or unobtainable because army purchasers found themselves outbid by native dealers. The other issue was the dominance of American agents buying up prime donkey studs in southern Europe. The combination of these two factors often resulted in chronic shortages of ordnance mules in particular, necessitating the ongoing quest for other sources of supply. As we saw in chapter 3, the shortages were addressed by importing mules from the United States, Argentina, and China. But this did not mean that the Army Remount Department wanted to see mule-breeding operations in India abandoned.

In order to gain a better understanding of military animal breeding issues,

18. Ibid., 79.

in 1900 the India Office appointed an independent commission to investigate current breeding schemes and recommend improvements. The commission was made up of British and Indian Army officers, as well as one civilian, Lord Arthur Cecil,[19] who had succeeded Charles Leslie Sutherland as the procurer of European donkey studs for India. After spending several weeks touring breeding farms, inspecting animals at depots, and visiting horse and mule fairs, the commission made several key suggestions. First, after concluding that the Civil Veterinary Department was unable to manage horse and mule breeding adequately, the commissioners urged the creation of a single breeding authority wholly within the British Indian Army. They also saw this as a means of reducing or ending the purported friction between the Army Remount and the Civil Veterinary Departments. Second, because they had determined that the mules bred in India from imported donkey sires were of high quality, commissioners recommended a greater investment in breeding donkey sires in India, using imported donkeys. Third, they urged that in order to achieve the latter, a stud farm be established in India expressly for raising donkey sires. Fourth, they proposed that the mule-breeding operations be concentrated in those areas of the Punjab where mule production was known to be popular. Fifth, the commissioners were concerned that mules were being bought at fairs, and put to work, much too young. They urged that the government buy up more of these mules and nurture them on breeding farms before setting them to work. Lastly, the commission urged that mule breeding be connected to the government's ambitious canal-building projects in the Indus River basin.[20] These recommendations were essentially put into place. A donkey stud program was begun at the government cattle-breeding farm at Hissar in 1903.[21] Over the next several years, the farm produced a small number of donkey studs, as well as mules, from the eleven sires on hand. But in one significant respect, the recommendations of the commission were almost immediately undermined by an unforeseen event.

In another corner of the British Empire, a vicious war had broken out in South Africa between Boer settlers and the British colonial state. Between 1899 and 1902, some 326,000 horses and over 50,000 mules perished in the

19. The half-brother of Lord Salisbury, foreign secretary and prime minister in a succession of Conservative cabinets at the end of the nineteenth century, Cecil was devoted to the improvement of equine stock in Britain, which he pursued on his estate in Kent.

20. IOR/L/MIL/17/TN 544: *Report of the Horse and Mule Breeding Commission, 1900–1901*, 20–21, 36–38, 62–63.

21. *The Imperial Gazetteer of India* (Oxford: Clarendon Press, 1908), 3:89.

conflict. After initial losses, a global scramble for replacements of both horses and mules ensued; this was reminiscent of a similar scramble to replace pack animals after the major losses in Afghanistan in 1879.[22] In the case of South Africa, however, the net was cast empirewide and beyond, sweeping up animals in Britain and North America as well as in British colonies. Frederick Smith, the veterinary surgeon discussed in chapter 4 who served throughout the Boer War, referred to the great loss of animal life as a "holocaust."[23] Unsurprisingly, the scale of loss in South Africa was attributed to a complete absence of organization and knowledge of animals. Many died much as the plains camels of India had—they were unable to acclimate to their new environment.[24] And although no one seems to have blamed the horses for their own deaths, these staggering losses only increased the reproductive pressures on pony and horse populations in India.

THE VICEROY'S COUNCIL AND THE REQUEST FOR PERMISSION TO RECONSTITUTE ARMY TRANSPORT

The rhetorical flourish that called for a downsizing of the army should the government find it unfeasible to fund the establishment recommended by the Sanford committee was, apparently, an empty gesture in a report that otherwise was a robust wish list with which others could tinker. Once in the hands of the viceroy, Lord George Curzon, and his council of advisors, the program of the committee report was deemed neither economical nor practical, and was itself downsized and reformulated. The key issue, as always, was the amount of money the colonial government felt it could commit to maintaining a permanent establishment as well as the amount Parliament would sanction. In other words, Curzon and his council had to convince the secretary of state for India in London of the necessity for change and argue for the expenditure of resources to reorganize. Other grand plans for army reform had foundered in the past precisely on contested questions of necessity and cost.[25]

22. The United States alone shipped some seventy-six thousand horses and mules to South Africa between October 1899 and January 1901; see US House of Representatives, Doc. no. 498, 56th Cong., 2nd Sess. (1901).

23. Frederick Smith, *A Veterinary History on the War in South Africa, 1899–1902* (London: H. W. Brown, 1919).

24. See the pathbreaking essay by Sandra Swart: "Horses in the South African War, c. 1899–1902," *Society and Animals* 18, no. 4 (2010): 348–66.

25. For example, in 1881, George Robinson, First Marquess of Ripon, the viceroy of India, submitted a lengthy report to the secretary of state for India, Spencer Cavendish, Lord Har-

Having digested the results of the Rawalpindi and Sanford Transport Committee reports over the course of a year, along with the recommendations of Edwin Collen, the military member of the viceroy's council, Curzon was prepared in early fall 1900 to present a case to the secretary of state for India, Lord George Hamilton. The memorandum to Hamilton began with the issue that had drawn so much attention in Parliament, the impressment of pack animals. The transport crisis during the Chitral expedition had demonstrated, Curzon and his council argued, the "inadequacy" of existing arrangements while disclosing the "many" evils resulting from hasty collection of large numbers of animals "without proper supervision and adequate control."[26] The memorandum moved on to summarize the findings of the two transport committees. The Rawalpindi committee, whose charge had been to consider impressment, concluded that compulsion was necessary, if animals were to be either bought or hired in time of crisis. And while the committee collected a substantial amount of testimony and material beyond its brief, and formulated a recommendation for reorganization, it had accepted, despite the distress that coercion caused owners and animals, the principle of impressment (1). Yet the campaigns of 1897–98 added, as if it were needed, additional proof of the evils of impressment, particularly that the practice resulted in the collection of inferior animals and the hiring of untrained attendants (2).

The Sanford committee that followed had a different charge, Curzon noted. It was to formulate a scheme to place the transport service of the Indian Army on a "sound footing" (ibid.). This meant considering the probable transport requirements of a "field army" (the portion of the army in India designated for mobilization) "as the primary basis of calculation." Since the field army, the Sanford committee surmised, was "intended to take the field rapidly and in an efficient condition, and to be maintained there in a position to strike effectively, it must be provided with sufficient transport suitably organized" (ibid.). In other words, regardless of its initial charge, the committee, in emphasizing

---

tington, produced by the Indian Army Reorganization Commission of 1879. The committee was formed before the Second Afghan War, and was thus able to draw from the experience of only the First Afghan War (1839–42), particularly with respect to transport, to make a case for reorganization of what were then the armies of the three Indian presidencies, Bombay, Madras, and Bengal, and those of the Punjab. After consultation with the War and India Office Military Department as well as retired officers with experience in India, Hartington rejected the proposal; see IOR/L/MIL/7/5445: *Report of the Army Reorganization Commission*, 1883. Hartington's final dispatch on the matter is dated 26 July 1883.

26. IOR/L/MIL/7/6702: Viceroy and Council to Lord Hamilton, 13th September 1900, 1. Page references to this memorandum are cited in the text unless otherwise indicated.

rapid deployment, effective strikes, and sufficient animals to carry out these objectives, was in fact drawing attention to the host of frictions that impressment and poor organization had engendered in time of crisis.

Curzon and his committee then explained that in exploring alternatives, the Sanford committee had offered a solution whose structure promised to make impressment a thing of the past. It recommended a robust and professional transport organization large enough to obviate the need for additional animals except under conditions of prolonged campaigns, such as an extended occupation of Afghanistan. But since most operations involved policing actions along the frontier, with only occasional multiple outbreaks like the ones that had occurred in 1897–98, the committee's proposal could be understood to address two of the three missions of the Indian Army—that is, mounting an expedition the size of the Chitral campaign and supplying movable columns along the North-West Frontier.

The committee's recommendations had been passed on for further evaluation to William Lockhart, the commander-in-chief of the Indian Army, and Gen. Collen. While both were in general agreement with the Sanford committee, they thought that it would be difficult to make others, presumably officials in London, recognize the need for such a large peacetime establishment. There was also concern that the financial resources of India would be unable to meet the expenditure involved (4). As a result, Lockhart and Collen recommended reductions.

With the support of the army command, the viceroy's council was now offering a scaled-back alternative consistent with a new frontier strategy, which Curzon had put in place the previous year. Convinced that forward fortified outposts in the mountains on the Afghan frontier were both indefensible and provocations to the mountain tribes, Curzon had troops withdrawn from these positions and concentrated in the rear. He had then organized mobile flying columns that could be expeditiously deployed in case of a conflict, and built outposts near key passes that were linked with the rear by light rail lines. Drawing from Sir Robert Sandeman's book on frontier administration, Curzon had British political officers introduce a "tribal service system," including the creation of local militias and trained units under the command of British officers. Finally, he restructured the administration of the frontier by creating a new province.[27]

With these cost-cutting elements in the management of frontier security

27. For Curzon's memorandum on military reform and India Office approval of his plan, see East India (North-West Frontier), Parliamentary Papers regarding British Relations with the

approved by London and having been put in place, Curzon sent the particulars of the new transport scheme to Lord Hamilton on 13 September 1900. Two months later, a response was received granting permission to proceed as requested.[28] The centerpiece of the peacetime structure to back up the new frontier strategy was thus to be an active-duty mule corps composed of 12,800 mules, with their establishment and drivers to be located at eleven depots based in Peshawar, Rawalpindi, Mian Mir, Umballa, Lucknow, Bareilly, Meerut, Bangalore, Poona, Mhow, and Quetta.[29] The preexisting mule units accompanying the frontier forces in the Punjab and Burma, some 6,000 animals in all, remained in place.[30] In addition, two camel corps, each composed of 1,068 animals, were to be created with full establishment of personnel, equipment, and sarwans.[31] For all practical purposes, these numbers were not substantially different from those of the early 1880s. The real change involved the reserve or cadre units of mules and camels.

In simple terms, these units fulfilled the desires of Lt. Edmund George Barrow for an establishment made up of trained men rather than trained animals. The idea governing the reserve was to create a military structure that could expand in an orderly fashion upon mobilization. As an example, the pack-mule cadre was organized as follows:

Establishment of a Pack-Mule Cadre
1 British officer
*2 subdivisional commanders (British warrant officers)
*1 sergeant-major (British noncommissioned officer)

Neighbouring Tribes of the North-West Frontier of India and Frontier Administration (London: Harrison and Sons, 1901): 115–21; on administrative reform, see pp. 121–50.

28. IOR/L/MIL/7/6704: Supply and Transport Corps, increase of subordinates.

29. The actual number of mule corps that would be created is not mentioned in the dispatch. Moreover, there were two different sizes of mule corps planned—one for infantry made up of 840 mules, the other for cavalry composed of 936 mules. If there were three mule corps for mobile cavalry units, enough would remain of the 12,800 to provide a corps of 840 for each of the eleven depots. See IOR/L/MIL/7/6702: Viceroy to Lord Harrington. Also see Maj. R. E. Vaughn, "The Transport Service in India," *JUSII* 35 (1906): 287, for the number and size of units.

30. These included camel and mule units with the Corps of Guides, the Sixty-Seventh Punjabis, the Fifty-Eighth Rifles, the Fourteenth Sikhs, and Eighty-Fourth Punjabis, and Supply and Transport units at Bannu and Dera Ismail Khan; see *Report of the Veterinary Officer Investigating Camel Diseases for the Year Ending 31st March 1909* (Simla: Government Central Branch Press, 1909), 3.

31. IOR/L/MIL/7/6702: Viceroy and Council to Lord Hamilton, 13th September 1900, 5.

*1 quartermaster sergeant (British noncommissioned officer)
*1 quartermaster *duffadar* (native noncommissioned officer)
*9 *kot-duffadars* (native noncommissioned officers, 8 of whom each commanded a troop of 96 mules, 1 for the depot troop)
4 *naicks* (corporals; head of a subdivision of 48 mules)
48 lance *naicks* (lance corporals; driver and head of a section of 12 mules)
144 drivers (130 to be drawn from reserve upon mobilization)
7 *syces* (attendants)
192 mules (two complete troops of 96; 648 additional to be purchased upon expansion)
14 ponies (for those personnel marked by an asterisk)
2 clerks
1 veterinary assistant (3 additional drawn from reserve on expansion)
1 shoeing smith (1 additional drawn from reserve)
4 saddlers (14 additional drawn from reserve)
1 carpenter
4 blacksmiths
4 hammer men
4 bellows boys

This is exactly the same structure as that of a full complement of an active-duty mule corps. Each of the latter was composed of 768 mules divided into sections, and 72 additional as a depot reserve used for replacements in the field and for training purposes. There were to be twelve pack-mule cadre units, which when expanded would provide 10,080 mules. Hence, upon full mobilization the army would have had available 22,880 mules in twenty-three corps. Equally significant, all the units would be made up of trained officers, noncommissioned officers, and qualified mule drivers.

With the exception of the British noncommissioned officers and, of course, the blacksmith establishment, the camel corps units were quite similar in structure to those of the mule corps. There was, however, one significant difference. The great bulk of the camel transport was organized in the reserve, which itself was composed of three forms: the Silladar, the Grantee, and the hired or cadre corps.[32] The first of these, the Silladar, were to be organized around depots and were composed of 356 sarwans, each of whom was expected to be responsible for three camels. The sarwans were divided into three groups

32. See *Quarterly Indian Army List, July 1908* (Calcutta: Office of the Superintendent for Government Printing, 1908), 405a–f, for the names and numbers of these units.

and rotated through the depots with their camels for inspection and training at least once a year. The off-duty sarwans received a stipend for the inactive time. Meanwhile, they were able to carry on trade and other activities with their animals while off duty. According to Maj. R. E. Vaughn, assistant quartermaster general for transport, the estimate was that each of the Silladar corps could be fully operational in ten to fifteen days after a mobilization order had been issued.[33] The Grantee camel corps were four units drawn from the camel land grants in the Chenab canal colony. They trained locally and probably participated in some rotational scheme as well.

The last group, the hired camel cadre, was essentially a skeletal command and service artificer structure, with a complement of 268 registered and trained sarwans. When mobilized, each of the hired cadres would be composed of 972 camels. Taken together, the camel reserve was made up of thirteen corps of the Silladar and Grantee units, each of which contained 1,068 camels, or 13,884 camels in total; and nine hired cadres of 972 camels each, for a total of 8,748. Thus, the reserve in its multiple forms totaled 22,632 camels and some 7,832 sarwans. When added up, upon full mobilization the British Indian Army would have available 22,880 mules and 24,768 camels, with a professional staff of officers, noncommissioned officers, enlisted men, artificers, and one attendant for every three transport animals.

This vast assemblage was, moreover, organized into units with a recognizable military hierarchy of ranks, producing a clear and legible chain of command. The ranks themselves were made consistent with the army in general, with the sarwan/camel compound agent the lowest and most common military rank. Lastly, the human reserve was to be made up of individuals who were (1) from the better classes and (2) enlisted in the army. In this way, under military discipline, the evil of sweeping up a "motley assemblage" from the bazaars was held to be no longer an issue.

When the Government of India sent its transport reorganization request to London in September 1900, some of the implementation work had already been done. Curzon had informed Hamilton that a plan for the hired camel cadre was already formulated, and he had forwarded the details in October 1899.[34]

33. See Vaughn, "The Transport Service in India," 285. For the camel corps, Vaughn gives a figure of 972 camels. However, a 1900 report by the Government of India on the newly formed Silladar camel corps sets the figure at 1068; see IOR/L/MIL/7/6695: Registration and inspection of camels and formation of Camel Corps from grantees of land on the Chenab canal.

34. IOR/L/MIL/7/6692: Organization of transport animals purchased or hired upon mobilization, 1902–12.

The following month, he sent correspondence outlining a similar plan for the creation of the mule cadre units.[35] Then in February 1900, he sent Hamilton a plan for the structure of the Grantee camel units. The particulars of the latter scheme included the branding of each camel with the letter and serial number of its corps. Once established, the intent was to have district transport officers, the same men who were to be responsible for registering pack animals in the Punjab's districts, make inspection tours of the canal camels. In July of 1902, Curzon was happy to report to Hamilton that three corps had been formed and were used effectively in the Waziristan blockade.[36]

The last piece, and perhaps the most critical part, of the reserve structure was the registration system. The idea was to assign a transport officer to operate within a specific territory designated as a circle. Within his circle, he would not only register and enumerate animals but become familiar with breeders, transport agents, local officials, and animal owners themselves. Because the transport officer would be expected to be able to make personal contact with owners and potential sarwans, a colloquial knowledge of Urdu and Punjabi was highly desirable. The original estimate was that seventeen officers would be required, but an additional four were added once registration began in 1901.

Over the next few years, this ambitions plan for transforming army transport and professionalizing the service began to be put in place. During this time, British understanding of pack animals, and how they conceptualized them in relation to the organized labor they were to perform, was subtly shifting. Animal life became a subject of concern and study for various units whose responsibilities overlapped within the new organization. This structure included the Army Remount Department, whose officers formed the pool from which transport registration officers were chosen and which now had the responsibility of breeding mules and donkeys. It also involved veterinary surgeons, some in the Army Remount Department, the bulk of the others in the Civil Veterinary Department.

At the beginning of the twentieth century, the new transport structure took administrative shape. The Commissariat was made the sole unit responsible for all supply and transport of the Indian Army, and the separate units existing within the Madras, Bengal, and Bombay armies were eliminated. By 1902, the renamed Supply and Transport Corps had an officer with the rank of general as

35. IOR/L/MIL/7/6694: Formation of a reserve of mule drivers and artificers, 1899–1926.

36. IOR/L/MIL/7/6695: Registration and Inspection of Camels. A military blockade, or denial of access to the Punjab plain, was a standard form of punishment for recalcitrant tribes.

its director-general. Below him were two deputy directors, two assistant directors, nine inspector generals and deputy inspector generals, and 117 transport officers ranked from first to sixth class.[37] In addition to this staff, all of whom were to have had some professional training in newly established transport schools and veterinary colleges, there was a section of registration officers; by 1908 they were twenty-two in number.[38] These officers were responsible for registering acceptable pack animals throughout the Punjab and monitoring the animals on the grantee plots in the Chenab, Jhelum, and Lower Bari Doab canal colonies. In turn, the holders of colony plots were increasingly made up of pensioners, soldier-settlers, and ex-soldiers.[39] Through these mechanisms, relations between animal life, military recruiting, agricultural development, and administrative routinization were drawn. The Punjab had become the premier militarized border region in the British Empire.

37. See *Quarterly Indian Army List, July 1902* (Calcutta: Office of the Superintendent for Government Printing, 1902) under Supply and Transport Corps.

38. See *Quarterly Indian Army List, July 1908*, 405a.

39. Tan Tai Yong, *The Garrison State: The Military, Government and Society in Colonial Punjab, 1849–1947* (New Delhi: Sage Publications, 2005), 90.

CHAPTER 7

Animal Management, Canal Colonization, and the Ecological Transformation of the Punjab

The new transport organization outlined in the previous chapter marked a watershed in human-animal relations in the Punjab. This chapter explores the impact of the reformed transport system on the Indian Army, the farmers and animals of the Punjab, and the ecology of northwestern British India. These reforms not only ended the ad hoc nature of army transport but established an enduring bureaucratic structure of animal management that firmly situated pack animals in a new relationship to the colonial state. On the British side, the new order promised to make transport animal procurement an orderly and systematic process. The new structure contained a clear chain of military command and set of responsibilities located in the Supply and Transport Corps, the Army Remount Department, and the Army and Civil Veterinary units. For animal herders and the Punjabi peasantry, the new administrative structure entailed a well-defined set of obligations to the colonial government. These obligations would be further solidified with the passage of a law in 1903 that effectively legalized pack animal registration and impressment in the Punjab. This combination of administrative rigor and legal codification placed unprecedented powers into the hands of Remount Department officers and veterinary surgeons in and outside the army. Not only was this new transport organization a critical historical shift from earlier British policy, it was also a major deviation from the logistical practices of previous imperial regimes in India.[1]

1. The Mughal administration did have some sense of the numbers of animals in rural communities, but primarily for taxation purposes. See Mahdav Gadgil and Ramchandra Guha, *The Fissured Land* (Berkeley: University of California Press, 1992), 107.

Remount Department officers were authorized to manage pack animal populations throughout the Punjab and adjacent provinces. Their duties included the census and registration of animals owned by Punjabis and the management of all breeding operations for army cavalry horses and transport mules. These responsibilities sometimes included determining when mule-breeding donkey studs had become biologically unproductive. Those that were had to be put down. For their part, army veterinary surgeons became the final arbiters on the fitness of pack animals to serve in transport units and on field expeditions. They were also responsible for consolidating old and generating new knowledge to guide the management of military animals. Meanwhile, veterinarians assigned to the Civil Veterinary Department took on the responsibility of investigating animal diseases, often through unregulated methods of live-animal experimentation, in the British colonies in South and Southeast Asia. This combination of census, registration, biological management of populations, fitness evaluations, and knowledge production through scientific experimentation penetrated ever more deeply into militarized animal life in India; the ways in which it did so among humans governed by state apparatuses we have come to understand as biopower regimes.

Biopower is a term coined by Michel Foucault to describe new forms of power that emerged in eighteenth-century Europe, procedures of governance that gradually displaced the arbitrary rule of the sovereign. For the absolutist monarchs, sovereign power had been power over life and death; the king could take life or let live. In place of sovereign power, Foucault identified dual poles of development in "governmentality." The first of these poles centered on the individual human body—"its disciplining, the optimization of its capacities, the extortion of its forces, the parallel increase of its usefulness and its docility, its integration into systems of efficient and economic controls." All these elements he characterized as *disciplines*: an "anatomo-politics of the human body." The other pole focused on the species body, the body as the basis of biological processes, including "propagation, births and mortality, the level of health, life expectancy and longevity." The supervision of each of these life processes in populations was effected through various interventions and *regulatory controls*: a biopolitics of a population. Emerging together, the disciplinary and regulatory elements of an emergent governmentality produced what Foucault termed a biopower regime.[2] Such a regime certainly affected the pack animals of the Punjab: we might consider animal census, registration, and branding to be essential disciplinary techniques, while breeding

2. See Michel Foucault, *The History of Sexuality* (New York: Vintage Books, 1980), 1:139.

programs and the medicalization of pack animal life served as regulatory and generative controls that produced and transformed animal populations.

As a result of the administrative changes brought about by Lord George Curzon's implementation of the Sanford Transport Committee recommendations, with their new forms of intervention into animal life, the pack animals of the Punjab were no longer merely a random collection of forced laborers. Instead, they were remade in terms that had already been advocated in the 1880s by the editors of the *Quarterly Journal of Veterinary Science in India and Army Animal Management*. Camels, mules, ponies, donkeys, and bullocks were now valuable members of the British Indian Army transport service. And as army animal management systems now suggested, their lives were thrown open to inspection, measurement, classification, and organization in biological terms that continuously assessed reproductive success and physical fitness for labor. They would come to be understood, if not as individuals, then as knowable kinds and types, some of these having particularly useful traits for specific tasks and environmental conditions. Pack animals became creatures of determinable and calculable military value, much as the martial races of India had become accountable before them. The result was that animals and their human handlers, along with the martial races, found themselves embedded in a reorganized and increasingly professionalized imperial security regime.

It is the purpose of this chapter to explore this new order as it pertains to pack animals. Central to my concerns will be an evaluation of the impact on the region's ecology wrought by changes in army transport requirements and related state development projects. There is little question that as animals throughout the Punjab were refigured and reimagined as administrable units, the many hands of the colonial state penetrated deeper into the everyday lives of both the animals and the humans of the region. It is less clear, however, precisely what lasting structural effects this extension of state power had. One way of tracking such effects is through the annual administrative reports sent to Indian Army headquarters and the Punjab government. Such reporting, which sometimes contained comparisons of vital statistics over time (e.g., mortality, biological reproduction), became a fundamental aspect of the new order, parts of which were governed by innovative regulations and legal codes. At the same time, because responsibilities often overlapped or because the activities of one unit affected, sometimes negatively, those of others, these reports also expose some of the fault lines in colonial political and economic administration. I begin with the new legal order and some of its problems.

THE DISCIPLINARY AND REGULATORY ORDER OF PACK ANIMAL LIFE

In 1903, the government of the Punjab enacted the Military Transport Animals Act. The act required the registration of all transport animals in the province and authorized the appointment of transport registration officers to enumerate and inspect animals. The officers were to identify all able-bodied transport animals and their owners, list them on a register, and set the "true value" of each animal. Once value was established, owners could opt to have their animal branded. Such a sign indicated that the animal could only be purchased, not hired, at a time of mobilization. The branding system was meant to ensure a guaranteed number of animals at a prefixed price for any needed expansion of the cadre reserve units. Should impressment for hire become necessary, owners were required to appear before a committee that would set the animal's replacement value.

Aware of the owners' reluctance in 1897–98 to leave their homes on long expeditions, the framers of the act included a provision that, should an expedition leave India, the animal would be deemed government property, and appropriate compensation would be paid to the owner. Moreover, the act did not call for owners to accompany their animals into the field or to supply attendants. These duties would be shouldered by the reserve cadres. All owners had to do was register their animals and produce them when called on by the government. Should owners refuse to comply with the provisions of the act, however, a hefty fine of up to Rs. 50 could be levied. Possible breaches of the act included denying transport officers access to animals, obstructing in any form the registration procedure, falsely branding animals, and failing to produce a registered animal when called to do so.[3]

Now made legible to the colonial state in two distinct ways, by registration and a brand, pack animals became accessible to Remount Department officers for a lifetime of inspection. Moreover, the various mechanisms of the act that disciplined the bodies of pack animals and their owners seem to have been responses to the reservations expressed by native officials during the Rawalpindi Transport Committee's deliberations in 1897 about hiring and impressment. But the law contained two flaws from the outset. First, it indicated that local government would appoint the registration officers. Yet the

3. See Government of India, Legislative Department, *The Punjab and North-West Code*, 3rd ed. (Calcutta: Superintendent of Government Printing, 1903), 518–27.

Remount Department had already begun appointing registration officers and assigning them to specific regions of the Punjab. There were no provisions in the act to indicate how the civil and the military aspects of registration would work in practice or in tandem. Second, the act assumed, on the one hand, that rational owners would want to have their animals branded, thus removing any ambiguity over an animal's status should a mobilization be called for. On the other hand, the act recognized another version of rationality—fraud and/or avoidance of authorities—and called for stiff penalties. In so doing, the new legal code seemed to recognize an ongoing agonistic relation between Punjabi animal owners and the colonial state. Put another way, the law and its implementation were hardly the sort of trust-building gestures recommended by Mirza Sultan Ahmed (see chapter 7).

Yet the apparent contradictions embodied in this law were not immediately evident to administrators. Instead, from the point of view of some civilian officials it seemed to have resolved the greater contradiction: the fact that the Punjab legal code was out of step with laws in other parts of colonial India. Such uniformity and regularity across the space of empire were generally seen as an essential condition for improvement, be it in economic development or military security. Moreover, standardization of rules and practices in one field of activity was often seen to have effects in others. In the case of the Military Transport Animals Act, the routinization of registration and impressment regularized the relation between the military needs of the state and the duties and responsibilities of animal owners, especially those in the newly established canal colonies. But perhaps most significantly, the law supported and encouraged practices designed to intervene in and regulate pack animal lives.

*

The regulation of pack animal life is discernible in army paperwork. This paperwork not only monitored the activities of the new transport scheme but effectively produced it as a unitary program for the scrutiny of higher-level administrators. The pertinent documents took three basic forms: annual reports, army manuals, and army regulations. In what follows, I will discuss both the form and the content of such documents in order to provide a sense of how the regulatory elements of the animal biopower regime were functioning in the first decades of the twentieth century.

Annual Reports

Under the new regime, reports were generated annually by all the units involved in army logistics. These reports were organized through a more or less stable set of categories. In the case of pack animals, relevant reports were generated by the Army Remount Department, the Army Veterinary Corps, the Civil Veterinary Department, and the Supply and Transport Corps. The reports generally provided statistical information on personnel, purchase of replacement animals, breeding activities, diseases and injuries and their treatments, and wastage rates from year to year.[4]

The early *Administration Reports* of the Supply and Transport Corps, for example, began soon after the formation of the active and reserve corps of transport animals, and highlighted the central problem in the early years—a shortage of trained personnel.[5] These reports also kept track of the registration system after the passage of the Military Transport Animals Act, the failed effort to extend the camel reserve system into the area near Quetta, and the developing insight that extending the canal system in the Punjab's "wastelands," as the British mistakenly named them, effectively undermined the camel reserve units.[6] The reports also verified that despite an expanded mule-breeding program, Indian Army transport remained dependent on imports from China, Persia, and, after World War I, the United States for replenishing the mule corps.[7] In addition, the reports recorded a gradual rise in the mar-

4. The primary source for the annual reports discussed here is the India Office collection in the British Library, London. Extant administrative reports of the Supply and Transport Corps begin in 1899–1900 and continue through 1912–13. The Civil Veterinary Department of India's reports run from 1892 to 1911, but none afterward. The Army Veterinary Service's reports run from 1921 to 1944.

5. See IOR/L/MIL/7/6700, which contains the reports for 1901–4; IOR/L/MIL/7/6712, those from 1906 to 1910; and L/MIL/7/6730, those from 1911 to 1913. They are all entitled *Administration Report of the Supply and Transport Corps for the Official Year* . . . (such as 1904–5) and were printed, in most cases, in Simla at the Government Central Printing Office. In the citations that follow, I will indicate the file in which the reports appear and the year of publication, followed by a page number.

6. Updates on registration are in all the reports and indicate a continual state of improvement. On the failed Quetta corps, see IOR/L/MIL/7/6712: 1906, 2; and 1908, 4. On the effects of the canals, see 1907, 4; and 1910, 10.

7. See IOR/L/MIL/7/6700: 1902, 4, indicating that 1,995 from China were delivered to India in 1901–2; IOR/L/MIL/7/6712: 1907, 5, indicating that 1,459 were shipped from Argentina over the previous two years; IOR/L/MIL/7/6712: 1909, 5, indicating imports from Persia; IOR/L/MIL/7/6712: 1910, 6, indicating imports from Persia and China; and IOR/L/MIL/7/6730: 1911,

ket price of camels and bullocks over the first decade of the twentieth century; this was identified as a factor contributing to peasant indebtedness in the canal colonies.[8] One report also indicated that the effort to introduce camels from Somalia in 1900 failed because the Somali camels proved to have weak hocks, narrow chests, poor muscular development, and inadequate carrying strength. They were also susceptible to colds.[9]

This careful parsing of the characteristics of Somali camels is indicative of how camels were now being evaluated in the professional language of the managers of animal populations. Other examples of this new professionalism involved the distribution of microscopes to the active and reserve pack animal units so that their veterinary assistants could identify from blood samples the parasitic ailment called surra (*Trypanosoma evansi*; see chapter 8).[10] In addition to noting the dissemination of scientific technologies into the transport units, the reports indicated that the army encouraged officers and NCOs, British and native, to enroll in courses that taught a variety of animal management techniques, including courses in veterinary medicine at Pune and Ambala; veterinary dressing at Lahore, Bombay College, and Pune; the proper uses of harnesses and saddlery at Cawpore and Madras; and the care of transport vehicles at the Jubblpore Gun Carriage Factory.[11]

But perhaps the most significant aspect of the annual reports was their reporting on the most critical elements of the new human-animal biopower regime: the reproduction and death of donkey studs and pack animals. Recall from the discussion in chapter 3 that in the 1880s, the imperial state had launched a mule-breeding program involving the importation of donkey studs to mate with Indian horse and pony mares. Initially, the program was

---

indicating imports from Persia and China, as well as from the Remount Depot in India. On postwar mule procurement in the United States, see IOR/L/MIL/7/9700: *Administrative Report of the Army Remount Department for the Year 1927–28* (Delhi: Government of India Press, 1929), 8, and 1930, 7–8.

8. IOR/L/MIL/7/6712: 1910, 7.

9. IOR/L/MIL/7/6700: 1901, 9. Attitudes toward Somali camels changed during World War I; see chapter 9.

10. IOR/L/MIL/7/6700: 1904, 3; and IOR/L/MIL/7/6712: 1908, 5. Surra is a wasting disease that caused many deaths in the camel corps. Upon identification of the disease, unit commanders received permission to destroy affected animals regardless of the number; see IOR/L/MIL/7/6712: 1906, 2.

11. See IOR/L/MIL/7/6712: 1910, 13. For the numbers of participants in these classes, see IOR/L/MIL/7/6730: 1912, 9; and 1913, 10. Two to three times the number of Indian NCOs as compared with British NCOs received such training.

in the hands of the Army Remount Department, but when the Civil Veterinary Department was created in 1892, it took over the program. Between 1892 and 1903, the CVD unit's annual reports included figures on the numbers of donkey studs it oversaw, the number of horse, pony, and donkey mares the studs "covered" (a term for *mating*), and the percentage of foals born from the coverings. The ARD continued this practice in its annual reports after 1903 and maintained it through 1913. There is no question that once the ARD became responsible for mule breeding, the numbers of births increased, as did the percentages of successful pregnancies from coverings. For example, in the reporting year of 1902–3, the CVD indicated that 423 donkey studs covered some 24,000 female horse and pony mares. From these couplings, 4,132 mules were born, a success rate of 17.2 percent. In 1904–5, the ARD reported that its stud population of 252 had produced 4,630 mule foals, or an average of 24.7 percent success rate to mares covered. From then until 1913, the percentage of foals to coverings hovered between 27 and 32 percent.[12] On the face of it, this jump in successful pregnancies seems to bear out the faith in army animal management expressed by the Horse and Mule Breeding Commission in 1901.

The other side of biological reproduction, however, was the death of breeding studs and pack animals in general. In the case of the donkey jacks, during CVD oversight of mule breeding, statistical charts were kept that included the names of deceased studs, their place of origin, and cause of death. Most of the animals died of one or another disease or injury, but there were also animals every year who were put down because they were "old and worn out," "failed to fill their mares," or perhaps most disturbing, refused to mount their mares.[13] In the reproductive regime of mules, there were no green pastures

12. The annual reports of the CVD are available from 1892 to 1911 on the website of the National Library of Scotland (http://digital.nls.uk, accessed 4 October 2017) under Medicine—Veterinary. The relevant statistics in CVD reports are organized in a section entitled "Mule-breeding." The ARD annual reports can be found in IOR/L/MIL/7/9687, 9691, 9697, and 9700. These files cover the years 1903 to 1913. The statistics on mule breeding are organized in the same manner as the CVD reports. It is difficult to determine how these percentages of successful pregnancies compare to mule breeding in other parts of the world. On the other hand, successful pregnancies in horse breeding appear to have been higher. In 1912, for example, the Lyallpur District registered a 44 percent rate, up slightly from the year before. See *Annual Reports of the Punjab Colonies* (Lahore: Civil and Military Gazette Press, 1913), "Chenab Canal Colony, Lyallpur," 1.

13. See, for example, IOR/V/4378: *Annual Administrative Report of the Civil Veterinary Department for the Official Year 1895–96*, xxvi. For ARD figures on donkey stud casualties, see the annual reports, appendix 11 in IOR/L/MIL/7/9687, 9691, 9697, and 9700.

TABLE 7.1 Mule and camel wastage rates, 1899–1902

Year	Pack animal	Number on rolls	Casualties	Cast	Wastage
1899–1900	Mules	17,780	320	948	7%
	Camels	2,975	745	154	30%
1900–1901	Mules	15,796	528	863	8%
	Camels	2,962	1,078	52	38%
1901–2	Mules	19,478	428	618	5.3%
	Camels	2,004	804	49	43%

Source: IOR/L/MIL/6700: 1901, 20; 1902, 16; and 1902, 17.

where male donkeys could spend their final days. If the donkey studs did not die of illness or injuries, they were destroyed when they either could no longer produce or resisted the harsh breeding regime.

The other kind of animal death occurred in service to members of supply and transport units. "No longer active" pack animals appear in annual reports as a component of wastage rates, a figure that combined animals lost as casualties and those who were cast (discharged or put down) as unfit for service. This statistical form produced the raw material that allowed authorities to rework camel, mule, donkey, and bullock life in actuarial terms as predictable patterns of a productive life of labor and wastage. With such data, the Supply and Transport Corps could estimate with increasing precision the annual number of new recruits required to replenish or even expand its standing and reserve corps for animal transport.

Such careful reporting of population losses also showed intriguing comparative data when populations were juxtaposed to one another. As table 7.1 indicates, the figures for the period between 1899 and 1902 indicate that not only were camel wastage rates higher than those of mules, but camel casualties were proportionally much higher.

These figures indicate two things. First, they provide clear and presumably unambiguous data on the replacement or remount rates for mules and camels at the inception of the new transport scheme. Second, they demonstrate the extraordinary cost to both the animals and the army of maintaining a camel establishment. The figures we have here are from a relatively peaceful period, yet the wastage rates approach those of the campaigns a few years earlier that had led to the complete overhaul of military transport. Later reports—from 1909 to 1913—show that the wastage rates for army mules remained relatively stable, while those for camels dropped to around 23 percent a year on average, although they were usually lower in Silladar reserve units than in the Government Camel Corps units.[14] How should the shift in wastage rates over time be accounted for? Was it simply the positive effect of the new animal management regime?

One possible answer to one difference in wastage rates is that the sarwans of the Silladar units took better care of their camels. Silladar sarwans, drawn from families that bred and raised camels, probably knew as much or more about the animals than did their counterparts in the government units. These sarwans also probably had strong affective ties with their animals as a result of raising them, living in close proximity to them, tending their ills, and herding them to grazing grounds. Hence, the degree of care afforded camels in the Silladar units was more than likely superior to that in the Government Camel Corps. Consider also that an owner of a Silladar camel, whether he be the sarwan or someone else, was required to replace the animal if it should be lost. This was a condition of service. The administration reports mention none of this, but note simply that at various times there were shortages of trained personnel in the active transport corps and a paucity of veterinary officers who understood camel diseases.

Thus, a second answer to the question of high attrition rates among government camels is that while the structure of the new transport system rationalized the management of pack animals, there was still a gap between the promises of better organization on paper and the realities of organization in practice. However, as more officers and enlisted men received training, particularly in veterinary medicine, the situation began to improve slightly. And although the statistical tables on wastage disappear in reports between 1904 and 1908, the officers reporting on the state of transport claim that casualties for those years showed either a "considerable" or a slight decrease. Yet camel

14. IOR/L/MIL/7/6730: 1911, 6; 1912, 10; and 1913: 10. No figures are given for the number of animals on the rolls, only percentages of wastage. The 1913 report included the following figures:

Year	Mules	Silladar CC	Government CC
1909–10	7.05	22.44	27.15
1910–11	10.6	16.74	22.97
1911–12	8.39	24.80	18.02
1912–13	9.06	13.60	21.61
Average	8.78	19.34	22.43

losses were still relatively high in the government units. These same reports suggest that the main reason wastage rates among camels remained high was the impact of surra and other communicable diseases.

But, as we will see shortly, camel mortality, far more than that of mules, was very much affected by ecological changes. Canal expansion significantly reduced camel grazing land and pushed browsing animals into areas rife with surra disease while the banks of the new irrigation canals provided more breeding grounds for the biting flies that spread surra.[15] How the colonial government addressed surra as well as other camel-related diseases will be taken up in the next chapter. Here it is sufficient to note that ecological problems related to canal development and resulting from the simultaneous reorganization of pack animal life placed many constraints on efforts to fully rationalize and routinize army transport. But as it happened, the British Indian Army never had to authorize a full mobilization of the Silladar and reserve pack animal units from at least 1905 to the beginning of World War I; so it is difficult to gauge the overall effectiveness of the reforms, which were, after all, oriented toward emergency deployments.

Army Regulations and Manuals

A second order of regulation involved situating pack animal lives within army regulations and manuals, which together produced an animal management regime overseen by transport and veterinary experts. These printed forms of military knowledge included field service regulations and field service manuals, newly formatted genres that emerged with the formation of a General Staff in Great Britain in 1904. Field service regulations for India appeared in 1906, followed in 1912 by regulations for the wartime establishment of supply and transport. Field service manuals for the Remount Department and native Silladar cavalry units appeared in 1911 and 1908 respectively. These publications provided a uniform set of rules and practices to govern the army in general and specific kinds of units in particular.[16]

15. See *Annual Report of Veterinary Officer Investigating Camel Diseases* (Calcutta: Superintendent of Government Printing, India, 1910), 3–5.

16. See *Field Service Regulations, India (Provisional Edition)* (Calcutta: Superintendent of Government Printing, India, 1906); *Field Service Manual: Supply and Transport (War, India)* (Calcutta: Superintendent of Government Printing, India, 1912); *Remount Manual (War), India* (Calcutta: Superintendent of Government Printing, India, 1911); and *Field Service Manual: Native Silladar Cavalry* (Calcutta: Superintendent of Government Printing, India, 1908). I have not found a manual for Silladar camel corps.

A second important genre for standardizing military practices was the specialist manual. This kind of publication comprised state-of-the-field knowledge about a particular subject, and protocols for the proper ordering and regulation of that subject. In the case of cavalry and pack animals, the manual assembled in one place a uniform body of knowledge and set of protocols for "army animal management."

In 1908, the Veterinary Department of the General Staff published the first edition of *Animal Management*, a manual addressing cavalry horses and transport mules, donkeys, camels, and bullocks.[17] It assembled a heterogeneous set of elements that included detailed descriptions of animal characteristics and commonsense practices for dealing with them; data drawn from the records of military campaigns; experiential knowledge transmitted across generations of animal handlers; hygiene and microbe theory; evolution; food science; and artisanal knowledge of saddlery and horseshoeing. The handbook was organized according to species, and the topics were presented in a military writing format that emphasized clear, unvarnished description and adopted the structural order of British military manuals in general. The effect of this compilation practice was to produce a comprehensive and authoritative set of relevant facts for the care and management of cavalry horses and transport animals.

However, *Animal Management* was not simply an ordering of elements pertinent to the health of military animals for its own sake. It also offered methods for ensuring that the functions of the military animal "be carried out with as great a perfection as possible." It was, therefore, a guide to the means through which military animals were physically maintained as fit for "the work required" of them.[18] And since the animals themselves tended to be located in spaces different from those occupied by humans (e.g., stables, grazing and exercise grounds), the knowledge assembled in the manual had to be transportable to where the animals were. Hence *Animal Management*'s format was that of a handbook (4⅞ × 6 inches), a mobile object designed to be carried in the pocket of a uniform, where it would be available in the field. And like all such manuals, it was organized around principles of easy accessibility, with clearly listed chapters and subsections about each type of military animal and a comprehensive index. It mirrored, in other words, the principles informing the restructured military as a whole, both in Great Britain and in India.

As with other military manuals, the writing style of *Animal Management*

17. Army Veterinary Department, General Staff, War Office, *Animal Management* (London: His Majesty's Stationery Office, 1908).

18. Ibid., 18, 131.

was a series of declarative sentences showing an efficient movement from the general to the particular. General principles were laid out in an introductory chapter that dealt with the "structure and function" of large-animal anatomy, with the particulars of the horse as the central example. After a discussion of the horse's "points" (i.e., those physical features that distinguish it from other military animals), the text moved to an explication of the horse's abode or stable, its "fittings," and the importance of good "ventilation." In such recommended spaces, horses were to be groomed, washed, clipped, clothed, and bedded down, with their surroundings kept orderly by the daily routines of the stable staff. The particular elements that made up the military horse's life were presented as a kind of domestic space not unlike that of the contemporary Edwardian household.[19] The part on grooming, for example, emphasized the importance of the practice as a "preventive of disease."

> Whilst it is quite true that mange and many other diseases are not produced by dirt, it is nevertheless equally true that they are most difficult to eradicate where dirty conditions prevail, and the regular brushing and cleansing of the coat is an undoubted preventive.[20]

No other animal discussed in the manual received this kind of attention. But perhaps that is understandable, for the horse was not simply part of an English aristocratic sport and hunting culture or the preferred working farm animal in rural Great Britain.[21] It was also a key participant in mobile infantry, cavalry, and scouting units.

And yet, because the horse is an herbivore like pack animals, the manual affirmed that horses share various elements with other military animals like mules and even camels. This point was made abundantly clear in the lengthy sections on animal feed, which related to all the animals covered by the manual. Not only were feeding techniques discussed, but much space was given over to the explication of the qualities of various kinds of grains and grasses, including sections on Indian and Egyptian types of fodder.[22] Other points

19. Ibid., 49–52, 57–85; the quotations are on p. 57.

20. Ibid., 57.

21. Harriet Ritvo, *The Animal Estate: The English and Other Creatures in the Victorian Age* (Cambridge, MA: Harvard University Press, 1987), 19–20. Also see Margaret Derry, *Horses in Society: A Story of Animal Breeding and Marketing, 1800–1920* (Toronto: University of Toronto Press, 2006).

22. Here can be found a clear description of *bhusa* (straw), the remnants of the threshing process. *Bhusa* came from two basic sources, cereal grains and legumes such as peas and beans.

of overlap included the discussion of techniques for proper saddling and the treatment of sore back, methods for transporting animals by sea. Descriptions of diseases that affect both horses and pack animals were also provided. In other words, the manual took up many of the topics present in the *Quarterly Journal of Veterinary Science in India and Army Animal Management* (see chapter 4).

Within a unifying and universalizing framework of expert information, the new system of animal management adopted the standard characteristics of General Staff publications. Military animals were now represented as enumerable entities subject to efficient management through a properly regulated human organization informed by expert knowledge that was derived from experience with and scientific knowledge of military animals. The mule, for example, was presented in the same positive terms as were discussed in chapter 3. His endurance, tolerance of thirst, adaptability to diverse climates and rations, and toughness were all said to make him the favorite among pack animals. Such a representation could only have been possible as a result of actual experience that army transport and veterinary staff had had with mules on military campaigns. But this characterization based on experience was complemented by one based on comparison. Mules are like horses. Since they share a similar anatomy and digestive system, they can be kept in good condition, like the horse, with proper stable management and feeding.[23] This pattern continued throughout the handbook—recovering and reaffirming established knowledge, highlighting best practices, and using comparisons of similarities and differences to make key points.

The mule chapter also demonstrated how the global reach of the British Empire was incorporated into the manual. The places in the Americas, Asia, southern Europe, the Mediterranean islands, and Africa where the British procured mules were listed, and this evocation of a global network in mule traffic was then juxtaposed to the qualities desired of the mules used in the Indian Army. The acceptable physical sizes of mules were presented in a table organized in terms of height in hands and girth at certain ages,[24] followed by descriptive prose outlining the optimum measures for chest, quarters, fore-

The former was called "white" *bhusa*, the latter "missa" *bhusa*. An excessive reliance on white *bhusa* for feed, as noted earlier, was one of the contributing factors in camel deaths during the Second Afghan War.

23. Army Veterinary Department, General Staff, War Office, *Animal Management*, 270.

24. So, for example, the approved girth of a five-year-old mule of thirteen hands is fifty-nine inches; ibid., 271.

head, legs, feet, and teeth. These points of the mule body essentially functioned to identify desirable features for transport work, but they also told agents what to look for when purchasing animals for the army. Following this explication of the ideal characteristics of transport mules were details on the care and management of the mule, including feeding, watering, loading, and marching with loads.[25] The entries on the donkey and ox were presented in much the same way.

In the case of the camel, however, this discursive structure could only be deployed partly, because they are, as the compilers were well aware, in many ways quite different from equines and bovines. Hence, the camel comprised the largest entry in *Animal Management* after the horse. It is perhaps not too surprising in this first manual on animal management to see the camel emerge as a pack animal that had been woefully misunderstood until quite recently. As a transport animal, compilers explained, the camel required special attention and a greater human understanding of its real capacities and needs. The animal was, for example, capable of carrying 250 to 450 pounds of supplies and equipment twenty miles a day, a range and carrying capacity that "must be looked upon as the limit of his normal powers when properly cared for."[26] Here norms of care were advocated to establish a baseline for proper management. Such norms were essential for transport officers to bear in mind, because "the animal's virtues are such that it is easy to unwittingly overtax him." Note the subtle shift here from the camel's inadequacies to its virtues, virtues that the uninitiated needed to know lest they overwork or otherwise mistreat the animal. These qualities were, moreover, those that had been highlighted by a few transport officers and veterinarians like Arthur Leonard and John Henry Steel two decades earlier. The innovation achieved by *Animal Management* is that the high value of camels was now fixed in military doctrine and authoritative prose.

In addition to providing a clear statement about what transport officers could expect from the camel in service, *Animal Management* regarded the animal as possessing some stellar qualities that presumably had been generally overlooked in the past.

> Patient to a degree, enduring hunger, thirst and pain with stoical courage *beyond all others*, the first sign that a camel may give that he is being asked to do the impossible is to drop down dead, on which account he has been classed

25. Ibid., 271–74.
26. Ibid., 276.

> as "delicate." The point on which a camel may be fairly regarded as delicate is, that he is peculiarly susceptible to changes in climate and surroundings. You cannot, for instance, work a desert camel successfully in the hills, or delta camel in the desert; but if properly selected and cared for they make excellent transport, are not more difficult to deal with than other animals, and on occasion are capable of a sustained effort which cannot be accomplished by others. They are, however, unintelligent; they cannot be taught much, but are willing machines and must be driven with care and judgment.[27]

This passage is a far cry from the conclusions drawn in 1880 regarding the causes of the high level of camel mortality during the Second Afghan War. Recall that at the time, some concluded that the fault lay with the failures of the camel itself, arguing that the army might be better off relying more on mule transport. Instead, in *Animal Management* the compilers incorporated specific knowledge produced about the camel in association with campaigns fought in Africa and India over the two and a half decades before the handbook's publication. The materials presented by John Henry Steel in his many works, as well as reports from the field by transport officers and veterinarians, clearly informed the text, beginning with the differentiation of types of camels (Indian, Egyptian, Arabian, Somali), instructions on how to select them, and an explanation of why a sensitivity to and awareness of a camel's age was important in the selection process.[28] Lurking in this last concern was an awareness that many camels perished on campaigns because they were put to work at too young an age.

Through this evocation of camels' special features and characteristics, the animal was moved from the status of a problematic, deficient Oriental Other into a position allowing its particular attributes to be effectively incorporated, through scientific management, into reliable service in regular animal transport units. But this incorporation could be managed only by way of attention to the "structural and other peculiarities of the camel." The lips, skin, hump, and feet are different from other pack animals, and its temper "peculiar." Camels suffer pain, for example, with unusual "stoicism" compared with other animals. Yet at the same time, there is at least one point of commonality. Like other ruminants, such as the bullock, they have four stomachs. This fact thus demanded special attention for grazing and diet.

The camel's physical particulars were followed in the handbook by de-

27. Ibid.

28. Ibid., 276–77.

tailed instructions on feeding, grazing, and watering it, as well as information about the wild plants to be found in Egypt, the Sudan, Somaliland, and India that it thrived on or which were poisonous to it. The locations in question were, of course, all places where camels had been on active service in military campaigns. *Animal Management* asserted that on such campaigns, care would be required in dealing with the amount of daily work per animal and the various physical obstacles of the terrain along the transport line. Marching, for example, ought to be about fifteen miles or six hours a day, with good rest and grazing between marches, and pack camels should be loaded only just before starting out. Concerning obstacles, steep-sided ditches, for instance, required special care—where such terrain existed, portable bridges like those used in Afghan campaigns were advised. Streams could also be a problem, but camels were reported to be good, strong swimmers. Advice followed on the setup of campgrounds so that they would afford camels adequate rest, grooming, clipping, and so on, all topics that had also been discussed regarding the horse.

Lastly, also like the horse, the question of equipment was addressed. The key items were the pad and saddle, and a blanket for protection during cold nights. The saddle and pad were presented as extremely critical parts of camel equipment. If they were improperly fitted, they produced the most common camel affliction—sore backs.[29] Thus, in one confident declarative sentence after another, each of which was grounded in experiences dating back to the Second Afghan War, the camel was officially rehabilitated and made a key member of military transport units in specific areas of the empire. Any ignorant complaints about the animal would have to deal with the formidable and authoritative pronouncements of *Animal Management*.

The practical and scientific knowledge embodied in the manual's camel entry dealt primarily with management of healthy animals. A second handbook published in 1910 provided a comprehensive overview of military animal illnesses. Organized by the veterinary section in the Quartermaster General's Division of the Indian Army, it was entitled *Handbook on Contagious and Infectious Diseases of Animals*.[30] The volume was less concerned with chronic and work-related afflictions of animals, such as sore backs, than with diseases caused by external pathogens. As will be discussed in the next chapter, many of these kinds of illnesses were contagions specific to certain ecologies and often transmitted by intermediate vectors like insects.

29. Ibid., 281–94.

30. Veterinary Section, Quartermaster General's Division, *Handbook on Contagious and Infectious Diseases of Animals* (Calcutta: Government Press, 1910).

The publication of works on the management of military animals and the communicable diseases affecting them stemmed from and reinforced the new role of veterinary surgeons in the British and Indian armies. That role, as defined by *Field Service Regulations, India* (1906), made veterinarians the final arbiter on the fitness of animals to serve, resolving, as it were, the problem of relatively weak authority that had plagued the profession within the imperial military establishment throughout the nineteenth century.[31] But these two handbooks did more as well. They emphasized the scientific nature of the veterinary enterprise, establishing veterinarians as one grade of expert professionals among those now staffing important parts of the improved British Indian Army. When their skills were combined with those of transport registration officers and supply and transport officers, all of whom were themselves subject to specialized training, we can begin to see the emergence of something like a pack animal biopower regime, one designed to maximize the effective working lives of military animals while ensuring, through various mechanisms, the biological reproduction of some of these species for military use. The next section will address the question of the effectiveness of the animal transport regime and its impact on animal life.

FRICTIONS AND TURBULENCE WITHIN THE NEW ORDER

From the inception of the new transport regime signaled by the 1903 Military Transport Animals Act, there were problems that particularly affected operations of the reserve components of Silladar and Grantee units. These included difficulties in coordinating overlapping civilian and military administrative responsibilities; chronic complications in replacing animals, especially camels, mules, and donkey studs, because of shortages; resistances from indigenous "colonists" in the canal projects against the rigid rules of the camel and mule land grants; excessive debt accumulation on the part of colonists, especially among the poorest of them; the steady elimination of grazing land for camels and a corresponding decline in their health; and problems associated with the engineering of water, including uneven distribution in the Punjab irrigation

31. See *Field Service Regulations, India*, 16. The pertinent regulations state that "a veterinary inspection will be made of all animals before proceeding on active service, with the object of weeding out those unsuitable owning to contagious or other diseases, or physical disability," and "all animals on active service will be under the professional supervision of the Army Veterinary department." In the field, veterinarians could remove from service any animal they deemed unfit.

system, floodwater damage to poorly constructed sections, silting, and waterlogging of areas around the canals, with concomitant salinization of soil.

The original idea animating the Punjab's irrigation projects had been to create a body of prosperous peasants cultivating their own land and living in a well-ordered, sanitary environment reliant on settled agriculture. In addition to relieving population pressure in congested districts in north India by repurposing wastelands, the intent of the irrigation scheme, as one anonymous gazetteer authority put it in 1904, was to

> colonize the area in question with well-to-do yeomen of the best class of agriculturalists, who will cultivate their own holdings with the aid of their families and of the usual menials, but as much as possible without the aid of tenants, and will constitute healthy agricultural communities of the best Punjab type.[32]

Thus, a hearty yeoman class was envisioned that would be established in the canal colonies, a class that would, through year-round agricultural production, enrich itself and the colonial state while producing the right sort of human and animal material for the Indian Army. But the scheme had even grander plans than those outlined in this gazetteer. The taming of the wasteland would also bring a number of other positive effects. Moved to an entirely new environment without historical roots and social obligations, the "best Punjab types" would be free to allow their best qualities and characteristics to flourish, ideally without the debilitating sheet anchors of caste or race to constrain them. The canal project was, in other words, a civilizing mission and a sociological experiment, one premised on unspoken assumptions about rural and "Oriental" human nature.

Not only was the project targeted at the Punjab's traditional agricultural groups, however. There was also the less dense population of the wasteland to consider, the pastoral herders of cattle and camels. From at least the mid-nineteenth century, as David Gilmartin has argued, the nomads of the doab (known by the British as the Bar) had been seen by the British as an atavistic remnant of a primitive past. Colonial good governance not only needed to liberate traditional agriculturalists from their past but sought to improve the nomad as well.[33] "Hemmed in" by the tentacles of the new canals, the nomads

32. *Gazetteer of the Chenab Colony, 1904* (Lahore: Civil and Military Gazette Press, 1905), 29.

33. David Gilmartin, *Blood and Water: The Indus River Basin in Modern History* (Oakland: University of California Press, 2015), 91–96.

and their animals would eventually have to either move on or settle down and become part of village-centered, agricultural property-owner communities, villages where colonial officials could better command and tax them and their goods.[34] What the state did not want in the new canal villages were shiftless wanderers addicted to cattle theft and prone to "turbulence."[35] The object, as Richard Temple, a Punjab administrator, explained in 1853, was to "take a wild wanderer of the Bar, give him some land to squat upon and call his own"; consequently, he would become a "wise and better man." Such a process of "improvement," presumably effective for all those now farming on their own land, would serve to foster and direct, like the water the British had bestowed on the colonists, those other key Punjabi attributes of "courage" and "military spirit."[36]

Colonization began in 1892 on land watered by the newly constructed canals off the Chenab River. The irrigation channels carried water into areas of what had been pastoral grazing lands, where square plots of land had been mapped out on a rectilinear grid, with new towns and villages laid out in the same manner. Configuring the land based on a geometry of squares overlaid a whole new geocosmology onto the terrain of Punjab. Unlike that relating to the shrines of Sufi saints and powerful invisible entities, or the seasonal oscillations of pastoral migration, the new geography inscribed a network onto the land that correlated with newly mandated proprietary or use rights to the measured plots. In so doing, the rectilinear structure was meant to capture, by means of enumeration and inspection, the full productivity of each household and plot, thereby generating a human-based biopower regime operating in tandem with that of working animals.

As the Lower Jhelum gazetteer described the process, a "geodic survey" of the "commanded area" began in 1888, which involved "laying out parallel lines, 1,100 feet apart, throughout the length of the Doab." At each of these intervals, a plot 1,100 × 1,100 was marked off, and the "entire area was thus demarcated." It was only once the grid was established that the contours of the land had to be taken into consideration. The highest point of each square became the target for the delivery of water to the plot. The channels of the

34. See Bernard H. Dobson, *Final Report of the Chenab Colony Settlement* (Lahore: Superintendent of Government Printing, Punjab, 1915), 8, on hemming in the nomads.

35. British administrators used the term *turbulence* to describe the effects of the nomads' movements as well as their lack of fixed property; see Gilmartin, *Blood and Water*, 94.

36. Cited in ibid., 91 and 95.

canals themselves were designed to follow the "main, and subsidiary, watersheds of the country."[37]

In this way, the natural landscape and the legislated cartography of the geodetic survey were brought into alignment. As Gilmartin has put it, the aim of the government was "to encompass the system of cultivation within a frame of technical and environmental management defined by a scientific, irrigational structure."[38] In turn, the relation between science and managed water flows constituted a novel geocosmology, one held to be objective and accountable because it was based on mathematical formulas and technical measurement, not invisible forces.

From the point of view of colonial authorities, the results of this aggressive and totalizing intervention into the wasteland bound living populations and land in a set of structured and legislated networks that could serve multiple ends of the state. These included expanding commercial agriculture in the region and thus producing higher state revenues. They also involved, as already suggested, the provision of military animals and the sons of farmers as army recruits, as well as an end to the social instability or "turbulence" believed to be caused by nomads. These intended outcomes in combination were expected to stabilize the western frontier of the British Indian Empire politically and militarily. They would also demonstrate to the indigenous population of the Punjab the effectiveness of scientific management and rational planning.

But this geometry of squares almost immediately ran into difficulties. Older settlements along the preexisting canals did not fit the geometric pattern, and government *rakhs* controlled by the Forestry Department did not either. As a result, the ideal of uniform plots, each assigned to an individual household, could be undermined by other proprietary uses of the land (say, hereditary claims on firewood from the wilderness). Adjustments in the course of surveying were, as a result, inevitable, with plots on the colonies' outer edges seldom conforming to the rectilinear symmetry of the other plots in the section. Asymmetrical plots were also frequently located at the end of an irrigation line, where they regularly suffered from water shortages. These were also the plots given to poorer peasants and to former pastoralists; through these land grants, many of them were locked into camel service grants.

As noted above, the British were keen to socially engineer the canal colo-

37. *Punjab Canal Gazetteers*, vol. 1, *Lower Jhelum Canal, 1920* (Lahore: Superintendent, Government Printing, Punjab, 1921), 16.

38. Gilmartin, *Blood and Water*, 160.

nies in order to stabilize a social and economic order that made sense to them. In effect, they established a class system in the colonies based on wealth and property rights. At the bottom of this class structure were the peasant grantees. They were made up of the following groups: immigrants from more congested areas where Punjabi agricultural traditions had been flourishing; the *janglis*, nomads of the wastelands; and the *hitharis*, hereditary landowners in the Chenab and Ravi river basins who had lost their holdings as a result of canal construction. Many *hitharis* received plots of land as compensation; in many cases, they rented these to more impoverished peasant tenants, an outcome that undermined the planners' goal of a freeholding rural peasantry.[39]

On the next rung up in the emergent class hierarchy, more fortunate than the peasant grantees, were the yeoman grantees whose wealth was somewhere between that of the richer gentry and the peasantry. Invariably, they were also from *zamindari*, or old landholding families, meaning that their role in the colonies was presumed to be that of setting a good example for others. A third group, the "capitalists," also were expected to "assist by example and precept," in this case with the investment of money and "brains" to develop the colony's commercial aspects. Finally, there were the auction purchasers, who were socially much like the capitalists.[40]

These four groups made up the "colonists," all of whose grants were primarily conditional upon their improvement of the land. That is, they were supposed to build houses, sink wells, plant trees, and comply with certain rules of sanitation. They also had to accept that common land remained in the hands and under the control of the government of the Punjab. There was, however, one major difference between the yeomen, capitalists, and auction purchasers and the *hitharis* and peasants, whether they were nomads or more settled farmers. The peasants held only use rights to the land for a twenty-year period, while the others either immediately, or soon after improvement, were able to gain property rights to their plots. This was a division of land based on British perceptions of proper rural hierarchies; it would become a source of much discontent and protest in the first decade of the twentieth century. Inequalities introduced by the system were further exacerbated when the engineers' vision of uniform water flow throughout the system failed to materialize, resulting in shortages in various parts. This shortfall not only caused friction between engineers and colonization and Remount Department officers, it also

39. I draw from Dobson, *Final Report of the Chenab Colony Settlement*, 5.
40. Ibid., 5–6.

resulted in landholders concluding that the government was reneging on its commitments to them.[41]

Matters boiled over in 1907, when Punjab authorities announced an increase in water rates and harsher terms for the land grants, which were made retroactive to the founding of the canal colonies. These changes met stiff and sustained resistance from all the classes of landholders. The government of the Punjab, certain that the agriculturalists to whom the state had been so generous were incapable of mounting such protests, initially claimed that discontent was being stoked by outside agitators. Eventually, however, the government had to back off from some of the 1907 regulations and, with the Colonization of Government Land Act of 1912, granted proprietary rights to those who had been holding twenty-year use-rights leases.[42] The general myopia regarding popular sentiment in this episode was paralleled by insensitivity to differences that were clearly present on the ground. These began with the locally important distinctions between agriculturalists and pastoralists, and there were finer-grained senses of social difference as well, based on language, ethnicity, and religious/cultural dispositions.

In addition to experiencing friction over the conditions of land grants in general, the camel reservists and camel land grant holders faced a number of difficulties unique to their arrangements with the government. The annual reports of the Chenab canal colony, where the bulk of the camel land grants were located, indicated a disturbing pattern. The camel grantees and the units they were attached to were regularly short of camels, primarily because each year so many of the animals were lost to the fatal disease called surra. Few grantees could afford to replace their camels, however, and were forced to take *takavi* (government loans) in order to do so. At the same time, colony reports indicated the shrinkage of suitable grazing land for these animals. The result was that grantees, already financially strapped, had to purchase animal feed, making it impossible for them to make a living, as one report put it.[43] Such problems were repeated in the reports of subsequent years, with de-

41. Gilmartin, *Blood and Water*, 170, 172.

42. See N. Gerald Barrier, "The Punjab Disturbances of 1907: The Response of the British Government in India to Agrarian Unrest," *Modern Asian Studies* 1, no. 4 (1967): 353–83; and the discussion of policy shifts in Gilmartin, *Blood and Water*, 174–79.

43. In the following parts of this section, I draw extensively from the annual reports of the Punjab's canal colonies. The titles vary; I have abbreviated them as ARPCC, followed by the year they cover. Full citations can be found in the bibliography. Also, because there are multiple paginations in the reports, I have added the specific colony report and page references. In this case, see ARPCC (1909), "Chenab Canal Colony," 1.

sired numbers in the four camel grantee corps falling short by 308 in 1910.[44] By 1914, the Chenab canal colony report indicated a general decline in the quality of replacement camels as a result of a lack of grazing grounds and stall feeding.[45] Concerned even earlier that the camel grantees were being forced into untenable positions, the Punjab government appointed a camel browsing committee, discussed below, to investigate matters in 1910.

A second kind of disturbing pattern involved an unexpected hydraulic consequence of canal expansion. By 1910, reports indicated that as a result of seepage in the new canal lines, the water table off the Jhelum River had risen from sixty to thirty feet below ground level, and "swamping" was evident in places.[46] Similar problems of "waterlogging" were reported in the Lower Bari Doab canal system, which included some of the Chenab colony camel grantee plots. Assurances were made that the chief engineer of the canal works was taking up the problem of "removing these blots on an otherwise admirable irrigation system."[47] The war in Europe intervened, however, before any action could be taken on either increased peasant indebtedness or the negative environmental impact of the canals.

An additional problem was conceptual, a failure of British imagination. The vision behind the canal colony development was the importation of an agricultural utopia into a space imagined as a historically empty wasteland that could then be brought under control and commanded to be productive. Yet as surveyors penetrated into the doab, to their surprise they found signs of extensive earlier sedentary habitation. Officials seem to have been unaffected, as well as unmoved, by the evidence at hand. As one of them put it,

> That this apparently desolate tract should have once supported a teeming population is incredible, but there is evidence of the fact in numerous mounds (*thehs*), strewn with debris of bricks and pottery, which can only mark the sites of human habitation of a by-gone age. Upon their means of subsistence, for these are no nomad camping-grounds but well-established settlements, *we cannot speculate*: our primary concern is with the present and our immediate concern with the steps, by which . . . this waste and inclement region was converted into a scene of unexampled agricultural prosperity.[48]

44. ARPCC (1911), "Chenab Canal Colony," 1.
45. ARPCC (1915), "Chenab Canal Colony," 2.
46. ARPCC (1910), cover letter to the report, 1.
47. ARPCC (1915), cover letter to the report, 1.
48. Dobson, *Final Report of the Chenab Colony Settlement*, 3; emphasis added.

This is the same kind of hubris that failed to grasp the reasons for peasant protests. Apparently few in authority felt it was important to ask why the settlements of the past had been abandoned. Drought and increased rain volume in monsoon cycles accounted for some of the region's ecological changes, but so too did the fragile nature of the alluvial plain the British were seeking to reengineer. Failing to fully grasp the meaning of the abandoned settlements, blinded by their dream of "unexampled agricultural prosperity," they then had to deal with silting, waterlogging, soil salinization, and rising rates of malaria as unfortunate side effects, judging that each should be managed by one or another department of experts.[49]

But perhaps there wasn't time enough for speculation about the natural and social vicissitudes of the past. Colonization officers in the new tracts had a substantial amount of friction to deal with just to get the colonies off the ground. Not the least of their problems were the people already resident in the wastelands. This population was lumped together by the British as janglis, and they hoped to tame them by turning them into farmers. In the early part of the twentieth century, official policy toward these peoples at first seemed to be working—they were applying for and receiving land grants. Upon closer inspection, however, colonization officers were said to have "erred deliberately on the side of generosity and allowed the benefit of the doubt in a good many very unlikely cases."[50]

Purported generosity on the part of colonization officers was a trope that glossed over a problem that seems to have arisen repeatedly. In a 1914 retrospective by the Montgomery District colonization officer, a Mr. Joseph, it is clear that the central problem was not so much a lack of jangli visibility in the colonial record as it was an overabundance of presence. As Joseph explained, *tirni*, a grazing rights tax, had been paid by many for years on "phantom camels," and house taxes were often paid on nonexistent dwellings; either tax could establish residency for census purposes. These "false" paper trails were created for the purpose of making occasional claims to plots of land for

49. The relationship between canal expansion and increased incidents of malaria was made in 1911 by S. R. Christophers; see *Malaria in the Punjab* (Calcutta: Superintendent of Government Printing, 1911): 101–4. As population increased in the canal colonies and sanitation measures failed to keep up with the rapid growth, there were also cholera and plague epidemics in 1892, 1899, 1900, 1903–4, 1907, and 1909. For a statistical overview of epidemics drawn from the colonial record, see Sasha, *Social History of Epidemics in the Colonial Punjab* (Gurgaon: Partridge India, 2014), 43–82.

50. Dobson, *Final Report of the Chenab Colony Settlement*, 5.

brief periods of subsistence agriculture.[51] And since there was always turnover in the colonies, especially on those asymmetrical marginal plots at the ends of canals, phantom camels and real camels, false sarwans and authentic ones, could slide in and out of the new colonial apparatus, with each move establishing a basis for a real claim in the records. In effect, pastoralists didn't so much give up their way of life as adjust themselves and their animals to the "turbulence" generated by the colonial state.

In this dance between colonization officers and a floating population of claimants, what seemed to have most substantively influenced manipulation of the system was the presence or absence of water in the canal runs. Water shortages had a direct impact on the camel grantee units' ability to maintain their full strength. The uncertainty of water availability, in other words, especially affected those grantees with plots at the ends of canal lines and contributed directly to jangli residents shifting in and out of the fringes of colonies. In this case, the so-called shiftlessness of pastoralists was a product of colonial policy, one that came with its own complex ideological imaginary. Jangli, it was asserted, were "accustomed to eke out the profits of camel and cattle rearing by tilling inferior soil"—wasn't that the very nature of their more primitive way of life?[52]

But there was also another factor in play, one that involved water shortages throughout the colonies. Such shortages may have persisted partly because the Irrigation Department hesitated to increase the volume of water in the system. The department's rationale for this was fear of waterlogging and salinization of soil(!), an outcome that would negatively affect the (more centrally located) plots of yeoman agriculturalists and their higher-class neighbors. But from around 1906 forward, annual reports from one or another of the canal districts repeatedly pointed to complaints about water shortages.[53] Matters apparently did not improve until the Army Remount Department added its voice to the complaints of the civilian officers, and water capacity in the canals was increased.[54] There were also other kinds of manmade water shortages. Some of the preexisting cultivators along the Punjab's rivers who had relied on the annual inundation of their fields found their land bypassed by the pe-

51. ARPCC (1915), "Lower Bari Doab Canal Colony, Montgomery District," 48–49.

52. ARPCC (1909), "Jhelum Canal Colony," 26.

53. Such complaints are present in the annual reports from 1906 to 1909. See, for example, ARPCC (1909), "Reports on the Colonization Operations in the Punjab," 2; and "Chenab Canal Colony," 2.

54. ARPCC (1913), "Chenab Canal Colony, I. Lyallpur," 1.

rennial canal system. At the same time, their wells, for unknown reasons, began to dry up. Some, of course, like the *hitharis*, received compensation. But others were uprooted and forced into the margins of the colonies, where they competed with the jangli for less favorable land.[55]

And water shortages were not the only problems associated with what were quickly becoming only partly perennial canals. In periods of high spring runoff from the Himalayas, canal banks might be breached, while in normal periods the rich silt that earlier farmers had relied on to enrich their fields through inundation went to waste, clogging canal heads.[56] In addition, water tables were rising throughout the area of canal construction. One effect of such a process was percolation of water upward to the surface, with the attendant transfer of salt and other minerals. The results might appear as waterlogged soil or as white, dried-out patches of land unfit for planting. Such scenes of despoiled land began to be seen in the 1890s, and they continued to appear right up to the end of British rule. Traveling through the Chenab colony on the eve of the British leaving India, Malcolm Darling noted that it was like "leprosy" affecting the entire countryside—"for miles our horse's hoofs padded through the soggy snow-white earth"—and that large areas of an otherwise rich colony were "sterile."[57]

How to account for this end-of-empire environmental disaster? On the one hand, within the Irrigation Department and the colonial bureaucracy in general was an undeviating refusal to face the facts at hand. A major report on waterlogging published in 1922 consistently referred to accounts and complaints as ones of "alleged" waterlogging,[58] while earlier reports argued, as noted above, that waterlogging was merely a "blot" on an "otherwise admirable system." This kind of myopia, as Gilmartin has concluded, resulted because few officials or engineers were willing to let the danger of waterlogging and salinity interfere with "new surface-flow projects,"[59] all of which promised advanced technical solutions to any problems at hand.

At the same time, however, colonial officials do seem to have been at least mildly stimulated to action as a result of imperial oversight. The 1928 Royal

55. Indu Agnihotri, "Ecology, Land Use and Colonization: Canal Colonies in the Punjab," *Indian Economic and Social History Review* 33, no. 1 (1996): 44–47.

56. Ibid., 47–48.

57. Malcolm Darling, *At Freedom's Door* (Oxford: Oxford University Press, 1949), 77–78.

58. IOR/V/25/734/31: *Punjab Irrigation Branch Papers*, no. 20—"Waterlogging of the Soil in the Vicinity of Irrigation Canals, and the Measures of Prevention of Water-Logging" (1922), passim.

59. Gilmartin, *Blood and Water*, 236–37.

Commission on Agriculture, for example, after extensive investigations into and testimony concerning the canal system, concluded that the root of the problem in the Indus basin involved the "failure to correlate the irrigation system with the natural drainage of the tract." In other words, the integrated perennial canal scheme had been poorly engineered from the outset. Moreover, as the report explained, the massive state-funded improvement projects of the previous decades had also inadvertently created a public health problem.

> There can be little doubt that certain districts have tended, as a consequence of the interference by man with the forces of Nature, to decline in fertility and to become the breeding ground of malaria and other diseases. This process is occasionally, and sometimes seriously, aggravated by the construction of railway and road embankments across the lines of natural drainage.[60]

Given this conclusion, the government had little choice but to act. Drains were dug to carry off water seepage from canals, water was either shut off for long periods or flows reduced as much as possible, and main canal channels were lined to prevent seepage.[61]

Water supply issues were not the only problem creating friction in the canal colonies. Colonization officers also had to regularly deal with colonists' complaints about the conditions stipulated in the grants. These complaints included what some colonists saw as harsh enforcement of improvement and sanitation rules. By the first decade of the twentieth century, officers also had to confront the manifold problems related to the steady growth of indebtedness among colonists. Debt mostly arose as a result of the necessity to borrow money to replace aging or deceased animals who were part of either the Silladar or the Grantee units.[62] To put this another way, while the decision about when animals required replacement was in the hands of Army Remount Department officers, the repercussions of such decisions were most keenly felt by the grantee, who then would complain to the civilian administrators of the colonies when they were forced to replace either their camel or their mules.

Complicating matters further was the fact that Remount registration officers appeared to have been far more comfortable and adept at dealing with horse-

60. *Royal Commission on Agriculture in India Report* (Bombay: Central Government Press, 1928), 360.

61. Agnihotri, "Ecology, Land Use and Colonization," 51–52.

62. ARPCC (1911), "Chenab Canal Colony, I. Lyallpur District," 1, which notes that many of the poorer Baluchis had to borrow in order to replace a camel.

and mule-breeding grantees than with camel raisers. The horse-breeding allotments tended to focus attention on people already in the horse-raising business, while the mule-breeding grants were given to a highly visible population of *lambardars* (village headmen). Free land plus access to free government breeding stallions proved to be an incentive to attract breeders into the Jhelum canal colony, which is where the vast majority of the horse-breeding grants were located. The annual reports from this colony indicate that the horse-breeding initiative was a marked success. However, mule-breeding grants were another matter. We have already seen that despite the Punjab government's ambitions for breeding mules in India, the numbers consistently fell short of the army's requirements, especially with respect to ordnance mules. So the practice of importing mules from outside India continued. Why was this the case? Why did the army remain reliant on imports to maintain sufficient numbers of ordnance and transport mules?

There are at least four factors reflected in reports. One involved grantees violating the conditions of the grant, which required them to maintain a horse or pony mare capable of breeding mules. In many cases after the initial grant, however, the mare had either disappeared, lived beyond breeding age, or died and wasn't replaced. It often took time for the registration officers to identify such noncompliant situations and intervene. At that point, the only recourse they had at hand was to confiscate the plot if the grantee was unable or unwilling to replace the mare.[63]

A second factor was the breeding system for mules. Recall that when the Army Remount Department took over mule breeding from the Civil Veterinary Department in 1903, the numbers of mules foaled increased. Yet as impressive as that accomplishment seems to have been, the ARD mule-breeding program produced only about four hundred more mules a year than the CVD had in the final years of its supervision of breeding. The numerical difference, moreover, might be accounted for by the conditions of the mule grants, which gave ARD officers far more direct control over the breeders than their predecessors in the CVD had enjoyed.[64] In addition, as noted earlier, all the mule-breeding grantees were *lambardars*, who were already part of the colo-

63. ARPCC (1913), "Proceedings of His Honour the Lieutenant-Governor of the Punjab," 1. No figures are given for the number of confiscations, only that they continued.

64. After reorganization, the Punjab CVD retained responsibility for reporting on the production of government donkey studs who were outside the "imperial" breeding scheme; e.g., the one supervised by the ARD. Several of the reports after 1903 indicate the difficulty veterinarians had in getting information on coverings and foals dropped without the "harassment" of breeders. See *Annual Report of the Punjab Veterinary College and the Civil Veterinary De-*

nial administration and thus under the scrutiny of officials. But even if the breeding system was more efficient, and officials' claims about the popularity and success of mule breeding were true, the army still faced the handicap of reliance on the animal marketplace as the primary procurement site. Put simply, the four hundred additional mules being bred did not automatically go to the army; they still had to be competed for at animal auctions.

Moreover, breeders tended to hold their mules off the market until they were considered old enough to bring maximum return.[65] When they reached maturity, owners would take their mules to periodic fairs, where they could be purchased by anyone. By the end of the first decade of the twentieth century, military procurement officers, stuck with purchase prices fixed by the government, found it difficult to outbid dealers from northern India and Central Asia who were willing to pay more for quality mules.[66] Thus, mule shortages in India were also a function of the government's commitment to a kind of political economy that at times seemed to undermine the colonial administration's stated objectives.

Other economic limitations on mule production were also evident, some of which involved a different sort of calculation. Since little if any pastureland was available in the canal colonies, mares and their progeny had to be stall-fed grain. As a result, fluctuations in grain prices affected whether or not an owner would see it as beneficial to continue to keep a mare for breeding purposes. Reports indicated that when the price of grain went too high, owners simply got rid of their breeding animals.[67]

Lastly, shortages of ordnance and transport mules were also a function of a phenomenon that was termed "breeding to extinction."[68] If pony mares, for example, were widely used to breed mules, it meant that a certain percentage of mares would not be producing fertile male and female ponies, only sterile hybrids, that is, mules. Unless pony mares were replenished in some other way, the gradual decline in pony foals would steadily reduce the number of available fertile females, which would eventually have an impact on the number of mules produced as well.

The careful recording of mule production by CVD and ARD officers told

---

partment, Punjab and the Cattle Farm (Lahore: Civil and Military Gazette Press), 1908: 10 and 1912: 8.

65. See ARPCC (1906), "Chenab Canal Colony," 1.

66. See the 1909–10 annual report of the ARD in IOR/L/MIL/7/9697, p. 5.

67. See the 1908–9 annual report of the ARD in IOR/L/MIL/7/9697, pp. 12–13.

68. ARPCC (1909), "Chenab Canal Colony," 1.

another story as well. Records were kept of the ages of donkey studs and annual wastage rates. By 1913, the population as a whole was getting older, with the number of studs over fifteen years of age steadily increasing. Since the ARD, like the CVD before it, had difficulty competing for donkey jacks with southern European markets, most replacements seem to have come through the local breeding of donkeys. The quality of the Punjab's donkeys is difficult to gauge, but the continued reliance on imported ordnance mules, which as noted earlier needed to be of a higher quality than baggage or draft mules, suggests that there may have been problems with the local supply of donkey studs.

The above summary of frictions in mule breeding reflected in the annual reports provides some sense of the interrelated and competing motives and forces affecting cultivators, grantees, and their animals, as well as civil and military officials. These pushed and pulled them all in often opposite directions at the same time, while perpetually postponing the scientific and social paradise promised by colonial development officialdom.

Camels and their owners were affected by these changes, but in somewhat different ways. Although suggestions were made at various times, the army never seems to have seriously considered engaging in camel breeding.[69] Instead, it relied solely on the hereditary camel breeders to provide animals that eventually, through the market, would be purchased either as government camels or as the replacements required to sustain the Silladar and Grantee camel corps. This might have worked well if it had not been for the expansion of irrigation canals into the wastelands, which were the camels' browsing and breeding grounds.

Indications of the shrinkage of camel grazing land began to be reported in 1902 in the Chunian colony, where roving camels seeking sustenance were eating up the colony's recently planted trees.[70] By 1904, the colonization officer in the Chenab colony, Mr. French, was beginning to express concerns about

69. One proposal came from Maj. G. E. M. Hogg, who commanded at various times the Fifty-Fourth and later the Fifty-Second Silladar Camel Corps. He thought that any Silladar commander could breed camels for his own units with the help of an expert camel man, "unfettered" control over 3,600 acres of prime grazing land in the Salt Range, eighteen squares of land under existing canal schemes, and about Rs. 15,000 to purchase ninety brood *dachis* (fertile female camels). The commandant could then use male camels from his Silladar unit to mate with his *dachis*, and move seasonally between his *rakh* headquarters and canal colony holdings. See Henry Eustace Cross, *The Camel and Its Diseases: Being Notes of Veterinary Surgeons and Commandants of Camel Corps* (London: Baillière, Tindall and Cox, 1917), 29–30, 42–44.

70. ARPCC (1903), "Chunian Canal Colony," 41.

the conditions afflicting the camel grantees. In a report, French explained that many of the grantees had been located at the end of irrigation lines so that their camels would have access to grazing lands. In these locations, as we have seen, the grantees received insufficient water to assure them of agricultural prosperity.[71] The water issue not only affected the grantees' agricultural endeavors but eventually reduced the fitness of their animals to serve in the corps.[72] At the same time, French, and perhaps other colonization officers as well, was beginning to speculate about the problems posed to camel owners by grazing land and water shortages. He averred at one point that stall-feeding camels was undesirable.

> The extension of the mule-breeding scheme is likely to prove a greater success and of wider utility. It seems to me, as a layman, questionable whether stall-fed camels of the plains (themselves imported into the Colony) will successfully cope with the hardships of expeditions among rocky mountain passes.[73]

He also expressed doubt that stall-fed camels would maintain the proper condition of fitness for military service. The following year, he noted that female and young camels were declining both physically and in terms of absolute numbers in the population.[74] In 1908, the deputy commissioner at Lyallpur in the Chenab colony quoted the ARD registration officer on the subject of the "absolute inadequacy" of the grazing available to grantees on half squares. These colonists, the registration officer concluded, could not possibly make a living as long as they had to stall-feed camels.[75] The only recourse for the grantee in such a situation was to borrow against his use rights to the land, but this invariably meant not only spiraling debt but the decline of the homestead and, incidentally, the health of the camel pledged to military service. A later report concluded that camels could not thrive in cultivated areas.[76]

The situation concerning the camel grants continued to deteriorate, as did the strength of the reserve transport units, partly because of losses due to contagious diseases such as surra (see the next chapter). As noted earlier, in 1910 the government of the Punjab appointed a Camel Browsing Committee to

71. ARPCC (1905), "Chenab Canal Colony," 3.

72. See, for example, ARPCC (1908), "Chenab Canal Colony," 1. The same observations were repeated in reports for the years 1908–9 and 1909–10.

73. ARPCC (1906), "Chenab Canal Colony," 10.

74. ARPCC (1907), "Chenab Canal Colony," 1.

75. ARPCC (1909), "Chenab Canal Colony," 1.

76. ARPCC (1911), "Chenab Canal Colony, I. Lyallpur District," 1.

investigate the situation and make a recommendation. From December 1910 until June 1911, the committee met on at least five occasions, culminating in a final session and delivery of its report at Simla on 9 June 1911. Between meetings, the committee gathered information from local civil officials, veterinary surgeons, and camel corps officers. Its brief included investigations into the conditions of both the eight Silladar units and the four canal Grantee corps. The key issue, as the committee identified it, centered on the question of the availability of camel grazing land, which in turn directed attention to troubled relations between camel corps units, villages with use rights in government *rakhs*, and the Forestry Department.[77]

Not surprisingly, the committee concluded that the main problem the transport camel corps faced was inadequate grazing land for both the Silladar and the Grantee camel corps. In the case of the latter, the committee found that the land available within the canal colonies was wholly inadequate for the numbers of camels comprising the four corps. They recommended that the units be dissolved, the grantees be allowed to purchase their plots, and four new Silladar units be created in areas where browsing was easily obtainable and free from surra. The committee suggested that one might be put in the northern Sind, two at Dera Ghazi Khan on the Indus, where browsing was said to be unlimited, and one at Jorala.[78]

Some pushback to the committee's rather radical conclusions was given by civilian authorities in the canal colonies. H. P. Tollington, the revenue secretary of the Punjab's government, observed in early 1913 that the lieutenant governor of the province was unconvinced of the necessity to disband the grantee units. He added that over the course of 1912, the units had returned to full strength, and that improvements in irrigation had accounted for some of the change. Access to the forest preserves was, from his perspective, the real issue. If they were opened up to the grantee units, as they had been for the Silladar corps, presumably many of the problems associated with camel health would be solved. He concluded that it would appear that "though camel-breeding and keeping in the colony may in time disappear, that time has yet to arrive, and every effort should be made to defer it in view of the great desirability from a military point of view of retaining these valuable transport corps."[79] No final decision seems to have been made to disband the units, and in 1914, with the

77. IOR/P/8672: *Report of the Camel Browsing Committee*, *Punjab Proceedings* (December 1911), *Punjab Revenue and Agriculture Proceedings*, no. 18, 41–49.

78. Ibid., 46, 48.

79. ARPCC (1913), cover letter to the report, 2.

advent of World War I, three of the four grantee units were mobilized for the first time. The canal colony report in which the mobilization notice appeared also mentioned that because of ongoing difficulties in replacing camels, camel fairs had been initiated.[80]

The issues identified by the Camel Browsing Committee involving the Silladar units proved to be even more complicated than those of the grantee units. They revolved around the shared authority of Silladar commanders and Forestry Department officials over managing access to the forest reserves. The committee reported that this dual authority was unworkable.

> On the one hand subordinates of the [Forestry] department are found to have connived at commission of illicit acts by attributing them to sarwans of the corps; on the other hand, these sarwans have committed such acts, and have defended themselves by pretending that they were due to actions of outsiders, with or without the connivance of forest officials. . . . Under the circumstances, the Committee is strongly of the opinion that an attempt should be made to ensure effective protection [of the *rakhs*], by placing control entirely in the hands of the Corps Commandants in those areas under browsing, and in the hands of the local Forest Officer in the areas allotted to the corps but actually under regeneration.[81]

The committee then calculated the amount of grazing land in the forest reserves required by each of the corps, determined if sufficient browsing resources were available near their base, and set figures for the maximum number of camels allowed to browse in the forests at any one time.[82] While its recommendations would appear to have been able to resolve the greatest frictions disrupting camel browsing (i.e., clashes between sarwans and forest officials), it also acknowledged that resources would be stretched, particularly with respect to breeding. The committee estimated that to maintain one thousand female camels and young stock, forty thousand acres of browsing land would be required. In the case of the Fifty-Fifth and Fifty-Sixth Camel Corps based at Montgomery, only about three thousand acres were left in the wastelands. Such a severe restriction of territory was exacerbated by the fact that nearby villages had long-standing rights in the *rakhs*, including access to firewood and various plants and herbs that grew in the jungle. Although no mention is

80. ARPCC (1915), "Lower Chenab Canal Colony, I. Lyallpur District," 2.
81. *Report of the Camel Browsing Committee*, 42.
82. Ibid., 43–46.

made concerning the other base areas, it seems safe to assume, given the ongoing canal expansion, that the story was not much different around the bases of other Silladar units. At the same time, however, the committee rejected the recommendation of one of the civil veterinarians that a camel-breeding farm be established. Instead, it thought that setting aside a certain amount of browsing land near each base for raising camels would suffice.[83]

Yet this conclusion on the part of the Camel Browsing Committee appears to ignore a key issue also affecting camel life in the Punjab. It turned out that it wasn't simply the availability of browsing land for camels but its quality that proved critical. Most menacing to camel life in the Punjab was the disease called surra, which by this time the committee well knew was spread by biting flies, the *Tabanus* horsefly in particular. The breeding cycle of the *Tabanus* was closely associated with the rainy season and wet ground, like that to be found around irrigation canals. The committee was also aware that breeding grounds for these flies had been detected near some of the camel corps bases, and that periodic surra outbreaks resulted. Hence, the only grazing land that made sense for camel welfare and the viability of the reserve camel corps was land free of surra and *Tabanus*.

Moreover, even before the Camel Browsing Committee was created, mortality from surra had become such an issue that the Civil Veterinary Department had assigned a specialist to study camel diseases. The first veterinary surgeon to hold the position was Arnold Leese, and it was Leese who recommended a camel-breeding farm, to be located away from the places he had identified as surra zones. That Leese's recommendation found little support in the Browsing Committee report provides another example of the difference in thinking about camels, as opposed to horses and mules, in the British Indian Army and the civilian establishment of the Punjab.

But the surra issue was another matter. It could not be ignored, because surra not only decimated units of the Silladar and Grantee Camel Corps, thus placing the owners of these animals in financial distress and weakening each corps that lost animals in this way. Surra also killed horses, ponies, and to a lesser extent mules. In that sense, the disease successfully threatened the entire new security structure that connected mobile cavalry, mountain artillery, and martial-race infantry units to army transport. It is to the colonial state's response to surra that I now turn. At the heart of this response were veterinary surgeons, who in the first decade of the twentieth century had gained

83. Ibid., 49.

much of the authority that the editors of the *Quarterly Journal of Veterinary Science in India and Army Animal Management* had called for in the 1880s.

*

In this chapter, I explored how the Government of India's decision to create a permanent army transport system served to link Remount Department officers, veterinarians, pack animals, and colonial improvement projects in novel ways. The primary effect of the construction of this assemblage was to produce an animal management biopower regime and a hydraulic engineering project that connected colonial agricultural expansion to military security. I also showed how these initiatives were disrupted by problems associated with mule-breeding practices, canal engineering mishaps, dwindling camel grazing land, and unanticipated responses to the new order by the indigenous population. Colonial order was also disrupted by an unanticipated subversive element, an actant made up of a parasitic microbe and a biting fly that produce surra. This disease attacked the essential nonhuman agents of the military security regime in the Punjab: camels, mules, and horses. It is to this disease and its impact on the colonial order that I now turn.

CHAPTER 8

Surra and the Emergence of Tropical Veterinary Medicine in Colonial India

In the processes of interaction between microorganism and host, it is necessary to take into consideration the interests of the parasite.

I. P. PAVLOV[1]

The parasite is an exciter . . . [that] enters the system as an element of fluctuation [and] changes its state . . . by despoiling actions, like ascarid worms or leeches; by toxic actions, like ticks or fleas; by trauma, like bilharzia or trichina worms; by infection, like dysenteric amoebas; by obstruction, like the filarial of elephantiasis; by compression, like those that form cysts; by irritations, inflammations, itching; by rashes.

MICHEL SERRES[2]

This chapter explores how the colonial state was excited into action to deal with a direct threat to the logistical organization of its frontier security system. The threat in question was a parasite that caused the disease named surra, which was killing camels and equines. Recall that surra was a name used by Punjabi sarwans (camel handlers) for the affliction. Since the late nineteenth century, veterinary scientists have known the agent of the disease as *Trypanosoma evansi*, a flagellated protozoan blood parasite dependent for its spread on a biting insect vector. *T. evansi* is one of a number of species that make up the genus *Trypanosoma*, whose members are distributed widely across the tropical regions of the world. Species can be found in a number of African, Asian, and South American domestic and wild animals, and at least two types have become pathogenic in human populations, causing African sleeping sickness and Chagas disease in Latin America. In all its hosts, trypanosomiasis causes anemia, edema, and emaciation; in many cases it is fatal.

1. Cited in Cecil Hoare, *The Trypanosomes of Mammals* (Oxford: Blackwell Scientific Publications, 1972), 113.

2. Michel Serres, *The Parasite* (Minneapolis: University of Minnesota Press, 2007), 191.

Trypanosomiasis in British India came into focus as an animal health issue only after 1880, when veterinary researchers demonstrated that this blood parasite was the primary cause of many deaths among Indian Army cavalry horses and Supply and Transport Corps pack animals. In this chapter, I explore the impact of surra and surra research on the camels and mules of the Indian Army transport service and its veterinary medical corps. It will be my argument that the surra parasite provided the useful object around which the civilian and army veterinary services in India could be refigured as the primary authority for defining army animal management. In addition, it was the nonhuman agent through which veterinary surgeons were transformed into tropical medicine experts.

DISCOVERING AND NAMING THE AGENT OF SURRA

Surra was discernible to sarwans as a "loss of condition" in camels. The disease developed gradually, with each stage carrying a distinct name. The first of these became visible when the animal refused food and passed urine of a high color (*khanhog*). In the second stage, the animal's chest became swollen (*doaia*). In the last stage, the swelling extended to the abdomen and legs, and the animal began to waste away (surra). Some British veterinary surgeons asked sarwans about the disease and its detection. Henry Pease, for instance, was told that it might be detected by dullness in the eye and change in odor of the urine.[3] Arnold Leese, another veterinary surgeon, noted that the Raibari, those Punjabi camel specialists on whom the Mughal had relied, allowed camels they suspected of having surra to urinate on a round, compacted piece of earth. Once the ball was dry, they would smell it to determine if surra was present. Raibari practitioners also plucked a hair from the camel's tail, and if the root did not stick to the palm of the hand, this also indicated the presence of surra.[4] Griffith Evans wrote about the various stages of the disease and also recorded a treatment method by Punjabi sarwans. If treated early enough with a formula of ghee and the boiled extracts of the "*sivah* or *vunna*" trees that grew in the hills, the camel could be cured.[5]

3. See Henry T. Pease, "Tibarsa Surra: Trypanosomiasis in the Camel," *Journal of Tropical Veterinary Science* (hereafter *JTVS*) 1, no. 1 (1906): 75. Pease added that he was unable to diagnose surra without the aid of a microscope.

4. Arnold Leese, *A Treatise on the One-Humped Camel in Health and in Disease* (Stanford, Lincolnshire: Haynes and Son, 1927), 240.

5. See Griffith Evans, "Report on 'Surra' Disease," which originally appeared in a *Punjab Government, Military Department* circular dated 13 November 1880 (no. 439-4467). Evans's

The cause of the disease was unknown to the Raibari and other indigenous camel men, but its pattern of occurrence was fairly well understood by northwestern Indian sarwans. It would arise in the rainy season, killing many of the camels who caught it, and it was known to be correlated with the arrival of the biting flies that came with the rains. The response of those who kept camels was to move them, if possible, away from water or marshy places, preferably into the dryer lands of the north or the arid elevated regions (doab) between the Punjab's five rivers. An infected camel would either die or, if it recovered, might be debilitated for up to two years.

In the wake of the Second Afghan War, the British understanding of surra, drawn primarily from indigenous camel men, began to change with the arrival of germ theory, the microscope, the hypodermic needle, and, eventually, younger veterinarians conversant with the emerging field of germ theory and microbiology. Sometime in September 1880, near Dera Ismail Khan on the Indus River, the Indian Army veterinary surgeon Griffith Evans put a blood smear taken from a sick horse of the Fourth Punjab Cavalry under a microscope and identified a small flagellated organism that he realized ought not to have been there (fig. 11). Evans then injected blood from the infected horse into an uninfected one, recorded the blooming of the microbe in the blood of the second horse, and declared the entity he had seen to be the cause of surra. He then performed a similar experiment with a dog and got the same results. Not long after, he found that the same microbe was present in the blood of sick mules and camels (63–64).

In his report on his methodology and discovery, Evans explained how he had carried out a number of autopsies on horses who had died of the disease, determining that there had been no damage to internal organs. He concluded that the disease was exclusively one of the blood, and described how single and sometimes multiple microbes could be seen simultaneously attacking and ripping apart red blood cells (70). This violent, swarming, and excited activity of the parasite, which seems to have awed Evans, was followed by its dying off and then reblooming over time. As for the mode of transmission into the horse's blood, Evans thought that it was probably through food or drinking water, but he also mentioned the indigenous notion that the disease was transmitted by large, biting flies called by the natives *bhura dhang* ("great needle-

---

report is reprinted in IOR/V/27/541/15 (1885), *Report of Veterinary Surgeon J. H. Steel, A.V.D., on His Investigation into an Obscure and Fatal Disease among Transport Mules in British Burma* . . . (India: Punjab Military Department, 1881–82), 59–89; see p. 65. Subsequent references to this source are given in the text.

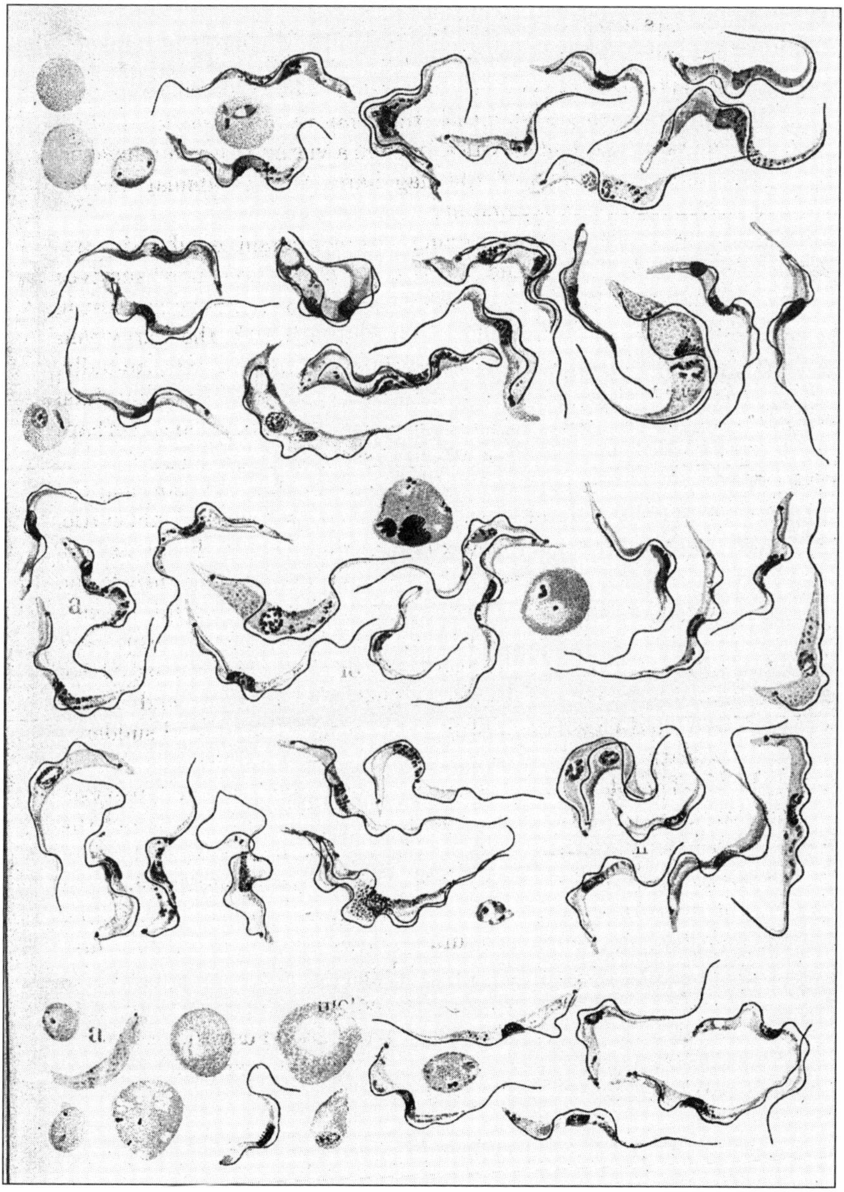

FIGURE 11. *Trypanosoma evansi.* From *Journal of Tropical Veterinary Medicine* 2, no. 1 (1907).

like sting"), which swarmed around horses (63). Evans recommended that additional experiments be conducted to establish the mode of transmission, also arguing that until more was known about the parasite, it might be wise to retain the indigenous name for the disease—that is, surra (59).

Evans's findings were printed locally in a Military Department circular of the government of the Punjab in November 1880. The following year, it was reprinted in installments between July 1881 and March 1882 in the London-based *Veterinary Journal and Annals of Comparative Pathology*, the major veterinary medicine publication in Great Britain. In India, however, Evans received little notice of his findings and no support for his experiments. Neither the surgeon general of India, Dr. J. M. Cuningham,[6] who as we saw in chapter 1 had a low opinion of veterinary surgeons, nor Evans's immediate superior, Dr. Timothy Lewis, thought that the parasite in question was pathogenic. Lewis based this conclusion on his study of rat blood, where flagellated entities like those that Evans had found were common in "healthy" rats (*T. lewisi*). Lewis added that the dog Evans had injected with surra blood was most probably suffering from "distemper." Both Cuningham and Lewis seem to have subscribed to the theory that no microbes in blood were pathogenic, but merely the result of a body's production of an unknown chemical that generated harmless entities.[7] In short, Evans was accused by his immediate superiors of having mistaken "effect" for "cause."[8] But in the view of George Fleming, the editor of the *Veterinary Journal* in London, this dismissal of Evans's research was outrageous; he saw it as just another example of the scorn the medical profession had for veterinarians.[9]

There matters stood until, in 1885, the veterinary surgeon John Henry Steel identified a microbe in the blood of sick army mules in Burma as the cause of their "relapsing fever." Steel duplicated the process of transmission from sick to healthy animals that Evans had pioneered and concluded that he was

6. Cuningham was a staunch opponent of germ theory and contagionist views; see David Arnold, *Science, Technology and Medicine in Colonial India* (Cambridge: Cambridge University Press, 2000), 83.

7. Griffith Evans, "Autobiographical Memoir," *Annals of Tropical Medicine and Parasitology* 12, no. 1 (July 1918): 7–14.

8. Somewhat later, this was the conclusion drawn by Sir Frederick Smith from his evaluation of the Cuningham and Lewis assessment of Evans's findings. Smith thought them both wrong and unnecessarily hostile to Evans. See his *A History of the Royal Army Veterinary Corps, 1796–1919* (London: Baillière, Tindall and Cox, 1927), 174.

9. Editorial, *Veterinary Journal* 13 (July 1881): 133.

dealing with the same pathogen as had been described by Evans. He made no special claims of originality, seeing himself instead as confirming Evans's work.[10] However, he also provided the first drawings of the parasite, the shape of which led him to compare it to "Spirillum Fever" and dubbed it *Spirochaete evansi*, a name that classified it among bacterial microorganisms.[11]

After Steel's characterization of the parasite in Burma, there followed what might be understood as, to use Andrew Pickering's insight, a "mangle of practice," wherein the nature of the being of the nonhuman agent remained elusive.[12] Cecil Hoare, the protozoologist and parasitologist and a historian of research on trypanosomiasis, noted that as researchers focused their microscopes on the organism, over a decade of "confusion in the nomenclature" resulted. *Haematomonas evansi*, *Trichomonos evansi*, *Spirochaeta evansi,* and *Trypanosomum evansii* appeared in the scientific literature, while virtually unnoticed at the time, Edouard Balbiani slipped the misspelled term "*Tripanosoma evansi*" into an 1888 publication.[13]

Meanwhile, as scientists strove to insert the entity into a familiar taxonomic scheme, little research was occurring in India to gain further understanding of the disease in camels or to determine how surra was transmitted.[14] Then in the early 1890s, Alfred Lingard, the holder of the newly created position of imperial bacteriologist, began a study in India of surra in equines. In this work, Lingard accepted the fact that the entity, designated as *Trypanosoma evansi*, after Evans, was pathogenic. He also insisted that the path of transmission of the parasite was through the digestive system of animals. In a summary of his findings that appeared in 1894, he wrote that

> there can be little doubt that many of the outbreaks are due to the ingestion of rats' or bandicoots' excrement with corn. In the hot season, the haematozoon or its resting form in the excrement would naturally be destroyed by the

10. IOR/V/27/541/15: *Report of Veterinary Surgeon J. H. Steel, A.V.D.*; Steel's report is on pp. 1–58.

11. John Henry Steel, "On Relapsing Fever of Equines," *Veterinary Journal and Annals of Comparative Pathology* 22 (1886): 166–74.

12. Andrew Pickering, "The Mangle of Practice: Agency and Emergence in the Sociology of Science," *American Journal of Sociology* 99, no. 3 (1993): 559–89.

13. Hoare, *The Trypanosomes of Mammals*, 555–56.

14. In his *A Manual of the Diseases of the Camel and of His Management and Uses* (Madras: Lawrence Asylum Press, 1890), John Henry Steel had little to say about surra research (46–47).

> continued drought; while in the rains, the moisture would be found sufficient to sustain the life of the infusoria, and enable the resting form to germinate.[15]

In other words, while Lingard recognized a relation between the rainy season and the spread of the disease, he seemed to think of the surra parasite as if it were much like a fungal spore. This led him to speculate further that one possible mode of moving such spore-like parasites among populations of animals was in the draft created by fast-moving trains.[16] Hence for Lingard, the expansion of the Indian railroad system had an obvious impact on equine ecology.

Not long after Lingard published his conclusions concerning the mode of transmission of surra, David Bruce, of the Royal Army Medical Corps in South Africa, was studying a debilitating disease in cattle referred to by the indigenous herders of "Zululand" as *nagana*. Bruce identified what he saw under his microscope as akin to the entities described by Evans in India and Steel in Burma over a decade earlier. More important, he argued that the disease was transferred from wild animals to healthy cattle by the Tsetse fly. His findings were published in two reports that appeared in 1895–96,[17] and they were summarized both in the *Veterinary Journal* and in *Nature* in 1896. The latter indicated that the nagana microbe was "allied to, if not actually identical with, *Trypanosoma evansi*, the haematozoon of 'Horse Surra.'"[18] Significantly, Bruce's research was the first clear indication that the trypanosome parasite required a living agent to carry it from one mammalian host to another. It also confirmed the long-standing observations of African herders[19] and Punjabi sarwans that the disease was connected to the presence of biting flies.

15. Alfred Lingard, *Summary of Further Report on Surra* (Bombay: Government Central Press, 1894), 8. *Infusoria* was a term used to encompass all microscopic life in water.

16. Alfred Lingard, *Report on Horse Surra* (Bombay: Government Central Press, 1893), 10–11.

17. David Bruce, *Preliminary Report on the Tsetse Fly Disease or Nagana, in Zululand* (Durban: Bennett and Davis, 1895), and *Further Report on the Tsetse Fly Disease or Nagana, in Zululand* (London: Harrison and Sons, 1896).

18. "The Tsetse Fly Disease," *Nature* 53, no. 1381 (April 1896): 566–67. The entry on surra and Lingard's research appeared in *Veterinary Journal* 42 (March 1896): 177–83. Also see the entry on the Tsetse fly, which speculates about the findings of Lingard and Bruce, 42 (June 1896): 410–13.

19. African agriculturalists combined the hunting of wild animals who were the reservoirs of trypanosomes with brush clearing in potential breeding areas of the Tsetse fly, producing what John Ford has called "a mobile ecological equilibrium with the wildlife ecosystems and

But the importance of Bruce's nagana research went beyond new connections he made between trypanosomes, flies, and pathology. On the one hand, the comparative references found in his reports, the rapidity with which his findings got into print, and the venues in which they appeared point to a new set of relationships in the domain of empire. The "polycentric" communication and transportation networks that connected Zululand, India, and Burma to London also allowed for horizontal connections,[20] ones that in this case put Bruce in touch with Lingard in India and repositioned London as more of a clearinghouse than a director of scientific developments.[21] This trend would continue into the twentieth century. Some researchers of pathogenic microbes began to think in terms of global latitudinal zones in which certain entities were specific to the "tropics," malaria being a prime example. In the British case, the proposed latitudinal zones covered colonies in southern and northeast Africa, South Asia, Southeast Asia, and the Pacific. This geographic range meant that research being done in German and French sub-Saharan colonies, the French colonies in North Africa and Southeast Asia, and the American colony of the Philippines could effectively be made relevant to the work of British veterinary surgeons in India.[22]

---

their associated diseases"; see his *The Role of Trypanosomiases in African Ecology: A Study of the Tsetse Fly Problem* (Oxford: Clarendon Press, 1971), 145. Also see John M. MacKenzie, *The Empire of Nature: Hunting, Conservation, and British Imperialism* (Manchester: Manchester University Press, 1988), 234–35.

20. I take the term from David W. Chambers and Richard Gillespie, who argue against a center/periphery and a diffusionist model of the history of science in their "Locality in the History of Science: Colonial Science, Technoscience, and Indigenous Knowledge," *Osiris* 15 (2000): 221–40. See especially p. 223 and their critique of "modernization theory," pp. 224–26. Also see Deborah Neill, *Networks in Tropical Medicine* (Stanford, CA: Stanford University Press, 2012), who traces many links and moments of cooperation between French, German, and British scientists as well as multinational participation in European conferences and publications in scientific journals, all of which, she argues, established productive international networks that furthered scientific discoveries of tropical diseases. Her approach appears, however, to be essentially diffusionist, with a focus that extends little beyond Africa and sleeping sickness.

21. On the Bruce-Lingard correspondence, see Bruce, *Further Report on the Tsetse Fly Disease or Nagana, in Zululand*, 17.

22. The tropical colonial network and the scale of research on trypanosomes can be discerned, for example, in C. A. Thimm, comp., *Bibliography of Trypanosomiasis . . .* (London: Sleeping Sickness Bureau, 1909). Also see the sources cited in Alphonse Laveran and Félix Mesnil, *Trypanosomes and Trypanosomiasis*, trans. David Nabarro (London: Baillière, Tindall and Cox, 1907).

On the other hand, Bruce's findings also disrupted and challenged accepted theories of how pathogens moved into healthy mammalian bodies. Yet his research did not change all minds. Even after he must have been aware of Bruce's findings in Africa, Lingard appears to have maintained his own view that surra was spread by air and ingestion, a position that continued to be repeated in the literature into the twentieth century, even after researchers had come to believe that biting flies were the only mode of transmission.[23] When Lingard went on sick leave between 1898 and 1900, his subordinate, Leonard Rogers, took over as the acting director of the imperial bacteriological laboratory at Muktesar in the Himalayan foothills. Rogers took the opportunity to carry out a series of experiments with biting flies to determine if they were indeed the vector of surra. By this time, Bruce's work on nagana and studies by several researchers on the transmission of malaria by the *Anopheles* mosquito reinforced the notion that diseases could be transmitted via insect vectors. Rogers's experiments were, therefore, not unusual. What was unusual was how he handled his results. He bypassed the medical establishment in India and sent his findings to the Tsetse Fly Committee of the Royal Society. In London, Bruce presented Rogers's report to a meeting of the society on 14 February 1901, and it was soon published in the society's *Proceedings*.

What Rogers had found was that biting flies, primarily the *Tabanus* species, transmitted the disease by carrying infected blood in their mouthparts from one animal to another. The process of transmission, as he described it, was somewhat hit or miss. It required that the fly be disturbed while feeding on one animal and thereupon almost immediately begin feeding on another. The longer the interval between feedings, the less likely it was that the pathogen would be passed from a diseased to a healthy animal. This suggested to Rogers that the surra microbe could live outside its host only for a very brief period of time, meaning that it was neither airborne nor an infusoria to be found in water or decaying matter. He dubbed this mode of microbial transmission "mechanical," because it involved no interaction between microbe and vector other than transportation.[24]

23. See W. E. Musgrave and Moses T. Clegg, *Trypanosoma and Trypanosomiasis, with Special Reference to Surra in the Philippine Islands* (Manila: Bureau of Public Printing, 1903), 75, 78–79.

24. Leonard Rogers, "The Transmission of the *Trypanosoma evansi* by Horse Flies, and Other Experiments Pointing to the Probable Identity of Surra in India and Nagana or Tsetse-Fly Disease of Africa," *Proceedings of the Royal Society of London* 68 (1901): 163–70.

A VETERINARY OFFICER FOR INVESTIGATING CAMEL DISEASES

As was noted in the last chapter, throughout the early years of the new transport system, the camel units had difficulty maintaining full strength, in part because of high levels of "wastage" and difficulties in acquiring replacement animals. The annual reports from 1901 to 1904 of the Supply and Transport Corps estimated camel wastage rates at the staggering levels of 30 to 40 percent annually.[25] By 1907, the corps was complaining of shortages of available camels and an increase in prices for replacements, factors that led to the demobilization of one of the Silladar units in 1908. Meanwhile, the problem of high levels of wastage caused by surra among government and Silladar camels was placed in the hands of the Civil Veterinary Department, which addressed it in a novel way.[26] As camel losses mounted, the CVD took the extraordinary step in 1905 of creating the position of the "Veterinary Officer Investigating Camel Diseases." If nothing else, the appointment signaled that the Government of India and the British Indian Army were still very strongly committed to camel-labor power as part of the logistics of the Indian security regime. R. M. Montgomery, a new arrival at the Imperial Bacteriological Laboratory in Muktesar, was given the position.[27] For reasons not made clear in the CVD's annual report the following year, Montgomery resigned the position. Soon after, he was replaced by a civilian veterinarian named Arnold Leese, who arrived from London in 1906. Leese proceeded to Kathgodam, near Muktesar, where he studied "Hindustani" and read up on surra.[28]

With a free hand given him by Col. Henry Pease, the inspector general of the CVD, Leese spent the next six years investigating camel diseases and the ways of life in which the animals were embedded. His work as veterinary

25. The reports are bundled together in IOR/L/MIL/7/6700. See *Annual Report Supply and Transport* (1901), 20; *ARS&T* (1902), 16; and *ARS&T* (1903), 17.

26. This seems an odd choice, given that all the transport units were under army control. On the other hand, most of the veterinarians in the CVD were army officers.

27. Originally, the laboratory was in Puna, but Lingard lobbied the government successfully to have it moved away from the heat and dust of the lowlands into the mountains. On Lingard's role in the establishment of the Muktesar laboratory, see Pratik Chakrabarti, *Bacteriology in British India: Laboratory Science and the Tropics* (Rochester: University of Rochester Press, 2012), 62–65.

28. Arnold Leese, *Out of Step: Events in the Two Lives of an Anti-Jewish Camel-Doctor* (Guildford, England: Arnold S. Leese, 1951), 16. Leese seems to have self-published all his works, including his book on camels cited in chapter 2.

scientist and military animal manager stands as an important transition in the colonial ecology of human-animal relations. Leese conducted his research almost wholly in the field, spending most of his time near camel grazing country in a base of operations at Sohawa in the Jhelum District. Although the afflictions he studied included a number of ailments, such as tuberculosis, Jhooling (skin tumors and lesions), anthrax, foot-and-mouth, *Filaria evansi* (parasitic worms; and yes, the same Evans), mange, and bilharziasis (intestinal parasites), he spent the bulk of his time investigating surra in camels. In annual tours built around what he identified as the surra season, Leese visited all the army's active and reserve camel units, took blood samples, identified the breeding grounds of biting flies such as *Tabanus* and *Stomoxys*, questioned sarwans on camel care and afflictions, and investigated the relation between weather patterns, grazing grounds, and animal health. He took, in other words, an epidemiological approach to the disease,[29] one that involved grueling work, with temperatures approaching and exceeding 100 degrees daily under a blinding sun. He later recalled that he might examine the blood of up to a hundred camels in one session, "squeezing a drop out of a very slight nick in the ear of the animal on to a slide" and then setting up his microscope on the ground for viewing.[30]

Leese's first major epidemiological observation occurred at the very beginning of his appointment, during an investigation into surra among the *tonga*, or fast postal transport service by pony between the hill towns of Kathgodam and Nainithal. While making a "fly survey" of the road, he ascertained that the conventional belief held by his CVD colleagues, that the disease spread only between October and December, was wrong. The *Tabanus* flourished during the monsoon season from late spring into summer, and had disappeared by fall (see box 8.1). Thus, flies could transmit trypanosomes between animals only during the rainy season. It followed that the disease must incubate for a period, showing signs of its presence only from the fall to early winter.[31] Leese concluded that if he was going to sort out the patterns of the disease, he would have to be in the field during the time the disease was spread, the months of June to October.

29. Epidemiology is, to quote Cecil Hoare, "a science based on the analysis and synthesis of the factors affecting the development of infections, involving knowledge of the ecology of mammalian hosts and their vectors, or their zoogeography and bionomics"; see *The Trypanosomes of Mammals*, 118.

30. Leese, *Out of Step*, 17.

31. Ibid., 16.

BOX 8.1: Tabinadae

The Tabinadae family is made up of some 4,300 species globally, including varieties of Tabanus to be found in India. Only female Tabanus feed on blood, but they can be persistent feeders. If interrupted at the start of breaking the skin of the host, they often return to the same place and complete the feeding process. They may also take blood from multiple animals in one feeding session. Since they essentially act as a mechanical vector for diseases, particularly *Trypanosoma evansi*, carrying microbes in contaminated blood on their mouthparts, biting rates, and interrupted feedings influence the transmission of pathogens. The females generally mate and feed before laying eggs.

The eggs are attached to the underside of leaves overhanging or close to relatively stable or moving water. Once they hatch, the larvae drop into shallow water, mud, or damp vegetation and burrow into the moist earth. They can undergo several larvae molts and remain in this state over the winter. In warmer climes, they leave watery areas to pupate for up to three weeks, but the timing of their transformation into flying invertebrates depends on a number of climatic factors—temperatures, rainfall, and barometric pressure. In South Asia, the monsoon patterns were part of the Tabanus reproductive cycle, but the cycle was only partly determined by the absence or presence of rain. The Punjab's rivers and canals, running through soft alluvial soil, and waterlogged areas near canals were also potential maturation sites, as was the timing of the spring flood. For a detailed discussion of the life cycle of the Tabinadae, see Gary Mullen and Lance Durden, *Medical and Veterinary Entomology* (Amsterdam: Academic Press, 2002), 263–71.

In the next surra season, he selected Mohand as the site for experiments to determine if biting flies were the vector of the disease. Surra had ravaged *tonga* ponies there as well, but the pony traffic had disappeared with the building of a rail line. Leese thought that by bringing both healthy and infected animals into a surra area with no others around, he would have an ideal situation for testing. Healthy ponies were purchased locally, and camels infected with surra were brought to Mohand by Leese and his assistants, Ata Mahommed and Kahan Singh. The three of them built an enclosure and covered part of it with mosquito netting. They put two healthy ponies under the netting (a control group kept away from flies), and four others, one of whom had been infected with surra, in open stalls. Leese eliminated grass and water as possible transmission agents by giving all the ponies the same water and local grass as portions of their feed. The same brushes, currycombs, and harnesses were used on all the animals in order to control for the possibility that such paraphernalia might be transmission agents. Although some flies were present in April and May, there were no indications that the disease had spread. When the rains arrived near the end of June, however, the situation changed dramatically.

Masses of large *Tabanus* "horseflies," along with *Haematopota* and *Stomoxys*, appeared at the start of July. Trypanosomes showed up in the blood of the three unprotected ponies between the fourth and seventeenth of August, or from six to seven weeks after the rains had started. Flies were caught and dissected, but no trypanosomes were found in their guts.[32] Leese concluded that transmission was purely mechanical, the biting fly acting as a conveyor of the pathogen on the surface of its mouthparts and proboscis, and no more.[33] His findings were summarized, with extensive quotation by Pease, in the 1909 annual report of the CVD.[34] The results also appeared, with handsome illustrations of the flies, in *Indian Civil Department Memoirs*.[35] However, when no recognition of the experiment was forthcoming in the London-based *Veterinary Journal*, Leese submitted his results in a letter to the *Sleeping Sickness Bulletin*, where it was printed in 1911. I will have more to say on this letter below. Here it is sufficient to note that Leese made two original observations in the letter, ones he presumably wanted others researching trypanosomiasis to be cognizant of. First, he explained that following an unusual rainy season, he had found surra present in the "sandy wastes" of the Bikaner desert in Rajputana. This was an area without canals where no *Tabanus* or *Stomoxys* flies were present. Second, he reported that he had identified a new biting fly vector, *Lyperosia*. Given the number of fly vectors he had now verified as

32. See *Sleeping Sickness Bulletin* 3, no. 26 (1911): 369.

33. Arnold Leese, "Camel Surra," in *Report of the Veterinary Officer Investigating Camel Diseases for the Year Ending 31st March 1909* (Simla: Government Central Branch Press, 1909), 9–11. In addition, Leese published a version of this report as "Experiments regarding the Natural Transmission of Surra Carried Out in Mohand in 1908," *JTVS* 4, no. 2 (1909): 107–32. He also briefly outlined the experiment in *Out of Step* (p. 19).

34. See *Annual Administrative Report of the Civil Veterinary Department, 1908–09* (Simla: Government Central Branch Press, 1909), 14–16.

35. See *Indian Civil Department Memoirs* 2 (1909): 1–26.

operating in India, Leese argued that there was no reason to doubt that the disease was spread by mechanical transmission on the mouthparts of flies.[36]

I emphasize the publication trail here, not only to demonstrate the venues then available for the circulation of medical and militarily useful information, but to make two other points. The first has to do with comparative research on trypanosomiasis in European colonies. In this case, as far as was known at the time, the vector of nagana and sleeping sickness in Africa was exclusively the Tsetse fly. By submitting his findings to the *Sleeping Sickness Bulletin*, Leese was announcing that if the trypanosome of surra in India was the same as or related to the African entity, then he had been able to show that it could be spread by many different kinds of biting flies.[37] Second, although Leese himself admitted there were a few questions still to be answered about transmission, he had demonstrated through live-animal experiments how an epidemiological approach to the disease could resolve long-standing speculation about the etiology of trypanosome infection in horses and pack animals.

Over the next four years, Leese refined these initial conclusions by expanding his range of observations across the Punjab and into Baluchistan and the Sind. As he inspected and tested for surra, he also recorded camel mortality rates, examined for other diseases, and distributed microscopes for diagnostic use by the Indian veterinary aides in the Silladar units. Since he had found surra present in all the units he visited, his idea was to enroll the commandants and camel men into a more comprehensive surveillance scheme. He no doubt sought in part to establish a firm statistical base for the disease. But his distribution of microscopes to the Silladar units was also intended to demonstrate to the natives the superiority of a modern visual technology in tracing the disease and identifying its causal agent.[38] In 1909, Leese was happy to report that the commandants of the Silladar corps and their veterinary aides had developed confidence in the microscope and had begun using it to cull infected animals from their units.[39]

At the same time that he was introducing a technoscientific system for iden-

36. *Sleeping Sickness Bulletin* 3, no. 26 (1911): 367–69.

37. Leese actually wondered at the time whether the trypanosomes were the same. Later research would indicate that *T. evansi* was a descendant of the trypanosome identified by Bruce (*T. brucei*) but distinctly different, because it could be transmitted only mechanically. See the discussion about the history of the discovery of this difference in Hoare, *The Trypanosomes of Mammals*, 382–83; and chapter 10.

38. *Report of the Veterinary Officer Investigating Camel Diseases for the Year Ending 31st Mach 1909* (Simla: Government Central Branch Press, 1909), 1, 5–6.

39. Ibid., 6.

tifying surra, Leese was also able to establish more firmly a relation between water, be it canal irrigation or monsoon rains, and the life cycles of biting flies. In the case of *Tabanus*, the fly's larvae were found on the leaves of plants overhanging the canals and in the areas where canals overflowed in flood season.[40] This led Leese to advocate what he thought of as a simple preventive measure. Camels ought to be moved out of areas where larvae had been identified and into grazing grounds free of canals and pooled water from monsoon rains. To exemplify the effectiveness of such a procedure, he pointed to the Sixty-Seventh Punjabi Transport Corps. During his tour of this unit, he learned that they habitually moved their camels into surra-free grazing areas during the rains and consequently had the lowest mortality rate among camel transport units.[41] Having established to his satisfaction the relation between bodies of water and biting flies, Leese increasingly used his field tours to identify naturally occurring surra-free havens.[42] As a result of his work, it may have become a regular practice to move at least some of the camel corps during the surra season.[43]

Yet Leese was aware that his search for safe grazing grounds was being undercut by the canal construction projects of the Punjab Public Works Department. He noted at one point that a good dry area in the Chenab colony should be used immediately for grazing, because canal construction was planned there. If expansion of the canal system was to continue, he repeatedly argued, then more government-owned *rakhs* as well as those controlled by the Forestry Department—free of surra but closed to pastoralists and, to a degree, to the camel corps—needed to be made available for the transport camel units, if surra mortality rates were to be lowered.[44]

Leese's field trips also led him to make a number of other recommendations. For example, concerned that periodic animal fairs in different parts of the Punjab appeared to be a source of surra, he advised that any camels purchased at these fairs be bought only outside the surra season, and after microscopic blood tests.[45] Moreover, since only one-third of the Silladar camels

40. *Report of the Veterinary Officer*, 1909: 6 and 1910: 5, 7.

41. *Report of the Veterinary Officer*, 1909: 8.

42. *Report of the Veterinary Officer*, 1910: 6.

43. See *Annual Report for the Punjab Canal Colonies* (1912), introductory summary, "Lower Chenab Canal Colony," 2. Titles of annual reports of the Punjab's canal colonies vary; I have abbreviated them as ARPCC. Also, because there are multiple paginations in the reports, I have added the specific colony report and page references.

44. On grazing issues, see *Report of the Veterinary Officer*, 1909: 4 and 1910: 2, 5.

45. *Report of the Veterinary Officer*, 1909: 7–8 and 1910: 1, 3.

were on duty at any time, Leese thought that the other two-thirds ought to have their grazing areas inspected for biting flies and their blood checked for the parasite. Further, he argued that the tenure of camel unit commandants was too short. As he put it, just when an officer learned about camels and developed a bond with his sarwans, his knowledge and experience would be lost through transfer. Lastly, he learned from sarwans that keeping camels in good condition involved a particular diet. Camels required a mixture of wild plants consumed while grazing and *missa bhusa* (pea straw) when not.[46] Such a combination aided ruminant digestion.

While all of Leese's ideas made sense from the point of view of animal management, disease control, and transport unit readiness, implementing them was another matter. It would have required the Indian Army to commit vast new resources to provide the personnel for carrying out the surveillance and policing that Leese was calling for. But if his ideas about improving the health of camels were probably unrealistic, his epidemiological approach to surra, which combined blood tests, avoidance of surra zones, knowledge of the life cycle of biting flies, the cooperation of unit commanders and their sarwans, and ruthless culling, had begun to show positive results by 1911. The CVD reported that mortality in the eight Silladar Camel Corps had fallen from around 30 percent annually to 13.3 percent on an average annual strength of 8,230 animals. This was deemed a "satisfactory" reduction in camel mortality rates.[47]

Once he had managed to reform camel transport unit practices and increase awareness of the pathology of surra, Leese then turned his attention to experimenting with possible cures for the disease. This research put him in direct competition with the Imperial Bacteriological Laboratory at Muktesar, where veterinarians had been investigating surra since Alfred Lingard had been in charge. The new director, J. E. D. Holmes, who had taken over when Lingard retired in 1908, was as keen as Leese to find a cure. Like the veterinarians at the laboratory, Leese began to experiment with drugs such as Atoxyl, an organic arsenic compound;[48] Soamin, a version of Atoxyl pro-

46. *Report of the Veterinary Officer*, 1909: 8, 11–12. These conversations with sarwans were no doubt the source of Leese's later writings on camel diet and care in his study of the one-humped camel; see chapter 2.

47. *Annual Administrative Report of the Civil Veterinary Department for the Official Year 1910–1911* (Calcutta: Superintendent of Government Printing, India, 1911), 5.

48. One of the earliest reports on the use of Atoxyl appeared in Great Britain in 1907. See Anton Breinl and John Todd, "Atoxyl in the Treatment of Trypanosomiasis," *British Medical Journal* 2403 (January 1907): 132–34.

duced by Burroughs Wellcome; tartar emetic (antimony potassium tartrate); and sodium arsenate.[49]

It is clear from Leese's initial foray into chemotherapy that there were a number of problems related to using this mixture of poisonous compounds on camels. First and foremost was the symptomatic pattern of the disease. Recall that John Henry Steel had pointed out that a symptom of surra was a "relapsing fever." During the paroxysms of fever, trypanosomes were abundant in the peripheral blood vessels of the animal's body. When the trypanosomes disappeared from the peripheral blood, the body temperature would return to normal (where the trypanosomes went and how they later regenerated was unknown). Even without treatment, a certain number of camels and horses would survive the initial attack and subsequent relapse incidents, eventually appearing surra free. Given this pattern, the question was, how could those animals who spontaneously recovered be distinguished from those who appeared to recover as a result of chemotherapy? A second question involved time and the tendency to relapse—how long should researchers continue testing blood until an animal was declared cured?

There was also some doubt about what had been achieved through live-animal experiments involving chemotherapy, even when treatments appeared successful. By 1911, both Leese and the researchers at Muktesar had demonstrated that a combination of Atoxyl, tartar emetic, and sodium arsenate spread over several days in alternating and carefully measured doses seemed to eliminate the parasite from some animals infected with *T. evansi*.[50] However encouraging this might have been for the veterinarians and the army transport corps, Leese spelled out some of the problems with using these drugs in one of his reports. The most obvious problem was that some animals died of arsenic poisoning, while others sustained internal damage. Some developed lung abscesses, heart dilation, and severe constipation wherein the third and

49. On his initial experiments, see Arnold Leese, "Summary of First Series of Experiments on the Treatment of Surra in Camels," *JTVS* 5 (1910): 57–64, 397–410, which involved alternating tartar emetic with Atoxyl and mercury bichloride; also see *Report of the Veterinary Officer*, 1911: 4–5.

50. *Report of the Veterinary Officer*, 1912: 2–9, which includes a list of instructions for administering the drugs; and Arnold Leese, "Third Series of Experiments on the Treatment of Surra in Camels, with Some Cures," *JTVS* 7, no. 1 (1912): 1–18. On research at Muktesar, see J. E. D. Holmes, "The Cure of Surra in Horses by the Administration of Arsenic," *JTVS* 6, no. 4 (1911): 447–67.

fourth stomachs of camels became impacted with dried food.[51] Even those deemed cured often remained in such poor condition that they required a lengthy recovery period. All these complications brought additional costs to the treatment.

There was another issue as well. This one concerned the kinds of animals being tested. Although none of the reports on drug therapy made much of the fact, the animals used by Leese and the Muktesar laboratory establishment were distinctly different. Leese treated camels with this drug cocktail, whereas Imperial Bacteriologist Holmes carried out his experiments on horses.[52] No one knew, for example, the significance of the animals' body weight for treatment dosage beyond the assumption that larger animals could manage larger amounts of chemotherapy drugs. Protocols and guidelines were also missing for the duration of testing required in order to declare that surra-free animals had been "cured" by Atoxyl or other compounds. Instead, arbitrary time periods were selected (ranging from 250 to 350 days), and success was announced if the animal's blood showed no return of trypanosomes. Nor was it clear how the physiologies of different animal species might interact with the parasites—or why some animals, like Timothy Lewis's rats, seemed immune to trypanosome-caused disease, while others died soon after exposure.

Similar questions had been raised in the *Veterinary Journal* in 1896. As the editor put it in a piece evaluating David Bruce's Tsetse fly research, the pathogen posed a variety of puzzles regarding its effects on different species of animals and on the same species in different locations. "Although the 'fly' disease trypanosome is pathological to the ox in Africa," the editor began,

> the "surra" trypanosome is not pathological, or only feebly so, to the ox in India. It would almost seem that the European, Indian, and the African trypanosomes, although closely resembling each other morphologically and biologically, belonging to probably the same species, yet differ in their pathological properties, the trypanosome of Europe being innocuous in the case of all animals, the trypanosome of India, if deadly to certain domestic animals, being almost innocuous to the ox of the country, whilst the African trypanosome is deadly to nearly all four-footed domestic animals, the ox included. *Seemingly,*

51. *Report of the Veterinary Officer*, 1911: 5; and Leese, "Third Series of Experiments on the Treatment of Surra in Camels," 8.

52. J. E. D. Holmes, "Investigation of an Outbreak of Horse Surra with the Result of Treatment with Atoxyl, Tartar Emetic, Mercury and Other Drugs," *JTVS* 3, no. 2 (1908): 157–72.

> *the pathological qualities of the three varieties are graded, as it were, by climate or by breed or by other circumstances.*[53]

That these puzzles were not addressed by the researchers in India but instead displaced by introducing poisonous drugs like Atoxyl in live-animal experiments indicates, perhaps more than anything, the outer threshold of the experimental biology of the time. That trypanosomes might change through interactions with the environment was certainly imagined by the editor of the *Veterinary Journal*. But in India, with camels dying at an alarming rate, the pressure to solve the surra problem by reducing mortality discouraged basic research into the biology of pathogen-host interactions. Instead, the emphasis was placed on killing the pathogen, seemingly without thought to what might result from pathogen-drug interactions. Nor was there any critique of investigators' moving infected blood from one species to another, as was the case with the relatively uncontrolled surra experiments at Muktesar, where dogs, goats, and guinea pigs, as well as horses, camels, and other live animals, became experimental subjects.

The choice, whether or not it was consciously made, to develop the arsenic-compound drug regime raised two other questions. Blood tests could find the pathogen present in what appeared to be perfectly healthy camels, thus making them candidates for chemotherapy. Not surprisingly, some sarwans were incredulous about allowing their apparently healthy camels to be treated by a method that could possibly kill them, an outcome that would leave the owner responsible for replacement. At one point, W. S. Hamilton, the successor of Henry Pease as inspector general of the CVD, suggested that the government offer suitable compensation to owners to encourage treatment.[54] Otherwise, he thought, there was the real danger of unwittingly retaining infected animals in the inactive reserve, where microscopic testing was less common. Whether or not his suggestion was taken up is unclear in the records.

The second issue involved ethics. Live-animal experimentation and Pasteurian methods using animal models had produced a public outcry in Great Britain, where a series of antivivisection laws were passed in the second half of the nineteenth century. And although there were discussions of such legislation being introduced in India, officials from the viceroy on down were opposed. Moreover, while the antivivisection laws in Great Britain built on long-

53. Editorial, *Veterinary Journal* 42 (June 1896): 412; emphasis added.

54. *Annual Report of the Camel Specialist for the Year 1912–13* (Lahore: Punjab Government Press, 1913), 2. Hereafter cited as *AR Camel Specialist* with year of publication.

standing legal codes against cruelty to animals, the only such protections that emerged in India involved cows. Pratik Chakrabarti has argued forcefully that the British in India, whatever moral convictions they may have had concerning animal cruelty, managed to ignore the live-animal experimentation being carried out by elements within the Indian government while claiming that the only animal cruelty in India occurred in the native treatment of animals. Indeed, a popular notion of Indian cruelty toward animals reinforced racial stereotypes of Indians among ordinary British people, and thrived in organizations like the Royal Society for the Prevention of Cruelty to Animals.[55] How else can one explain the uproar in Britain following World War I when it was suspected that demobilized animals, of which there were some 250,000 in France and the Middle East, might be sent to India and sold into "slavery"?[56] Most animals avoided such an imagined fate by being sold to animal traders, butchers, or animal rendering factories in France and Belgium.[57]

The problems associated with chemotherapy and live-animal experimentation seem, however, to pale in the face of the resurgence of the disease following Arnold Leese's departure for England in 1912. Annual reports of the canal colonies between 1912 and 1916 indicate increases in camel mortality and shortages of replacements, with one report exclaiming that it was high time to stamp the disease out.[58] In its annual report of 1915, the Punjab Veterinary Department added that despite chemotherapy, surra deaths among camels had gone from twenty-five in 1912–13 to 218 in the current year, requiring a substantial number of replacements. It concluded that in addition to the gen-

55. Pratik Chakrabarti, "Beasts of Burden: Animals and Laboratory Research in Colonial India," *History of Science* 48 (2010): 125–51.

56. See IOR/L/MIL/7/9707: Secretary of State's Orders for Prevention of Cruelty to Army Animals. On 3 March 1917, the chief secretary of the Royal Society for the Prevention of Cruelty to Animals wrote the secretary of state for India, requesting that no demobilized or "cast" (unfit) animals be sold into "slavery" to "lower class Indians." The figure for animals to be demobilized comes from the estimate given by Winston Churchill, the secretary of state for war, in Parliament in March 1919. Other materials in this file indicate that the issue did not disappear soon after the war but lingered into the late 1930s, with additional requests from the RSPCA that castoff cavalry horses in India not be sold to the natives. Also see the documents in IOR/L/MIL/7/9706: Postwar Market for Army Horses, Mules, and Camels.

57. See Layton John Blenkinsop and John Wakefield Rainey, eds., *Veterinary Services* (London: His Majesty's Stationery Office, 1925), 681–91, for a detailed official accounting of the disposal of military animals after the war.

58. ARPCC (1913), cover letter to the report, 2; ARPCC (1914), "Lower Chenab Canal Colony, I. Lyallpur District," 1; ARPCC (1915), "Lower Chenab Canal Colony, I. Lyallpur District," 1–2; and ARPCC (1916), "Lower Chenab Canal Colony, I. Lyallpur District," 2.

erally known causes of the spread of the disease (e.g., canals producing *Tabanus* breeding grounds), "until the movement of [nonmilitary] animals can be restricted (which is a very big problem), the disease is bound to spread."[59] The department was speaking not only of traditional patterns of pastoralist seasonal migration in the Punjab's wastelands but also of camel owners from outside the region who were moving animals in to meet the demands of the military transport market there. The perceived problem was that these owners might see the high levels of demand as a way to get rid of infected or aged animals.

Moreover, movement of camels was, in a sense, already restricted by the Forestry Department's control of government *rakhs*.[60] As Leese had noted earlier, while good grazing grounds existed outside surra zones, camel herders were generally barred from the dry areas that were part of *rakhs*. Yet as grazing land shrank because of canal expansion, and Forestry Department *rakh* restrictions remained in place, pastoralists and the reserve camel corps units were forced to move to other areas, sometimes very far from their usual grazing grounds. Thus, at the same time that Leese was calling for much tighter control over camel life in order to contain surra, the policies of other government units such as the Forestry and Public Works Departments were making it difficult for the CVD to manage the camel population at all. Indeed, other than the CVD camel specialist and registration officers of the Army Remount Department, who were in short supply, few personnel were on hand to track the camel men's movement as they sought surra-free grazing lands, let alone to conduct epidemiological surveys for animal diseases. Concurrently, camel reservists and camel land-grant holders continued to face the problem of diminished grazing grounds, high prices for replacement animals, water shortages, and mounting debt.

CONFLICT WITHIN THE CVD

Disagreements within the colonial bureaucracy generated by competing and conflicting policies were not confined to those between the Forestry, Public Works, and Civil Veterinary Departments and the Indian Army. Such disputes

59. *Annual Report of the Punjab Veterinary College, Civil Veterinary Department, Punjab and the Government Cattle Farm, Hissar for the Year 1914–15* (Lahore: Superintendent Government Printing, 1915), 7.

60. On *rakh* policies, see David Gilmartin, *Blood and Water: The Indus River Basin in Modern History* (Oakland: University of California Press, 2015), 81, 157–58.

existed within the CVD itself. Leese's empirical fieldwork between 1908 and 1912 not only produced new knowledge about surra and other camel diseases. Through his intrepid on-the-ground technique, it also challenged earlier speculation about and laboratory experimentation on surra, beginning with Alfred Lingard's published speculations in the 1890s about the oral ingestion mechanism of surra transmission. Although he made no mention of Lingard's work in his own reports, Leese confirmed Leonard Rogers's earlier studies of the mechanical transmission of surra—not in a laboratory, of course, but out in wastelands, where the camel, biting fly, and pathogen interacted.

Leese might have quietly but successfully superseded earlier work were it not for the publication of several other pieces concerning current trypanosome research in the same issue of the *Sleeping Sickness Bulletin* in which his seminal letter appeared. One of these was by Friedrich K. Kleine, a military doctor studying sleeping sickness in German East Africa. His findings demonstrated that part of the trypanosome life cycle identified by Bruce took place inside the Tsetse fly, indicating a physiological, rather than a mechanical, path of transmission with respect to nagana.[61] The *Bulletin* noted that Kleine's work was unknown when Leese had published his initial findings. Following mention of Kleine, the editor of the *Bulletin* abstracted an article by Maj. F. S. H. Baldrey, acting imperial bacteriologist at Muktesar while Holmes was on leave. Apparently influenced by Kleine's findings on the developmental cycle of *T. brucei* in the Tsetse fly, Baldrey claimed that the trypanosomes he had taken from an infected animal in India showed signs of change within the gut of the fly, suggesting that the *Tabanus* was more than a passive conveyor of trypanosomes.[62] In addition to showing results consistent with those of Kleine, Baldrey no doubt claimed a certain authority through the substantial number of abbreviations around his name (Maj., F.R.I.P.H., F.R.C.V.S., and F.R.G.S.)[63] as well as his professorship in sanitary science at the Punjab Veterinary College. Taken together, the research of Kleine and Baldrey, and the latter's professional standing, called into question Leese's assertion that surra was exclusively transmitted mechanically.[64] As a result, the mode of

61. Kleine's work appeared in "Sleeping Sickness Investigations in German East Africa," *Sleeping Sickness Bulletin* 3, no. 26 (1911): 165–75.

62. Maj. F. S. H. Baldrey, "The Evolution of *Trypanosoma evansi* through the Fly," *JTVS* 6, no. 3 (1911): 271–82.

63. Fellow Royal Institute of Public Health, Fellow Royal Civil Veterinary Society, and Fellow Royal Geographic Society. He had also been involved in producing the ninth edition of William Williams's *The Principles and Practices of Veterinary Medicine* (1909).

64. See *Sleeping Sickness Bulletin* 3, no. 30 (1911): 369–73.

transmission became a point of controversy in India between Leese and the Muktesar establishment, especially because, morphologically, the African and Indian trypanosomes appeared via microscopy to be identical.

Leese may have seen the article or known of Baldrey's work, which might have been why, in the letter he sent to the *Sleeping Sickness Bulletin*, he made it clear that he was in fact aware of Kleine's research with Tsetse flies. He explained, however, that he was unable to duplicate Kleine's experiment, largely because the *Tabanus* was extremely difficult to keep alive in captivity.[65] Recall also that he had reported the discovery of a new vector.[66] Leese thought it completely implausible that *T. evansi* could carry out part of its life cycle in three or more fly species. Moreover, did it really matter, he wondered, whether part of the trypanosome's life cycle occurred inside the *Tabanus*? Wouldn't research time be better spent experimenting on treatments for the disease, instead of dissecting flies?[67]

The following year, the *Journal of Tropical Veterinary Science* in India published an article by Leese that expanded on the points he had made in the letter. He began by noting that Kleine's findings on the life cycle of trypanosomes in the African Tsetse fly seemed to have "cast grave doubt" on arguments for the direct spread of surra, and that "high authorities" in India now believed that development of the parasite in an invertebrate host in that country was "very probable."[68] After repeating his Bikaner findings (21–23), he then proceeded to call into question Baldrey's laboratory research, emphasizing that the whole process of biting flies transmitting surra can be "seen in the Monsoon season in any *Tabanus*-afflicted grazing ground" (24)—that is, it was clearly visible in the field! Or, as he put it on another occasion, any observer of camels in a heavily infested *Tabanus* region can see the flies themselves experimenting with "direct inoculation."[69] But Leese didn't stop there—he then turned to the publications of the current imperial bacteriologist, J. E. D. Holmes, who in 1906 had expressed doubts about the mechanical transmis-

65. Ibid., 367.

66. For Leese's official report on his Bikaner research, see *Report of the Veterinary Officer*, 1911: 2–3. The years 1908 and 1909 were La Niña years, which meant increased water volume in the monsoon.

67. *Sleeping Sickness Bulletin* 3, no. 30 (1911): 367–68.

68. Arnold Leese, "Biting Flies and Surra," *JTVS* 7, no. 1 (1912): 19. I cite page numbers from this source in the text unless otherwise indicated.

69. Arnold Leese, "'Tips' on Camels, for Veterinary Surgeons on Active Duty," *Veterinary Journal*, n.s., 24 (1917): 86.

sion of surra, as well as about the possibility that an animal infected with surra could be imported into an area and become the source of the spread of the disease.[70] Leese had demonstrated just the opposite in his very first surra experiments, apparently without any acknowledgment from Holmes. Parenthetically, whether he was aware of it or not, Leese was also making a case for the superiority of veterinary field observation over laboratory work.

Leese then moved the discussion into another realm, where perhaps only a veterinarian steeped in practical fieldwork might venture. Infected animals that survived the initial onslaught of the disease carried surra from one season to the next, thus becoming a reservoir for the next cycle of biting flies to spread the disease (28–30). With this notion of camel as reservoir, Leese then speculated about how surra had come to India. He thought that at some earlier date, camels had entered the African Tsetse belt region in the normal course of trade between northern and more southern African groups. Camels had been bitten and infected with nagana or bovine trypanosomiasis in Africa. Because the animal could carry the trypanosomes for up to three years or longer in its system, trypanosomiasis could move north and east following trade routes, finding new vectors along the way (31–32). This deduction, based partly on studies of trypanosomiasis in Africa with support from comparative genetic studies of *T. evansi* and various Tsetse belt trypanosomes, would become the standard interpretation of the blood parasite's globalization.[71]

There Leese's speculations about the surra parasite ended. He did not take the next step that the idea of mechanical transmission suggested. That is, he did not argue that the African trypanosome, wedded as it was to the Tsetse fly, might be morphologically similar to *T. evansi* but biologically different. And, in fact, even in Africa questions arose over whether the nagana parasite, *T. brucei*, was the same entity that infected humans and caused sleeping sickness. The uncertainty ran right through the period of Kleine's publications, with at least two names applied to the disease in different parts of Africa. One disease was identified with *T. rhodesiense*, a parasitie that lived in forests and the bush, and fed off wild animals and humans. The other parasite was *T. gambiense*, which dwelled in the shade of riverbanks and fed off humans and the occasional reptile. Both shared the Tsetse fly or *Glossina* as their vector, although where *T. rhodesiense*, which causes the more virulent form of

70. Leese, "Biting Flies and Surra," 25.

71. See, for example, Hoare, *The Trypanosomes of Mammals*, 558; and Lorne E. Stephen, *Trypanosomiasis: A Veterinary Perspective* (Oxford: Pergamon Press, 1986), 187.

sleeping sickness, appeared, it was carried by *Glossina moritans*, a bush fly.[72] Moreover, as research in Africa morphed into a multinational enterprise of staggering proportions compared to the work of the small complement of veterinarians in India, the numbers and names of trypanosomes also increased. If there had been a mangled confusion of nomenclature in the 1890s regarding trypanosomiasis, there was now confusion over the infectious potential for mammals from the many versions of trypanosomes that were turning up in different parts of Africa. More to the point, this absence of clarity concerning trypanosomiasis in Africa appears not to have had any effect on the debate in India.

Leese's response to Baldrey and to laboratory science was his final publication on surra in India. In 1912, he went on leave. When he returned, he was informed that his position as camel specialist had been rescinded, and that the government wanted him to take up the study of diseases of the elephant, an animal that had more or less been eliminated from army transport. Leese said little about the circumstances of this transfer decision in his memoir, and there seems to be nothing in the archival records indicating that he had been "rifted" by "higher authorities." Yet his open challenge as a scientist and a civilian to the work of his superiors would not have stood well with many. In his memoir, Leese mentions only that at the time, he thought it was too late in life to begin the study of another highly unusual animal. Given his often-articulated disdain for discipline and the "social conventions" of "station life" in India, coupled with his appreciation of Henry Pease's willingness to give him a free hand in his earlier investigations,[73] it also seems possible that he felt some resentment toward the army-officer veterinary surgeons who held virtually all the other positions in the CVD and the Muktesar laboratory. Moreover, he may have bridled at the fact that, other than his one-time superior Col. Pease, few of the higher authorities in the CVD acknowledged his contributions, though none had his field experience.

But something else was involved in Leese's outbursts in the biting-fly papers. They highlight tensions between a fieldwork-oriented epidemiological approach to disease and one focused on laboratory experimentation. Recall Leese's comment on the life cycle of the trypanosome. From his point of view, research time spent on trying to determine whether part of its life occurred in

72. Luise White, "Tsetse Visions: Narratives of Blood and Bugs in Colonial Northern Rhodesia, 1931–39," *Journal of African History* 36, no. 2 (1995): 222–23; and Hoare, *The Trypanosomes of Mammals*, 500–505.

73. Leese, *Out of Step*, 18.

the fly helped little in solving the bigger problem of keeping the camel transport units near their full complement. Knowledge of the dynamics of the surra season, of surra and non-surra territorial zones, and of the costs and benefits of drug cures for the disease made sense in relation to the primary needs of the military. And those needs were for professional animal management in the service of readiness for mobilization of military transport and cavalry units. Put simply, like other epidemiologically oriented researchers, Leese placed an emphasis on health and hygiene as a means of avoiding or preventing infection. As such, he was in agreement with scientists like Ronald Ross, who argued that sound public health practices were more important than launching expensive research wars on microbial diseases, as had been advocated by Patrick Manson, head of the London School of Tropical Medicine.[74]

As Deborah Neill has noted about laboratory research in general, for their part CVD laboratory researchers lived in a space that was isolated from the social and environmental world where disease existed.[75] Indeed, when Muktesar was being contemplated as a site for government laboratories, Lingard argued that India's teeming and pestilential cities were no place to carry out serious microbiological research. What was needed was a site with the "salubrious climate" afforded by the hill stations, where productive work could be done.[76] Freed from environmental constraints and unconcerned with the multifactorial ecology of diseases, enfolded in a site of "somatic control and closure," as Warwick Anderson has put it,[77] CVD laboratory researchers could set about, like their imagined counterparts in Berlin, Paris, and London, producing a comprehensive knowledge of the workings of a single organism, like the trypanosome.

Their form of epistemophilia demanded that the morphology, life cycle,

74. On Ross and his conflict with Charles Manson over public health vs. laboratory science, see Michael Worboys, "The Emergence of Tropical Medicine: A Study in the Establishment of a Scientific Specialty," in *Perspectives on the Emergence of Scientific Disciplines*, ed. Gerard Lemaine et al. (Mouton: Aldine, 1976), 91–92; and "Mason, Ross, and Colonial Medical Policy: Tropical Medicine in London and Liverpool, 1899–1914," in *Disease, Medicine and Empire*, ed. Roy Macleod and Milton J. Lewis (London: Routledge, 1988), 30–32. For a brief outline of Ross's research concerning malaria and the controversies surrounding it, see Gordon Cook, *Tropical Medicine* (Paris: Academic Press, 2007), 88–97.

75. Neill, in *Networks of Tropical Medicine* (16), makes this point about the seeming disconnect between laboratory research and the quotidian world.

76. Chakrabarti, *Bacteriology in British India*, 62–63.

77. Warwick Anderson, "Excremental Colonialism: Public Health and the Poetics of Pollution," *Critical Inquiry* 21, no. 3 (1995): 652.

and transmission mechanisms of pathogens be intimately understood, particularly at the biological level; hence the concern about the possible life cycle of the trypanosome in the digestive system of the fly. This orientation appears consistent with the approach to tropical diseases promoted by Manson, who, Michael Worboys has argued, built his version of tropical diseases not on germ theory but rather on a concern with single-celled and multicellular pathogens transmitted by vectors that produced diseases like surra, nagana, and malaria.[78] If this was also the case for those working at Muktesar, the human-animal-plant-climate complex in which camels were embedded was secondary to the questions on which their microbiological endeavors were centered. These scientists tended to ask less epidemiological questions. Instead, the questions they sought answers to looked something like this: Were other animals susceptible to surra in the same way horses and camels were? Was there one kind of surra, or, as some research suggested, were there dog, horse, camel, and bovine versions? How could animal models best be used to answer such questions? Arsenic compounds showed some promise as a treatment, but were also debilitating to the host. If arsenic compounds were to be employed, in what proportion or combination with other drugs would they be most effective? What was the exact relationship of contiguity between vectors of transmission and the parasite's animal host, and how would such knowledge help in the battle against the disease?

These were the sorts of questions that animated Muktesar laboratory scientists and structured their tropical veterinary research apparatus. In it, camels, horses, and mules took on a new form of military service as laboratory animals. Along with a menagerie of other animals, they were impressed as forced laborers, even apart from military campaigns and frontier warfare. As symptom complexes and living laboratories, they were the object of the scrutinizing eye of the veterinary surgeon as scientist. As providers of blood, they became laboratory natural resources. Their blood, in turn, entered a structured epistemological complex made up of microscopes, glass slides, photographic equipment, veterinary scientists and native lab technicians, statistical forms of representation, and entries in professional veterinary journals in and outside India. Horses, mules, and camels were re-embodied as blood smears, temperature graphs, and photographic images of diseased and experimental animals. They became receptors for carefully timed and calculated doses of poisonous synthetic drug mixtures, each of which was numbered, like the

78. Michael Worboys, "Germs, Malaria and the Invention of Masonian Tropical Medicine: From 'Diseases in the Tropics' to 'Tropical Diseases,'" *Clio Medica* 35 (1996): 181.

animal, for record-keeping evaluation, comparison, and eventual archiving. Animals that had been "macroscopically complex," incorporating masses of uncontrollable variables, were translated and reduced, through the laboratory regime, into "docile specimens."[79]

At the same time, the laboratory complex was perfectly capable of appropriating and correcting Arnold Leese's critical insights and field research, in part because he had deployed certain laboratory techniques. Such was the case with Leese's successor, Henry Eustace Cross. An assistant bacteriologist at Muktesar beginning in 1906, Cross worked with J. E. D. Holmes on early experiments with Atoxyl, tartar emetic, and other drugs in treating surra in horses.[80] In his first annual report after becoming camel specialist, Cross set about correcting Leese's findings. He pointed out that the latter's cure for surra in camels was no more than a modification of the drug regime that he and Holmes had pioneered at Muktesar, and he argued that Leese's results were based on too small a sample size ("only" nine animals).[81] The next year, Cross challenged Leese's insistence that surra was transmitted mechanically. He referenced Tsetse fly research and then argued that if transmission were mechanical, far more animals would be infected than actually were. This observation led him to question whether the *Tabanus* fly species was as big a culprit in spreading surra as Leese had suggested.[82] Later, in his book on the camel published in 1917, Cross granted that sometimes transmission of surra was mechanical, but added that "it is probable that the trypanosome undergoes a cycle in the fly (and in a particular species of fly only), a percentage only of these flies being capable of infecting healthy camels."[83]

Cross's concerns and speculation about modes of surra transmission were, in a sense, also a research agenda. Over the next decade, he became fixated on finding the right dosage and timing for exclusive use of tartar emetic as a treatment for surra while formulating a seemingly endless series of experiments to

79. I take the quotations from Warwick Anderson, where he is speaking of humans under the care of the American colonial regime in the Philippines. See *Colonial Pathologies: American Tropical Medicine, Race and Hygiene in the Philippines* (Durham, NC: Duke University Press, 2006), 6.

80. Holmes, "Investigation of an Outbreak of Horse Surra with Results of Treatment with Atoxyl, Tartar Emetic, Mercury and Other Drugs," 158–72.

81. *AR Camel Specialist*, 1913: 4.

82. *AR Camel Specialist*, 1914: 11–12.

83. Henry Eustace Cross, *The Camel and Its Diseases: Being Notes of Veterinary Surgeons and Commandants of Camel Corps* (London: Baillière, Tindall and Cox, 1917), 94.

establish the feeding habits of multiple kinds of biting insects.[84] Yet he never found the elusive fly species in whose body the trypanosome underwent a part of its life cycle.

These examples of differences between a field-oriented veterinarian like Leese and a laboratory-oriented one like Cross might be read as a personality clash or representations of the rivalries common to the scientific production of truth, in the metropole as in the colonial field station. They might also be understood as exemplifying the difference highlighted by Worboys as the "essential tension" between two forms of scientific knowledge. The form that Leese was producing was gained through research that was "problem"-oriented or "subject-based," creating knowledge that was "particular" or "empirical." Muktesar scientists, in contrast, oriented to the production of "universal" or theoretical knowledge, produced it through "distinguishable cognitive structures and technical resources."[85] Cross's critique of Leese's seat-of-the-pants methodology and conclusions drawn from small sample sizes seems to exemplify a contrast between a universalistic versus a particularistic approach to research. To Leese's credit, however, his approach, particularly that involving the identification of surra-free territories, drew from and left a space for indigenous knowledge. He might not have understood existing local patterns of seasonal animal movement had he not followed a problem-based approach that had led him to listen to the sarwans. The laboratory scientists, by contrast, had little use for premicrobiological understandings of animal diseases.

On the other hand, Leese and Cross shared certain assumptions. Both put a great deal of emphasis on the technoscientific apparatus that included the microscope and the hypodermic needle; both seemed to understand the importance of publication to any factual claims they might make based on scientific research and practice; and both were clearly committed to laboratory-

84. See IOR/V/25/125: *Bulletin no. 95, Agriculture Research Institute, Pusa*, "A Note on the Treatment of Surra in Camels by Intravenous Injections of Tartar Emetic" (1920): 1–4. Cross also conducted or directed many studies of the habits of biting flies, only to conclude that surra was, in fact, transmitted mechanically. See IOR/V/25/541/31-35: H. E. Cross and G. Patel, "Surra Transmission Experiments," *Department of Agriculture, Punjab: Veterinary Bulletin no. 5 of 1921*, 1–13; H. E. Cross, "A Note on the Transmission of Surra by Ticks," *Department of Agriculture, Punjab: Veterinary Bulletin no. 6 of 1921*, 1–3; H. E. Cross and G. Patel, "A Note on the Transmission of Surra by Tabanus nemocallosus," *Department of Agriculture, Punjab: Veterinary Bulletin no. 7 of 1921*, 1–7; and "Surra Transmission experiments with Tabanus albimedius and Ticks," *Department of Agriculture, Punjab: Veterinary Bulletin no. 12 of 1923*, 1–11.

85. Worboys, "Mason, Ross, and Colonial Medical Policy," 22.

made synthetic drugs and vaccines. These commitments reflected the kinds of changes evident in veterinary medicine in the early twentieth century.

In India, British veterinarians like John Henry Steel had, for much of the nineteenth century, tended to rely on a small number of basic drugs they had brought from England while also drawing from large numbers of local herbs that were part of the Indian pharmacopeia, as we saw in chapter 4. And while they might disdain Indian formulary for its ignorance of the chemical properties of medicinal herbs, veterinarians found that they had no choice but to rely on medicines available in the bazaar, because of both their low cost and the lack of alternatives.

By the 1890s, however, veterinarians operating in the colonial tropics increasingly had access to new kinds of drugs, products of the chemistry laboratories and manufacturing enterprises that produced chemicals like Atoxyl and tartar emetic. More to the point, veterinarians found that they had a readily available animal population and no restrictions on using these military animals for testing the efficacy of synthetic organic and inorganic compounds in treating a variety of afflictions.[86] Parasitic infections, for which there were no clear cures or treatment protocols, were ideal targets against which to direct manmade compounds such as Atoxyl. More to the point, the veterinary experimental regime was fueled by the desire to evaluate new drugs made from organic and inorganic elements combined in chemical laboratories. Medical scientists and chemists both seemed to revel in their newfound freedom from nature.

In 1926, not long after Cross published his final study of the use of tartar emetic to cure surra, Capt. R. H. Knowles, of the Royal Army Veterinary Corps and a veterinary research officer for the Sudanese government, called Cross's approach into question. In addition to being "somewhat prolonged," Knowles argued, Cross's method was problematic because trypanosomes, more often than not, reappeared "after a variable period." Knowles then provided data on his tests with a new pharmaceutical drug, Bayer 205. This was a synthetic urea-based compound invented in the laboratories of the German drug manufacturer Bayer in 1916. Later known as Naganol, the compound not only cured surra in Knowles's tests but didn't seem to have the negative physiological effects found in camels treated with Atoxyl and tartar emetic.

Naganol's arrival in Africa, and soon after in India, repeated the established

86. Organic compounds are ones that contain carbon and often hydrogen. They are found in biological systems. Inorganic compounds are found in geological systems, and are made up of salts, minerals, and so on.

pattern of field-testing chemotherapeutic drug compounds in colonial settings.[87] The linkage between field, manufacturer, and army veterinary practice was institutionalized almost immediately. The section on surra to be found in the third edition of the *Hand Book of Contagious and Infectious Diseases of Animals*, issued by the Quartermaster General's Branch of the British Indian Army in 1929, directed the use of four grams of Naganol and three grams of tartar emetic, which, like a magic bullet, was given in a single intravenous injection. The simplicity of the method, the text tells us, could "obviate the evacuation of Surra cases for treatment to [Lines of Communication] and Base Camel Hospitals during campaigns, as camels in good condition can be cured and returned to duty within a few days"—rather than months.[88] Put simply, Naganol promised to finally solve the logistical problem surra had created during the frontier campaigns that had relied on camel and equine labor.

*

Surra was, of course, not the only disease that affected military animals in India, but its impact on the Indian security regime seems to have been far more profound than any of the others. That surra killed all animals key to the operations of that regime while disrupting the biopower logic of army animal management set it apart from the other afflictions plaguing animals in India. In this chapter, I have emphasized both how the disease was approached by various actors in the civil veterinary corps and how polycentric communication networks affected their work. The contributions of various veterinarians in South Asia to the emerging field of tropical medicine were significant precisely because of the links between their research and the needs of empire. In the colonial Punjab, the imperial state both created the surra crisis by expanding the *Tabanus* fly's breeding grounds through one sort of development project, and battled surra with another, contemporary bacteriological and parasitological science. In both cases, those who were most af-

87. Testing of Naganol had begun by 1926 in India. See J. T. Edwards, "The Chemotherapy of Surra in Horses and Cattle in India," *Journal of Comparative Pathology and Therapeutics* 39, no. 2 (June 1926): 82–112; and 39, no. 3 (September 1926): 169–201. For accounts of successful treatments with Naganol, also see S. K. Sen, "Prophylaxis against Equine Surra by Means of 'Bayer 205' (Naganol)," *Indian Journal of Veterinary Science and Animal Husbandry* 1, no. 4 (1931): 283–95; hereafter *IJVSAH*.

88. *Hand Book of Contagious and Infectious Diseases of Animals* (Calcutta: Government of India Central Publication Branch, 1929), 302–3.

fected, who saw their lives and well-being most thoroughly transformed, were not the British canal colony officials, Army Remount Department officers, or veterinary surgeons but the pastoralists and peasantry of the region and their animals. They would continue to pay a price for colonial development long after the British left India.

CHAPTER 9

The Great War and Its Aftermath

One of the great ironies of the restructuring of British Indian Army transport in the early twentieth century was that when the anticipated full mobilization did occur, it had little to do with a crisis in India. Instead, large-scale mobilization was triggered by the start of World War I in Europe in August 1914. Moreover, once mobilized, the vast majority of Indian Army regular and reserve transport units, along with personnel from the military and civil veterinary corps, were deployed outside India. They were posted to theaters of military operations in Egypt, the Sinai, Palestine, Gallipoli, Salonika, and Mesopotamia. Not all went overseas, however. Anticipating a possible invasion from the Ottoman Empire through Afghanistan, the Government of India retained a number of units that could support frontier forces. As the war continued into 1916, some tribal groups on the frontier, such as the Mahsuds of Waziristan, rebelled against British rule; the transport units thus became involved in campaigns that stretched into the postwar era. The central theme of this chapter is the nature of the service performed by working animals in a conflict that dwarfed the previous mobilizations along the Indian frontier.

Although camels remained an important part of the British army's transport system in Middle Eastern operations, some also became part of the camel cavalry units used in the Sinai and Palestine campaigns. Under these circumstances, human perceptions of camels were altered, from seeing the camel as a beast of burden to recognizing a reliable partner in a kind of warfare dominated by harsh and unfamiliar environments. After reviewing the conditions under which animals labored and served during the war, in the final part of this chapter I consider postwar changes in army transport systems. These changes were brought on primarily by the fiscal crisis the war caused for Britain and its empire. The tremendous cost of the war forced officials to reconsider virtually all aspects of public finance. Dubbed "retrenchment" in India, the colonial state organized itself around notions of greater efficiencies, scientific management, and cost cutting. As a result, animal transport, always an expensive proposition, was reevaluated once more and found to be wanting, particularly when considered together with the new form of mechanical transport now available to the army: the truck.

TRANSPORT IN MIDDLE EASTERN THEATERS OF OPERATIONS

In 1919, with the Indian Army already engaged in dealing with uprisings among hill tribes on the frontier and anticolonial demonstrations in many parts of India, including the Punjab, armies of the amir of Afghanistan crossed the border known as the Durand line and invaded the Northwest Provinces.[1] The compiler of the official history of the ensuing conflict, known to the British as the Third Afghan War, explained the desperate straits in which the transport service found itself.

> Animal transport had been exploited to the uttermost and the reserve of animals left in the country had sunk very low. The supply of mules had been completely exhausted, and ponies, which are greatly inferior to mules in general utility and endurance, had to be employed as draught animals even in the Field Army. There was also a shortage of camels, due to heavy shipments overseas and to the ravages of surra.[2]

1. The boundary was negotiated with the amir of Afghanistan in 1893 by Henry Mortimer Durand. It artificially separated groups in the hills and was a major cause of the uprisings in 1897–98. The government of Afghanistan repudiated the boundary treaty in 1948, and the border remains controversial to the present day. See Bijan Omrani, "The Durand Line: History and Problems of the Afghan-Pakistan Border," *Asian Affairs* 40, no. 2 (2009): 177–95.

2. General Staff Branch, Army Headquarters, India, *The Third Afghan War 1919, Official Account* (Calcutta: Government of India Central Publication Branch, 1926), 20–21. Memos from the viceroy of India and from the Military Department of the Government of India in 1917 indicate the desperate need for replacements of horses and mules. Some 26,000 horses were ordered from Australia and 8,000 mules from Argentina, 400 mules from China, and 800 ordnance mules from the United States. Another 955 mules were ordered from Argentina at the end of 1917; see IOR/L/MIL/7/1079: Supply of Ordnance and Transport Mules, India, 1917.

Where had all the animals gone, and what were their fates? The disposition of the first transport units from India provides some answers to these questions. In November 1914, Indian Army regiments occupied the port of Basra in Mesopotamia. Included in these forces were the Fifty-Second Silladar Camel Corps and two transport corps from the Baluchistan native states of Las Bela and Kalat. For a variety of reasons, the campaigns in Mesopotamia stretched over the entire four years of the war; Baghdad was not taken until March 1917. Over the course of multiple campaigns, six mule corps and several other units known as mule columns provided transport services. The Third, Fourth, Fifth, and Sixth Government Camel Corps also participated in the Mesopotamian campaigns.[3] When the war ended in 1918, over forty-three thousand Indian Army mules remained in Mesopotamia, although a good number of them seem to have been shipped back to India eventually.[4] The camel corps, meanwhile, had been decimated by surra. In the final year of the war, 2,158 camels out of a force of 2,498 had perished, a wastage rate of 86 percent. Since most of these animals were probably replacements bought locally, it is doubtful that any were returned to India.[5]

In addition to whole units being dispatched abroad, smaller groups of animals were shipped as replacements to other theaters of operation. The drain on camels in the Punjab and the Sind was such that the Indian Army Remount Department, in order to maintain the strength of camel corps units remaining in India, had to import replacement camels from Persia.[6] The department was only able to sustain the number of mules needed in Mesopotamia and on the Egypt-Palestine front by purchasing large numbers of animals in China, Australia, and Argentina, as well as in Indian markets. In other words, the Remount Department was required to tap the global network for mule and donkey stud procurement that had been established in the late nineteenth century (see chapter 3). In addition, after the worrying visit of a "Turco-German" mission to Kabul in 1915, the government determined that sufficient levels of animal transport had to be maintained in India as a defense against a possible

3. Mention of these units can be found in Frederick Moberley, *The Campaign in Mesopotamia*, 4 vols. (London: His Majesty's Stationery Office, 1923–27). See 1:347; 2:489; 3:411, 417; and 4:342, 376, 392.

4. War Office, *Statistics of the Military Efforts of the British Empire during the Great War, 1914–1920* (London: His Majesty's Stationery Office, 1922), 398, 861, and 878.

5. Layton John Blenkinsop and John Wakefield Rainey, eds., *Veterinary Services* (London: His Majesty's Stationery Office, 1925), 339–40, 348.

6. Ibid., 353.

invasion by Ottoman forces as well as for use in possible operations against rebellious Pathan tribes on the Indo-Afghan frontier.[7]

Although it appears that many more mules than camels served in the campaigns on the peripheries of the Ottoman Empire, camels were still seen as necessary participants in the war. This was because much of the warfare that took place in Mesopotamia, the Sinai, and Palestine was in desert terrain and in arid zones, with poor roads or none at all.[8] In such terrain, camels were well adapted, and replacement animals were also readily obtainable in these areas. For operations on the southern and western edges of the Ottoman Empire, camels were bought in Egypt, the Sudan, and Somalia by veterinary surgeons of the Royal Army Veterinary Corps. One of these officers was Arnold Leese, who had enlisted in the army sometime in 1915, following his civilian career in India (see chapter 8) and East Africa. While serving in France, he wrote "'Tips' on Camels" for veterinary officers in the field who were now having to deal with an unfamiliar animal.[9] When the British offensive into Palestine faltered in early 1917, Leese was sent to Egypt to buy replacement camels; he was able to acquire substantial numbers in Somalia.[10] By the end of the war, Leese, other veterinary surgeons, and Army Remount officers had been able to purchase some 32,644 camels, 44,738 mules, and over 10,000 donkeys for the Egyptian Expeditionary Force transport units.[11]

These numbers were substantially larger than those of the prewar active-duty Indian Army Supply and Transport Corps; more important, the camels, mules, and donkeys represent only one small part of what was probably the largest collection of animal laborers ever assembled for a human war. The process began in Britain with the declaration of war; in the first two weeks of mobilization, Army Remount officers had "requisitioned" 165,000 horses in

7. On the Turco-German mission, see Asta Olsen, *Islam and Politics in Afghanistan* (New York: Routledge, 1995), 106.

8. Geoffrey Inchbald describes the Sinai as composed of "soft sand" and "hard gravel," with some areas made up of impenetrable sand dunes, mounds, and hillocks that had to be marched around. He also noted that the available maps contained large areas labeled "unexplored"; see *Camels and Others* (London: Johnson Publications, 1968), 45–47.

9. Arnold Leese, "'Tips' on Camels, for Veterinary Surgeons on Active Duty," *Veterinary Journal*, n.s., 24 (1917): 79–89, 136–40, 167–73, 214–18, 253–59, 294–98, 323–36.

10. Arnold Leese, *Out of Step: Events in the Two Lives of an Anti-Jewish Camel-Doctor* (Guildford, England: Arnold S. Leese, 1951), 29–30.

11. War Office, *Statistics of the Military Efforts of the British Empire during the Great War, 1914–1920*, 878.

the British Isles. That number would grow to 450,000 by war's end,[12] with another 428,608 horses and 275,097 mules imported from the United States and Canada, and 28,000 horses sent to Egypt and France from Australia.[13] At the peak of the conflict in 1917, some 878,000 horses, mules, camels, and bullocks were part of British operations in Europe and western Asia,[14] and literally millions more were operating in the armies of all the belligerents in Europe and the Middle East, including large numbers of camels in the Ottoman army.[15] No one knows how many of this vast sea of forced animal labor perished while in service, but the British alone lost over 250,000 horses in France and Flanders, while an estimate of French losses was 376,000 horses.[16] In the British campaigns in the east against the Ottoman armies, the official count of dead horses and mules exceeded 66,000. A less precise official count of camel deaths placed the number at 12,189 in a population of around 120,000 camels serving in those areas.[17] But given the earlier record of the British army's campaigns in India and Africa and the numbers cited above for losses in Mesopotamia, an official wastage rate for camels of only 10 percent seems far fetched. It was very likely higher. At any rate, most of the staggering number of deaths to be found in the official record, it was later acknowledged, could be attributed to "debility and exhaustion," although many also died of diseases such as surra and mange, as well as wounds received from bullets, shell bursts, and aerial bombardment.[18]

The scale of animal losses in the Middle Eastern campaigns appears to have been proportionally lower than on the western front in Europe, largely because forces were more mobile in the desert campaigns than in the stationary

12. The numbers for the requisition at the beginning of the war and for later ones come from Capt. Sidney Galtrey, *The Horse and the War* (London: Country Life, 1918), 16.

13. War Office, *Statistics of the Military Efforts of the British Empire during the Great War, 1914–1920*, 396, 861.

14. Of this total, approximately 293,000 were with British forces in Egypt, Mesopotamia, Salonika, and Italy. See Blenkinsop and Rainey, *Veterinary Services*, 511.

15. John Keegan estimated that during the war, the Austrians mobilized 600,000 horses, the Germans 715,000, and the Russians well over 1 million. Although perfectly plausible, Keegan's sources for these figures are unclear; see *The First World War* (New York: Alfred A. Knopf, 1999), 73.

16. War Office, *Statistics of the Military Efforts of the British Empire during the Great War, 1914–1920*, 397.

17. Blenkinsop and Rainey, *Veterinary Services*, 510–11.

18. Maj. Gen. John Moore, *Army Veterinary Service in War* (London: H. and W. Brown, 1921), 64–68.

trench warfare of the European theater, with its explosive artillery bombardments. Nevertheless, large numbers of transport animals died or were cast as unfit for service during all these campaigns. Some of these losses can be traced through the records of a few of the Indian Army camel units sent to Egypt. They included the Fifty-Ninth and Sixty-Second Grantee Camel Corps and the Seventieth Hired Camel Corps. The three units arrived in Egypt in the first few months of 1916, and as one might expect, the Indian camels did not fare well in the unfamiliar environment. Of the original complement of 972 in the Fifty-Ninth Corps, some 484 were lost between March and December of 1916, a wastage rate of 50 percent. Most died of vomiting and diarrhea as a result of inappropriate diet, the same cause of many deaths during previous British Indian Army campaigns in Afghanistan, Egypt, and the Sudan. Others died of ingesting desert sand. There is no reason to believe that the situation was any better in the Sixty-Second. In addition, for those camels who survived, mange was a constant nuisance, and seems to have been a problem throughout the camel units (see box 9.1).[19] There were also instances reported in which mange passed from camels to soldiers in the British army.[20]

Entries in war diaries of other units suggest that heavy losses in the Indian transport units were not exceptional; losses in units made up of Egyptian and Somali camels also appear to have been high. Although wastage rates were not reported in the war diaries consulted here, that of the Camel Transport Corps no. 2 Depot based at Kantara did, at one point, provide a running tally of camels transferred in and out of the unit. The diary for April 1917, for example, indicated that there were some 1,183 camels at the depot. Of these, only 234 were deemed fit for heavy burdens, and 274 were usable for light burdens. The rest were apparently soon shipped off, and replaced with over 600 camels acquired in Egypt and Somalia by the Remount Department. This pattern continued through the year, with from 10 to 20 sent to a veterinary hospital and one or two reported as deceased every few days.[21] These numbers suggest that despite better knowledge and understanding of camels produced, in part, by

19. NA/WO95/4404: GHQ Troops: "59th Grantee Camel Corps," "62nd Grantee Camel Corps," "191st Hired Camel Corps, February 1916 to September 1917," and the "70th Hired Camel Corps June to November 1916."

20. Geoffrey Inchbald, *The Imperial Camel Corps* (Driffield, Yorkshire: Leonaur, 2005), 159.

21. The War Diaries in question are available at the Australian War Memorial website (https://www.awm.gov.au, accessed 9 October 2017) in its digitized collection. See AWM Subclass 11/4—no. 1 Depot, Camel Transport Corps, and AWM Subclass 11/5—no. 2 Depot, Camel Transport Corps. The figures and discussion in this paragraph are based on sources to be found in the latter; see digital files RCDIG101-2067, 2710, 2711, and 2713.

BOX 9.1: Mange

Mange is a contagious skin disease caused by acari mites. These parasites are oval and about 1/50th of an inch in length and width. They can be detected by taking a deep scraping of an animal's skin and observing the sample under a low-powered microscope. Female mites are more numerous than males, and given the right conditions, the parasites multiply rapidly. They burrow into the skin, where they deposit up to two dozen eggs. The mites are sexually mature fifteen days after hatching. While they require a host for long-term reproduction, they can exist for extended periods in the lining of saddles, in blankets, and on the ground. They can also lie dormant in a treated animal and reproduce the disease at a later time. Humans can be the hosts of these parasites as well, which can be transmitted from human to animal. Grooming and cleanliness of equipment and sleeping areas are important for controlling the spread of the disease. Veterinary manuals advise that infected areas be clipped of hair, washed, and dressed. The most effective dressing in the field is made up of whale oil, sulfur, and carbonate of soda. Two weekly dressings suffice for mild cases. See Blenkinsop and Rainey, eds., *Veterinary Services*, 265, 715–18.

the routines of ever-more expert animal managers, camel mortality remained high. So apparently did sore backs. In many cases, camel back pain resulted from well-known factors—badly engineered or damaged saddles, improper loading, and overloading. High wastage rates can also be attributed to causes already familiar from the Second Afghan War. These included poor diet, excessive work without proper rest, and incompetent animal handlers. Within the reformed army transport scheme, however, there was a distinct difference from nineteenth-century campaigns. Camel transport officers or veterinarians were able, on their own authority, to move debilitated animals out of the line and into veterinary hospitals, where they could rest and get treatment. The war diaries testify to the large number of animals being sent to and returning from the hospitals.

The sort of ground-level view provided by individual unit reports and war diaries both supports and challenges some of the statistics to be found in the official histories, such as the surprisingly low 10 percent wastage rate of camels. These sources also suggest another factor that influenced the survival rate of animals. While great advances had been made in the veterinary corps in both Britain and India between 1900 and 1914, the sheer scale of the war outpaced the availability of trained personnel, in both human and geographic terms. When the war began, there were a total of 216 army veterinary officers in Great Britain and the colonies combined. At war's end there were 1,200. This still-modest number of veterinary surgeons was responsible for treating or supervising the treatment of an *average daily total* of 74,000 sick animals in 1916, and 110,000 by the end of the war.[22] During one six-month period in Egypt in 1917, for example, veterinarians handled 139,780 cases out of a total population of horses, mules, and camels numbering 130,706. The vast majority of these patients, clearly some more than once, suffered from wounds and other forms of injury, including lameness. At the same time that they were treating thousands of injured animals, veterinarians also had to deal with mule replacements from North America that arrived already infected with glanders. All American mules had to be isolated from the other animals and checked using a mallein test before they could be released into the general population (219–21).

In addition to a limited number of qualified personnel in the Indian Army, veterinarians in the field were unevenly distributed across units. At Gallipoli, for instance, the Eighth Corps, with some 4,100 horses and mules, had eleven veterinary officers, while the Anzac and Suvla units had only four veterinarians for their 4,000 animals (116–17). Hence, some animals had access to more, though not necessarily more experienced, care.

There were also special factors that seemed to have affected camels more than other animals, the chief problem being surra. Recall the decimation of camel corps units in Mesopotamia at the end of the war. An incident early in the war is comparable: 400 camels of the Bhawalpur Camel Corps, a unit from the Indian native state of the same name, were sent to Mesopotamia. All of them died (301).[23] Although there was some question about the diagnosis, surra was presumed to be the main cause. In another case, while not as catastrophic as the Bhawalpur incident, the Camel Transport Corps in Egypt reported a high prevalence of surra infections. These included an unsubstantiated claim that among the 45,000 camel casualties during operations to seize

22. Blenkinsop and Rainey, *Veterinary Services*, 23–24, 510–11. Subsequent page citations are given in the text.

23. This particular entry shows only limited knowledge of the state of surra research at the time, and suggests that the camels might have been killed by some other disease.

the Suez Canal, a large number of the deaths were caused by surra. In contrast, when camel companies of the corps were tested for surra during the campaign in the Jordan valley in 1918, the percentage of those infected, from a combined strength of 16,279 camels, was only 2.59 percent. Although six varieties of *Tabanus* were identified in the valley, reports suggest that the rate of infection was low because officers of the Camel Transport Corps, perhaps on the recommendations of their sarwans, knew enough to keep the animals away from water where biting flies were common (251–53).

As satisfying as it is to find that procedures like those advocated by Arnold Leese in India had filtered into some parts of the veterinary corps, other cases can be pointed to indicating disturbing repetitions of past mistakes. The campaign involving the Seistan Field Force in northern Persia provides one such example. The force was made up of three Silladar camel corps plus the Sixty-Fifth Government Camel Corps and the Sixty-First Grantee Camel Corps. Silladar losses were insignificant, while the Government and Grantee units lost large numbers, the bulk of which were attributed to surra. The report of the campaign observed that the trek from Nushki in Afghanistan to Saidak in Persia could be made simply by "following the camel skeletons along the route," an observation eerily reminiscent of the losses between Quetta and Kandahar over three decades earlier. Yet the Seistan report acknowledged that there was more than disease at work in bringing about losses. Among these factors were some that had been long noted, including general ignorance about camels and poor supervision of subordinates on the part of officers; the failure to allow animals proper rest or time to ruminate after they had browsed; and the refusal of veterinary assistants in one unit to treat sick animals in another. These explanations of camel deaths not only are reminiscent of the Second Afghan War, but indicate that the regimental ethos that had led to problems in the past lingered on (354–57).

The Seistan campaign of 1916–17 also pointed to another problem faced by military animals—a shortage of competent camel handlers for units operating in western Asia. In 1916, when forces were being mobilized in Egypt to invade Palestine, Indian sarwans were sent to serve in transport units made up of Egyptian, Sudanese, and Somali camels. According to the few reports we have on these units, the animals were worked continuously, veterinary assistants were in short supply, and Indian sarwans were steadily reduced in number by disease, the most common being "relapsing fever" (probably malaria).[24]

24. NA/WO95/4404: 59th Grantee Camel Corps, 191st Hired Camel Corps, and 70th Hired Camel Corps War Diaries.

Extant figures indicate a steady stream of ill sarwans entering hospitals, with about a third of them later being invalided home. In order to replace them, and to expand the number of transport units, military authorities in Egypt had to hire camel men locally. Some of these handlers came from Egypt and others from Somalia. Here again, patterns familiar from campaigns in India repeated themselves. Local camel men, or those purporting to be camel men, were gathered up by British procurement officers and stationed where they were needed. Few, one presumes, had knowledge of the animals to whom they were assigned. Work was grueling for all and illness common, so not surprisingly more than a few of the hired camel handlers deserted.[25]

Yet despite the evident repetition of past abuses of pack animals, especially considering that the army had to scale up well beyond its peacetime levels of trained personnel, a small number of camels had completely different war experiences from those working in supply and transport units. Some were incorporated as animal stretcher bearers in field hospitals, where they would carry up to two wounded soldiers at a time in specially designed cacolets (litters mounted on the backs of animals).[26] Other camels had a far more "romantic" experience, becoming part the Imperial Camel Corps, a cavalry unit that was formed in 1916. The camel's role in this unit was quite different from the experience of rank-and-file pack camels. Nevertheless, it is worth considering the relations that developed between these camels and their riders and handlers. A few sources reflect an unusual understanding of the value of camels to warfare developing in western Asia during the Great War.

The Imperial Camel Corps was staffed by British officers and by officers and enlisted men from Australia and New Zealand. In a memoir, one of the Australian troopers, Oliver Hogue, wrote a poem reminiscent of Rudyard Kipling's "Oonts,"[27] the latter of which was an extended lament on the frustrations of commissary personnel who were forced to deal with camels. In the first two stanzas of "To My Camel," Hogue expressed his initial negative impressions of the animal, ones that were shared by many of his fellow soldiers.

> You're an ugly smellful creature:
> You're a blot upon the plain:

25. See NA/WO95/4454 for examples of records on illnesses and desertions.

26. William G. MacPherson, *Medical Services, General History* (London: His Majesty's Stationery Office, 1921–24), 4:598–603.

27. Rudyard Kipling, *Barrack-Room Ballads* (New York: Signet Classics, 2003), 23–25. *Oonts* is a Punjabi or Hindi word for "camels."

I have seen Mohamed beat you,
And it gave me no pain.
You're spiteful and you're lazy,
You'd send a white man crazy,
But I reckon you're a daisy
When the Turks come out again.

Your head is most unsightly,
And so is your humpy back;
I hear you roaring nightly,
When you're loading for the track.
You're bow-legged and you're bandy,
But in this desert sandy
It's as well to have you handy;
You're a mighty useful hack.[28]

Here the physical and olfactory otherness of the camel, its refusal to spend the night peacefully, driving white men crazy, is somewhat balanced by bald human necessity. Unlike Kipling, who characterized the camel as a "devil an' a ostrich an' a orphan-child in one,"[29] and who saw few if any virtues in the beast, Hogue seemed to recognize that if one was going to survive in the desert, a camel was a "mighty useful" companion. This slight shift in human awareness came to full fruition at the close of Hogue's memoir, where he seems to be correcting Kipling. In the "Anzacs Farewell to his 'Steed,'" Hogue recalled his own transformation as he became more intimate with "Old Hoosta."

In the days when I was younger, when I never knew your worth;
When I thought a prancing palfrey was the finest thing on earth;
When a ride upon a camel seemed a punishment for sin;
And made a man feel fed up with the land we're living in:
It was then my errant fancy lightly turned to thoughts of verse,
And I libeled you, Old Hoosta, in a wild iambic curse.
I know you now for better; but for I might be dead.
So I recant, Old Hoosta: I take back all I said.

28. Oliver Hogue, *The Cameliers* (Driffield, Yorkshire: Leonaur, 2008), 11.
29. Kipling, *Barrack-Room Ballads*, 24.

You have borne me late and early o'er the sands of Sinai,
When the khamseen[30] lashed our faces and our water-bags were dry;
You somehow found the pathway, and you lobbed in camp again.
All through the mud and slush and mire of rain-soaked Palestine
You struggled like a hero. Now all gratitude is mine.
I once hurled maledictions at your supercilious head—
I'm sorry now Old Hoosta; I take back all I said.

When winter nights were freezing on the hills of old Judaea,
You humped my load of blankets and a ton of surplus gear;
When summer's sun was scorching and my head seemed like to burst,
You bore a full fantassie, and quenched my raging thirst.
I have never yet gone hungry, I have never yet gone dry;
That's something to your credit in a place like Sinai.
You have been my board and lodging, you even humped my bed—
Honest Injun! Oont, I'm grateful; I take back all I said.[31]

The change in attitude evident in Hogue's second poem makes it clear that his camel had become more than a beast of burden to him. The Camelier, as he terms himself, was, after all, mounted on the camel and in close tactile contact with the animal's body, swaying with his distinctive gait. Hogue's physical contact with and dependency on the camel, much like that of a transport sarwan, transformed his perception, making the camel more than just a handy and useful tool. Other accounts suggest that attitudes toward camels may have changed as a result of experiences of watching grooms care for them much as horses were being managed. Geoffrey Inchbald, a British officer in the Imperial Camel Corps, explained that during training, camels were kept "beautifully clean" by their Arab grooms. The animals were tethered nightly in a square facing inward; there they were washed, combed, scraped, brushed, and de-ticked.[32]

Such affective and tactile intimacies between cameliers, grooms, and Imperial Camel Corps camels may have been reinforced in another unusual way, through competitive play. Hogue described how soldiers participated in games

30. A hot, sandy wind common in the Egyptian desert.

31. Hogue, *The Cameliers*, 174–75.

32. Recall the inward-facing nightly encampment of camels in the cold mountains leading into Afghanistan; see chapter 1. Inchbald, *Camels and Others*, 39.

while astride their camels. There were, of course, camel races, and wagering on them. But there were also a number of more inventive competitions—soldiers wrestling each other while aboard their camels, or participating in camel-mounted egg and spoon races. Somehow they also managed to play a version of musical chairs aboard camels. Hogue observed, however, that it seemed that the camels "hardly entered into the spirit of the chase." This led him to conclude that if camels did think, they must have wondered why Allah had allowed the cameliers to cross the ocean in order to make merry at the expense of "dignified dromedaries."[33] Such playfulness and self-deprecation in human relations with camels are rare, as we've seen from the many sources cited throughout this study. With the exception of the positive comments of a few transport officers and veterinarians discussed earlier, any affirmative statements expressed about camels were usually like that of Pvt. Atkinson during the Second Afghan War—empathy for the animal's degree of suffering, and admiration for the its determination to work until it dropped dead from exhaustion. And yet, as unusual as Hogue's sentiments were, he was not alone.

In a piece published in the wartime journal *Cacolet*, Capt. J. Barber of the Imperial Camel Corps wrote that

> much maligned by timid riders, cheap trip tourists and writers who have seen it only in pictures or in the Zoological Gardens, the camel has proved itself a valuable servant of man, both in peace and war . . . they are not beautiful, and yet, swinging across the desert against an orange golden sunset, a string of camels makes a fine picture. There is, too, a touch of grace about the dromedary when he exalts his head and gazes afar like an alert sentinel.

Barber went on to extol the virtues of the animal in desert warfare, and added that it was futile to resort to violence in dealing with camels.[34]

Respect and affection for the camel can also be found in the reminiscences of Inchbald, who served with the Imperial Camel Corps unit from its creation

33. Hogue, *The Cameliers*, 143–45; the quotation is on p. 145. One of the military publications of the army in Egypt also mentioned the "Group Alarm Race" and the relay race as part of camel sports. See *Barrack: The Camel Corps Review*, 1 July 1917, Cairo. The issue of 1 September 1917 contained a souvenir program for "Imperial Camel Brigade Sports" scheduled for 12–13 February 1918 somewhere in Palestine. A copy of the former issue can be found in the British Library, London, the latter at the Imperial War Museum, London.

34. J. Barber, "Camels in Peace and War," *The Cacolet: Journal of the Australian Camel Field Ambulance*, ed. Charles Barrett and Tom V. Brennan, Palestine (September 1917): 5–6. A copy is in the British Library, London.

in early 1916, and who was involved in the Sinai and Palestine campaigns. He spoke, for example, of the close ties that developed between himself and his men and their mounts. In one instance he recalls, his unit had arrived at a fenced-in camp of British infantry. The camp commandant refused to allow the camels inside, so the cameliers slept with their mounts outside the barbed wire. These affective relations between trooper and animal, Inchbald suggested, were grounded in the greatheartedness of the camel and his innate intelligence(!). At the same time, he acknowledged that despite the fact that service in the Camel Corps was probably the last instance of "romance" in war, combat could still be unforgiving and brutal, especially when he and his comrades had to kill an injured or exhausted animal to put it out of its misery. In one particularly brutal instance, in which he and his men had to shoot a number of ill and exhausted camels, creating an "endless line of corpses" leading into the distance, he was clearly moved: "They had served us faithfully, poor devils, and we had become very attached to them."[35]

THE WAR IN INDIA

As these intense relationships emerged between cavalry camels and soldiers from Australia, New Zealand, and Great Britain fighting the Great War on the edges of the Ottoman Empire, the political situation in India was undergoing dramatic changes. Despite the great number of men and animals that had left that country to fight in Europe and the Middle East, a substantial number had been kept behind to defend the North-West Frontier. The reason for this, as noted earlier, was the fear that Ottoman leaders in Istanbul would encourage and support unrest and rebellion along the frontier, and perhaps even mount an invasion of India from Afghanistan. Matters remained relatively quiet until 1917, when Mahsud groups in Waziristan began attacking British posts.[36] An estimated 10,000 transport camels were engaged in a series of battles and skirmishes.[37] At the same time, as transport was being deployed to deal with the emergency, large numbers of camels were being lost to surra. In fact, a two-year epidemic was raging. According to Maj. Gen. Sir John Moore, director of the Veterinary Service in India, in 1917–18 there were 9,262 cases of surra, which resulted in 4,181 deaths. Of these, only 117 were horses, mules, ponies, or oxen.

35. Inchbald, *The Imperial Camel Corps*, 59–61, 90–93, 156, 159.

36. See General Staff Branch, Army Headquarters, India, *Operations in Waziristan, 1919–1920* (Calcutta: Superintendent of Government Printing, 1921), 30–63.

37. Blenkinsop and Rainey, *Veterinary Services*, 351.

The remainder of the dead were camels; their wastage rate in the epidemic was 25 percent. The following year there were 2,059 camel deaths, a lower wastage rate of 14 percent. Amid the surra epidemic, the amir of Afghanistan chose to invade India. The invasion was accompanied by outbreaks all along the frontier, similar to those of 1897–98. The difference now, however, was that the rebellious groups included former British Indian Army soldiers who either had been demobilized or had deserted from frontier militias.[38] This kind of violent anticolonial opposition continued into 1920, further straining the army's transport system, but also demonstrating the key role that camel and mule transport still played in the defense of British India.

As for the surra epidemic, by 1920 it had fortunately begun to wane, with the mortality rate dropping dramatically to .16 percent. Now back in India after service in northern France, Gen. Moore attributed the sharp decline in surra infections to two factors. One involved the transfer of camels to the newly created Surra Corps animal hospital, which exclusively dealt with animals infected with the disease. In the Surra Corps, affected animals were essentially quarantined and treated, presumably with Atoxyl and tartar emetic. If they could not be cured, they would be destroyed and the carcass burned. The other factor Moore believed had led to a decline in surra infections was regulations that prevented government camels from browsing. Instead, they were stall fed and kept in sanitary surroundings. Such an approach, Moore explained, was only possible among government-owned camels; those that were privately owned by Silladar and grantee sarwans were beyond his reach.[39] This radical transformation of government camel life may well explain why, from 1921 to 1929, surra infections were relatively low according to the annual reports of the Army Veterinary Service.[40]

Yet one cannot help but wonder whether Moore understood camel life. Recall earlier discussions of browsing in chapters 2 and 7. For camels, browsing was an essential part of ruminant digestion and of physical recovery from heavy work, as well as the basis of a kind of animal sociality. Also recall earlier

38. On these conflicts, see Andrew Roe, *Waging War in Waziristan* (Lawrence: University of Kansas Press, 2010), 94–95; and Tim Moreman, "'Watch and Ward': The Army in India and the North-West Frontier, 1920–1939," in *Guardians of Empire*, ed. D. Killingray and D. Omisso (Manchester: Manchester University Press, 1999), 137–56, especially 139–40.

39. Moore, *Army Veterinary Service in War*, 85–86.

40. The reports for these years contain in chart form all sick animals treated and the specific affliction for which they were admitted to veterinary care. The reports are in L/MIL/17/5/2361 and are entitled *Statistical and General Report of the Army Veterinary Service in India* for specific reporting years beginning in 1921–22.

reports from the canal colonies; they indicated that stall feeding was a major contributor to the decline in strength and vigor of the Punjab's camels. In Moore's formula for dealing with surra, camels avoided infection, but only by being thoroughly uncamel-like. While this logic may have made sense in an animal management regime where reducing wastage rates among government camels was a major goal, Moore's support of stall feeding seems a rather surprising outcome within a system that also claimed to understand camels better than ever before. His views on camel health can also be understood as akin to the state's policies toward pastoralists; it was argued that the nomad's life would be vastly improved if he would cease wandering about and take up the sedentary life of an agriculturalist.

But matters did not end with this confinement and constriction of camel life. Soon after the Third Afghan War ended in 1920, committees were appointed to address what to do with the postwar army and its transport system, which were still quite large. The watchwords for these "retrenchment" committees were *cost cutting* and *reduction in scale*.

RETRENCHMENT

Over the course of the war, personnel in the Supply and Transport Corps had grown from around 2,500 military and civilian members in 1914 to over 17,000 in 1921.[41] Also in 1921, the Army Veterinary Service counted a total population of 82,000 military animals under its care—a fourfold increase over prewar levels.[42] After an initial review by a committee headed by Gen. Walter Braithwaite, the Indian Army Retrenchment Committee of 1922–23 began to determine what needed to be eliminated. The key decision the committee made was that given the present "financial circumstances" of the Government of India and considering the growing availability of mechanical transport in the form of the truck, maintaining a transport reserve of large animals was no longer justified. In other words, the reserve system that had been set up specifically to deal with multiple outbreaks on the North-West Frontier was to be downsized, even though frontier disturbances continued.

In place of maintaining the pack animal reserve, the Retrenchment Committee recommended that a permanent system relying on light rail and lorries be established. And although it seemed to have skirted the issue of the

41. IOR/L/MIL/17/5/1781: *Report of the Indian Retrenchment Committee 1922–23* (Delhi: Superintendent of Government Printing, 1925), appendix B. Hereafter cited as *IRC*.

42. *Statistical and General Report of the Army Veterinary Service in India* (1923), 1.

inadequacy of roads for motor vehicles along the frontier, and the limits the frontier's mountainous terrain would place on rail extension, the committee thought that a combination of trucks and light rail would obviate the need for an animal reserve and also make it possible to downsize the active animal transport units.[43]

In fact, this process had already begun. In 1921, due to a shortage of grazing land, peasant indebtedness, and surra, the camel land-grant leases in the canal colonies as well as the grantee system were allowed to lapse.[44] Thereafter, cuts being considered mainly involved the Silladar camel transport units and the mule cadres. The questions were, how many animals and associated troops were to be eliminated, and how quickly could changes be made by replacing them with mechanical transport? To answer these questions, the Retrenchment Committee had to resolve a number of issues, beginning with assessing the present condition of mechanical transport systems.

Most of the trucks the Indian Army had on hand were prewar vehicles that were both obsolete and almost impossible to repair because of an absence of spare parts. Resources would have to be found to purchase new vehicles, along with an adequate supply of parts to maintain them.[45] A second problem involved the relative inefficiency of mechanical transport. The committee found that the cost of keeping a truck on the road was excessive (Rs. 4,250 per year) and suggested a number of possible solutions. These included improving gas mileage from the current level of fourteen miles to the gallon. No recommendation was made, however, on how this was to be done. A second suggestion was to reduce the use of vehicles to only fully justified and necessary operations, although no definition was provided for determining which circumstances would be deemed justified and necessary. But then perhaps none was needed, if, as the committee also proposed, gasoline was to be rationed.[46]

After determining that mechanical transport could be made more efficient by using it less, the Retrenchment Committee then concluded that the reduction of animals and attendants in the army would have the salutary effect of lessening the need for a large veterinary establishment, resulting in a reduction in the current number of veterinary hospitals. The smaller number

43. *IRC*, 14.

44. *Punjab Colony Manual* (Lahore: Superintendent of Government Printing, Punjab, 1922), 1:52–55. Peasants were permitted to purchase the land under colony tenure arrangements.

45. *IRC*, 15.

46. Ibid., 16.

of veterinary hospitals could, moreover, be made more efficient and medical stores reduced. The committee estimated that reductions in the overall animal establishment would produce an annual savings of 55 lakhs (Rs. 5.5 million), or about 8 percent of the current supply and transport budget.[47]

These proposals seemed to sidestep two other kinds of issues, though the Retrenchment Committee was fully aware of them. One involved the reason why Indian Army vehicles were obsolete. It seems that the trucks had been manufactured in Great Britain to Indian Army specifications in order to deal with poor roads and rugged terrain (e.g., they had extra-hefty gearboxes). This meant that the parts the manufacturers were providing for vehicles sold in Great Britain were not interchangeable with the parts needed by those in India. The absence or shortage of replacement parts in India was because British manufacturers did not stock them for these nonstandard vehicles.[48] Thus, because vehicles presumably still needed to be specially constructed for India's terrain, the decision to emphasize mechanical transport hardly seems to have been a significant step forward, particularly if the aim was efficiency and cost cutting. The army remained dependent on the importation of specially made trucks, just as in the past it had been dependent on the importation of mules with specific qualities.

The second obstacle to retrenchment involved ongoing military deployments in Waziristan.[49] In addition to the enormous cost of these operations (173 lakhs, or Rs. 17.3 million, in 1922 alone),[50] the terrain reinforced the army's continued dependence on animal transport to prosecute the war, especially ordnance mules that could move material on treacherous mountain trails. Hence, the need for animal transport to prosecute mountain warfare was not disappearing; it was an unavoidable fact on the ground. Indeed, the official history of operations on the North-West Frontier noted the army's ongoing reliance on mule and camel transport well into the 1930s. A diagram in this work showed the setup of the transport system for supply lines into Waziristan. Mechanical transport carried supplies between a base and an advance supply depot. Material was then moved forward on camel and mule transport to supply depots at the head of the road, and then onward to oper-

47. Ibid., 16.

48. IOR/L/MIL/7/6778: Dispatch from Army Department, Simla, to Secretary of State for India, London, 2 July 1925, 2.

49. On the continued problems the British had in Waziristan after the Great War, see Roe, *Waging War in Waziristan*.

50. *IRC*, 34.

ational camps. This meant that the action of the fighting units took place two stages beyond the limits of truck transport.[51] Thus, the retrenchment issue was not whether to eliminate animal transport but rather to determine how deeply it could be cut while still allowing the British Indian Army to police the recalcitrant occupants of the frontier highlands.

By 1925, the scale of the desired reductions had begun to come into focus. Total numbers of mules fell to 19,787, camels to 5,808, and bullocks to 870. The reduction in the number of camels included elimination of four of the eight Silladar reserve corps.[52] In 1930, additional cuts were made, beginning with the complete elimination of bullocks as transport animals. Mule transport was reduced to 12,576 animals, and camels to 864 on active duty and 3,840 in Silladar reserves.[53] No mention was made of donkeys or ponies. Nevertheless, these numbers were still relatively high; they provide some sense of the limits of mechanization. Moreover, mule breeding continued apace; one source noted that in 1937, 92 donkey studs were operating in the Punjab and 12 in the North-West Frontier Province.[54] Conditions on the ground dictated that as long as the Indian Army had to deal with armed anticolonial resistance in rugged mountain terrain, pack animals had a place in the imperial security regime.

As if to acknowledge the continued relevance of animal transport to the British military, in 1937 the War Office published a volume with the curious title *Manual of Horsemastership, Equitation and Animal Transport*. In the transport chapters, detailed instructions were provided for how to load horses and mules properly, and how to drill them in training. The instructions began, as most military manuals did, with general principles, followed by specific directions. For example, for lashing boxes to animals' backs, only certain kinds of knots were appropriate, and diagrams were provided for how to tie them. Instructions followed on the loading of equipment, all of which came in standard-size boxes of identical weight for each equipment type. Hence, six boxes of hand and rifle grenades, each box weighing twenty-three pounds, were to be loaded two on each side of a mule and two on top for balance; or

51. *Official History of Operations on the N.-W. Frontier of India* (New Delhi: Government of India Press, 1945), 147–48, 192, 196, 249; the diagram is on p. 253.

52. IOR/L/MIL/7/6780: "Reorganization of Animal Transport, 1924–1930," 3.

53. IOR/L/MIL/7/6780: Government of India to the Secretary of State for India, 28 August 1930.

54. IOR/V/24/11: Imperial Council of Agricultural Research, *Agriculture and Animal Husbandry in India, 1936–37* (Delhi: Manager of Publications, 1939), 283–84.

three boxes could be loaded per side. Once the mules were loaded, directions were given for organizing and moving a mule column, including no-nonsense instructions for march discipline, ascent and descent of hills, and so on. For questions concerning mule care, readers were referred to the *Animal Management* manual of 1908, which, as noted earlier, conceived the subject as an empirewide matter. A similar pattern of detailed explanation was provided in chapters about transport animals other than mules.

It should come as no surprise, therefore, that instructions on how to operate camel transport could be found in this volume. The layout was identical to that of the section on mules. There were instructions for organizing a camel transport column, loading the animals, and marching them in an orderly manner. Ideally, camels were understood to operate in a convoy system, in which they hauled loads to a meeting point where their loads could be transferred to front-line transport, which presumably meant mules, donkeys, or ponies. With one exception, the camel entry was presented in a matter-of-fact tone, with no reference to any of the difficulties the British had experienced with camel transport in Asian campaigns over the last sixty years. The exception involved camel drivers. "Camels require skilled handling," the manual asserted, and then—presumably invoking historical experience—cautioned the reader that native drivers are "rarely reliable camelmasters." Those skills were now all presumed to be in the hands of members of the British transport units.[55]

Taken as a whole, this manual might be viewed as just another, albeit belated, instantiation of the rule of experts, animal transport division. In its careful diction, it tied up loose ends concerning the loading and moving of military transport animals, thus establishing a triumvirate of expertise with the companion volumes *Animal Management* and *Handbook on Contagious and Infectious Diseases of Animals*. And like the other manuals, it asserted an authority that superseded all others. Moreover, with its companions it could claim to provide adequate foundations for the humane treatment of military animals and the efficient execution of field operations.

Indeed, a manual on frontier warfare in India, published soon after *Manual of Horsemastership*, underscored the importance of properly loading pack animals while on campaigns. Emphasizing that all movement of animals must be expeditious because they were potential targets of mountain fighters, the manual asserted that

55. *Manual of Horsemastership, Equitation and Animal Transport* (London: His Majesty's Stationery Office, 1937), 198–207; the quotation is on p. 199.

> all ranks of *all* arms must be expert in the tying and adjustment of loads for mules and camels. Badly tied loads may entail great delays and so cause casualties which might otherwise have been avoided. Thorough and constant practical training is necessary to attain proficiency in this most important subject.[56]

In other words, tying and adjusting loads were more than matters of practical efficiency or humane means of preventing unnecessary injuries to pack animals. Tying and adjusting were security issues that *all* participants, human and animal alike, were to have drilled into them. In this way, the manuals discussed here provided a kind of ceaseless professional refining and honing of the mundane militarization of pack animal life.

State-of-the-art instruction manuals, combined with the reduction in animals being kept for Indian Army transport, might also be seen as a humane development for the transport animals of the Punjab. Indeed, substituting mechanical labor for animal labor was quite generally assumed to be a positive sign of human progress and the advance of civilization.[57] On the other hand, while fewer and fewer animals were called on to serve their imperial masters, the masters themselves did not rescind their right to do so. The Punjab Military Animals Transport Act, revised in 1916, remained firmly established in colonial law, and later became part of the legal code of the new nation-state of Pakistan.

SURRA DEVELOPMENTS

With its arrival as a treatment regime for surra in the latter part of the 1920s, Naganol fit nicely with the other watchwords of the postwar era. It too was efficient, scientifically rational, and cost cutting, since it eliminated the need for prolonged treatment of animals and got them back into service quickly. It also had a number of other intriguing effects besides curing some animals of the disease. Naganol treatment made older knowledge produced by British veterinarians obsolete. Ironically, much of the research conducted on surra by John Henry Steel, Arnold Leese, Henry Eustace Cross, J. E. D. Holmes, and others was relegated to the dustbin of history. As the principal of the Punjab Veterinary College in Lahore put it in 1934, the records of treating surra with

56. Army Headquarters, India, *Frontier Warfare—India* (New Delhi: Government of India Press, 1939), 158.

57. See Michael Adas, *Machines as the Measure of Man* (Ithaca, NY: Cornell University Press, 1989).

Atoxyl and tartar emetic "have come to be regarded as so many 'dead' chapters in the history of chemotherapeutic endeavors." On the other hand, the disease, as the principal also noted, was alive and well, occasionally assuming "terrifying proportions" in the Punjab.[58] A few years after his statement was published, the parasite surprised everyone by infecting the historically resistant bovine population of India and killing huge numbers of cattle.[59] Whether this development was related to the experimental transfer of blood between species in live-animal experiments, as noted in chapter 8, is not clear; but at least one contemporary group of researchers of the trypanosome has referred to the "incredible plasticity of this amazing parasite."[60] There seems to be little doubt that the parasite was transformed in a complex relation with landscape and habitation changes, military occupation, and scientific interventions in animal population biology. Surra is still in the Punjab, of course, and it still kills camels; the difference now is that, like the vast and environmentally flawed canal network of the region, it is a management problem for the postcolonial development state.[61]

58. W. Taylor, "Surra in the Punjab," *IJVSAH* 4, no. 1 (1934): 29.

59. Bachan Singh, "Bovine Trypanosomiasis in Central Provinces with an Account of Some Recent Outbreaks," *IJVSAH* 6, no. 3 (1936): 243–50; and Imperial Council of Agricultural Research, *Agriculture and Animal Husbandry in India*, 270–71.

60. Robert Jensen, Larry Simpson, and Paul Englund, "What Happens When *Trypanosoma brucei* Leaves Africa," *Trends in Parasitology* 24, no. 10 (October 2008): 430.

61. Muhammad Ali Shah, Kalili Ur Rehman, Fawad Ur Rehman, and Nongye He, "Present Status of Camel *Trypanosomiasis* in Pakistan: A Review of Literature," *Science Letters* 1, no. 1 (2013): 30–33.

CHAPTER 10

Colonial Legacies: The State, Water, Surra, and Camels

In this final chapter, I explore some connections between practices of the colonial and the postcolonial state. Thematically, this involves tracing the long-term impact of the militarization of the Punjab and the reengineering of the canals of the Indus River basin. I then take up surra research over the last four decades, and explain why early twentieth-century veterinarians and microbiologists had difficulty understanding the nature of the surra parasite. In conclusion, I explore the present place of camels in Pakistan, particularly their location in a discourse on national development and food security.

GARRISON STATE

The militarization of the Punjab that began in the 1880s produced what Tan Tai Yong has referred to as a "garrison state." Building on the work of Imran Ali, Tan has emphasized that the British continued a policy, adapted from the Mughals and Sikhs, of making land grants in exchange for military service.[1] However, the close tie between landownership and military service took another twist under the British. The land grants were tied to an agricultural development scheme for exporting wealth from the colony while linking army service with a military structure specifically designed to permanently police the North-West Frontier of British India. Well into the twentieth century, the link between agricultural development and military security involved complex

1. Tan Tai Yong, *The Garrison State: The Military, Government and Society in Colonial Punjab, 1849–1947* (New Delhi: Sage Publications, 2005), 90–97.

relationships between privileged landowners and British civil administrators. But the present study has also shown that the garrison state included the pack animals needed for army transport. The garrison state thus eventually mounted a comprehensive animal management regime that incorporated in its repertoire the general oversight of animal life and health. To what extent is such a colonial regime still discernible in contemporary Pakistan?

When partition occurred in 1947, Pakistan and India almost immediately went to war. Since then, occasional skirmishes have occurred along their shared border, and an almost permanent state of cold war exists between them.[2] The garrison state thus not only has remained in place—it effectively reproduced itself by taking advantage of foreign military aid, acquiring nuclear weapons, and retaining the previous colonial ties between the army and landowners. Today, that link is further strengthened with generous government pensions and welfare organizations for retired soldiers, along with privileged access to jobs and business opportunities.[3] Meanwhile, Pakistan's defense budget, in which military spending has increased 11 percent annually over the last five years, is the single largest outlay of the Pakistani state. Recent defense budgets are somewhat deceptive, however, in that they do not include expenditures for operations in the Federally Administered Tribal Areas (i.e., the Afghan frontier zones), the nuclear program, or pensions for military veterans.[4] Moreover, as had been the case with the British, the relations between the government of Pakistan and the Pathan peoples living in the Federally Administered Tribal Areas continue to be fraught. The region in question remains in a state of almost permanent martial law, the basic legal code being the much-amended Punjab Murderous Outrages Act of 1867.[5] The "fanat-

2. The wars are covered in Brian Cloughley, *A History of the Pakistan Army: Wars and Insurrections*, 4th ed. (Oxford: Oxford University Press, 2014).

3. See, for example, Ayesha Siddiqa, *Military, Inc.: Inside Pakistan's Military Economy* (Karachi: Oxford University Press, 2007).

4. On the increase in military spending, see the article "Defense Budget Hiked by Usual 11pc," *Dawn* (Karachi), 4 June 2016, https://www.dawn.com/news/1262657; accessed 6 October 2017. The defense budget is Rs. 860 million, comprising 22 percent of the total budget, while economic development programs are about half that of defense outlays. Foreign debt service is also high, and is projected to exceed Rs. 440 million. See Finance Division, Government of Pakistan, *Budget in Brief, Federal Budget 2016–17* (Islamabad, 2016), 23, which is available at http://budget.par.com.pk/2016-17/; accessed 6 October 2017.

5. The act is posted, with amendments, at http://www.commonlii.org/pk/legis/pj/consol_act/pmoa1867302/#_ftnref7; accessed 6 October 2017. Some of the more offensive features of the law, including ones that hold groups collectively responsible for the acts of their individual

ics" designated in the colonial-era act are now referred to as "terrorists," who like their predecessors are accorded few civil rights or legal protections. Most recently, the Pakistani state's military domination was exercised in Waziristan, where operations continue at the time of this writing, and in Swat.[6]

These strong continuities between former imperial and current nation-state security regimes have also carried over in certain respects to still-militarized animals. Recall that the British Indian Army maintained camel and mule transport units for use in mountainous frontier regions well into the 1930s. Today, while camels no longer seem to be part of army transport, mule companies are still operating. According to a documentary film describing the functions of the current Pakistani Army Service Corps, mules are used to carry supplies to units in terrain where helicopters cannot land and air drops are difficult.[7] In India, some six thousand mules continue to serve in Ladkh and other parts of the Himalayan highlands.[8] Moreover, perhaps learning from the Pakistanis, the United States Army trains soldiers in the use of pack mules at the Mountain Warfare Training Center at Bridgeport, California, in the Sierra Nevada. According to one report, mules can supply US troops in the mountains of Afghanistan where neither helicopters nor mechanical transport can go.[9] In

---

members, were amended in 2011. However, given continued military operations in the Federally Administered Tribal Areas, it is difficult to gauge the effects of the changes; see http://www.slideshare.net/fatanews/regulation-to-amend-the-frontier-crimes-regulationfcr-august-2011; accessed 17 October 2017.

6. See, for example, Hassan Abas, "The Political Landscape of the Taliban Insurgency in Pakistan," 262–88, and Daud Khan Khattak, "The Taliban in Swat," 289–313, in *Talibanistan*, ed. P. Bergen and K. Tiedemann (Oxford: Oxford University Press, 2013). Also see "The Pakistan Army and Its Role in FATA" (15 January 2009) and "Evaluating Pakistan's Offensives in Swat and FATA" (31 October 2011). Both can be found at the website of the Combating Terrorism Center at West Point, https://ctc.usma.edu; accessed 17 October 2017.

7. See *Army Service Corps Documentary* at https://tune.pk/video/3853125/army-service-corps-asc-documentary-pakistan-army; accessed 6 October 2017.

8. "The History that Mules, Mountains and the Military Share," *Economic Times*, 11 June 2017, at http://economictimes.indiatimes.com/news/defence/replacing-mules-with-new-vehicles-for-army-a-good-idea/articleshow/59088926.cms; accessed 6 October 2017.

9. Gordon Lubold, "Fighting a High-Tech War with a Low-Tech Mule," *Christian Science Monitor*, 22 October 2009. The use of American mules in Afghanistan was preceded by a shipment of some twelve hundred mules to *mujahidin* forces fighting the Soviet invasion of Afghanistan in the late 1980s. See Susan Orlean, "Riding High: Mules in the Military," *New Yorker*, 15 February 2010; http://www.newyorker.com/magazine/2010/02/15/riding-high, accessed 6 October 2017. The mules, some twelve hundred in number, were purchased in Tennessee and flown to Pakistan as part of CIA programs in support of the *mujahidin*.

other words, precisely the same sorts of imperatives that sent American mules to the Punjab in the late nineteenth and early twentieth centuries are repeating themselves in the twenty-first. One other continuity is worth mentioning. Despite a whole new jargon that embeds militarized animals' lives in "liberation" or "counterinsurgency" operations,[10] the Pakistanis, perhaps recalling the seminal work of one of the British frontier agents, Robert Sandeman,[11] speak of the necessity to win the "hearts and minds" of Pathan tribes once military operations cease in areas like Waziristan.[12]

CANAL COLONIES

The canal system bequeathed by the British to the new state of Pakistan almost immediately became a part of nation-building projects. Like other developing countries, Pakistan relied on an expansion of agricultural output that could then be used as exports to generate foreign exchange credits. Agricultural expansion was dependent, however, on successfully managing the water of the Indus basin, a proposition complicated by the partition. The Indus River basin canal system was split in half in 1947, with the Sutlej, Beas, and Ravi Rivers kept under Indian sovereignty. Just how the waters of the border-crossing rivers were to be used was not resolved until 1960, when the World Bank brokered an agreement known as the Indus Water Treaty. The treaty awarded the Chenab, Jhelum, and Indus to Pakistan and left the other three under Indian control. Pakistan thereupon began an ambitious reengineering project affecting the three rivers, including the building of major dam and reservoir complexes on the northern parts of the Indus and Jhelum Rivers. In addition, five water diversion barriers called barrages were constructed in order to direct water from the Jhelum and Chenab Rivers to new canals linked

10. See, for example, James L. Hevia, "Small Wars and Counterinsurgency," in *Anthropology and Global Counterinsurgency*, ed. John Kelly et al. (Chicago: University of Chicago Press, 2010), 169–77, as well as the other articles in this volume.

11. See Thomas H. Thornton, *Colonel Robert Sandeman* (1895; reprint, Quetta: Gosha-e-Adab, 1977), 253.

12. "Fata: Beyond Military Operations," Institute of Policy Studies, Islamabad, 20 October 2014; http://www.ips.org.pk/whats-new/92-seeminar/1829-fata-beyond-military-operation, accessed 6 October 2017. The operations in Waziristan continued into 2016; see "Operation in Fata Nearing Completion," *Dawn* (Karachi), 15 March 2016, https://www.dawn.com/news/1245732; accessed 6 October 2017.

with the empty courses of the Sutlej, Beas, and Ravi Rivers that remained in Pakistan.[13]

Yet modern reengineering has not resolved the problems that plagued the system from the early twentieth century (e.g., waterlogging, salinization). Moreover, standing water in pools and along canal banks continues to provide breeding areas for *Tabanus* and other biting flies, as well as anopheles mosquitoes.[14] The canal system is now further plagued by industrial pollution, the runoff of chemical fertilizers from fields, and the increase in human effluent in the rivers. And because the natural process of silt distribution by seasonal inundation of fields was curtailed with the construction of perennial canals and, more recently, large hydroelectric dams, silting of the canal runs remains a major problem.[15] Lastly, with more than a century of human reengineering of the Indus basin, natural drainage patterns have been seriously disrupted. As a result, the region remains very vulnerable to flooding when monsoon rains are particularly heavy. This was the case in 2010, when embankments in the Punjab and the Sind were breached, killing some 1.6 million domestic animals and affecting the lives of some 20 million humans. Events like this one have led to calls for less "heroic engineering" and more sensitivity to the natural rhythms

13. M. A. Kahlown, A. D. Khan, and M. Azam, "The World's Largest Contiguous Irrigation System: Developments, Successes and Challenges of the Indus Irrigation System in Pakistan," in *A History of Water*, ed. T. Tvedt and E. Jakobsson (London: I. B. Tauris, 2006), 1:37–39.

14. Even an economic historian who finds great virtue in the British canal system, especially from a cost-benefit point of view, acknowledges that among the "negative externals" (e.g., waterlogging and salinization) related to canals, the most serious is that they provide breeding grounds for malaria vectors and consequently pose a serious public health problem (Ian Stone, *Canal Irrigation in British India* [Cambridge: Cambridge University Press, 1984], 144–57).

15. There is a substantial amount of literature on the subject of soil salinity, waterlogging, and silting in Pakistan. See, for example, A. S. Qureshi et al., "Managing Salinity and Waterlogging in the Indus Basin of Pakistan," *Agricultural Water Management* 95, no. 1 (2008): 1–10; and M. H. Malik, "Hazard of Erosion and Its Effects on the Water Resources of Pakistan," http://lib.icimod.org/record/23024/files/c_attachment_203_2025.pdf; accessed 6 October 2017. In some cases, farmers have organized their own desilting campaigns; in others, the Pakistani state closes the entire irrigation system for desilting operations. See Salim Malik, Waheed-u Zaman, and Marcel Kuper, *Farmers' Organized Behavior in Irrigated Agriculture in Pakistan's Punjab: A Case Study of Six Watercourse Command Areas in Junejwala Minor, Lower Chenab Canal System* (Colombo, Sri Lanka: International Irrigation Management Institute, 1996), 30–32; and "IRSA to Close Canals Dec 26 to Jan 31 for De-silting," *Pakistan Today* (Lahore), 23 November 2016, https://www.pakistantoday.com.pk/2016/11/23/irsa-to-close-canals-from-dec-26-to-jan-31-for-de-silting-2/; accessed 6 October 2017.

of the river basin.[16] Given the enormous fiscal and intellectual commitment to scientific management of the Indus and its tributaries, it seems unlikely that this kind of program will be implemented. Moreover, if the Mississippi basin is any example, the effect of flooding has historically been to build higher levees or embankments along the river, introducing greater risks still.[17]

One program of the government of Pakistan that has had some effect in addressing both salinity and waterlogging has been the installation of tube wells. These are round metal cylinders that can be sunk fairly deeply to access groundwater deposits. Lack of financial resources to support the tube-well program forced the government to close it down around 2000, and salinity and waterlogging have returned. Farmers have attempted to address the issue by installing their own tube wells, but as thousands have now been put in place, groundwater pollution and water depletion have ensued. These "fixes" and recurring problems serve to highlight the fact that the canal development project, from its beginning, was overly ambitious, and initiated changes that have gone far beyond human control.

Some farmers have attempted to address salinity, waterlogging, and pollution by mixing old and new methods. Instead of chemical fertilizers, some are using human and animal manure, mixing rotten vegetables into their soil, planting salt-resistant crops such as barley instead of wheat, and introducing salt-resistant palm and eucalyptus trees around the edges of fields. Equally important, officials and agricultural specialists in government and experts at universities are beginning to listen to farmers concerning the effectiveness of these low-cost "appropriate technologies."[18]

But not all the problems that farmers face in the Indus River basin can be attributed to inefficiencies within the canal system and the unexpected consequences of expanding agriculture into the wastelands (see the prologue to part 2). When the government of the Punjab passed the Canal and Drainage Act in 1873, one intention seems to have been to provide an authority that could govern the use and development of canal irrigation. The act gave substantial power to engineers, in the expectation that they would be able to

16. David Gilmartin, *Blood and Water: The Indus River Basin in Modern History* (Oakland: University of California Press, 2015), 250–51.

17. Andrew Pickering and Keith Guzik, eds., *The Mangle in Practice* (Durham, NC: Duke University Press, 2008), 5–9.

18. This paragraph is based on materials collected by Alina Alam in "Analysis of Salinity Control and Reclamation Project in Pakistan" (2015), 1–14; at https://ecommons.cornell.edu/bitstream/handle/1813/40312/SCARP-Report-M.Eng.pdf?sequence=2; accessed 6 October 2017.

rationally manage water. From the perspective of the engineer, the ideal result would be an equitable and fair distribution of water throughout the expanded irrigation system. As the canal colonies developed in the 1880s and 1890s, however, this goal was undermined by two factors.

The first involved the fact that engineers did not have either the technical knowhow or the hydraulic technologies to produce such an egalitarian system. Recall, for example, the perennial problem of water shortages at the tail ends of irrigation runs. Engineers could deliver water to some of these locations, but only if they reduced flows in other parts of the system. There was no situation in which it all evened out. The second problem was built into British officials' notions of how they wanted the new colonies to function and grow. They did this in part by creating, through the process of allocating land, a hierarchy of privileges. A social and economic pecking order was envisioned in the colonies, such that the colonial state would find natural allies at the top of the pyramid it had created. This class- and interest-based structure was meant to be further reinforced by providing land grants as rewards for service to the state. Those with status could use their embedded positions to ensure privileges, one of the primary ones being a greater access to water than other landowners had. Put simply, the sociopolitical structure the British preferred ultimately served to undermine any efforts at creating equitable water distribution, even when relatively equal distribution became more technically feasible in the 1920s.[19]

Scholars who have addressed the historical issues related to the Indus River basin have seen this tension between privilege and equity as defining an ideological split in British governance; or, as David Gilmartin has put it, a conflict between the "science of empire," embodied in the actions of colonial administrators such as colonization officers, and "imperial science," as represented in the actions of hydraulic engineers.[20] G. E. van Halsema and L. Vincent have questioned this dichotomy, arguing that hydraulic engineers were also administrators. They add that more often than not, there was a consensus among these officials that sought to maintain the status quo in the colonies. This may be true; but, as I have tried to emphasize throughout this study, the

19. The technical changes were to outlets off the canals that could be used to regulate water flow more evenly through branch channels. For a discussion, see G. E. van Halsema and L. Vincent, "Of Flumes, Modules and Barrels: The Failure of Irrigation Institutions and Technologies to Achieve Equitable Water Control in the Indus Basin," in Tvedt and Jakobsson, *A History of Water*, 70–72.

20. David Gilmartin, "Scientific Empire and Imperial Science," *Journal of Asian Studies* 53, no. 4 (November 1994): 1127–49.

friction wasn't simply a matter of canal colony officers posed against engineers. Multiple parts of the colonial government had an interest in maintaining the canal colonies as they were perceived to be, not the least important being the Indian Army, where the status quo meant easy access to transport animals and recruits. Peasants, particularly those at the far ends of canals, and pastoralists were the odd men out in this colonial configuration. The postcolonial link of powerful landowners and pensioners with the state and the military continues to skew the canal system, making equitable distribution of water impossible.[21]

SURRA TODAY

Throughout the earlier discussion of *Trypanosoma evansi* in chapter 9, I emphasized that the keys to the spread of the parasite were an exploitable camel and equine population and an abundance of vectors. The latter was especially critical because *T. evansi* only seemed to be transmissible from one host to another mechanically; that is, in the blood carried on the mouthparts of feeding female flies. The primary agent of transmission in the Punjab has been the *Tabanus* fly, but other biting flies have also been involved. At the same time, it seems to be the case that the flies, while capable of transmitting the disease, were probably inefficient vectors. Often disturbed in their feeding and frequently in motion, they no doubt lost microscopic passengers along the way. Plenty of trypanosomes must have died of extended exposure outside any hosts' body. Hence, an abundance of flies and bites was necessary to guarantee transmission.

But there could be large numbers of flies only if there was sufficient water available for the fly to complete its life cycle. In the arid plains of the Punjab and the Sind (before the construction of irrigation canals), and in the deserts of Bikaner and Baluchistan, there were only two sources of water: the Indus and its tributaries, and pools produced during the monsoon. This was why canal expansion, with its concomitant waterlogging, aided the biting flies. The wet banks of canals and water-soaked spots enabled by rising water tables became new breeding grounds for flies as well as for mosquitoes. Already an opportunist, *T. evansi* found naïve helpers in the form of colonial administrators bent on agricultural development, and hydraulic engineers certain they could command the waters of the Indus River basin to be more "efficient."

In the twentieth century, the only treatment for the disease in pack animals and cavalry horses that resulted from this unwitting pathogen-human

21. Van Halsema and Vincent, "Of Flumes, Modules and Barrels," 78–81.

relationship had been synthetic chemical poisons that killed trypanosomes. But very little was known about the parasite itself, beyond its morphology and suspicions that the trypanosomes in India were related in some way to those in Africa. After World War II, trypanosomiasis was transformed into a "third world" or "developing country" disease that was seen as a bane to the development process because of its impact on domestic animals such as cattle, goats, and camels. As a result, by the 1970s joint research projects conducted by microbiologists across Asia and Africa were launched to better understand the disease and find a cure.[22] Current understanding of *Trypanosoma evansi* as a biological mechanism helps explain some of the earlier confusion over its modes of transmission while also explaining why it has been so difficult to develop a serum to treat those infected by it.

Recall Arnold Leese's speculations about how trypanosomes came to India. He argued that camels traveling close to the Tsetse belt in sub-Saharan Africa must have been infected by these flies. As the camels moved north, they encountered multiple vectors (flies), which mechanically transmitted *T. evansi* to other animals. Leese was more or less correct, but the problem remained that if the trypanosome identified by David Bruce as the cause of nagana in cattle and sleeping sickness in humans was related to *T. evansi*, how did the latter reproduce outside the body of the fly?

Recent genetic research has determined that *T. evansi* and *T. equiperdum*, a version that affects only horses and is transmitted during coitus, are "petite mutants" of *T. brucei*. That is, they are genetically less complex versions of their ancestor, having dropped some of the DNA coding related to the part of their reproductive process that took place in the Tsetse fly.[23] No longer dependent on an intermediating vector for reproduction, *T. evansi* was able to escape southern Africa and spread across North Africa; western, southern, southeastern, and eastern Asia; and even to some Pacific islands, living in

22. On international research from 1970 forward, see M. M. Mahmoud and A. R. Gray, "Trypanosomiasis Due to *Trypanosoma evansi* (Steel 1885) Balbani, 1888: A Review of Recent Research," *Tropical Animal Health and Production* 12 (1980): 35–47; and R. Boid et al., "Trypanosomiasis Research at the Center for Tropical Veterinary Medicine (CTVM) 1970 to 1995," *Tropical Animal Health and Production* 28 (1996): 5–22. On the geographical distribution of *T. evansi* and hosts, see M. Desquesnes et al., "*Trypanosoma evansi* and Surra: A Review and Perspectives on Origin, History, Distribution, Taxonomy, Morphology, Hosts and Pathogenic Effects," *BioMed Research International* (2013): 1–22.

23. De-hua Lai, "Adaptations of *Trypanosoma brucei* to Gradual Loss of Kinetoplast DNA: *Trypanosoma equiperdum* and *Trypanosoma evansi* are *Petite* Mutants of *T. brucei*," *Proceedings of the National Academy of Science* 105, no. 6 (February 2008): 1999–2004.

the bodies of camels and other mammalian hosts. Moreover, descendants of some of the escapees were carried into the Americas, probably in the bodies of the horses of the Spanish conquistadors; as a mutation termed *T. cruzi*, they infected both animals and humans. The latter infection, known as Chagas disease, is common in South and Central America, and through an expanding number of mammalian reservoirs, it has begun to appear in the southern United States.[24] It seems reasonable to assume that it may move even further north as a result of climate change. Michel Serres's representation of the parasite as an "exciter" seems particularly appropriate in the case of trypanosomes.

But if a change in its DNA structure accounts for *T. evansi*'s escape from Africa, it doesn't explain its success in adapting to a wide range of hosts across Africa and Asia. Put simply, *T. evansi* has the capacity, after the initial attack by a host's immune system, to change its form. It does this by altering the surface protein (variant surface glycoprotein, or VSG), or antigen, on its outer layer, so that the host's immune system is no longer able immediately to detect the original form of the invader.[25] Even more impressive, trypanosomes carry with them an "archive" of some two thousand proteins from which to draw for these alterations.[26] As the host immune system feverishly produces antibodies to respond to a succession of VSGs, a condition of immunosuppression results. This ability to suppress the host's immune system not only makes it impossible to limit the reproduction of trypanosomes, but results in a general reduction of the host's immune responses and a diminished effectiveness of any vaccine-produced antibodies the host may carry to combat other common animal diseases.[27] And because animals often carry the parasite without any evident signs of disease in the early stages of the infection, *T. evansi* can spread rather quickly through a population before being detected.

The ability of trypanosomes to alter their own surface proteins is the fundamental reason why no serum or treatment has been developed to contain the disease. Instead, methods identical to those of the 1920s continue to be used;

24. See the review article by F. Noireau et al., "*Trypanosoma cruzi*: Adaptation to Its Vectors and Its Hosts," *Veterinary Research* 40, no. 26 (2009): 1–23.

25. This particular feature of the trypanosome was initially understood by researchers in the 1960s as its ability to produce multiple antigens; see Hoare, *The Trypanosomes of Mammals* (116–17) and the sources he cites. Also see George Roelants and Margaret Pinder, "Immunobiology of African Trypanosomiasis," in *Immunobiology of Parasites and Parasite Infections*, ed. J. J. Marchalonis (New York: Plenum, 1984), 225–77.

26. J. David Barry, James Hall, and Lindsay Plenderleith, "Genome Hyperevolution and the Success of a Parasite," *Annals of the New York Academy of Sciences* 1267 (September 2012): 11–17.

27. Desquesnes et al., *Trypanosoma evansi*, 12–13.

that is, administering synthetic chemicals to kill the parasites is the only treatment. But the trypanosomes have proved adaptive here as well, developing their own immunities to Naganol (Suramin) and other trypanocidal drugs.[28]

A more recent tactic on the part of microbiologists involves an attempt to discover potential weaknesses of the parasite through the sequencing of the trypanosome genome. This has been accomplished, for example, with *T. brucei* and *T. cruzi*, which has led to the identification of "a large number of potential drug targets."[29] This seems to be the likely direction of future research, that is, the development of synthetic drugs that can be directed at specific parts of the parasite's genetic makeup. Given sufficient resources, something similar may soon be in the works with respect to *T. evansi*. It was announced at the beginning of 2015 that its genome had been successfully sequenced, which opens the possibility of new, albeit costly, forms of treatment for camels, cattle, and other domestic animals in Asia and Africa.[30]

Meanwhile, in Pakistan and India, where resources for the development of new drugs are limited, veterinarians confront surra in long-familiar ways. One involves dealing with periodic outbreaks of the disease by using available trypanocidal drugs to treat the infected animals. One of the more recent examples occurred in Rajasthan, India, on the border with Pakistan, where within seven days of the report of infection, sixteen camels out of a herd of two hundred had died. In this case as in others, however, veterinarians have been left with a menu of drugs to which they know that trypanosomes have already developed immunities.[31] The other way of dealing with the disease recalls the

28. Much of the research to date on trypanosome resistance to trypanocidal drugs appears to have been done in Africa, and primarily on the *T. brucei* subspecies that causes sleeping sickness. References to recent research can be found through an Internet search on trypanocidal resistance. In addition, S. R. Wilkinson and J. M. Kelly provide an overview of research and tests on drug efficacy; see "Trypanocidal Drugs: Mechanisms, Resistance and New Targets," *Expert Reviews in Molecular Medicine* 11 (October 2009): 1–24.

29. Wilkinson and Kelly, "Trypanocidal Drugs," 12–13. Also see the discussion in B. Khan, A. Iqbal, and M. Riaz, *Production and Management of Camels* (Faisalabad: University of Agriculture, 2003), 92–93, at http://169.237.124.123:8082/AfghanAg/c_livestock/camels/Man_Live_Camel_Prod_Mgt_UAF.pdf; accessed 6 October 2017.

30. The sequencing was carried out by an international group of researchers, numbering twenty-seven in all and including M. Desquesnes and Lai. See Jason Carnes et al., "Genome and Phylogenetic Analyses of *Trypanosoma evansi* Reveal Extensive Similarity to *T. brucei* and Multiple Independent Origins of Dyskinetoplasy," *PLOS: Neglected Tropical Diseases* 9, no. 1 (January 2015): 1–21. The strain sequenced was from China.

31. V. Mandovera et al., "An Outbreak of Trypanosomiasis in Camel at Rajasthan," *Indian Journal of Applied Research* 4, no. 4 (2014): 566–67.

epidemiological methods of Leese, which involved screening populations to identify infected animals. Pakistani and Indian veterinarians are experimenting with ways to detect *T. evansi* when the parasite is not prevalent in the peripheral circulation system.[32] Presumably, when a successful early detection method is found, those animals determined to be infected will be culled.

The only other way of managing the disease at present is to target its vectors. In the postwar era of development in both South Asia and Africa, this has meant the use of insecticides. Not only do these chemicals have an impact in the food chain, the targeted insects also develop immunities to them. Or, as is the case with *Tabanus*, the vector insects have such a wide range (e.g., the entire Indus River basin and canal system) that it becomes impossible to spray all potential breeding grounds.[33] Thus, although a substantial amount is now known about the biology of surra, dealing with the disease on the ground has not moved very far from Leese's recommendations in the early twentieth century. Moreover, in Africa, researchers are considering whether it might be best to abandon chemical warfare against Tsetse and return to some of the practices of precolonial African agriculturalists. These approaches involved concentrating populations and clearing the brush where flies bred from around settlements. It also involved culling wild animals and allowing pastoralists to move their animals freely in order to avoid known areas of infection. As one report put it in 2001, these means of dealing with African trypanosomiasis have "achieved effective control of the disease over more extensive regions of Africa than any other strategy."[34]

CAMELS AND DEVELOPMENT

Although camels are no longer relied on by the military as transport animals or used by merchants in long-distance carrying trade, they remain an impor-

32. See, for example, M. Hasan, "Prevalence of *Trypanosoma evansi* Infection in Equines and Camels in the Punjab Region, Pakistan," *Annals of the New York Academy of Sciences* 1081 (2006): 322–24. Also see Muhammad Ali Shah, Kalili Ur Rehman, Fawad Ur Rehman, and Nongye He, "Present Status of Camel *Trypanosomiasis* in Pakistan: A Review of Literature," *Science Letters* 1, no. 1 (2013): 30–33.

33. A. K. Jaiswal, V. Sudan, N. Verma, and A. Verma, "Insight into Trypanosomiasis in Animals: Various Approaches for Its Diagnosis, Treatment and Control; A Review," *Asian Journal of Animal Sciences* 9, no. 1 (2015): 172–86. See the section "Prevention and Control."

34. David Bourn et al., *Environmental Change and the Autonomous Control of Tsetse and Trypanosomiasis in Sub-Sahara Africa: Case Histories from Ethiopia, the Gambia, Kenya, Nigeria, and Zimbabwe* (Oxford: Environmental Research Group, 2001), 148.

tant part of life in Pakistan and northwestern India. Camels still work as farm laborers and intermediate-/short-distance carriers of various kinds of goods to local markets.[35] They have also become an object of a new discourse on "food security," itself stimulated not only by population growth in Pakistan but also by global climate change. As one set of researchers puts it, the camel's unique adaptability to the environment of Pakistan "makes this an ideal species for exploitation under . . . arid and semi-arid land conditions."[36] The main point many authors make is that since the formation of the state of Pakistan, the camel has been grossly ignored as a potential contributor to national development. It is as if, once this animal's military usefulness had been replaced by mechanical transport, the state lost interest, and left it to live its life among the remaining pastoral and semipastoral populations.

Those who have imagined the camel as part of an economic development and food security regime are composed of a new group of Pakistani experts, some of whom are in government ministries, while others are at universities and research institutes. Unlike their British counterparts in the past, they see the camel as more than a transport animal involved in either caravan trade or military undertakings. While many acknowledge that some of these animals are still used in trade by nomadic merchants, they see camels' economic promise in two other areas. One involves the efficient manner in which camels convert marginal plants to labor power that can then be used to turn grinding wheels, plow fields, level land, draw water from wells, and transport agricultural goods to markets. They also recognize the important role camels still play in moving household goods, salt, and firewood.[37] As discussed in chapter 3, these are, of course, tasks that enmeshed camels in a moral ecology of small households and kept them subject to the seasonal cycles of pastoralists. As in the past, camels contribute to linking farmers and nomads with larger villages and market towns, where mosques and Sufi shrines also remain as major sources of spiritual sustenance, annual celebrations, and healing.[38] These latter aspects of camel life do not seem to figure into the development calculations of contemporary experts, however.

But if camels are now occasionally being recognized for what they have

35. Khan, Iqbal, and Riaz, *Production and Management of Camels*, 4–5.

36. S. Ahmad et al., "Economic Importance of Camel: A Unique Alternative under Crisis," *Pakistan Veterinary Journal* 30, no. 4 (2010): 191. Also see Khan, Iqbal, and Riaz, *Production and Management of Camels*, 108–27, on camel products.

37. S. Ahmad et al., "Economic Importance of Camel," 192–93.

38. Katherine Ewing, "The Sufi as Saint, Curer, and Exorcist in Modern Pakistan," *Contributions to Asian Studies* 18 (1984): 106–14.

always done well, development experts also see new economic potentials they appear to offer. These are the products camels can produce in life and in death. Camel milk, for example, is high in vitamin C and more nutritious than bovine milk. Various kinds of cheeses can be made from the milk, and it can be soured for longer shelf life. Camels could be raised for slaughter, like cattle, their meat being low in fat content, and their hides and hair useful in making a variety of products. Camel bones can be either carved into jewelry or used as a source of calcium in supplements.[39] From a development point of view, it is not simply that the parts of the camel have economic value; it is that camels can survive in hostile environments, making it possible to imagine the virtual nothingness of the wastelands of the Punjab, the Sind, and Baluchistan being magically transformed into wealth via the camel's body.

There is, however, one problem with this vision of camel-mediated plenty. At present, most of the animals are in the hands of nomads, who are still presenting problems for the orderly planned development schemes of the experts. As in the past, nomad turbulence disturbs the enumerative technologies of the state. And while mobile populations are less common than in the past, some of the old patterns are still evident. Many nomadic groups, with their camels, still migrate from the highlands along the Afghan frontier to the lowlands in the winter. Among these are the Brahui and a Pashtun group identified as "Pawinda," which can only be a remnant of the larger seasonal Powindah migration discussed in chapter 3. Seasonal migration, even when it is relatively predictable, offers no assurances that camel products will reliably enter the markets of Pakistan. Moreover, during roughly half the year, the nomads and their camels are nowhere near these markets, even while themselves consuming valuable commercial products.[40]

A second kind of human mobile pastoralist also poses problems for development officials. This group, referred to as transhumants, spend part of the year raising a winter wheat crop at higher elevations, and then migrate into the Indus valley in the spring to graze their herds, pick up seasonal labor, and probably also pass through villages selling their various skills, services, and goods. As such, transhumants seem to be the descendants of the multitasking pastoralists discussed in chapter 3. Like the nomads, they pose the same sort of problem for development officials as they did for the British dis-

39. S. Ahmad et al., "Economic Importance of Camel," 194–96.

40. A. W. Jasra, Atiq-Ur-Rehman, and M. Afzal, "Socio-economics of Pastoralists Communities of Highland Baluchistan, Pakistan," *International Journal of Agriculture and Biology* 3, no. 2 (2001): 257.

trict commissioners—they are far too mobile. That mobility means that while some of the products of the camel, especially milk, might enter the marketplace when transhumant groups move through a region, at other times suppliers, like the nomads, are far from bazaars. When they are not actually in Pakistan, however, transhumants consume the milk and other camel products themselves.

Development experts would like to find ways to encourage these mobile groups to become sedentary. Perhaps they might be subsidized to sink tube wells out at the end of the canal runs, alter the camels' diet, or let veterinary scientists treat their animals with modern medicines rather than their own less effective traditional herbal preparations. Only through such alterations in behavior, as one report puts it, could an "unexploited species" like the camel thrive and become productive, especially under conditions of climate change. From the experts' point of view, what is needed is better management, scientific breeding, and a better camel diet if humans are going to be able to exploit the animal's genetic potential to its "maximum."[41] To put this bluntly, what is being proposed here is a biopolitical camel regime that goes well beyond anything imagined or put in place by the British. On the other hand, this sort of thinking is a logical extension of colonial notions of efficiency and improvement, especially in its insistence that experts know, in theory, what is best for pastoralists and their camels.

Fortunately, these experts are not the only voices in the discussion. Advocates of a more traditional pastoralism are more concerned with ways and means of supporting nonsedentary lifeways, including sustaining camels as something other than objects to be maximally exploited. And while notions of food security might also be evoked by advocates of pastoralism, these activists do so in another context, one involving conservation of scarce resources. In the case of contemporary Pakistan, a conservationist argument is used, for instance, in relation to the ecosystem of the Cholistan desert, a territory shared with Rajasthan in India. Here, on both sides of a manmade border, plants, camels, and pastoralists live in a delicate balance. The problems these pastoralists face appear similar to those faced in the Sind and Baluchistan—formerly arid lands are being transformed by canals in order to expand grain and cotton production. The supporters of pastoralism argue that the delicate ecosystem of the desert is an irreplaceable asset. And they point to earlier studies that highlight how camel browsing, because the animals keep moving

41. S. Ahmad et al., "Economic Importance of Camel," 196.

and nibble only a bit here and a bit there, actually allows plants adapted to arid climes to thrive.[42]

Their main point, then, is that if camels are to contribute to national development, their browsing lands must be preserved and the encroachment by canals halted. These critics also disapprove of the way state planners ignore the views of pastoralists in their planning. Veterinarians come in for criticism too, primarily because they can only offer expensive advice and drugs to pastoralists, who in turn see this unrealistic intervention as typical of city people. On the other hand, critics also recognize that some major changes have occurred in what I previously referred to as the moral ecology of the Punjab. Underpinned as it has been by Islamic notions of human responsibility to all God's creation, ideas that linked pastoralists, animals, and agriculturalists together, the moral ecology of the region is increasingly under extreme stress because of claims on water by an expanding human population. Drought exacerbates these stresses, and conflicts between animal herders and farmers become, as a result, more common.

These kinds of complaints could easily have been expressed under British rule, but there is one major difference since decolonization. Pastoralists in Pakistan, as in many other parts of the world, are nowadays connected to international agencies and nongovernmental organizations. Among these is the League of Pastoral Peoples and Endogenous Livestock Development. Organizations like this one are concerned with both conserving pastoralism and sustaining biodiversity, which for them includes not only camels but the unique plants of the desert on which they browse. The task pastoralists and their supporters face, however, is daunting. As we have seen, camels and other animals that rely on grazing lands for health and sustenance have suffered from the incursions of expansive state projects since the nineteenth century. Even when camels were made useful in a militarized security regime, their habitats were intentionally shrunk to increase the acreage for food and commercial crops, such as cotton and sugarcane. Camels may have received a brief respite from exploitation when they became obsolete in the frontier security regime. But as the human population has grown in Pakistan, and as nation-state boundaries

42. For this and the next paragraph, I draw from A. Kakar et al., "Rapid Change in Strategy Is Necessary for the Development of Dromedary Camel Pastoralism in Cholistan Desert of Pakistan," *Pastoralism: Research, Policy, Practice* 1, no. 3 (2011): 1–9. This piece also mentions pastoralist-farmer conflicts, with water at the heart of the matter. On camel browsing and plant interaction, Kakar et al. cite Hilde Gauthier-Pilters and Anne Innis Dagg, *The Camel: Its Evolution, Ecology, Behavior, and Relationship to Man* (Chicago: University of Chicago Press, 1981), 59.

have solidified, the relief camels and their handlers received from the colonial state in the 1930s has disappeared. Although it is encouraging to see transnational efforts to preserve diverse forms of life threatened by development on the one hand, and programs to adapt to climate change and water scarcity on the other, the pressure for camels to become productive members of national economies will only increase.

Postscript

This study began with questions about animal service in wars "throughout time"; about claims that animals marched "alongside" British and Allied soldiers in conflicts that aimed to preserve freedom; I asked how we could reconcile these statements with the recognition that animals had no choice in the matter. The Animals in War Memorial in London's Hyde Park embodies a fundamental contradiction that cannot easily be reconciled. If animals had no choice, it meant that they were forced labor—how, then, could they march beside soldiers supposedly fighting for the preservation of freedom? The monument both hinted at this question and hid the actual conditions of animal servitude behind an expression of human gratitude for the "sacrifices" animals made. The historical question I then posed concerned the nature of animal service, and how humans thought about such service at the time it was happening.

Rather than venture into the temporally vague territory gestured at by the monument, I have directed attention to a particular moment of change, one involving a shift between the impressment of animals into military service and a complex set of overlapping developments that produced both an animal management regime and conditions of permanent military service for animals. Had the study stopped there, it would have amounted mostly to an administrative history of change within the transport system of the British Indian Army. Such changes could then have been situated within the broader context of bureaucratic alterations instituted under Lord Curzon, viceroy of India from 1899 to 1905. From that limited perspective, it might have looked as if administrative change at the turn of the century had produced a newly humane order for pack animals, providing a positive example of colonial modernization and rational, scientific planning.

The administrative history is certainly present in this study. But because of the questions raised by the Hyde Park Animals in War Memorial and other questions that arose over the course of my research, it could not stop there. What, for example, are we to make of all those dead camels in the Second Afghan War, leading to the British conclusion that mules were a more reliable pack animal? More important, how were animals thought of and engaged with in the world of the Indian colonial subjects from whom they were taken, camels in particular? In order to answer these questions, it was necessary to explore what I have termed a moral ecology of the Punjab before the region's militarization and colonization. This was an ecology in which camels played a critical part as both a material and a symbolic link between pastoralists, agriculturalists, townspeople, and powerful invisible agents of many kinds, including Sufi saints. In exploring precolonial animal-human orders, it became possible to gain a sense of the real impact and cost, for both animals and humans, of pack animal impressment and other forms of colonial "animal management." This broader consideration of animal lives, inspired in part by philosophical and empirical studies of human-animal relations, served as a means of critiquing the large-scale projects launched by the colonial state: invasions of Afghanistan, securing the frontier of British India, and extending canals into the so-called wastelands of the Indus River basin.

At the heart of what I take to be the early twentieth-century neocolonization of the Punjab was a collection of ambitious and multifaceted imperial state-formation projects, undertakings that went beyond rules of property and tax collection to essentially recolonize the Punjab in technocratic form. This was a process of deterritorialization and reterritorialization by means of canal building, restrictive legal codes, and population redistribution, coupled with the military and veterinary reorganization of animal life. The rationale for this aggressive alteration to colonial governance, aptly described by David Gilmartin, was that it was an effort to end the turbulence and waste thought to be caused by troublesome and unproductive others, including the land and water themselves. This assault on a host of human and nonhuman agents connected a newly imagined imperial security regime to public works projects designed to "improve" the land, rivers, and population of the Punjab and make them more efficient. The latter aims were accomplished in novel ways. Land grants were offered to a preferred group of hardworking "martial" peasants, some of whom received plots of land because they agreed to raise camels and mules. The land was to be stabilized, and social turbulence eliminated, by grounding the new order on these idealized colonial subjects. In turn, their sons would provide an ample supply of soldiers for the army, and their camels and mules would be integrated into a robust reserve transport corps.

Under the sign of constructive colonialism, the dual projects of economic development and military logistics were imagined as essentially complementary. Yet there were clearly also frictions within and between the projects themselves as well as between nonmilitary government units, such as the Forestry Department, the manager of the wasteland. Moreover, camels, mules, and their owners were caught up in these frictions. Camels required ranges of uncultivated land with wild local plants to browse in if they were to remain healthy and fit for service. Making arid zones productive by way of canals meant reducing camel browsing territory. At the same time, such projects expanded the reproductive range of disease-causing biting flies and disrupted life in general for the plants and pastoralists who had adapted to the rigors of an arid ecology.

Mules, though they could be produced in India, were held to a military transport standard, particularly for ordnance, that was difficult for Indian breeders to achieve. The inability of the domestic breeding scheme to produce military-grade mules led to the development of a global supply chain that linked India with China and the Americas, while creating and expanding life pathways for pathogens that caused diseases in animals. The mule supply question also led to a much finer parsing of mule bodies and mule attributes than was the case with camels. The difference in British attitudes toward the reliable mule and the problematic camel mirrored British notions about the shortcomings of "Orientals" in general.

The shift in the latter part of the nineteenth century to a more precise accounting of mule traits was an aspect of a broader shift in imperial governance, one oriented toward a rule of experts and a more invasive penetration of pack animal life through such expertise. These changes in colonial governance in India and their consequences are reminiscent of other studies of large-scale colonial projects, namely the British reengineering of the Nile in Egypt, discussed by Timothy Mitchell, and the French transformation of the Mekong Delta in Vietnam, as described by David Biggs. Hence, this study not only follows upon this work but extends the insights of Mitchell and Biggs into new areas, specifically the reconfiguring of pack animal life in the Punjab; the development of tropical veterinary medicine as an aspect of that reconfiguration; and a new army logistical system that in its scale and ambitions was unprecedented historically among empire builders in South Asia. To make such connections, one need not ask if the camel can speak. The links materialized in this animal's body are palpably there in the colonial archive, sometimes as elements in expressions of imperial hubris and other times as complaints about the unintended and bothersome effects of animal breeding or canal construction (e.g., too few mules, waterlogging and salinization). Moreover, the imperial connections between Egypt, Vietnam, and India can clearly be seen in the rise of the authority of the hydraulic engineer and in the emergence of tropical medicine, particularly with respect to malaria and trypanosomiasis. The impact of ambitious engineering is also evident in the unexpected, although certainly not unpredictable, environmental effects created through what Biggs refers to as "schizophrenic flows." In the case of Vietnam, such flows produced highly acidic irrigation waters and much abandoned land.[1] In Egypt, new flows moved malaria into northern Egypt and shifted agriculture from food crops nurtured by river silt and animal manure to cotton and sugarcane production fertilized by expensive synthetic chemicals.[2]

The global spread of colonial meddling is also clear in how the ecological transformations of the river systems of Egypt and the Punjab opened new territories for insects and pathogenic microorganisms. Camels and mules stood at the intersection of these developments, sometimes as the symptoms of emerging pathological relationships; and the camel, because it was such an unknown creature for the British, provided an unusual entry point into the transregional emergence of research in tropical medicine and the field testing of synthetic chemical compounds to treat veterinary diseases. Instructive in this case was the early adoption of live-animal experimentation by microbiologists in the colonies, which included the moving of blood from infected to healthy animals, with consequences that are only now beginning to be understood through genetic analysis of pathogens like *Trypanosoma evansi*.

The British military-administrative transformation of the Punjab had other effects as well. The Pakistani security regime of today is organized around the identical topographical dynamic that the British faced, and still requires, on the extreme edges of state sovereignty, the service of mules, as we have seen. In addition, the close ties between landholders and the army, fixed in place as part of the militarization of the Punjab, has hardly become obsolete. Most modern state-sponsored development projects are essentially an extension of the imperial improvement projects begun in the 1890s. The difference now is that the experts are Pakistani citizens with advanced academic degrees. These experts, judging by some sources, tend to have the same dismissive attitude

1. David Biggs, *Quagmire: Nation-Building and Nature in the Mekong Delta* (Seattle: University of Washington Press, 2010), 96, 123.

2. Timothy Mitchell, *Rule of Experts* (Berkeley: University of California Press, 2002), 33.

toward pastoralism and indigenous camel knowledge as the British had from the late nineteenth century forward. Like their predecessors, experts today also seem to believe that indigenous remedies for animal ills, while perhaps useful in some cases, are at root wholly unscientific, because native practitioners do not understand the chemistry of their drugs. Further, these experts seem unaware of the complexity of the moral ecology of the arid ranges, which they seek to displace with "realistic" planning imposed from above. Transhumants and pastoralist had an astute assessment of the carrying capacity of their region, and they were apparently willing to live within its constraints. Along with agriculturalists, they produced and handed down knowledge of how to work in concert with an easily stressed environment. This was knowledge that sustained a symbiotic relationship between the two groups, and constructed both animals and humans as something more than merely economic resources.[3] The technoscientific assault on the Punjab's rivers and the imposition of a robust imperial security regime changed this delicate balancing act.

This study has attempted to get at the scale of those changes by incorporating nonhuman agents into the analysis. The multiagent approach deployed here provides, I believe, a critical perspective on colonialism that differs from earlier studies. For a very long time, colonial studies have been caught up in debates about the positive or negative effects of colonialism, about the political relations between imperial centers and peripheries, and about the agency of the colonized, as was brought into sharp focus by Edward Said's study of Orientalism. Mitchell's work on Egypt has rendered these debates more equivocal by (1) introducing nonhuman agents (notably, mosquitoes) as actors into the colonial arena and (2) questioning approaches to colonialism that carve up analysis based on the disciplinary divisions to be found in the Western academy and intellectual community. In a sense, we might interpret Mitchell's intervention as one that criticizes scholars for constructing false objects of investigation: false in the sense that in order to have a bounded unit of analysis, one had to subtract phenomena that were perceived as extraneous to the research questions of a particular discipline. Mosquito behavior was in

3. Although he does not discuss pastoralism, Alan Mikhail makes a similar point about the knowledge of peasant farmers in the maintenance of a balanced ecosystem in the Nile valley. This system was gradually subverted by ever-larger dam and water control projects on the river beginning in the mid-nineteenth century and including the projects Mitchell discusses. See *Nature and Empire in Ottoman Egypt: An Environmental History* (New York: Cambridge University Press, 2011).

the domain of the natural scientist, not the political scientist. Who the mosquito bit was in the domain of university-trained public health professionals, not philosophers. The physical effects of the bite belonged to medical science, certainly not social science. Overlooked in this parsing of the mosquito was the relation between large-scale colonial "improvement" projects, ecological change, and the crises the world finds itself in today—water shortages, environmental degradation, and microorganisms immune to manmade chemical cures.

The inclusion of nonhuman actors in a study of colonialism also makes it possible to see other effects, both material and conceptual, brought on by the changes in colonial governance that began at the end of the nineteenth century. These changes involved the globalization of projects to scientifically reengineer nature and to declare war on entities that obstructed these manmade projects. The production of trypanocidal drugs, for example, was paralleled by the invention of chemical "pesticides" to eradicate the vectors of such pathogens. Such approaches stand in stark contrast to so-called premodern methods of disease management. To give but two examples: before colonization, Africans in the Tsetse zone limited the breeding grounds of the flies, while culling the wild animals of the forest who were the reservoirs for trypanosomes.[4] The other example is the one discussed here. Camel herders were aware of the connection between biting flies, surra, and the seasonal rains. They moved their animals into what they had identified as safe zones to avoid, not eradicate, the disease. In both cases, agriculturalists and pastoralists also developed and used knowledge about the plants of the forest and the drylands that were helpful for keeping themselves and their domesticated animals healthy.

These sorts of methods for interacting with a multiagent universe seem quaint in the world of today. Our age is one of rational management and scientific expertise partnered with corporate transnational capital in the form of chemical and drug conglomerates, agribusiness, and technologically sophisticated engineering firms that build well-watered cities in the deserts of the Arabian Peninsula. Late nineteenth-century colonialism anchored and encouraged these developments, giving them legitimacy as they supposedly uplifted populations and improved the lives of the colonized. Yet the cost for this progress has tended to be hidden or willfully ignored. I have attempted in this study to highlight suppressed or marginalized elements of the historical record, and to fashion an archive that brings those elements into view. The

4. See John MacKenzie, *The Empire of Nature: Hunting, Conservation, and British Imperialism* (Manchester: Manchester University Press, 1988), 234–36.

picture that has resulted is disturbing, and it doesn't offer a great deal of hope for the future.

I would argue, however, that the first step in coming to terms with the global crises of environment and human population is to seek a clearer understanding of how the world has come to this moment; how food security has suddenly become a pressing issue for human life on earth; and why state-sponsored militarized security regimes appear today to be just as ineffectual a response to perceived threats as they have been since the end of the nineteenth century. This study, I hope, helps clarify some of these issues. We might also recognize that the power of the imperial pack animal biopower regime proved to be more limited than the totalizing ambitions of committees and planners had envisioned. It was constrained, in part, because of the turbulence and excitation caused by a microbial parasite as well as by shortages of personnel and resources, and by the frictions between different parts of the colonial state's administrative structure. Or, to put this another way, it would seem that the on-paper pack animal biopower regime was mangled in practice.[5]

The reengineering of the Indus basin can hardly be seen as an imperial success story. The vast plans of engineers and administrators were undone by water itself, water that refused to be "trained" and took every opportunity to neglect its "duty." Seeping out of irrigation channels, pooling in low areas, puddling along canal banks, and sinking below the surface and thereby raising its "table," water defied imperial science and its hegemonic authority more effectively than most other "natives." Sometimes it overflowed the banks designed to contain it; other times it disappeared for extended periods of time. And, all along its paths of flow, water became a participant in the activities of other nonhuman agents. Minerals, salts, biting flies, and bothersome "weeds" were nudged into action, whereupon they expanded their range and sometimes colonized new areas.

Finally, a few words are in order concerning the camel, the nonhuman agent that stimulated this study. Despite dire predictions by some colonial officials, camels have hardly disappeared from South Asia. In Bikaner, the local government holds an annual camel festival in mid-January, where camels dance and compete in contests for the most beautifully decorated.[6] Meanwhile, the Bikaner Camel Corps, now the Border Security Force of the Indian Army, marches annually in India's National Day Parade, holding open a ritual space

5. Andrew Pickering and Keith Guzik, eds., *The Mangle in Practice* (Durham, NC: Duke University Press, 2008).

6. See http://camelfestival.com; accessed 7 October 2017.

for the cavalry camel.[7] In other parts of South Asia, camel owners compete with one another to produce the most intricate geometric designs by clipping their camel's hair.[8] And in the arid border region between India and Pakistan known as the Cholistan Desert, camels still browse, nibbling a bit here and a bit there, and rub up against other camels, not to mention the occasional tree or rock. And as the camels browse, their human companions and dependents follow along, in annual circulations through what the British mistook as "wasteland."

7. The unit can be seen on Youtube at https://www.youtube.com/watch?v=H73zLzm_hFI; accessed 7 October 2017.

8. See http://viola.bz/camel-beauty-festival/; accessed 7 October 2017.

ACKNOWLEDGMENTS

The completion of projects like this one depends on the generosity, cooperation, and labor of many people. First and foremost, I would like to thank the staff of the Asian and African reading room at the British Library, London, and the library staff at the Regenstein Library at the University of Chicago, especially James Nye and Laura Ring. Head librarian Clare Boulton of the Royal College of Veterinary Science helped me sort out the research activities of a number of British veterinarians in India.

Much of my research time in London was possible because of the research funds afforded me by the College at the University of Chicago, whose dean, John Boyer, has always supplied encouragement and support. I also benefited from funding provided by the GlaxoSmithKline Senior Fellowship at the National Humanities Center, Research Triangle Park, North Carolina. The staff of the center provided much-appreciated help and daily cheerfulness that made my year there a pleasure. Lunch and daily conversations with fellows, especially Bill Schwarz, Norman Kutcher, Owen Flanagan, Colleen Lye, April Marsten, Jane Newman, Michelle O'Malley, Mark Pozzanza, Janice Radway, and Nelihan Senocak, moved the project along. Colleagues in the History Department at Chicago, including Mark Bradley, Michael Geyer, and Moishe Postone, were invariably tolerant and helpful when I turned conversations to the subject of camels, mules, and trypanosomes.

I have benefited enormously from the suggestions of several anonymous reviewers, and thank them very much for their willingness to engage my manuscript and my frequently vague prose. Sabrine Datoo, Larisa Jasarevic, and Judith Farquhar did me the incredible favor of reading the entire manuscript and making wonderful and challenging suggestions and corrections. As the project unfolded and began to take shape, I also much appreciated the comments and help of graduate students at the University of Chicago, including Stacie Kent, Elizabeth Sartell, Usama Rafi, and Kyle Gardner, as well as the graduate students in the ongoing Animal Studies/Non-human Workshop. Stacie, in particular, was a sounding board for a good deal of what made it into this book. Joshua Oxley and Aaron Hill tirelessly helped put critical pieces of the manuscript together, and for that I am very grateful. Dennis McClendon did a superb job producing map 1.

Finally, I should say something about the staff at the University of Chicago Press. My editor, Priya Nelson, encouraged and supported this project when it was only at the prospectus stage. Dylan Montanari, Ruth Goring, and Kristen Raddatz kept the production process moving along. Sandra Hazel not only performed a superb job of copyediting on the final draft of the manuscript but also made a number of suggestions that have now been incorporated into the body of this book. To all of you, I wish to express my deep gratitude and thanks.

SELECTED BIBLIOGRAPHY

NOTE ON ARCHIVAL SOURCES

The two primary archives drawn from in this study are the National Archives (NA) and the India Office Records (IOR) of the British Library, both of which are in London. Sources in the National Archives are from the War Office (WO) Records. Those in the India Office Records are designated *L/MIL* for Military Records; *L/P&S* for Political and Secret; *P* for Proceedings and Consultations of the Government of India; and *V* for Official Publications of the Government of India.

MANUSCRIPTS

Curzon Papers, British Library.
Atkinson, William. "Journal of Private William Atkinson, H.M. 67th (South Hampshire) Regiment." IOR/MSS Eur D1093, British Library.

ARCHIVAL DOCUMENTS

Below are the collections from the India Office Records and the National Archives, London, from which individual files were consulted. Each file and its title are cited in the footnotes.

Collections

IOR/L/MIL/5/678–88: Government of India Military Proceedings on the "Kabul Expedition" (Second Afghan War), 1879–81
IOR/L/MIL/7/830–93: Veterinary Department in India (1878–1927)
IOR/L/MIL/7/1001–84: Donkey Stallions, Mules and Mule Breeding Operations (1874–1928)
IOR/L/MIL/7/5441–509: Reorganization of the Army in India (1861–1936)
IOR/L/MIL/7/6666–821: Commissariat-Transport: Supply and Transport Corps (1881–1939)

IOR/L/MIL/7/9626–716: Horse Breeding Operations and Army Remount Department (1851–1927)

NA/WO95: Royal Army Medical Corps, World War I and Army of Occupation War Diaries

Individual Documents

IOR/P/8672: *Report of the Camel Browsing Committee. Punjab Proceedings* (December 1911), *Punjab Revenue and Agriculture Proceedings*, no. 18, 41–49.

IOR/L/MIL/17/5/2361: *Statistical and General Report of the Army Veterinary Service in India.* 1921–22.

IOR/L/MIL/17/TN 544: *Report of the Horse and Mule Breeding Commission*, 1900–1901.

IOR/L/P&S/20/203: "Statement of Fanatical Outrages in the North-West Frontier Province and Baluchistan, 1905." Simla, 1 December.

NA/WO 32/6129: Gen. Gerald Graham's Report on the Suakin Field Force, 1885.

PARLIAMENTARY PAPERS

Correspondence Relating to the Estimates for the War in Afghanistan: Presented to Both Houses of Parliament by Command of Her Majesty. London: Eyre and Spottiswoode for Her Majesty's Stationery Office, 1880.

East India (Military Accounts). *Report of the Committee Appointed by the Secretary of State for India, by Minute Dated 2nd July 1880, to Enquire into the System of Military Account and Estimate in India.* London: House of Commons, 17 February 1881.

East India (North-West Frontier). Parliamentary Papers regarding British Relations with the Neighbouring Tribes of the North-West Frontier of India and Frontier Administration. London: Harrison and Sons, 1901.

Further Correspondence Relating to the Estimates for the War in Afghanistan. London: Eyre and Spottiswoode for Her Majesty's Stationery Office, 1881.

OFFICIAL PUBLICATIONS

Several of the sources listed below are annual reports of administrative departments in British India. These reports were published by government presses. Rather than list each of them, I provide titles, date ranges, and, where appropriate, archive file numbers.

Administration Report of the Supply and Transport Corps., 1899–1913. [IOR/L/MIL/17/5/1859]

Administrative Report of the Army Remount Department, 1889–1928. [IOR/L/MIL/17/5/2184 and L/MIL/7/9700]

Annual Administrative Report of the Civil Veterinary Department, 1896–1901. [IOR/V/4378]

Annual Report of the Camel Specialist, 1909–25.

Annual Report for the Chenab, Jhang, Chunian, and Jhelum Canal Colonies, 1903–13.

Annual Report of the Punjab Veterinary College and the Civil Veterinary Department, Punjab and the Cattle Farm, 1908, 1912, 1915, 1917.

Army Headquarters, India. *Frontier Warfare—India*. New Delhi: Government of India Press, 1939.

———. *Manual of Operations on the North-West Frontier of India*. Calcutta: Government of India Central Publication Branch, 1925.

Army Remount Department. *Annual Administrative Report of the Bengal, Punjab, Madras, and Bombay Commands*. 1898–1913. [IOR/L/MIL/7/9665]

Barrow, Lt. E. G. *The Military Geography of Afghanistan*. Simla: Government Printing Office, 1893.

Blenkinsop, Layton John, and John Wakefield Rainey, eds. *Veterinary Services*. London: His Majesty's Stationery Office, 1925.

Christophers, S. R. *Malaria in the Punjab*. Calcutta: Superintendent of Government Printing, 1911.

Commissary-General-in-Chief. *From the Commissary-General-in-Chief to the Secretary to the Government of India, Military Department*. Simla: Government Central Printing Office, 1899. [IOR/L/MIL/7/6694]

Commissary-General's Office, Punjab Command. *Report on the Commissariat-Transport Arrangements of the Tirah Expeditionary Force, 1897–98*. Calcutta: Government of India, 1899. [IOR/L/MIL/17/5/1855]

Cross, H. E. "A Note on the Transmission of Surra by Ticks." *Department of Agriculture, Punjab: Veterinary Bulletin no. 6 of 1921*, 1–3.

———. "Note on the Treatment of Surra in Camels by Intravenous Injections of Tartar Emetic." *Agricultural Research Institute, Pusa: Bulletin no. 95 of 1920*. [IOR/V/25/125]

Cross, H. E., and G. Patel. "A Note on the Transmission of Surra by Tabanus nemocallosus." *Department of Agriculture, Punjab: Veterinary Bulletin no. 7 of 1921*, 1–7.

———. "Surra Transmission Experiments." *Department of Agriculture, Punjab: Veterinary Bulletin no. 5 of 1921*, 1–13. [IOR/V/25/541/31-35]

———. "Surra Transmission Experiments with Tabanus Albimedius and Ticks." *Department of Agriculture, Punjab: Veterinary Bulletin no. 12 of 1923*, 1–11.

Dobson, Bernard H. *Final Report on the Chenab Colony Settlement*. Lahore: Superintendent of Government Printing, Punjab, 1915.

Douie, James M. *Punjab Settlement Manual*. 1899. Reprint, Delhi: Daya, 1985.

Field Service Manual for Commissariat and Transport Officers of the Indian Army. Simla: Commissary-General-in-Chief, 1887. [IOR/L/MIL/17/5/752]

Field Service Manual for Commissariat and Transport Officers of the Indian Army (Preliminary Edition). Simla: Commissary-General-in-Chief, 1887. [IOR/L/MIL/17/5/752]

Field Service Manual: Native Silladar Cavalry. Calcutta: Superintendent of Government Printing, India, 1908.

Field Service Manual: Supply and Transport (War, India). Calcutta: Superintendent of Government Printing, India, 1912.

Field Service Regulations, India (Provisional Edition). Calcutta: Superintendent of Government Printing, India, 1906.

Gazetteer of the Attock District, 1907. Lahore: Civil and Military Gazette Press, 1909.

Gazetteer of the Chenab Colony, 1904. Lahore: Civil and Military Gazette Press, 1905.

Gazetteer of the Dera Ismail Khan District, 1883–4. Lahore: Arya Press, 1884.

Gazetteer of the Jhelum District, 1883–4. Calcutta: Calcutta Central Press, 1884.

Gazetteer of the Jhelum District, 1904. Lahore: Civil and Military Gazette Press, 1907.

Gazetteer of the Montgomery District, 1883–4. Lahore: Arya Press, 1884.

Gazetteer of the Multan District, 1901–02. Lahore: Civil and Military Gazette Press, 1902.

Gazetteer of the Shapur District, 1883–4. Calcutta: Central Press, 1884.

General Staff Branch, Army Headquarters, India. *Operations in Waziristan, 1919–1920*. Calcutta: Superintendent of Government Printing, 1921.

———. *A Study of the Existing Strategical Conditions on the North-West Frontier of India*. 1909. Simla: Government Monotype Press, 1912. [IOR/L/MIL/17/13/7]

———. *The Third Afghan War 1919, Official Account*. Calcutta: Government of India Central Publication Branch, 1926.

General Staff, War Office. *Animal Management*. London: His Majesty's Stationery Office, 1908.

Government of India, Legislative Department. *The Punjab and North-West Code*. 3rd ed. Calcutta: Superintendent of Government Printing, 1903.

Hailey, W. M. *W. M. Hailey to the Officiating Chief Secretary to Government, Punjab, 18th August 1898*. In *Report of the Transport Committee, 1897*. Simla: Government Central Printing Office, 1897. [IOR/L/MIL/7/6687]

Imperial Council of Agricultural Research. *Agriculture and Animal Husbandry in India, 1936–37*. Delhi: Manager of Publications, 1939. [IOR/V/24/11]

Kennedy, Lt. Gen. Michael. *Memorandum Proposing a Permanent and Organized Transport Service in India*. Simla: Government Central Branch Press, 1880. [IOR/L/MIL/7/6666]

———. *Memorandum on Supply and Transport Arrangements and Operations during the Campaign in Northern Afghanistan and the Kuram Valley in 1879–80*. Simla: Government Central Branch Press, 1880.

Leese, Arnold. "Camel Surra." In *Report of the Veterinary Officer Investigating Camel Diseases for the Year Ending 31st March 1909*. Simla: Government Central Branch Press, 1909.

Lingard, Alfred. *Report on Horse Surra*. Bombay: Government Central Press, 1893.

———. *Summary of Further Report on Surra*. Bombay: Government Central Press, 1894.

MacGregor, Charles Metcalfe, comp. *The Second Afghan War, 1878–80*. 2 vols. Simla: Government Central Branch Press, 1908.

MacPherson, William G. *Medical Services, General History*. 4 vols. London: His Majesty's Stationery Office, 1921–24.

Manual of Horsemastership, Equitation and Animal Transport. London: His Majesty's Stationery Office, 1937.

Moberley, Frederick. *The Campaign in Mesopotamia*. 4 vols. London: His Majesty's Stationery Office, 1923–27.

Musgrave, W. E., and Moses T. Clegg. *Trypanosoma and Trypanosomiasis, with Special Reference to Surra in the Philippine Islands*. Manila: Bureau of Public Printing, 1903.

Official History of Operations on the N.-W. Frontier of India. New Delhi: Government of India Press, 1945.

Provincial Report of the Civil Veterinary Department, Punjab, 1897–98. Lahore: Civil and Military Gazette Press, 1898.

Punjab Canal Gazetteers. Vol. 1, *Lower Jhelum Canal, 1920*. Lahore: Superintendent, Government Printing, Punjab, 1921.

Punjab Colony Manual. Lahore: Superintendent of Government Printing, Punjab, 1922.

Quarterly Indian Army List. Calcutta: Office of the Superintendent for Government Printing, 1902, 1908.

Remount Manual (War), India. Calcutta: Superintendent of Government Printing, India, 1911.

Report of the Commissariat-Transport Arrangements of the Tochi Field Force, 1897–98. Calcutta: Superintendent of Government Printing, India, 1898. [IOR/L/MIL/17/5/1855]

Report of the Indian Retrenchment Committee 1922–23. Delhi: Superintendent of Government Printing, 1925. [IOR/L/MIL/17/5/1781]

Report of the Transport Committee, 1897. Simla: Government Central Printing Office, 1897. [IOR/L/MIL/7/6687]

Report of the Transport Committee, 1898. 2 vols. Simla: Government Central Printing Office, 1899. [IOR/L/MIL/7/6688]

Résumé of Pony and Mule Breeding Operations in the Madras Presidency. Madras: Superintendent, Government Press, 1888.

Roe, C. A., and W. E. Purser. *Report on the Revised Land Revenue Settlement of the Montgomery District, in the Mooltan Division of the Punjab*. Lahore: Central Jail Press, 1878.

Rose, H. A. *A Glossary of the Tribes and Castes of the Punjab and North-West Frontier Province: Based on the Census Report for the Punjab, 1883*. Lahore: Civil and Military Gazette Press, 1911.

Royal Commission on Agriculture in India Report. Bombay: Central Government Press, 1928.

Sheriff, Moodeen. *Supplement to the Pharmacopeia of India*. Madras: Government Gazette Press, 1869.

Steel, John Henry. *Report of Veterinary Surgeon J. H. Steel, A.V.D., on His Investigation into an Obscure and Fatal Disease among Transport Mules in British Burma, Which He Found to Be a Fever of the Relapsing Type, and Probably Identical with the Disorder First Described by Dr. Griffiths Evans under the Name "Surra," in a Report (Herewith Reprinted) Published by the Punjab Government, Military Department, no. 439-4467, of 3rd December 1880—vide the* Veterinary Journal. India: Punjab Military Department, 1881–82. [IOR/V/27/541/15]

Thimm, Carl A., comp. *Bibliography of Trypanosomiasis: Embracing Original Papers Published prior to April, 1909, and Reference Works and Papers on Tsetse-Flies Especially Glossina Palpalis*. London: Sleeping Sickness Bureau, 1909.

Tucker, H. St G. *Report of the Settlement of the Kohat District*. Calcutta: Calcutta Central Press Company, 1884.

Veterinary Section, Quartermaster General's Division. *Handbook on Contagious and Infectious Diseases of Animals*. Calcutta: Government Press, 1910.

War Office. *Statistics of the Military Efforts of the British Empire during the Great War, 1914–1920*. London: His Majesty's Stationery Office, 1922.

"Waterlogging of the Soil in the Vicinity of Irrigation Canals, and the Measures of Prevention of Water-Logging." *Punjab Irrigation Branch Papers*, no. 20, 1920. [IOR/V/25/734/31]

Willoughby, Maj. M. E. *Report on the Mules and Ponies of the Province of Yunnan (West China)*. Calcutta: Office of the Superintendent of Government Printing, India, 1905. [IOR/L/MIL/7/1061]

BOOKS AND ARTICLES

Abas, Hassan. "The Political Landscape of the Taliban Insurgency in Pakistan." In *Talibanistan*, edited by P. Bergen and K. Tiedemann, 262–88. Oxford: Oxford University Press, 2013.

Adas, Michael. *Machines as the Measure of Man*. Ithaca, NY: Cornell University Press, 1989.

Agamben, Giorgio. *Homo Sacer*. Stanford, CA: Stanford University Press, 1998.

Agnihotri, Indu. "Ecology, Land Use and Colonization: Canal Colonies in the Punjab." *Indian Economic and Social History Review* 33, no. 1 (1996): 37–58.

Ahmad, S., et al. "Economic Importance of Camel: A Unique Alternative under Crisis." *Pakistan Veterinary Journal* 30, no. 4 (2010): 191–97.

Alam, Muzaffar, and Sanjay Subrahmanyam. *Indo-Persian Travels in the Age of Discoveries, 1400–1800*. Cambridge: Cambridge University Press, 2007.

Ali, Imran. *The Punjab under Imperialism, 1885–1947*. Princeton, NJ: Princeton University Press, 1988.

Anderson, Warwick. *Colonial Pathologies: American Tropical Medicine, Race and Hygiene in the Philippines*. Durham, NC: Duke University Press, 2006.

———. "Excremental Colonialism: Public Health and the Poetics of Pollution." *Critical Inquiry* 21, no. 3 (1995): 650–69.

Arnold, David. *Science, Technology and Medicine in Colonial India*. Cambridge: Cambridge University Press, 2000.

———. *The Tropics and the Traveling Gaze*. Delhi: Permanent Black, 2005.

Atkinson, James. *Expedition into Afghanistan*. London: W. H. Allen, 1842.

Attewell, Guy N. A. *Refiguring Unani Tibb: Plural Healing in Late Colonial India*. Hyderabad: Orient Longman, 2007.

Baldrey, Maj. F. S. H. "The Evolution of *Trypanosoma evansi* through the Fly." *JTVS* 6, no. 3 (1911): 271–82.

Balland, Daniel. "Nomadism and Politics: The Case of Afghan Nomads in the Indian Subcontinent." *Studies in History* 7, no. 2 (1991): 205–29.

Banerji, Arup. *Old Routes*. Gurgaon: Three Essays Collective, 2011.

Barber, J. "Camels in Peace and War." *The Cacolet: Journal of the Australian Camel Field Ambulance*, ed. Charles Barrett and Tom V. Brennan, Palestine (September 1917): 5–6.

Barrier, N. Gerald. "The Punjab Disturbances of 1907: The Response of British Government in India to Agrarian Unrest." *Modern Asian Studies* 1 (1967): 353–83.

Barrow, Lt. E. G. "The Government's Transport Scheme." *JUSII* 12, no. 55 (1883): 109–10.

———. "A Transport Service for Asiatic Warfare." *JUSII*, special number (1880): 1–30.

Barry, J. David, James Hall, and Lindsay Plenderleith. "Genome Hyperevolution and the Success of a Parasite." *Annals of the New York Academy of Sciences* 1267 (2012): 11–17.

Beinart, William, Karen Brown, and Daniel Gilfoyle. "Experts and Expertise in Colonial

Africa Reconsidered: Science and the Interpretation of Knowledge." *African Affairs* 108, no. 432 (2009): 413–33.

Bernier, Francis. *Travels in the Mogul Empire*. Translated by Irving Brook. 2 vols. London: William Pickering, 1826.

Bhattacharya, Neeladri. "Lenders and Debtors: Punjab Countryside, 1880–1940." *Studies in History* 1, no. 2 (1985): 305–42.

———. "Pastoralists in a Colonial World." In *Nature, Culture, Imperialism: Essays on the Environmental History of South Asia*, edited by David Arnold and R. Guha, 49–85. Oxford: Oxford University Press, 1995.

———. "Predicaments of Mobility: Peddlers and Itinerants in Nineteenth-Century Northwestern India." In *Society and Circulation: Mobile People and Itinerant Cultures in South Asia 1750–1950*, edited by Claude Markovits, Jacques Pouchepadass, and Sanjay Subrahmanyam, 163–214. Delhi: Permanent Black, 2003.

Bingley, Capt. A. H. "The Improvement of the Present Transport Organization in India." *JUSII* suppl. (July 1896): 1–32.

Blandford, W. F. H. "The Tsetse Fly-Disease." *Nature* 53, no. 1381 (1896): 566–67.

Blochmann, Henry, trans. Abu al-Fazl's *A'in-i Akbari*. 1927. Reprint, Lahore: Quasain, 1975.

Boid, R., et al. "Trypanosomiasis Research at the Center for Tropical Veterinary Medicine (CTVM) 1970 to 1995." *Tropical Animal Health and Production* 28 (1996): 5–22.

Breinl, A., and J. L. Todd. "Atoxyl in the Treatment of Trypanosomiasis." *British Medical Journal* 2403 (January 1907): 132–34.

Brereton, J. M. "The Panjdeh Crisis, 1885." *History Today* 29, no. 1 (1979): 46–52.

Brooke, Henry Francis. *Private Journal of Henry Francis Brooke: Late Brigadier-General Commanding 2nd Infantry Brigade Kandahar Field Force, Southern Afghanistan, from April 22nd to August 16th, 1880*. Dublin: William Curwen, 1881.

Brown, Karen, and Daniel Gilfoyle. *Healing the Herds: Disease, Livestock Economies, and the Globalization of Veterinary Medicine*. Athens: Ohio University Press, 2010.

Bruce, David. *Further Report on the Tsetse Fly Disease or Nagana, in Zululand*. London: Harrison and Sons, 1896.

———. *Preliminary Report on the Tsetse Fly Disease or Nagana, in Zululand*. Durban: Bennett and Davis, 1895.

Buck, Maj. Cecil Henry. "Canal Irrigation in the Punjab." *Geographic Journal* 27, no. 1 (1906): 60–67.

———. *Faiths, Fairs, and Festivals of India*. Calcutta: Thacker, Spink, 1917.

Buckler, F. W. "The Oriental Despot." *Anglican Historical Review* 10 (1927–28): 238–49.

Bulliet, Richard W. *The Camel and the Wheel*. Cambridge, MA: Harvard University Press, 1975.

Cambridge, Richard. *An Account of the War in India*. London: T. Jefferys, 1761.

Cameron, Charles. *A Romance of War; or, How the Cash Goes in Campaigning*. London: Baillière, Tindall and Cox, 1884.

Carroll, Patrick. *Science, Culture, and Modern State Formation*. Berkeley: University of California Press, 2006.

Caton, Brian. "The Transition from Animal Capital to Land Capital in the Colonial Punjab, 1850–1900." *Capitalism Nature Socialism* 26, no. 3 (2015): 64–72.

Chakrabarti, Pratik. *Bacteriology in British India: Laboratory Medicine and the Tropics*. Rochester, NY: University of Rochester Press, 2012.

———. "Beasts of Burden: Animals and Laboratory Research in Colonial India." *History of Science* 48, no. 160 (2010): 125–51.

———. "Medical Marketplaces beyond the West: Bazaar Medicine, Trade and the English Establishment in Eighteenth-Century India." In *Medicine and the Market in England and Its Colonies, c. 1450–c. 1850*, edited by M. Jenner and P. Wallis, 196–215. New York: Palgrave, 2007.

Chambers, David W., and Richard Gillespie. "Locality in the History of Science: Colonial Science, Technoscience, and Indigenous Knowledge." *Osiris* 15 (2000): 221–40.

Chapman, E. F. "The March from Kabule to Kandahar in August and the Battle of the 1st September, 1880." *JUSII* 25 (1881): 282–315.

Choudhary, R. B. Azad. "The Mughal and the Trading of Horses in India." *International Journal of History and Cultural Studies* 3, no. 1 (2017): 1–18.

Cloughley, Brian. *A History of the Pakistan Army: Wars and Insurrections*. 4th ed. Oxford: Oxford University Press, 2014.

Cohn, Bernard. *Colonialism and Its Forms of Knowledge*. Princeton, NJ: Princeton University Press, 1996.

Colquhoun, James Andrew Sutherland. *With the Kurram Field Force, 1878–79*. London: W. H. Allen, 1881.

Cook, Gordon. *Tropical Medicine*. Paris: Academic Press, 2007.

Corrigan, Philip, and Derek Sayers. *The Great Arch*. Oxford: Basil Blackwell, 1985.

Cross, Henry Eustace. *The Camel and Its Diseases, Being Notes of Veterinary Surgeons and Commandants of Camel Corps*. London: Baillière, Tindall and Cox, 1917.

Curth, Louise Hill. *The Care of Brute Beasts: A Social and Cultural Study of Veterinary Medicine in Early Modern England*. Leiden: Brill, 2010.

———. *English Almanacs, Astrology, and Popular Medicine: 1550–1700*. Manchester: Manchester University Press, 2007.

Darling, Malcolm. *At Freedom's Door*. Oxford: Oxford University Press, 1949.

———. *The Punjab Peasant in Prosperity and Debt*. 4th ed. Oxford: Oxford University Press, 1947.

Davis, Mike. *Late Victorian Holocausts: El Niño Famines and the Making of the Third World*. London: Verso, 2001.

Deleuze, Gilles, and Felix Guattari. *A Thousand Plateaus*. Minneapolis: University of Minnesota Press, 1987.

Deloche, Jean. *Transport and Communication in India prior to Steam Locomotion*. Translated by James Walker. Vol. 1, *Land Transport*. Delhi: Oxford University Press, 1993.

Derry, Margaret. *Bred for Perfection*. Baltimore: Johns Hopkins University Press, 2003.

———. *Horses in Society: A Story of Animal Breeding and Marketing, 1800–1920*. Toronto: University of Toronto Press, 2006.

Desquenes, M., P. Holzmuller, De-hua Lai, A. Dargantes, Zhao-rong Lun, and Sathaporn Jittaplapong. "Trypanosoma evansi and Surra: A Review and Perspectives on Origin,

History, Distribution, Taxonomy, Morphology, Hosts and Pathogenic Effects." *BioMed Research International* (2013): 1–22.

Dewey, Clive. *Steamboats on the Indus: The Limits of Western Technological Superiority in South Asia*. Oxford: Oxford University Press, 2014.

Digby, Simon. *War Horse and Elephant in the Delhi Sultanate*. Oxford: Orient Monographs, 1971.

Doniger, Wendy. *On Hinduism*. New York: Oxford University Press, 2016.

Duke, Joshua. *Recollections of the Kabul Campaign, 1879 and 1880*. London: W. H. Allen, 1883.

Eastwick, Capt. William Joseph. *Lord Lytton and the Afghan War*. London: R. J. Mitchell and Sons, 1879.

Eaton, Richard. "The Political and Religious Authority of the Shrine of Baba Farid." In *India's Islamic Traditions, 711–1750*, edited by Richard Eaton, 263–84. Oxford: Oxford University Press, 2003.

———. "Sufi Folk Literature and the Expansion of Indian Islam." *History of Religions* 14, no. 2 (1974): 117–27.

"Editorial: Microbiology." *QJVSI* 7.26 (April 1889): 198–208.

"Editorial: On the Inter-relations of Human and Veterinary Medicine." *QJVSI* 2, no. 7 (April 1884): 308–21.

"Editorial: On the Specialties and Scope of Veterinary Science in India." *QJVSI* 2, no. 6 (January 1884): 169–82.

Edwards, J. T. "The Chemotherapy of Surra in Horses and Cattle in India." *Journal of Comparative Pathology and Therapeutics* 39, no. 2 (1926): 82–112.

———. "The Chemotherapy of Surra in Horses and Cattle in India." *Journal of Comparative Pathology and Therapeutics* 39, no. 3 (1926): 169–201.

Elsmie, G. R., ed. *Field-Marshal Sir Donald Stewart, G.C.B., G.C.S.L., C.I.E.: An Account of His Life Mainly in His Own Words*. London: John Murray, 1903.

Engels, Donald W. *Alexander the Great and the Logistics of the Macedonian Army*. Berkeley: University of California Press, 1978.

Ernst, Carl W. "An Indo-Persian Guide to Sufi Shrine Pilgrimage." In *Manifestations of Sainthood in Islam*, edited by Grace Smith and Carl Ernst, 43–67. Istanbul: Isis Press, 1993.

———. *Sufism: An Introduction to the Mystical Tradition of Islam*. Boston: Shambhala, 2011.

Evans, Griffith. "Autobiographical Memoir." *Annals of Tropical Medicine and Parasitology* 12, no. 1 (1918): 5.

Ewing, Katherine. "The Sufi as Saint, Curer, and Exorcist in Modern Pakistan." *Contributions to Asian Studies* 18 (1984): 106–14.

"Extracts from Resumé of Horse and Mule Breeding Operations in India, 1880." *JUSII* 11, no. 51 (1882): 139–40.

Fairholme, Edward G., et al. *A Century of Work for Animals: The History of the R.S.P.C.A., 1824–1924*. London: John Murray, 1924.

Farquhar, Judy. *Knowing Practice*. Boulder, CO: Westview Press, 1996.

Fenton, V.S. "Veterinary Report on the Suakin Field Force, 1886." *QJVSI* 7, no. 26 (1889): 127–36.

Ferdinand, Klaus. *Afghan Nomads: Caravans, Conflicts, and Trade in Afghanistan and British India, 1800–1980*. Copenhagen: Carlsburg Foundation, 2006.

Ferrari, Fabrizio M., and Thomas Dahnhardt. *Charming Beauties and Frightful Beasts: Non-Human Animals in South Asian Myth, Ritual and Folklore*. Sheffield: Equinox, 2013.

Foltz, Richard. *Animals in Islamic Tradition and Muslim Cultures*. Oxford: Oneworld, 2006.

Ford, John. *The Role of the Trypanosomiases in African Ecology: A Study of the Tsetse Fly Problem*. Oxford: Clarendon Press, 1971.

Fothergill, J. Milner. *A Manual of Dietetics*. New York: William Wood, 1886.

Franklin, Sarah. *Dolly Mixtures: The Remaking of Genealogy*. Durham, NC: Duke University Press, 2007.

Furse, Maj. G. A. "A Transport Service for Asiatic Warfare." *JUSII*, special number (1880): 125.

———. "Various Descriptions of Transport." *JUSII* 7, no. 34 (1878): 464.

Gadgil, Mahdav, and Ramchandra Guha. *The Fissured Land*. Berkeley: University of California Press, 1992.

Galtrey, Capt. Sidney. *The Horse and the War*. London: Country Life, 1918.

Gauthier-Pilters, Hilde, and Anne Innis Dagg. *The Camel: Its Evolution, Ecology, Behavior, and Relationship to Man*. Chicago: University of Chicago Press, 1981.

Giersch, C. Patterson. "Across Zomia with Merchants, Monks, and Musk: Process Geographies, Trade Networks, and the Inner-East–Southeast Asian Borderlands." *Journal of Global History* 5, no. 2 (2010): 215–39.

Gilbey, Walter. *Horse-Breeding in England and India and Army Horses Abroad*. London: Vinton, 1906.

Gilchrist, William. *A Practical Memoir on the History and Treatment of the Diseases of the Camel, with Instructions for Preserving Its Efficiency as an Animal of Transport and a General Outline of Its Anatomy, Also, an Account of the Medicines Used in the Cure of Its Diseases*. Calcutta: G. H. Huttmann, Bengal Military Orphan Press, 1843.

Gillham-Thomsett, Richard. *Kohat, Kuram, and Khost; or, Experiences and Adventures in the Late Afghan War*. London: Remington, 1884.

Gilmartin, David. *Blood and Water: The Indus River Basin in Modern History*. Oakland: University of California Press, 2015.

———. "Scientific Empire and Imperial Science." *Journal of Asian Studies* 53, no. 4 (November 1994): 1127–49.

Ginn, Franklin, Uli Beisel, and Maan Barua. "Flourishing with Awkward Creatures: Togetherness, Vulnerability, and Killing." *Environmental Humanities* 4, no. 1 (2014): 113–23.

Gladstone, W. E. *The Approaching General Election: A Political Catechism Containing an Indictment and a Programme*. London: H. J. Infield, 1879.

Golamreza'i, Mohammad-Nasar. "Camel." In *Encyclopædia Iranica*, 4:374. London: Routledge and Kegan Paul, 1983.

Gommans, Jos. *Mughal Warfare*. London: Routledge, 2002.

———. *The Rise of the Indo-Afghan Empire c. 1710–1780*. Leiden: E. J. Brill, 1995.

Gooch, John. *The Plans of War: The General Staff and British Military Strategy, c. 1900–1916*. London: Routledge and Kegan Paul, 1974.

Green, E. H. H. "The Political Economy of Empire, 1880–1914." 346–68. In *Oxford History of the British Empire: The Nineteenth Century*, edited by Andrew Porter, 3:346–68. Oxford: Oxford University Press, 1999.

Green, Nile. *Making Space: Sufis and Settlers in Early Modern India*. Oxford: Oxford University Press, 2012.

———. "Stories of Saints and Sultans: Re-membering History at the Sufi Shrines of Aurangabad." *Modern Asian Studies* 38, no. 2 (2004): 419–46.

Greene, Ann M. "The Now-Opprobrious Title of 'Horse Doctor': Veterinarians and Professional Identity in Late Nineteenth-Century America." In *Healing the Herds*, edited by Karen Brown and D. Gilfoyle, 42–58. Athens: Ohio University Press, 2010.

Hallen, J. H. B. "Address." *JUSII* 15, no. 76 (1887): 177–97.

Halsema, G. E. van, and L. Vincent. "Of Flumes, Modules and Barrels: The Failure of Irrigation Institutions and Technologies to Achieve Equitable Water Control in the Indus Basin." In *A History of Water*, edited by T. Tvedt and E. Jakobsson, 1:55–91. London: I. B. Tauris, 2006.

Hamilton, T. C. *Diary of the March of the 15th "the King's" Hussars to Kandahar: October 1878 to April 1879*. Meerut: "Charles and Co." Medical Hall Press, 1879.

Hanna, Henry B. *The Second Afghan War 1878–79–80: Its Causes, Its Conduct and Its Consequences*. Vol. 1. Westminster: Archibald Constable, 1899.

———. *The Second Afghan War 1878–79–80: Its Causes, Its Conduct and Its Consequences*. Vol. 2. Westminster: Archibald Constable, 1904.

Haraway, Donna Jeanne. *When Species Meet*. Minneapolis: University of Minnesota Press, 2008.

———. "Value-Added Dogs and Lively Capital." In *Lively Capital*, edited by Kaushik Sunder Rajan, 95–120. Durham, NC: Duke University Press, 2012.

Hardiman, David, and Projit Mukharji, eds. *Medical Marginality in South Asia*. London: Routledge, 2012.

Harrison, Mark. "Science and the British Empire." *Isis* 96, no. 1 (2005): 56–63.

Harrison, Michael. "Tropical Medicine in Nineteenth-Century India." *British Journal of the History of Science* 25 (1992): 299–318.

Hasan, M. "Prevalence of *Trypanosoma evansi* Infection in Equines and Camels in the Punjab Region, Pakistan." *Annals of the New York Academy of Sciences* 1081 (2006): 322–24.

Hassanien, Ahmed. *The Lost Oases*. New York: Century, 1925.

Haynes, Douglas M. "Social Status and Imperial Service: Tropical Medicine and the British Medical Profession in the Nineteenth Century." In *Warm Climes and Western Medicine*, edited by David Arnold, 208–26. Amsterdam: Rodopi, 1996.

Hevia, James L. *The Imperial Security State: British Colonial Knowledge and Empire-Building in Asia*. Cambridge: Cambridge University Press, 2012.

———. "Small Wars and Counterinsurgency." In *Anthropology and Global Counterinsurgency*, edited by John Kelly et al., 69–77. Chicago: University of Chicago Press, 2010.

Hickman, John. "Sir Frederick Smith—his Life and Work." *Equine Veterinary Journal* 16, no. 5 (1984): 403–10.

Hoare, Cecil Arthur. *The Trypanosomes of Mammals*. Oxford: Blackwell Scientific Publications, 1972.

Hogg, G. E. M. "Camel Breeding." In *The Camel and Its Diseases, Being Notes of Veterinary Surgeons and Commandants of Camel Corps*, by H. E. Cross, 29–44. London: Baillière, Tindall and Cox, 1917.

Hogue, Oliver. *The Cameliers*. Driffield, Yorkshire: Leonaur, 2008.

Holland, Maj. Treven, and Capt. Henry Hozier, comps. *Record of the Expedition to Abyssinia*. 2 vols. London: Harrison and Sons, 1870.

Holmes, J. E. D. "The Cure of Surra in Horses by the Administration of Arsenic." *JTVS* 6, no. 4 (1911): 447–67.

———. "Investigation of an Outbreak of Horse Surra with the Result of Treatment with Atoxyl, Tartar Emetic, Mercury and Other Drugs." *JTVS* 3, no. 2 (1908): 157–72.

Hume, John C. "Rival Traditions: Western Medicine and Yūnān-i Tibb in the Punjab, 1849–1889." *Bulletin of the History of Medicine* 51, no. 2 (1977): 217–19.

Ibn Khaldun. *The Muqaddimah: An Introduction to History*. Translated by Franz Rosenthal. Vol. 2. New York: Pantheon Books, 1958.

The Imperial Gazetteer of India. Vol. 3. Oxford: Clarendon Press, 1908.

Inchbald, Geoffrey. *Camels and Others*. London: Johnson Publications, 1968.

———. *The Imperial Camel Corps*. Driffield, Yorkshire: Leonaur, 2005.

Intelligence Department, Army Headquarters. *The Second Afghan War, 1878–1880*. Abridged Official Account. London: John Murray, 1908.

Irvine, William. *The Army of the Indian Moghuls*. London: Luzac, 1903.

———. "The Mughal Army." *Journal of the Royal Asiatic Society* (January 1896): 509–70.

Irwin, Robert. *Camel*. London: Reaktion Books, 2010.

Jacobi, Renate. "The Camel-Section of the Panegyrical Ode." *Journal of Arabic Literature* 13 (1982): 1–22.

Jasra, A. W., Atiq-Ur-Rehman, and M. Afzal. "Socio-economics of Pastoralists Communities of Highland Balochistan, Pakistan." *International Journal of Agriculture and Biology* 3, no. 2 (2001): 257.

Johnson, Forrest Bryant. *The Last Camel Charge: The Untold Story of America's Desert Military Experiment*. New York: Berkley Publishing Group, 2012.

Kahlown, M. A., A. D. Khan, and M. Azam. "The World's Largest Continuous Irrigation System: Developments, Successes and Challenges of the Indus Irrigation System in Pakistan." In *A History of Water*, edited by T. Tvedt and E. Jakobsson, 1:35–54. London: I. B. Tauris, 2006.

Kakar, A., et al. "Rapid Change in Strategy Is Necessary for the Development of Dromedary Camel Pastoralism in Cholistan Desert of Pakistan." *Pastoralism: Research, Policy, Practice* 1, no. 3 (2011): 1–9.

Katewa, S. S., P. K. Galav, and Anita Jain. *Traditional Folk Veterinary Medicines*. Jodhpur: Scientific Publishers (India), 2010.

Kean, Hilda. "Animals and War Memorials: Different Approaches to Commemorating the

Human-Animal Relationship." In *Animals and War*, edited by Ryan Hediger, 237–62. Leiden: Brill, 2013.

Keegan, John. *The First World War*. New York: Alfred A. Knopf, 1999.

Kerr, Ian J. *Building the Railways of the Raj, 1850–1900*. Oxford: Oxford University Press, 1995.

Khan, B., A. Iqbal, and M. Riaz. *Production and Management of Camels*. Faisalabad: University of Agriculture, 2003.

Kipling, John Lockwood. *Beast and Man in India: A Popular Sketch of Indian Animals in Their Relations with the People*. London: Macmillan, 1904.

Kipling, Rudyard. *Barrack-Room Ballads*. New York: Signet Classics, 2003.

Kirksey, S. Eben, and Stefan Helmreich. "The Emergence of Multispecies Ethnography." *Cultural Anthropology* 25, no. 4 (2010): 545–76.

Kleine, Friedrich K. "Sleeping Sickness Investigations in German East Africa." *Sleeping Sickness Bulletin* 3, no. 26 (1911): 165–75.

Köhler-Rollefson, Ilse, Paul Mundy, and Evelyn Mathias. *A Field Manual of Camel Diseases*. London: ITDG, 2001.

Kohn, E. "How Dogs Dream: Amazonian Natures and the Politics of Transspecies Engagement." *American Ethnologist* 34, no. 1 (2007): 3–24.

Kolff, Dirk H. A. *Nauker, Rajput and Sepoy*. Cambridge: Cambridge University Press, 1990.

Kubicek, Robert V. *The Administration of Imperialism: Joseph Chamberlain at the Colonial Office*. Durham, NC: Duke University Press, 1969.

Kumar, Deepak. "Adoption and Adaptation: A Study of Medical Ideas and Techniques in Colonial India." In *Science between Europe and Asia*, edited by Feza Günergun and Dhruv Raina, 233–43. Dordrecht: Springer, 2011.

Lambert, Helen. "Plural Traditions? Folk Therapeutics and English Medicine in Rajasthan." In *Western Medicine as Contested Knowledge*, edited by Andrew Cunningham and Bridie Andrews, 191–211. Manchester: Manchester University Press, 1997.

Latour, Bruno. "Drawing Things Together." In *Repersentation in Scientific Practice*, edited by M. Lynch and S. Woolgar, 19–68. Cambridge, MA: MIT Press, 1990.

———. *Science in Action: How to Follow Scientists and Engineers through Society*. Milton Keynes, Buckinghamshire: Open University Press, 1987.

Laveran, Alphonse, and Félix Mesnil. *Trypanosomes and Trypanosomiases*. Translated by David Nabarro. London: Bailliére, Tindall and Cox, 1907.

Lawrence, Thomas E. *Seven Pillars of Wisdom: The Complete 1922 "Oxford" Text*. Fordingbridge, Hampshire: J. and N. Wilson, 2004.

Leach, H. M. "Human Domestication Reconsidered." *Current Anthropology* 44, no. 3 (2003): 349–68.

Leese, Arnold. "Summary of First Series of Experiments on the Treatment of Surra in Camels." *JTVS* 5, no. 1 (1910): 57–64.

———. "Summary of Second Series of Experiments on the Treatment of Surra in Camels." *JTVS* 5, no. 3 (1910): 397-410.

———. "Third Series of Experiments on the Treatment of Surra in Camels, with Some Cures." *JTVS* 7, no. 1 (1912): 1–18.

———. "Biting Flies and Surra." *JTVS* 7, no. 1 (1912): 19.

———. "'Tips' on Camels, for Veterinary Surgeons on Active Duty." *Veterinary Journal*, n.s., 24 (1917): 79–89, 136–40, 167–73, 214–18, 253–59, 294–98, 323–36.

———. *A Treatise on the One-Humped Camel in Health and in Disease*. Stanford, Lincolnshire: Haynes and Son, 1927.

———. *Out of Step: Events in the Two Lives of an Anti-Jewish Camel-Doctor*. Guildford, England: Arnold S. Leese, 1951.

Le Messurier, Augustus. *Kandahar in 1879: Being the Diary of Major Le Messurier, R.E.* London: W. H. Allen, 1880.

Leonard, Maj. Arthur G. *The Camel: Its Uses and Management*. London: Longmans, Green, 1894.

Li, Chien-hua. "Mobilizing Christianity in the Antivivisection Movement in Victorian Britain." *Journal of Animal Ethics* 2, no. 2 (2012): 141–61.

Luttwak, Edward. *The Grand Strategy of the Roman Empire: From the First Century A.D. to the Third*. Baltimore: Johns Hopkins University Press, 1976.

MacKenzie, John M. *The Empire of Nature: Hunting, Conservation, and British Imperialism*. Manchester: Manchester University Press, 1988.

Mahmoud, M. M., and A. R. Gray. "Trypanosomiasis Due to Trypanosoma evansi (Steel 1885) Balbani, 1888: A Review of Recent Research." *Tropical Animal Health and Production* 12 (1980): 35–47.

Major, Andrew. "State and Criminal Tribes in Colonial Punjab." *Modern Asian Studies* 33, no. 3 (1999): 657–88.

Markovits, Claude. "Indian Merchants in Central Asia." In *India and Central Asia: Commerce and Culture, 1500–1800*, edited by Scott C. Levi, 123–51. Oxford: Oxford University Press, 2007.

Marsh, George Perkins. *The Camel: His Organization, Habits and Uses*. Boston: Gould and Lincoln, 1856.

Mayuer-Jaouen, Catherine. "Badawi and His Camel: An Animal as the Attribute of a Muslim Saint of Mamluk and Ottoman Egypt." In *Animals and People in Ottoman Egypt*, by Suraiya Faroqhi, 113–28. Istanbul: Eren, 2010.

Mazumder, Rajit K. *The Indian Army and the Making of the Punjab*. Delhi: Permanent Black, 2003.

Meisami, Julie S. *Medieval Persian Court Poetry*. Princeton, NJ: Princeton University Press, 1987.

Mikhail, Alan. *The Animal in Ottoman Egypt*. Oxford: Oxford University Press, 2014.

———. *Nature and Empire in Ottoman Egypt: An Environmental History*. New York: Cambridge University Press, 2011.

Miller, David, and Peter Reill, eds. *Visions of Empire: Voyages, Botany, and Representations of Nature*. Cambridge: Cambridge University Press, 1996.

Mishra, Saurabh. *Beastly Encounters of the Raj: Livelihoods, Livestock, and Veterinary Health in India, 1790–1920*. Manchester: Manchester University Press, 2015.

———. "Beasts, Murrains, and the British *Raj*: Reassessing Colonial Medicine in India from the Veterinary Perspective, 1860–1900." *Bulletin of the History of Medicine* 85, no. 4 (2011): 587–619.

Mitchell, Timothy. *Rule of Experts*. Berkeley: University of California Press, 2002.

Moore, Col. H. "A Transport Service for Asiatic Warfare." *JUSII*, special number (1880): 125, 132, 136, 148, 156.

Moore, Maj.-Gen. John. *Army Veterinary Service in War*. London: H. and W. Brown, 1921.

Moosvi, Shireen. *The Economy of the Mughal Empire c. 1595*. Delhi: Oxford University Press, 1987.

Moreman, Tim. "'Watch and Ward': The Army in India and the North-West Frontier, 1920–1939." In *Guardians of Empire*, edited by D. Killingray and D. Omisso, 137–56. Manchester: Manchester University Press, 1999.

Morrison, Alexander. "Camels and Colonial Armies: The Logistics of Warfare in Central Asia in the Early 19th Century." *Journal of the Economic and Social History of the Orient* 57 (2014): 443–85.

Murphey, Rhoads. *Ottoman Warfare, 1500–1700*. New Brunswick, NJ: Rutgers University Press, 1999.

Neill, Deborah. *Networks in Tropical Medicine*. Stanford, CA: Stanford University Press, 2012.

O'Brien, Aubrey. "The Mohammedan Saints of the Western Punjab." *Journal of the Royal Anthropological Institute of Great Britain and Ireland* 41 (1911): 509–20.

Official Yearbook of New South Wales. Sydney: Government of New South Wales, 1907.

Oliver, Edward Emmerson. *Across the Border; or, Pathan and Biloch*. London: Chapman and Hall, 1890.

Olsen, Asta. *Islam and Politics in Afghanistan*. New York: Routledge, 1995.

Omrani, Bijan. "The Durand Line: History and Problems of the Afghan-Pakistan Border." *Asian Affairs* 40, no. 2 (2009): 177–95.

Paget, William Henry, and A. H. Mason. *A Record of the Expeditions against the North-West Frontier Tribes, since the Annexation of the Punjab*. London: Whiting, 1884.

Palgrave, William. *Personal Narrative of a Year's Journey through Central Asia and Eastern Arabia (1862–63)*. London: Macmillan, 1869.

Parkyn, Lt. Samuel Spence. *Transport in Southern Afghanistan, between Sukkur and Quetta, 1878–1880*. 2nd ed. London: Harrison and Sons, 1882.

Paxson, Heather, and Stefan Helmreich. "The Perils and Promises of Microbial Abundance." *Social Studies of Science* 44, no. 2 (2014): 165–93.

Pease, Henry T. "Tibarsa Surra: Trypanosomiasis in the Camel." *JTVS* 1, no. 1 (1906): 75.

Pickering, Andrew. "The Mangle of Practice: Agency and Emergence in the Sociology of Science." *American Journal of Sociology* 99, no. 3 (1993): 559–89.

Pringle, V.S. Robert. "Report on the Working of the Veterinary Department of the Zhob Valley Field Force." *QJVSI* 4, no. 13 (1885): 82–83.

Quartaert, Donald. *The Ottoman Empire, 1700–1922*. 2nd ed. Cambridge: Cambridge University Press, 2005.

Queripel, V.S. Alfred. "Nile Expedition." *QJVSI* 5, no. 17 (October 1886): 44–58.

———. "Nile Expedition (continued)." *QJVSI* 5, no. 19 (April 1887): 213–34.

Qureshi, A. S., et al. "Managing Salinity and Waterlogging in the Indus Basin of Pakistan." *Agricultural Water Management* 95, no. 1 (2008): 1–10.

Raffles, Hugh. *Insectopedia*. New York: Pantheon Books, 2010.

Rayment, V.S. "With the Indian Contingent at Suakin." *QJVSI* 4, no. 15 (1886): 284–85.

Richard, D. "Camel Mange." *Revue Scientifique et Technique* 6, no. 2 (1987): 475–77.

Ritvo, Harriet. *The Animal Estate: The English and Other Creatures in the Victorian Age.* Cambridge, MA: Harvard University Press, 1987.

———. *Noble Cows and Hybrid Zebras: Essays on Animals and History*. Charlottesville: University of Virginia Press, 2010.

Robinson, J. A. *Notes on Nomad Tribes of Eastern Afghanistan.* 1934. Reprint, Quetta: M/S Nisa Traders, 1978.

Roe, Andrew. *Waging War in Waziristan.* Lawrence: University of Kansas Press, 2010.

Rogers, Leonard. "The Transmission of the *Trypanosoma evansi* by Horse Flies, and Other Experiments Pointing to the Probable Identity of Surra in India and Nagana or Tsetse-Fly Disease of Africa." *Proceedings of the Royal Society of London* 68 (1901): 163–70.

Rose, Deborah Bird, and Thom van Dooren. "Guest Editors' Introduction." *Australian Humanities Review* 50 (2011): 1–5.

Sasha. *Social History of Epidemics in the Colonial Punjab.* Gurgaon: Partridge India, 2014.

Scott, James. *Seeing like a State.* New Haven, CT: Yale University Press, 1998.

Sells, Michael. "Mu'akkaqa of Tarafa." *Journal of Arabic Literature* 17 (1986): 21–33.

Sen, S. K. "Prophylaxis against Equine Surra by Means of 'Bayer 205' (Naganol)." *IJVSAH* 1, no. 4 (1931): 283–95.

Serres, Michel. *The Parasite.* Minneapolis: University of Minnesota Press, 2007.

Shah, Lal. "Notes on Some Frontier Shrines." *Indian Antiquary* 35 (1906): 119–25.

Shehada, Housni. *Mamluks and Animals: Veterinary Medicine in Medieval Islam.* Leiden: Brill, 2013.

Siddiqa, Ayesha. *Military, Inc: Inside Pakistan's Military Economy*. Karachi: Oxford University Press, 2007.

Siddiqui, Iqtidar Husain. "The Early Chishti Dargahs." In *Muslim Shrines in India: Their Character, History and Significance*, edited by Christian W. Troll, 24–43. Delhi: Oxford University Press, 1989.

Singh, Bachan. "Bovine Trypanosomiasis in Central Provinces with an Account of Some Recent Outbreaks." *IJVSAH* 6, no. 3 (1936): 243–50.

Slack, Paul. *The Invention of Improvement: Information and Material Progress in Seventeenth-Century England.* Oxford: Oxford University Press, 2015.

Sleeping Sickness Bulletin 3, no. 26 (1911): 165–75, 367–69; 3, no. 30 (1911): 367–68, 369–73.

Smith, Frederick. *A History of the Royal Army Veterinary Corps, 1796–1919.* London: Baillière, Tindall and Cox, 1927.

———. *A Veterinary History of the War in South Africa, 1899–1902.* London: H. W. Brown, 1919.

Smith, Frederick, and Fred Bullock. *The Early History of Veterinary Literature and Its British Development.* 4 vols. London: Baillière, Tindall and Cox, 1919–33.

Speziale, Fabrizio. "The Relation between Galenic Medicine and Sufism in India during the Delhi and Deccan Sultanates." *East and West* 53 (2003): 149–78.

Spivak, G. C. "The Rani of Sirmur: An Essay in Reading the Archives." *History and Theory* 24, no. 3 (1985): 247–72.

Steel, Charles. "Camels in Connection with the South Afghan Expedition 1878–1879." *JUSII* 8, no. 39 (1879): 455–62.

Steel, John Henry. *A Manual of the Diseases of the Camel and of His Management and Uses*. Madras: Lawrence Asylum Press, 1890.

———. "On Relapsing Fever of Equines." *Veterinary Journal and Annals of Comparative Pathology* 22 (1886): 166–74.

Stephen, Lorne E. *Trypanosomiasis: A Veterinary Perspective*. Oxford: Pergamon Press, 1986.

Stetkevych, Jaroslav. "Name and Epithet: The Philology and Semiotics of Animal Nomenclature in Early Arabic Poetry." *Journal of Near East Studies* 45, no. 2 (1986): 89–124.

Stevens, Christine. *Tin Mosques and Ghantowns: A History of Afghan Camel Drivers in Australia*. Melbourne: Oxford University Press, 1989.

Stone, Ian. *Canal Irrigation in British India*. Cambridge: Cambridge University Press, 1984.

Suvorova, A. A. *Muslim Saints of South Asia: The Eleventh to Fifteenth Centuries*. London: RoutledgeCurzon, 1999.

Swart, Sandra. "Horses in the South African War, c. 1899–1902." *Society and Animals* 18, no. 4 (2010): 348–66.

Tan, Tai Yong. *The Garrison State: The Military, Government and Society in Colonial Punjab 1849–1947*. New Delhi: Sage Publications, 2005.

Taylor, W. "Surra in the Punjab." *IJVSAH* 4, no. 1 (1934): 29–35.

Tegetmeier, W. B., and Charles Lindsay Sutherland. *Horses, Asses, Zebras, Mules, and Mule Breeding*. London: Horace Cox, 1895.

Thornton, Thomas H. *Colonel Robert Sandeman*. 1895. Reprint, Quetta: Gosha-e-Adab, 1977.

———. "The Vernacular Literature and Folklore of the Panjab." *Journal of the Royal Asiatic Society of Great Britain and Ireland*, n.s., 17, no. 3 (1885): 373–414.

Tirmizi, S. A. I. "Mughal Documents Relating to the Dargah of Khwaja Mu'inuddin Chishti." In *Muslim Shrines in India: Their Character, History, and Significance*, edited by Christian W. Troll, 48–59. New Delhi: Oxford University Press, 1989.

Tlili, Sarra. *Animals in the Qur'an*. New York: Cambridge University Press, 2012.

Trevaskis, Hugh Kennedy. *The Land of the Five Rivers: An Economic History of the Punjab from the Earliest Times to the Year of Grace 1890*. Oxford: Oxford University Press, 1928.

Tuchsherer, Michel. "Some Reflections on the Place of the Camel in Ottoman Egypt." In *Animals and People in Ottoman Egypt*, by Suraiya Faroqhi, 171–85. Istanbul: Eren, 2010.

Tucker, H. St George. *Report of the Land Revenue Settlement of the Dera Ismail Khan District of the Punjab, 1872–79*. Lahore: W. Ball, 1879.

Vaughn, Maj. R. E. "The Transport Service in India." *JUSII* 35 (1906): 287.

Waring, Edward J. *Pharmacopeia of India*. London: Allen and Sons, 1868.

White, Luise. "Tsetse Visions: Narratives of Blood and Bugs in Colonial Northern Rhodesia, 1931–9." *Journal of African History* 36, no. 2 (1995): 219–45.

Wilkinson, S. R., and J. M. Kelly. "Trypanocidal Drugs: Mechanisms, Resistance and New Targets." *Expert Reviews in Molecular Medicine* 11 (October 2009): 1–24.

Wilson, R. T. "Nutritional Requirements of the Camel." *Options Méditerranénnes* 2 (1989): 171–79.

Wise, M. Norton, and Crosbie Smith. "Work and Waste—political Economy and Natural Philosophy in Nineteenth-Century Britain." *History of Science* 27, no. 77 (1989): 263–301; 27, no. 78 (1989): 391–449; 28, no. 81 (1990): 221–61.

Worboys, Michael. "The Emergence of Tropical Medicine: A Study in the Establishment of a Scientific Specialty." In *Perpectives on the Emergence of Scientific Disciplines*, edited by Gerard Lemaine et al., 75–98. Chicago: Aldine, 1976.

———. "Germs, Malaria and the Invention of Masonian Tropical Medicine: From 'Diseases in the Tropics' to 'Tropical Diseases.'" *Clio Medica* 35 (1996): 181–207.

———. "Germ Theories of Disease and British Veterinary Medicine 1860–1900." *Medical History* 25 (1991): 308–27.

———. "Mason, Ross, and Colonial Medical Policy: Tropical Medicine in London and Liverpool, 1899–1914." In *Disease, Medicine, and Empire*, edited by Roy MacLeod and Milton J. Lewis, 21–37. London: Routledge, 1988.

Yule, Henry, and A. C. Burnell. *Hobson-Jobson: A Glossary of Colloquial Anglo-Indian Words and Phrases, and of Kindred Terms, Etymological, Historical, Geographical and Discursive*. Delhi: Munshiram Manoharlal, 1994.

Zimmermann, Francis. *The Jungle and the Aroma of Meats: An Ecological Theme in Hindu Medicine*. Delhi: Motilal Banarsidass, 2011.

INDEX